ALL IS GRACE

A Biography of Dorothy Day

(Credit: Jon Erikson)

ALL IS GRACE

A Biography of Dorothy Day

JIM FOREST

NOVALIS

ORBIS BOOKS
Maryknoll, New York 10545

Founded in 1970, Orbis Books endeavors to publish works that enlighten the mind, nourish the spirit, and challenge the conscience. The publishing arm of the Maryknoll Fathers and Brothers, Orbis seeks to explore the global dimensions of the Christian faith and mission, to invite dialogue with diverse cultures and religious traditions, and to serve the cause of reconciliation and peace. The books published reflect the views of their authors and do not represent the official position of the Maryknoll Society. To learn more about Maryknoll and Orbis Books, please visit our website at www.maryknollsociety.org.

Manufactured in the United States of America.
Design: Roberta Savage

Library of Congress Cataloging-in-Publication Data

Forest, Jim (James H.)
  All is grace : a biography of Dorothy Day / Jim Forest.
    p. cm.
  Revised edition of: Love is the Measure. c1994.
  Includes index.
  ISBN 978-1-57075-921-5 (pbk.)
  1. Day, Dorothy, 1897-1980. 2. Catholics—United States—Biography.
  3. Social reformers—United States—Biography. 4. Catholic Worker
Movement. I. Forest, Jim (James H.) Love is the measure. II. Title.
  BX4705.D283F67 2011
  267'.182092—dc22
  [B]
                              2010039646

Published in Canada by Novalis.
Publishing Office: 10 Lower Spadina Avenue, Suite 400, Toronto, Ontario, Canada M5V 2Z2.
Head Office: 4475 Frontenac Street, Montréal, Québec, Canada H2H 2S2.
www.novalis.ca

Cataloguing in Publication is available from Library and Archives Canada.
ISBN 978-2-89646-370-1

We acknowledge the financial support of the Government of Canada through the Canada Book Fund for business development activities.

To my parents
Jim and Marguerite
who were among the people
on Union Square
May 1, 1933
the day the first issue
of The Catholic Worker
was distributed

and to
Tom Cornell
and
Robert Ellsberg

Our life of grace and our life of the body goes on beautifully intermingled and harmonious. "All is grace," as the dying priest whispered to his friend in The Diary of a Country Priest. *The Little Flower also said, "All is grace."*

— Dorothy Day, "On Pilgrimage" column,
May 1954

Contents

May Day

A clear contralto voice filled Union Square in New York with the words, *"Arise, ye prisoners of starvation."* In moments tens of thousands of voices joined in singing together the *Internationale*, the socialist anthem. *"Arise, ye wretched of the earth."* Tears sparkled in the eyes of those whom editorial writers and politicians sometimes described as godless, heartless and witless radicals. *"For Justice thunders condemnation."* Large numbers of police, some on horseback, watched from the sidelines of the huge crowd. *"A better world's in birth."*

Workers and radicals gather for the annual May Day rally in New York's Union Square, 1933.

It was May Day, 1933. Franklin Delano Roosevelt had been in the White House only a hundred days. The Great Depression was in its fourth year. Industrial production was barely half what it had been in 1929. In a population of 123,000,000, more than 13,000,000 workers were unemployed. The majority of America's banks had collapsed, while those which survived were busily repossessing houses, shops and farms whose owners couldn't make mortgage payments. Hoovervilles—shanty towns for the homeless made of tin, cardboard, canvas and scrap wood—had sprung up in vacant lots all over the country. No Social Security program yet existed. Beer could be legally purchased once again—the end of Prohibition was in sight. "King Kong" was a hit on movie screens. Mickey Mouse was five years old. The first modern sighting of the Loch Ness Monster had been reported in Scotland. Hitler was the new chancellor of Germany. Stalin had been ruling Soviet Russia for five years and was thought of, by those on the Left, not as a tyrant or mass murderer, but as a benevolent liberator.

Denouncing Hitler and praising Stalin, the speakers at Union Square called for worker ownership and control of

First issue of *The Catholic Worker*, May 1933.

industry. Despite hard times, their audience was in a festive mood. There were brass bands, red flags, and faces that were hopeful about the future, as if to say, "In my lifetime the revolution will happen."

One of those present, a young writer named Dorothy Day, remembered that the square was filled with "a hot undulant sea of hats and sun-baked heads, over which floated a disordered array of banners, placards and pennants." But Dorothy Day wasn't carrying a placard or paying attention to the speeches. She was one of four people handing out the first issue of a small, eight-page tabloid newspaper, *The Catholic Worker*, and wasn't even asking for its penny-a-copy cover price. An Irishman objected that a "penny" was an English coin and therefore was far too much to ask.

Dorothy found more bewilderment than enthusiasm from those who had the paper thrust into their hands. They all knew *The Daily Worker*, a Communist paper that was a militant supporter of unions and strikes. But a radical paper, a paper for workers, put out by *Catholics*? Everyone knew that the Catholic Church was far more anti-Communist than pro-worker.

Many copies of the first *Catholic Worker* quickly found their way into the nearest trash barrel, but some were read and seen as a welcome sign that a fresh wind was blowing in the Catholic Church.

An editorial on page four declared this new paper was published "for those who are huddling in shelters trying to escape the rain, for those who are walking the streets in the all but futile search for work, for those who think that there is no hope for the future, no recognition of their plight." *The Catholic Worker* would let its readers know "that the Catholic Church has a social program" and that there are people "who are working not only for their spiritual, but for their material welfare. . . . Is it not possible to be radical and not an atheist? Is it not possible to protest, to expose, to complain, to point out abuses and demand reforms without desiring the overthrow of religion?"

The editorial made light of the paper's fragile economic foundations: "The first number of *The Catholic Worker* was planned, written and edited in the kitchen of a tenement on 15th Street, on subway platforms, on the 'El' [the elevated railway], on the ferry. There is no editorial office, no overhead in the way of telephone or electricity, no salaries paid." The cost of printing 2,500 copies of the first issue— $57—was paid by a few small contributions, plus the editors' savings, and what could be spared by not paying gas and electric bills. "By accepting delay, the utilities did not know that they were furthering the cause of social justice."

What they were doing, the editorial declared, was no more reckless than the way Jesus and his friends had lived in Galilee. "It is cheering to remember that Jesus Christ wandered this earth with no place to lay his head. 'The foxes have holes and the birds of the air their nests, but the Son of Man has no place to lay his head.' And when we consider our fly-by-night existence, our uncertainty, we remember (with pride in sharing the honor) that the disciples supped by the seashore and wandered through cornfields picking the ears from the stalks wherewith to make their frugal meals."

The text was modestly signed "The Editors." Who were "The Editors" who had delayed paying their gas and electric bills? It was just one person—Dorothy Day, thirty-five years old.

Dorothy Day in the early 1930s.
(Maryknoll archives)

From Brooklyn to San Francisco

Dorothy Day was born on the 8th of November 1897 at 71 Pineapple Street in Brooklyn, a short walk from the east end of the Brooklyn Bridge. The third of the Day children, she had been preceded by Donald in 1895 and Sam Houston in 1896. Two others followed Dorothy: Della in 1899 and John in 1912. All but Della grew up to become journalists, with Sam Houston Day ending his career as managing editor of *The New York Journal American*, a popular right-wing paper that featured crime news.

Their father, John Day, was a newspaperman as well—a sports writer whose specialty was the race track. A tall man with sandy hair, he was born in Tennessee in 1870. He was of Scotch-Irish descent, proud that his ancestors had fought both in the Revolutionary War and the Confederate side of the Civil War. He liked whiskey and disliked foreigners, Jews, Catholics, blacks and radicals. "Nobody but Irish washwomen and policemen are Catholic," Dorothy recalled him saying. He regarded a particular New York hotel as "all right but full of Jews." Though describing himself as an atheist, he often quoted the Bible, carrying one with him whenever he traveled.

In Dorothy's autobiographical writings, John Day emerges as an unsympathetic and hot-tempered figure, easily irritated by the presence of children. He firmly believed that sparing the rod spoils the child. When the children ate Sunday dinner in the company of their parents, Dorothy found it a grim event. "None spoke; all ate in gloomy silence. We could hear each other swallow." Because of him, it was a family in which "there was never a close embrace." John seems to have found it easier to be with horses than with children. Later in his life, he wrote a racing column, "On and Off the Turf," for *The New York Morning Telegraph*. For a time he was an inspector for the New York State Racing Commission, and later a steward and partner of the Hialeah race track in Florida. In his senior years, friends called him "Judge Day."

"We did not search for God when we were children. We took Him for granted. We were at some time taught to say our evening prayers. 'Now I lay me,' and 'Bless my father and mother.' This done, we prayed no more unless a thunderstorm made us hide our heads under the covers and propitiate the Deity by promising to be good."

—The Long Loneliness

He was deeply disapproving of the direction Dorothy's life took both in faith and politics.

His wife, Grace Satterlee, was always remembered by Dorothy with grateful affection, a mother as near to her as her father was remote. Grace had been born in Marlboro, New York, in the Hudson Valley, in 1870. (Marlboro is now the location of the Peter Maurin Catholic Worker Farm.) One wing of the Satterlee family had gone to sea. In one generation, nine brothers had been captains of whalers and all but one had been lost. The one survivor, Christian Satterlee, married Charity Hummel Washburn, Dorothy Day's great-grandmother. Christian had nearly died under sail. "He fell from a mast," Dorothy wrote in *The Long Loneliness*, "and cracked his head and was never quite right after that, running down Delafield Street in his night shirt and finally drowning in a brook." He lasted long enough to father Napoleon

The Brooklyn Bridge, c. 1900. (Library of Congress)

5

John Day at the racetrack with
Dorothy's older brother Donald
(Marquette University archives)

*"I wonder if those stories of our ancestors
took away the fear of death that comes to
us all, or whether it mitigated it."*
—The Long Loneliness

Bonaparte Satterlee, who went off to fight in the Civil War on the northern side, returning home from a prison camp with a damaged larynx. For the rest of his life he only spoke in a hoarse whisper which he treated with eggnog brought to him by his daughter Grace, or Graceful, as he preferred to call her.

Then there was Aunt Cassie, Grace's sister, who on winter days used to skate down the Hudson River from Poughkeepsie to Marlboro to bake bread and cookies and then skate home again, all because she was in love with one of the engineers who helped build the railway bridge that spanned the river. Dorothy marveled at how love gives strength to one's limbs and wings to one's feet.

Grace delighted in telling her children stories of what it was like when she was a little girl and who was in the family before Dorothy was born. "How we loved these stories," Dorothy wrote, "and how welcome our warm house was as we heard of terrible winters with the Hudson freezing over so that skating and ice-boating was commonplace." Stories gave Dorothy a sense of connection with the past. "Tradition! How rich a word that is. To a thinking child it means a great deal. Children all love to hear stories of when their parents were young, and of their parents before them. It gives a child a sense of continuity."

Grace's father died when she was nine. Three years later, to help her hard-pressed family, Grace found work in a shirt factory, but at last a government pension came through which allowed her to continue her education. In 1894, while studying at Eastman's Business School in New York City, Grace met John Day. Soon after they were married at the Perry

Left: Grace Satterlee (Day), Dorothy's mother, as a teenager. (Marquette University archives)

Below: Dorothy (center) with her brothers Sam and Donald. (Marquette University archives)

Street Episcopal Church in Greenwich Village. Within a year, Donald was born, with four more children to follow in the coming years. None were baptized. Though John had been raised a Congregationalist and Grace came from an Episcopal family, after their wedding they kept their distance from churches.

Brooklyn, Dorothy's home for her first six years, was less urban at the time than it is today. "I can remember well the happy hours on the beach with my brothers," Dorothy wrote, "fishing in the creeks for eel, running away with a younger cousin to an abandoned shack in a waste of swamp around Fort Hamilton, and pretending we were going to live there all by ourselves."

Dorothy recalled an early experiment with solitude: "On one occasion I went away all alone, spending what I felt to be long hours one sunny afternoon, blissful enchanted hours until the sudden realization came over me that I was alone, and the world was vast and that there were

John Day with a jockey. (Marquette University archives)

"It seems to me I spent much time alone in spite of the fact that I had two brothers and a sister."
— The Long Loneliness

evil forces therein . . . then suddenly the black fear overwhelmed me at being alone, so that I ran all the way home."

Her last year in Brooklyn was her first year in school. In those days, students in public school started the day with prayer. "We prayed . . . every morning, bowing our heads on our desks and saying the Our Father, and I can still smell the varnish, and see the round circle of moisture left by my mouth on the varnish as I bent close to the desk."

In 1904 John Day accepted a job in California covering racetrack news for a San Francisco newspaper. While waiting for their furniture to make its way by ship around Cape Horn, the family moved into a rented house in Berkeley on the San Francisco Bay. When the ship arrived, the Days moved a few miles south to Oakland, terminus of the transcontinental railroad and home of Idora Park, a racetrack John Day covered for his paper. Their house was surrounded by trees and flowers and had a view of the softly sloping hills to the east.

"There were hours working in the garden," Dorothy remembered, "playing with dolls made of calla leaves with roses for heads, making perfume by crushing flowers and putting them in bottles with water, playing with dirt and sand, watching anthills, gopher hills, sitting and listening to a brook, smelling geranium leaves."

Sometimes Dorothy's explorations of wildlife in Oakland were shared. On one occasion, several children joined in making tunnels through a field of thistles "looking for what we considered little rooms in those sheltered recesses among the weeds. It was like living in a green sea, a shallow sea with sunlight sifting through and the odor of the earth, and the hum of insects and the drowsy heat all around us. In one of these rooms one boy, he might have been ten or so, wanted to 'play house, mama and papa,' but this was an intrusion on my happy mind, and I rejected him."

But love already had its fascinations. At school Dorothy passed a note to a little boy with the simple message, "I love you." The teacher intercepted the note and kept the two after school so that she could probe "to find the wickedness that my simple words were not meant to convey. I had merely thought he was beautiful."

Dorothy kept her temper at school, but at home, if sufficiently provoked by her brothers, she could be explosive. Her biting and kicking were supplemented by name-calling that on one occasion was so sailor-like that her mother scrubbed Dorothy's mouth out with soap.

Dorothy's childhood confessions from her Oakland days include the theft of a nickel from her mother's purse and the sale of a school book for ten cents. She bought candy with her stolen wealth, but once the candy was eaten, remorse drove her sorrowfully to Mother Grace to confess her wrongdoing.

One rainy Sunday afternoon, Dorothy explored the attic and came upon a musty old Bible which she spent hours reading. "I remember nothing that I read, just the sense of holiness in holding the book in my hands." Before long, under the influence of a Methodist family next door, the Reeds, Dorothy had a first go at religion. "I became disgustingly, proudly pious. I sang hymns with the family next door. I prayed on my knees beside my bed. I asked my mother why we did not pray and sing hymns and got no satisfactory answer. No one went to church but me. I was alternately lonely and smug. At the same time, I began to be afraid of God, of death, of eternity. As soon as I closed my eyes at night the blackness of death surrounded me. . . . If I fell asleep God became in my ears a great noise that became louder and louder, and approached nearer and nearer to me until I woke up sweating with fear and shrieking for my mother. I fell asleep with her hand in mine, her warm presence by my bed."

Dorothy's contact with the Reed family and their church ended when Dorothy, in a dispute over hamsters, called one of the Reed boys "a bad name." No longer welcome in the Reed home, Dorothy found company instead with kids who played at the nearby racetrack.

On the evening of April 17, 1906, John Day was at the Idora Park racetrack. The weather was sultry and the horses were strangely restless, neighing and stamping in their stalls. He sensed panic in their behavior. At 5:13 the next morning, with a pale crescent moon hanging in the dawn sky, the bell of Old Saint Mary's Church in Chinatown began to toll of its

"In the family the name of God was never mentioned. Mother and father never went to church, none of us children had been baptized, and to speak of the soul was to speak immodestly, uncovering what might better remain hidden. . . . In all the first years I remember nothing about God except that routine chapter and prayer in school which I did not feel. It was that Sunday afternoon up in the dim attic and the rich, deep feeling of having a book, which would be with me through life, that stands out in my mind now."

—From Union Square to Rome

9

own accord, and was quickly joined by other bells across the city. For forty seconds the surface of the city rolled as if it were liquid. There were ten seconds of rest, and then a greater shock than the first that lasted twenty-five seconds. In just over a minute, an earthquake had shifted the ground under parts of San Francisco twenty feet. Fires started at hundreds of locations. As the water mains as well as gas lines had broken, little could be done to prevent the blaze from spreading.

The visiting opera singer, Enrico Caruso, who had sung Don Jose in "Carmen" the night before, woke in his bed in the Palace Hotel less in dread of death than of damage to his voice. To reassure himself, he stood at an open window of his suite and sang a passage from Umberto Giordano's "Fedora," a performance that must have astonished the panicking people in the streets below as much as the earthquake. Unintentionally, Caruso gave them courage.

Dorothy remembered waking to deep rumbling, feeling convulsions in the earth, "so that the earth became a sea which rocked our house." Water splashed from the windmill and water tank that she could see from her window. Her father took the three boys from their beds while Grace carried Dorothy's younger sister, Della, to safety, but Dorothy was "left in a big brass bed, which rolled back and forth on a polished floor." She had dreamed of "blackness and death surrounding me" and now discovered, wide awake, not only that the hard earth was unreliable, but so were her parents. No one had come to her rescue.

Across the bay, the fires raged. Before they burned out, half the city's population, 250,000 people, were homeless. Nearly 700 had died. Though badly damaged, Oakland was far enough off the fault line to have escaped devastation. "When the earth settled," Dorothy wrote, "the house was in shambles, dishes broken all over the floor, the house cracked from roof to ground. But there was no fire in Oakland." (The writer Bret Harte remarked that Oakland was spared "because there are some things the earth cannot swallow.")

For two days refugees poured into Oakland by ferry and boat, emerging from San Francisco's flames and smokey black cloud bank. "Idora Park and the racetrack made camping

"While the crisis lasted, people loved each other. They realized their own helplessness while nature 'travaileth and groaneth.' It was as though they were united in Christian solidarity. It makes one think of how people could, if they would, care for each other in times of stress, unjudgingly, with pity and with love."

—From Union Square to Rome

Aftermath of the San Francisco Earthquake in 1906. (Library of Congress)

grounds for them," Dorothy remembered. "All the neighbors joined my mother in serving the homeless. Every stitch of available clothing was given away. All day, following the disaster, there were tremblings of the earth and there was fear in the air."

"What I remember most plainly about the earthquake," Dorothy recalled, "was the human warmth and kindliness of everyone afterward. Mother and all our neighbors were busy from morning to night cooking meals. They gave away every extra garment they possessed. While the crisis lasted, people loved each other."

The worst was over and the Day family had survived without physical injury, but the plant that printed John Day's newspaper had burned, the paper was out of business, and John was out of a job. The house and much of the property that had been shipped around Cape Horn were shattered. What was still usable, John sold for cash. In short order the Day family was on its way by train to Chicago, a city with big shoulders, built on ground that behaved itself.

Chicago

The Day family moved into a dingy six-room tenement apartment over a tavern in a long block of flats three-stories high on 37th Street. One window had a view of Lake Michigan. Until John Day found a job, the apartment was all they could afford. Grace Day had to work hard, Dorothy recalled, "washing for six in a large common basement which stretched almost the length of the block and was like a series of caverns where the children played on rainy days. Outside was a cement-paved yard with neither tree nor blade of grass. The nearest green was that of a vacant lot on the corner, where I wheeled my doll carriage and smelled the sweet clover, gathering sheaves of it for mother to dry in pillowcases and put in linen chests."

Lake Michigan was only two blocks away. A breakwater had been made of slabs of limestone, and, in the pools that formed behind the rock barrier, the Day brothers used to swim in the summer. Here two neighbor children drowned one sunny day. "The little boy had found himself beyond his depth and his sister . . . had taken off her dress to twist into a rope for him to catch hold of; instead he had dragged her in too and they had died in each other's arms." Dorothy looked out over "the vast sunny lake, calm and treacherous, the weeds and grasses among the sands where little children played while older ones stood in awe close to their parents, that long quiet afternoon. When the bodies were found, we did not run to the spot, but mother hurried us home and doubtless there was panic in her heart."

It was Dorothy's first close encounter with death "and yet it did not touch me nearly as those forebodings of death which came to me at night after I had closed my eyes in the dark room and the universe began to spin around me in space."

The family's plunge into poverty was humiliating. Not

Chicago, early twentieth-century. (Credit: Chicago Historical Society)

"[Chicago] was the first time we had been really poor. There was no upstairs, no garden, no sense of space. I remember how hungry I became for the green fields during the long hot summer that followed."

—From Union Square to Rome

wanting to be seen by school friends entering a tenement door, Dorothy pretended to live elsewhere, passing by her own door and instead entering a more impressive building on nearby Ellis Avenue.

When Dorothy was sent shopping, she had to leave untouched the more appealing items and bring home potatoes, bread, jelly, tea and bananas—and the last only in their dead ripe condition at ten cents a dozen. Yet Grace Day managed to bring a special dignity to the household. She made curtains from remnants and hung them from fishing rods. She transformed fruit crates into bookcases, nail kegs into kitchen stools. Lacking a sewing machine, she hand stitched the family's shirts and dresses. "All our clothes were beautifully made and laundered no matter how poor we were." It seemed to Dorothy that her mother "reigned over the supper table as a queen and had as much interest in entertaining her four children as if we were adult friends at a party." Dorothy felt privileged to assist in her mother's evening bath ritual, adding a drop of cologne to the water so that its scent might briefly transform life in a tenement.

Grace Day's bravado rarely cracked, but one night after supper she became hysterical and one by one broke all the dishes. Perhaps it was brought on by exhaustion and hopelessness, or criticism from John, or was caused by the blinding headaches she sometimes suffered. This was a period in her life when she experienced four miscarriages. The next day she seemed her usual self. "I lost my nerve," she explained to the children.

Dorothy shared in the work of the house. "I scoured the faucets until they shone" and had many household chores. Without knowing it, she realized later in her life, "I had imbibed 'a philosophy of work,' enjoying the creative aspects of it as well as getting satisfaction from a hard and necessary job well done."

If there was no yard, at least there was a large back porch. Here Dorothy could arrange tea parties with the dolls her mother made from remnants and wooden clothes pins, creating faces with buttonhole mouths. It was on the porch one night, while gazing at the stars, that Mary Harrington, a

Grace Day. (Marquette University archives)

Dorothy and her younger sister Della.
(Marquette University archives)

Chicago neighbor four years older, told her the story of a saint. In later years Dorothy couldn't remember who it was or anything of the saint's life, only that the story filled her with enthusiasm so that her heart "almost burst with desire to take part in such high endeavor. . . . I was filled with a natural striving, a thrilling recognition of the possibilities of spiritual adventure."

Dorothy received another positive impression of Catholic life from another neighbor, Mrs. Barrett. Searching for a playmate, she discovered Mrs. Barrett praying on her knees at the side of her bed. She looked up at Dorothy without dismay or embarrassment, told her where to find her daughter, and returned to her prayer. "I felt a burst of love toward Mrs. Barrett that I have never forgotten, a feeling of gratitude and happiness that warmed my heart." For a time Dorothy prayed at bedtime. One night, while a hurdy-gurdy played on the street below, she convinced Della that they should both sleep on the floor, thinking of saints sleeping on the cold stone floors of their monastic cells. She fell asleep listening to the snoring of the drunken lady who lived upstairs.

During his period of joblessness, John Day labored over what he assured Grace would be a best-selling adventure novel. His typewriter stood poised in front of him, an ashtray on one side and a glass of whiskey on the other. But the novel never found a publisher.

Making the neighborhood rounds, the pastor of the local Episcopal church came to visit one day, hoping to recruit new members for his congregation. While failing to win over either parent, he got their agreement that the children could attend church if they wished. The two brothers joined the choir, and Dorothy and Della listened eagerly to the music and prayers. Several years later, Dorothy was baptized and confirmed in the Episcopal Church.

Dorothy "loved the Psalms and the Collect prayers and learned many of them by heart, and the anthems filled me with joy. I had never heard anything so beautiful as the *Benedictus* and the *Te Deum*. The words remained with me ever since:

> All ye works of the Lord, bless ye the Lord.
> Praise Him and glorify Him forever.
> O ye sun and moon, O ye stars in the sky,
> O ye winds and hoarfrosts, ye rain and dew,
> Bless ye the Lord, praise Him and glorify Him forever. . . .

"The song thrilled in my heart, and though I was only ten years old, through these Psalms and canticles I called on all creation to join me in blessing the Lord. I thanked Him for creating me."

From childhood onward, Dorothy had a marked capacity for awe and a vulnerability to beauty. "I wanted to cry out with joy. . . . I always felt the common unity of all humanity; the longing of the human heart is for this communion. If only I could sing, I thought, I would shout before the Lord, and call upon the world to shout with me, 'All ye works of the Lord, bless ye the Lord, praise Him and glorify Him forever.'"

At last John Day found work—sports editor of a Chicago paper, *The Inter Ocean*—and could bring to an end the family's tenement sojourn. The Days moved first to Oakwood Boulevard and then to a large house near Lincoln Park on Webster Avenue on Chicago's North Side. Here there was privacy for all, a bedroom fireplace for Grace and, great treasure, a library, in the center of which was a "large round table with a green cover and a lamp in the middle, a gas lamp, green shaded, with a long green hose that always smelled slightly of gas." The chairs were arranged so that all could read by the same light.

Dorothy loved words, rejoiced in the way they could be sewn together to change seasons, leap across time and space,

"Natural goodness, natural beauty, brings joy and a lifting of the spirit, but it is not enough, it is not the same. The special emotions I am speaking of came only at hearing the word of God. It was as though each time I heard our Lord spoken of, a warm feeling of joy filled me. It was hearing of someone you love who loves you."
—From Union Square to Rome

"It seems to me as I look back upon it that I had a childhood that was really a childhood and that I was kept in the status of a child until I was sixteen."
—From Union Square to Rome

or simply describe the ordinary things around her that she found most captivating. By the age of ten, she had become a passionate reader. Sitting with her back to the gas lamp in the library of the Webster Avenue house, she read Victor Hugo, Charles Dickens, Robert Louis Stevenson, James Fenimore Cooper and Edgar Allan Poe, even *The Imitation of Christ* by Thomas à Kempis. She also was drawn to books that her father banned as "trash." The romances that Dorothy borrowed, and the dime novels her brothers enjoyed, had to be kept out of sight. "I can remember one book with a lurid cover of ten robed and hooded men walking in single file along a mountain path with a boa constrictor gliding along behind them." Dorothy hid Swinburne's poem, "Tristram," with an illustration of lovers in the grass, behind a bookcase.

The Day daughters weren't allowed out of the house without permission, restrictions Dorothy later looked back on in a positive light. "The fact that father kept us from going out, and did not want company to come in, saved us from the busy existence that most persons had," she recalled with a remarkable lack of annoyance.

In fact, books were not full-time companions and life was not simply to be read about. She could recollect "sad summer afternoons when there was nothing to do, and suddenly everything palled and life was dull and uninteresting." But on Sundays, at least, there was worship at the Episcopal church and during the warmer months there were Sunday afternoon band concerts at Lincoln Park, where large crowds of picnickers gathered. Dorothy fell madly in love with the band's violinist and shuddered if he happened to glance at her. "We never exchanged a word but I hungered for his look." On Sunday afternoons, Dorothy and Della were allowed to go to the movies—films made by Mack Sennett and D.W. Griffith and comedies with the Keystone Kops and Charlie Chaplin.

Dorothy turned fifteen in 1912, and in May of that year the last of the Day children was born, a baby brother named John who was often put in Dorothy's care. Before two in the morning, when John Day returned from his newspaper, the baby was brought to Dorothy's bed, where Dorothy was required to keep him from crying so that her father's sleep

wouldn't be disturbed. Every night Dorothy had to rock him to sleep, singing from the Episcopal hymnal until her back and shoulders ached, "but the very hardship of taking care of him, the hours I put in with him, made me love him all the more."

Before dawn, with baby John fed and sleeping, Dorothy could turn to her homework—Latin and Greek, English composition, and history. History seemed to her a dull topic, but the ancient languages delighted her. She was one of several students who signed up for a voluntary class in Greek and Latin after school. For ten cents, she bought a second-hand copy of the Greek New Testament and worked on her own translation.

While her experiment several years earlier at sleeping monk-like on the floor had been a one-night event, Dorothy continued to be fascinated with piety. In her journal she declared what "poor weak creatures we are" and what hard work it is to overcome temptation. "I am working always,

Dorothy as a teenager, reading at home. (Marquette University archives)

"I had a special seat by the fire with a pile of books beside me. It was never one book that engrossed me but a dozen. I was hungry for knowledge and had to devour volumes."
—From Union Square to Rome

17

"The call to my youth was the call of Kropotkin, and the beauty of his prose, the nobility of his phrasing, appealed to my heart. . . . This was Kropotkin, to me at that time a saint in his way."
—From Union Square to Rome

Russian anarchist and "revolutionist" Peter Kropotkin, whose writings made a lasting impression on Dorothy. (Library of Congress)

always on guard, praying without ceasing to overcome all physical sensations and be purely spiritual . . . the only love is of God and is spiritual without taint of earthliness. I am afraid I have never really experienced this love or I would never crave the sensual love or the thrill that comes with the meeting of lips. . . . Oh, surely it is a continual strife and my spirit is weary."

If her writing was painfully adolescent, the subject was one that she never lost interest in: the tug-of-war between flesh and the spirit. In fact, the only thing close to a "meeting of lips" that Dorothy had yet experienced was "a firm, austere kiss from my mother every night."

In her last year at high school, radical political sensitivities began to take root. Her oldest brother Donald got his first newspaper job with *The Day Book* (no connection to the Day family). Refusing to publish advertisements, the journal exposed harsh working conditions in factories and department stores without fear of lost revenue. It was thanks to *The Day Book* that Dorothy first became aware of the American labor movement and the "Left"—such groups as the Socialist Party, led by Eugene Debs, and the Industrial Workers of the World.

The books Dorothy was reading in her mid-teens drew her to the Left. She read not only Jack London's adventure books—*The Call of the Wild, White Fang, On the Rails*—but his essays on the class struggle. In the Russian writer Peter Kropotkin she discovered a scientist who had renounced his princely title and become a "revolutionist." Kropotkin's vision of a decentralized, anarchist social order based on cooperation rather than competition had a lifelong impact. Later in life, she often recommended some of his books: *The Memoirs of a Revolutionist, Mutual Aid, The Conquest of Bread,* and *Fields, Factories and Workshops.* Kropotkin, she said, "brought to my mind the plight of the poor."

It was Upton Sinclair that took Dorothy away from the library and the bandstand in the park and turned her toward areas of urban poverty in which she had earlier lived in such shame. Sinclair's novel *The Jungle* was set in and around Chicago's vast stockyards and slaughterhouses. Its protagonist, a Lithuanian immigrant named Jurgis Rudkus, was the only member of his family not utterly destroyed by squalor and injustice. Finally, after suffering a series of tragedies caused by social injustice, he committed himself to fighting for a just social order by joining the Socialist Party. The novel's depiction of filth, violence and corruption in the meat industry so shocked its readers that the book is given credit for Congressional passage of tough meat inspection laws, although Sinclair had hoped to stimulate more profound social change. His intention had been, he said, to expose "the inferno of exploitation" endured by American factory workers. "I aimed at the public's heart," he commented, "and by accident hit it in the stomach."

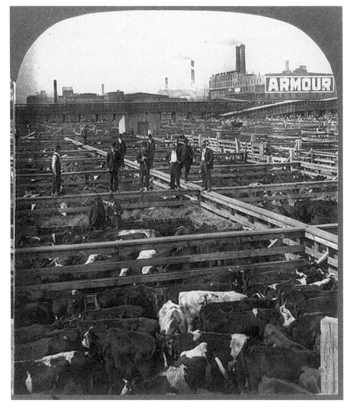

Chicago stockyards. (Library of Congress)

Sinclair's book reached Dorothy's heart. She began taking long walks toward the West Side of Chicago, where the meat-yards were, rather than along the lake or in the green of Lincoln Park. "I walked for miles, pushing my brother in his carriage," exploring "interminable gray streets, fascinating in their dreary sameness, past tavern after tavern, where I envisioned such scenes as the Polish wedding party in Sinclair's story."

Exploring the slums of Chicago was Dorothy's first experience of finding beauty in the midst of desolation. "There were tiny flower gardens and vegetable patches in the yards. Often there were rows of corn, stunted but still recognizable, a few tomato plants, and always the vegetables were bordered by flowers, often grateful marigolds, all sizes and shades with their pungent odor." The drab streets seemed to be transfigured by pungent odors: "The odor of geranium leaves, tomato plants, marigolds; the smell of lumber, of tar, of roasting

"I felt even at fifteen that God meant man to be happy, that He meant to provide him with what he needed to maintain life in order to be happy, and that we did not need to have quite so much destitution and misery as I saw all around and read of in the daily press."
—The Long Loneliness

coffee; the smell of good bread and rolls and coffee cake coming from the small German bakeries. Here was enough beauty to satisfy me."

Dorothy's view was no longer that of so many people she knew who regarded the poor as shiftless and worthless people whose sufferings were no one's fault but their own. Walking such streets as a fifteen-year-old, she pondered the poor and the workers and felt "that from then on my life was to be linked to theirs, their interests were to be mine: I had received a call, a vocation, a direction in my life."

The vocation Dorothy had begun to discover during her long walks on the West Side distanced her from churches. "I am sick and tired of religion," she announced to Della. Dorothy had lately turned sixteen and was in her last year of high school. It was better for the soul, she explained, to bask in the sun or read beautiful poetry than to go to church. And were churches not silent partners to injustice? If Christians shed occasional tears for the poor and their tragedies and made donations to charities, they did not raise a cry against those who piled up fortunes at their expense. Rather, "the rich were smiled at and fawned upon by churchgoers." Dorothy didn't "see anyone taking off his coat and giving it to the poor. I didn't see anyone having a banquet and calling in the lame, the halt and the blind."

While Della never became a radical, she too felt no more need for church services. As a celebration of their newfound freedom, Dorothy and Della climbed out a window and slipped off to the movies. "What do we care," Della asked, "if we get a scolding when we get back?"

My Universities

In 1914, with a world war breaking out in Europe and Charlie Chaplin's baggy-trousered tramp new to the silver screen, Dorothy graduated from Waller High School. Thanks to her accomplishments in Latin and Greek, she was one of three students at Waller to win a scholarship. This not only made college possible, but offered her the welcome prospect of being some distance from her father's irritation with foreigners, agitators, radicals and trashy books. There would be no more climbing out of windows to go to the movies.

In September, "filled with a great sense of independence," seventeen-year-old Dorothy took the two-hour train ride south to the Urbana campus of the University of Illinois. She had no clear idea what directions her studies might take her. Though she had signed up to study Latin, English, history, biology and rhetoric, in fact she felt no special interest in a particular course of studies or even in gaining a degree. The main thing was that "I was on my own, and no longer to be cared for by the family. The idea of earning my own living, by my own work, was more thrilling than the idea of an education."

Dorothy made no attempt to join a sorority, obtain a campus job or settle into student housing. "While I was free to go to college, I was mindful of girls who worked in stores and factories through their youth and afterward married men who were slaves in those same factories. The Marxist slogan, 'Workers of the world, unite! You have nothing to lose but your chains,' seemed to me a most stirring battle cry . . . a clarion call that made me feel one with the masses [and] apart from the bourgeoisie, the smug, and the satisfied."

Choosing physical labor as her means of support, she found a succession of domestic jobs—washing and ironing and child care—in exchange for bed and board. "Many a time I scrubbed the skin off my knuckles," she recalled. Making a

Alma Mater, University of Illinois in Urbana.

"I was happy as a lark at leaving home. I was sixteen and filled with a sense of great independence. I was on my own, and no longer to be cared for by my family."
—The Long Loneliness

A young Dorothy. (Marquette University archives)

"Even as I talked about religion I rejected religion. . . . I had read the New Testament with fervor. But that time was past." —The Long Loneliness

start in journalism, she also earned small amounts writing for the local paper. Support occasionally came from home, but it wasn't much, as John Day's paper had folded and he was again unemployed. What money Dorothy had was largely spent on books. The words of the sixteenth-century scholar Erasmus of Rotterdam could have been her own: "When I get a little money I buy books, and, if anything is left over, I buy food and clothes." In her own case, money not spent on books went to food and cigarettes, the latter a newly acquired taste.

Kropotkin had stirred her interest in Russian authors, and now she discovered several others whom she would read again and again for the rest of her life: Gorki, Chekhov, Tolstoy and Dostoevsky. Dostoevsky especially provided a thread of connection with Christianity, a faith she was otherwise attempting to shrug off, convinced that "religion would only impede my work."

She found classes less interesting than her reading. "Really, I led a very shiftless life," she wrote in *The Long Loneliness*, "doing for the first time exactly what I wanted to do, attending only those classes I wished to attend, coming and going at whatever hour of the night I pleased. My freedom intoxicated me. I felt it was worth going hungry for."

Reading histories of the labor movement, Dorothy became familiar with the speeches and writings of Big Bill Haywood, Mother Jones, Elizabeth Gurley Flynn, Eugene Debs, Carlo Tresca, and the Haymarket Anarchists—Chicago labor organizers, four of whom had been hanged in 1887.

It disturbed Dorothy that far more was done to provide a degree of relief for victims of social evils than to get rid of those evils. "There were day nurseries for children . . . but why didn't fathers get money enough to take care of their families so that mothers would not have to work?" She was haunted by her growing awareness of the world's cast-off people: "Disabled men, without arms and legs, blind men, consumptive men with all their manhood drained out of them by industrialism; farmers gaunt and harried with debt; mothers weighed down with children at their skirts, in their arms, in their wombs; people ailing and rickety—all this long procession of desperate people called to me. Where were the saints to try to change the social order, not just to minister to the slaves but to do away with slavery?"

Her heroes were those who, at great risk and sacrifice, were building up unions and cooperatives and struggling for the eight-hour workday and the five-day week. In 1915, the ten-hour workday was common, and only eight percent of America's workers were union members. Many men and women had died or been crippled to win small gains in union growth. "My heart thrilled at those unknown women in New England," Dorothy wrote, "who led the first strike to liberate women and children from the cotton mills." She was grateful that her mother's heart was touched by such events as well. Grace Day reminded Dorothy of a period in her own childhood when her family's poverty was such that she had to work in a Poughkeepsie shirt factory.

Dorothy took the symbolic step of joining the Socialist Party, whose base of support was made up of trade unionists, social reformers, populist farmers and immigrant communities. Its candidate, Eugene V. Debs, had won nearly a million votes in the presidential election of 1912. But Dorothy found the Socialist Club meetings in Urbana unbearably dull. Her involvement as a dues-paying member was short lived.

Socialist leader Eugene Debs. (Library of Congress)

She joined a campus writers' club, the Scribblers, which accepted her on the basis of an essay on the experience of hunger, in which, "with grim relish," she described going for three days with no food other than salted peanuts while living in a frigid attic room that contained a bed, table, chair and tiny stove which in those few days was of no use. (Accounts of surviving on very little money became a recurrent theme of Dorothy's early journalism.) As a Scribbler, she got to wear the club symbol: a small golden pen nib.

Friendships developed with two fellow Scribblers: Samson Raphaelson and Rayna Simons. Raphaelson was a gifted writer and satirist who went on to become an immensely successful playwright. He wrote the script for Hollywood's first "talkie," "The Jazz Singer." His later film credits include "The Little Shop Around the Corner," "Trouble in Paradise," "Heaven Can Wait," and, with Alfred Hitchcock, "Suspicion."

Yearbook photo of Rayna Simons (later Prohme). (Marquette University archives)

"Whatever [Rayna] did she did with her whole heart. If she read, she read. If she was with you, all her attention was for you. She was single-minded, one of the pure of heart, and her interest in life was as intense as her interest in books."
—The Long Loneliness

The more important friendship for Dorothy was with Rayna Simons, three years older than herself, "slight and boney, deliciously awkward and yet unself-conscious, alive and eager." She had a mass of curly red hair, "loose enough about her face to form . . . a flaming aureole, with sun and brightness in it. Whatever she did, she did with her whole heart." The fact that she was Jewish meant that, despite family wealth, personal warmth and brilliance as a student, Rayna was invited into no sorority. Through Rayna, Dorothy had her first personal contact with the social reality of anti-Semitism.

Their friendship was "clear as a bell, crystal clear, with no stain of self-seeking." The two became inseparable. During the summer, Dorothy stayed on a farm owned by Rayna's father, and in the fall she accepted Rayna's invitation to share her room in an Urbana boarding house for Jewish girls. Together they attended concerts, heard lectures on socialism and feminism, and attended readings by such poets as Edgar Lee Masters, Vachel Lindsay and John Masefield.

Rayna was loved by many, Dorothy wrote in *The Long Loneliness*, "because she was so unself-conscious, so interested in others, so ready to hear and discuss all that interested them." While still at the university, Rayna's selfless love of people had not yet drawn her toward any political ideology. She didn't yet share Dorothy's radical views, while Dorothy found Rayna too intellectual. (Not many years later, Rayna's thinking turned as red as her hair. In 1927, while Americans were waiting in long lines to see "The Jazz Singer," Rayna was in Moscow to take part in a massive celebration of the tenth anniversary of the Russian Revolution. While there she made arrangements to enter the Lenin Institute, a graduate school for revolutionists, but in mid-November she fell ill and a week later died. The next morning her body was carried by mourners to Moscow's New Crematorium. The journalist Vincent Sheean was among those weeping. "The bier was draped in the red flag and covered with golden flowers," he wrote in *Personal History*. "Then a signal was given, a switch was turned, and the golden mass of Rayna, her hair and her bright flowers and the Red flag, sank slowly before us into the furnace.")

In June 1916, Dorothy—now eighteen—decided she had

had enough schooling. She joined her parents in moving to New York where John Day had been hired by *The New York Telegraph*. Dorothy found it easy to be with her mother again, as well as with Della and four-year-old John, but sharing a house with her father was more difficult than ever. Neither hesitated to bait the other with their contrary opinions. Realizing that she needed an apartment of her own and her own income, Dorothy began searching for employment as a reporter. With a portfolio of her clippings from Urbana, she set out applying at various New York daily papers, but quick-

"For weeks I was oppressed by the misery of human existence. The people I saw in subways, in crowded eating places, walking the streets, sitting on park benches, or looking for work, all seemed miserable and hopeless. I walked the streets in solitude and my heart wept within me for the ugliness of all I saw."
—From Union Square to Rome

ly found that she was lucky to get past the office boys. The two city editors she managed to talk with assured her that urban reporting was definitely not for girls, a view shared by John Day. One editor gave her the address of a rural newspaper he thought she might try, but Dorothy was determined to stay in New York and persisted with her search despite a deep anguish that she later called "the long loneliness." "In all that city of seven millions, I found no friends; I had no work; I was separated from my fellows. Silence in the midst of the city noises oppressed me. My own silence, the feeling that I had no one to talk to, overwhelmed me so that my very throat was constricted; my heart was heavy with unuttered thoughts; I wanted to weep my loneliness away."

"House Tops," an etching of passengers on the "El" train by Edward Hopper.

The weeks of futile job-hunting made her feel more at home in New York. Each day she walked the streets and discovered the autonomous ethnic communities that were packed side by side like ragged squares in a patchwork quilt. She became familiar with the bus and subway routes and the several bridges "that were strung like jewels over the East River."

She found the poverty of New Yorkers even worse than in Chicago. Homeless and jobless men haunted the streets. The loud clatter of the "El"—the elevated trains—and the subways jarred her nerves. The rotting tenements shed a "smell like no other in the world and one never can become accustomed to it. . . . It is not the smell of life, but the smell of the grave." Yet she found her burden of loneliness was eased when she walked through the slum neighborhoods. Here life had more texture, more contact, and not all the smells were unpleasant.

It took five months before she arrived at the place where, given her leftward tilt, she might have first applied: the offices of New York's one Socialist daily, *The Call*, down on Pearl Street, near the Brooklyn Bridge in lower Manhattan, just across the river from where she was born. A small and struggling paper with office space over a printing plant, here no one felt obliged to ward off visitors who wanted to talk to the managing editor, Chester Wright. A copy boy rushing downstairs to the press room ignored her. There were a few men busy at their typewriters and several others reading copy at another desk. She introduced herself to Wright and asked him for a job. He had no objection to women journalists, nor did he mind that she was young and new to urban reporting. The problem was, Wright told her, that *The Call* didn't have the money to add anyone to its staff. "Why, we hardly have enough money to pay the office boy!"

"That's all right," Dorothy assured him. "I wasn't expecting a big salary." She argued that a socialist paper needed a woman reporter on the staff. There are people who find it easier talking to a woman than a man. There are doors a woman might get through that men would find locked. "I know, women reporters are always a good thing," Wright agreed, "but we're broke, simply broke."

While showing him her portfolio, Dorothy had an inspiration. She remembered there were some city policemen who had organized themselves into "diet squads" in order to demonstrate that the poor could live well enough on $5 a week. Also some wealthy women in Chicago were feeding themselves on twenty-five cents a day to prove that the relief

The Call, a Socialist daily.

the unemployed received was more than adequate. If *The Call* would pay her just $5 a week—what a lot of factory girls were getting, she pointed out—she could be a "diet squad of one" and write from a more radical perspective about the experience for *The Call.*

Perhaps the idea appealed to Chester Wright, or perhaps he had developed admiration for the sheer bravado of this eager, ambitious, attractive young woman who wouldn't take no for an answer. He agreed to hire her for a month at $5 a week, and, if he decided to keep her, somehow he would find the money to pay her $12 a week afterward.

The next morning Dorothy packed, said goodbye to her parents, left her suitcase at *The Call,* and went out in search of her own lodging. On Cherry

Hester Street on the Lower East Side. (Library of Congress)

Street there were many tenements displaying "furnished room" signs and in one of them she found something that seemed suitable. The rent was $5 a month. There were vermin in the mattress, she found out during the first night, and the loose panes in her window rattled with the steady draft from the narrow air shaft beyond. With the draft came the stench of the hall toilets. At night the neighborhood cats "shrieked with almost human voices." Even so, Dorothy was delighted with what she had found and felt that she had been led to her new home—and away from her old one—by a guardian angel.

Having a room and a job, her sense of isolation evaporated. The staff of *The Call* quickly absorbed Dorothy into their

Mulberry Street on the Lower East Side. (Library of Congress)

social life, inviting her to join them at Child's Restaurant on Park Row in the small hours of the night, after the day's edition had gone to press. Here they nightly renewed their permanent debates about their competing radical ideologies. Some favored the anarchist "Wobblies"—the nickname for members of the Industrial Workers of the World (the IWW)—who were attempting to gather all laborers into one vast union; Wobbly heroes included Big Bill Haywood and Joe Hill, the labor organizer who had been executed by a firing squad in Utah but whose songs were heard on every picket line. Others aligned themselves with the American Federation of Labor, whose membership was restricted to skilled industrial workers, the elite of labor, and who took a less revolutionary view of change than Wobblies. There were other factions as well, but no Communists—the Communist Party hadn't yet been founded. Socialism, in all its varieties, was well represented on *The Call*'s staff. Dorothy found much to agree with on all sides but saw herself as a Wobbly and was proud of her recently-issued red IWW membership card.

Her new neighborhood seemed more interesting than any political theory. "It was a cheerful and lively street with horse carts which jogged every half hour through the crowds of children playing in the gutters and hiding among ash cans. The air was full of shrill child voices, shouted admonitions from the mothers hanging over their fire-escapes which fronted the buildings like stage props. Street organs surrounded by little girls played the latest popular tunes and every once in a while a merry-go-round set on a wagon was drawn to the curb by a lean and deafened horse. Rides were a penny and the music which the man ground out as he turned the handle which set the carousel spinning held an invitation which gathered the children from blocks around."

Nearby was Mulberry Street with its Greek and Turkish coffee shops and "shops where long cheeses and sausages and chains of red pepper and garlic contributed their smell to the cluttered air." But streets that seemed almost heavenly in the day turned sinister late at night, when Dorothy made her way home. The noise of her footsteps so disturbed the silence that she bought rubber heels for her shoes. People were rarely to be seen, but she discovered she wasn't alone. "A whole silent world was alive, a world that slept at dawn. . . . There were huge sleek cats, furtive pariahs that prowled through the hallways and gutters."

Yet even the night world revealed delights, such as the bakeries filling the darkness with the smell of bread just out of the ovens. A tobacco shop gleamed brightly on one corner, a harbor of warmth. The night world had its own population. One of them was a woman who ran along the streets calling out the name of her long-dead son. One winter night, when Dorothy stopped to talk with two policemen who had built a small fire in a shelter under the Manhattan Bridge and were having a midnight meal of coffee and rolls, the woman came running down the street. The policemen welcomed her. "How about it, mother. You haven't found him yet? Better come and get warm and have a cup of coffee. You've hunted

"I have learned since that the poverty of the East Side is comparatively well-fed poverty. There are always the pushcart markets with all kinds of fruits and vegetables. Mussels were the cheapest of the sea foods, and you could buy a leg of chicken and cook up a pot of soup. The Jews and Italians knew how to cook and they did not mind haggling at the push-carts over pennies. . . . I enjoyed that winter in the slums and have never lived any place else since."
—From Union Square to Rome

"I was only eighteen, so I wavered between my allegiance to Socialism, Syndicalism (the I.W.W.'s) and Anarchism. When I read Tolstoy I was an Anarchist. My allegiance to The Call kept me a Socialist, although a left-wing one, and my Americanism inclined me to the I.W.W. movement."

—From Union Square to Rome

long enough tonight." The woman's name was Audrey, and despite her age and her beaten face she was able to make a slight living as a prostitute. She was known locally as "Dis-Audrey conduct," in recognition of the charge under which she was often arrested.

From such adventures, Dorothy returned to her tiny room, with its bed, table and chair and small library. She had decorated the dingy walls with pictures of a bullfighter, a famous explorer, and a postcard of a bust of Amenemhat III, an Egyptian ruler of thirty-seven centuries earlier, a handsome image despite a blow to the stone that had cost it part of the nose. Dorothy in fact liked "the desolate line of his broken nose, and the pleasant sensuousness of his expression." She had a record player as well. By limiting her food budget to twenty-five cents a day, she would be able to pay a dollar a week for this mechanical roommate. Grace Day contributed fifteen records.

Dorothy wrote up her diet, the purchase of record player and other details of her life in a series of four articles for *The Call*, one of which ran under the headline, REPORTER EATS FARINA AND CHEESE AND READS WORDSWORTH. She had become a working journalist in New York City.

If the first month's diet was meager, Dorothy's work provided well for her huge appetite for experience. "There was much to do—meetings to attend of protest against labor, capital, the high cost of living, war-profiteering, entering the war, not entering the war, conscription, anti-conscription. There were meetings to start strikes, to end strikes, to form unions, to fight against unions. Food riots came. . . . There were birth control meetings—trials of birth control leaders . . . and interviews galore."

While covering one demonstration for *The Call*, Dorothy was clubbed by a policeman. She was

Socialist demonstration in Union Square. (Library of Congress)

surprised at how easily she had herself been caught up in "the spirit of the mob." When the club struck her ribs with a hollow thud, she was in such a state that it didn't hurt nor did it even anger her. All she felt was a "curious, detached, mad feeling . . . as the crowd seethed and shouted and fought." She looked at the policeman whose club had struck her and noticed blood was flowing from a gash in his forehead, blurring his vision. He wiped the blood from his eyes and was distressed to discover he had hit a young woman wearing a press card. "Excuse me," he said. "I can't see." He then renewed his use of the club on others in the crowd. It happened it wasn't a radical crowd that day, but flag-waving youth impatient with America for not yet having joined in the European war with Germany.

Dorothy was sent up to East 15th Street to write about a shelter for probationers, which turned out to be a warm, caring house of hospitality to which judges occasionally sent women—mainly young prostitutes—who might otherwise have gone to prison. Miss Prince, the house's founder and fund-raiser, spoke with Dorothy of her hope that someday there might be enough such houses so that prisons would no longer be needed.

One night in 1917, Dorothy covered a speech by Elizabeth Gurley Flynn, who later in her life went to prison for her leadership of the American Communist Party. At the time, Flynn was still a "Wobbly." She was in New York to raise financial help for iron miners on strike in Mesabi, Minnesota. Many in the audience, including Dorothy, wept as twenty-seven-year-old Flynn described the brutality that was being heaped upon the strikers, the appalling conditions of the mines, and the destitution being suffered by the miners' families. "History has a long-range perspective," Flynn declared. "It ultimately passes stern judgment on tyrants and vindicates those who fought, suffered, were imprisoned, and died for human freedom, against political oppression and economic slavery." When a collection was taken up for them, Dorothy emptied her purse to the last coin, "not even saving carfare, so that I had to borrow the fare back to the office and go without lunch for some days afterward." (When Flynn died in 1964, she left her rocking chair to Dorothy.)

One day Dorothy was assigned to interview Leon Trotsky, who at the time was living in exile in an apartment on the Lower

Elizabeth Gurley Flynn, "The Rebel Girl." (Library of Congress)

IWW demonstration in New York.

"Our function as journalists seemed to be to build up a tremendous indictment against the present system, a daily tale of horror which would have the cumulative effect of forcing the workers to rise in revolution."

—From Union Square to Rome

East Side across the street from one of Manhattan's oldest churches, Saint Mark's in the Bowery. Soon after the interview, Trotsky was on his way back to Russia where he became one of the principal figures of the November Revolution and a co-founder, with Lenin, of the Soviet state. Little of Dorothy's interview was published in *The Call*, however, as the editors didn't appreciate Trotsky's criticisms of the American Socialist Party. He regarded it as naive due to it emphasis on avoiding violence.

The 1917 revolution in Russia came in two stages, both in one year. The first, pre-Soviet stage—a short-lived attempt to establish democracy in Russia—was in March. Faced by strikers and an army that ignored his orders, Czar Nicholas II abdicated. In the midst of the social chaos brought on by massive Russian losses in World War I, an ancient monarchy had collapsed and a provisional government, headed by Alexander Kerensky, had taken its place without any bloodshed. Radicals throughout the world responded with jubilation to the vacating of the imperial throne. (Eight months later, the Kerensky government was ousted at gunpoint and the Soviet Union established.)

Celebrating phase one, on March 21 Dorothy was among the many thousands who gathered for an exultant rally in New York's Madison Square Garden. "I felt the exultation, the joyous sense of the victory of the masses as they sang . . . the workers' hymn of Russia":

Arise, ye prisoners of starvation!
Arise, ye wretched of the earth!

For justice thunders condemnation,
A better world's in birth.
No more tradition's chains shall bind us,
No more enslaved, no more enthralled,
The earth shall rise on new foundations.
We have been naught, we shall be all.
'Tis the final conflict,
Let each stand in his place . . .
The international working class
Shall be the human race.

The night was a festival of hope. There was a feeling among the celebrants that heaven was descending to earth—a world without oppression, without homelessness, without hunger, without injustice, without war. If such an event could happen in backward Russia, surely it could happen in resourceful, inventive, forward-looking America.

Among those singing the "Internationale" with Dorothy that night was Mike Gold, a co-worker at *The Call* who had already become her closest friend. Gold had been born into an Orthodox Jewish family in 1893 on the Lower East Side. He had "no politics except hunger" until 1914, when he strayed into a demonstration at Union Square and was knocked down by the police when they attacked the demonstrators. The same day he bought a copy of *The Masses*, the Socialist monthly magazine, and began to gravitate into the Socialist Party. When the Communist Party was founded in the United States in 1919, Gold became a member and later in his life was editor of the Communist paper, *The Daily Worker.* (In 1930, his book, *Jews Without Money*, was published; it remains a classic memoir of the urban poor.)

Gold was twenty-three years old when Dorothy met him. He, too, had joined the paper's staff when he was eighteen. After midnight, when *The Call* had been turned over to the printers, they both were among the reporters who went to Child's for pancakes and coffee. During a period when she was sick, it was Gold who came after work one night to bring her cough medicine, lemons and some whiskey, as well as an essay on Maxim Gorki, a radical Russian writer they both

Dorothy's friend Mike Gold, later editor of the Communist *Daily Worker.* (Library of Congress)

Dorothy in 1917, with copies of *The Call* opposing U.S. entry into war. (Marquette University archives)

liked. The landlady came to her own conclusions about why Mike Gold was in Dorothy's room and called Grace Day to notify her of Dorothy's immoral conduct. Grace Day quickly came to visit and accepted Dorothy's reassurance that she and Gold were friends, not lovers.

It is not surprising that gossip about them continued to be plentiful. The two spent long hours walking the streets, sitting on piers along the waterfront on the East River, talking about life and sharing experiences about the passion that had brought them both to *The Call*—the sufferings of the poor. They both loved books and rejoiced to talk about their reading. Sometimes Gold broke into song—whether in Hebrew or Yiddish, Dorothy didn't know.

Another friendship that began in 1917 was with Peggy Baird, whom Dorothy met through Gold. Peggy was an artist who lived in a large, wildly unkempt room and who was baffled at Dorothy's seeming immunity to sexual temptation. Peggy rejoiced to find lovers. She assured Dorothy that sex was "a barrier that kept men and women from fully understanding each other, and thus a barrier to be broken down." Love affairs, she said, were "incidents in an erotic education." Dorothy neither agreed nor disagreed, but was fascinated with Peggy's openness and sense of adventure. The fact that Peggy "sexed," as she called it, and Dorothy didn't wasn't a barrier between them. Peggy recruited Dorothy as a model. "Just strip off your clothes," she said to Dorothy after coffee was brewed one morning. "The room's warm enough. And while you're drinking your coffee, I'll sketch you." It struck Dorothy that she wouldn't dream of undressing before her mother or sister, and yet it was impossible to refuse Peggy's request. She slipped out of her clothes, curled up on the sofa, and comforted herself with a cigarette. "You'll probably have a beautiful figure by the time you're thirty," Peggy said reassuringly. (Half a century later, Peggy settled at the Catholic Worker farm, and, while there, was received into the Catholic Church. Even when she was slowly dying of cancer, people were drawn to her just as they had been when she was a young woman in Greenwich Village. "It is wonderful," Dorothy wrote in her journal during Peggy's last months, "how young and old turn to Peggy, who is always calm, equable, unjudging. She has something.")

Dorothy's work experiences at *The Call* came so thick and fast that she found it impossible to piece them together in a coherent way. "Life on a newspaper," she wrote, "whether radical or conservative, made me lose all sense of perspective. . . . I was carried along in a world of events, writing, reporting, with no time at all for thought or reflection, one day listening to Trotsky, and the next day interviewing Mrs. Vincent Astor's butler." The emerging pattern of Dorothy's life, with its fierce intellectual and spiritual needs, required more space for reflection than was possible on a daily paper.

Her last *Call* assignment brought her to Washington where, on April 2, 1917, President Wilson addressed both houses of Congress and war was declared. On her return, she went to Webster Hall in lower Manhattan to attend a dance which had been organized to raise money for a group of anarchists opposing the draft. Attracted to Dorothy, one anarchist approached Dorothy so assertively that she slapped

"There were other kinds of protests for me to cover: street-corner meetings, marches to City Hall as well as appeals for playgrounds, recreation centers, babies' clinics, and better schools. Usually the protests grew out of some case of human misery. . . . There were always leaders to rush in trying to sway the people to their cause, either I.W.W.'s, Anarchists, or Socialist leaders, all of them combating each other vigorously the while."
—The Long Loneliness

him. He slapped her back. Others intervened on behalf of Dorothy and roughly ushered the anarchist out. Mike Gold had watched it all, was critical of Dorothy's part in the event, and told her so. She responded by resigning her job and walking out. Her stay with *The Call* had lasted seven months.

For several weeks she worked with the Collegiate Anti-Militarism League at Columbia University, then joined the staff of *The Masses*, the monthly magazine whose staff and contributors were the intellectual aristocracy of America's Left. Max Eastman, the editor, was a poet and speaker who, in the early years of the Russian Revolution, was one of its uncritical admirers, but who later in life became a disillu-sioned and bitter anti-Communist and an editor of *The Reader's Digest*. Floyd Dell, who hired Dorothy, had quit high school at sixteen, worked in a factory, become a Chicago jour-nalist, made a name as a poet, and finally started writing for *The Masses*. Later he was best known as a novelist. Jack Reed, after graduating from Harvard, became a combination labor organizer and radical reporter. His eyewitness account of the Russian Revolution, *Ten Days That Shook the World*, became an international best-seller. (In 1919, at the age of thirty-two, he became a founder of the American Communist Labor Party. In 1920, he died of typhus while back in Moscow. Honored as a "Hero of the Revolution," his ashes were buried by the Kremlin wall.)

Max Eastman, editor of *The Masses*. (Library of Congress)

The offices of *The Masses* looked out over Union Square. The walls were decorated with drawings and cartoons by the leading artists of the Left: Art Young, Hugo Gellert, Boardman Robinson, Maurice Becker, Henry Glintencamp and others. Delivering new work, the artists often paused for conversation and coffee away from the drawing board. The magazine's poets were often there as well, and on occasion there were spontaneous poetry readings.

The government took *The Masses* seriously. "Max Eastman," Dorothy recalled, "was carrying on a scholarly con-troversy with President Wilson: the letters they exchanged were printed monthly in the magazine, which I helped to dummy up at a printer's on Park Row with Floyd Dell, who patiently taught me how to be an editor along these mechanical lines."

IN GEORGIA
The Southern Gentleman Demonstrates His Superiority

Dorothy's main work was to sort through the many sub-missions the magazine received and to decide which ones merited being read by the senior editors. It was meditative, quiet work, in contrast to reporting for a daily, and gave her a chance to think more and gain perspective.

Dorothy's rift with Mike Gold was short-lived. Soon they were reading Tolstoy together and renewing their explorations of the slums and waterfront. Together they welcomed Dorothy's college friend, red-haired Rayna Simons, when she came visiting from Chicago. They went to visit the younger brother of artist Hugo Gellert, held in a military prison for his refusal to wear a uniform or take part in the war. There was at the time no legal provision for conscientious objectors. Despite everything, the boy was cheerful; he had been allowed to keep his violin. A few weeks later he was dead, officially a suicide. Those who knew him couldn't believe it— Hugo Gellert took for granted his brother had been murdered. "I could see the blind greed of the industrialist, but the cold, calculating torture and killing of prisoners was a mystery that left me shuddering," Dorothy wrote.

The February 1917 issue of *The Masses* was suppressed by the postal authorities for its "pornographic" cover." (Library of Congress)

No one could miss the fact that Gold and Dorothy were in love. "In our radical ardor [Mike and I] made friends with the world; many a time, coming home late at night, we picked up men from the park benches and gave them whatever bed was empty in the place, ourselves sitting up all night, continuing to talk." Yet they never married and seem never to have lived together. In conversation with Stanley Vishnewski about her younger years, Dorothy recalled once suggesting marriage to Gold, but he turned the idea down. Once asked why he hadn't married Dorothy, Gold replied, "Because she was too radical."

Repression wasn't only for young men who refused to kill, like Hugo Gellert's brother. It came in milder forms to those who opposed the war with words and gestures. Each issue of *The Masses* was studied by the postal authorities before being accepted for delivery. One issue was refused because it included a poem about Mary, the mother of Jesus, becoming pregnant out of wedlock. Another was judged undeliverable on the grounds that it contained pornography—there was a drawing on the cover of a bare-breasted woman. An issue that offered prizes to winners of an essay contest was refused because the contest was deemed a lottery.

The harassment of the magazine, however, generated news and, despite post office suppression, circulation via the newsstand managed to climb steadily until September, when federal officers raided the magazine, seizing back issues, manuscripts, financial records, subscriber lists and all the files of correspondence. The U.S. Post Office rescinded the magazine's mailing permit. Five of the editors and two leading contributors were indicted on the charge of sedition.

As Dorothy's name was new to the magazine's masthead, she wasn't arrested and managed to get out the last issue of *The Masses*, dated November-December 1917. It included her own lyrical description of Manhattan's South Street, "where truckmen and dockmen sit around on loads of boxes and wait for a boat to come in, where men idle in the September sunlight and dream and yawn and smoke . . . where kids sit on the edge of the dock and look into the water below that swirls with refuse and driftwood."

From Jail to the Golden Swan

Suffragists protesting in front of the White House. (Library of Congress)

In the spring of 1917, U.S. participation in the European war was close at hand. Pacifists were demonstrating in Washington, and so were suffragists. The latter had been picketing at the White House all year to protest the exclusion of women from the voting booth and public office.

Among those arrested and jailed for thirty days was Peggy Baird. On her release in November, she briefly returned to New York, met Dorothy and Mike Gold in a basement café in Greenwich Village, and described "the stir" the imprisoned women were making. "I wouldn't use the vote if I had it," Peggy said, "but that doesn't keep me from joining them when they're making such a good fight." She planned to return to Washington the next day and wondered if Dorothy would like to take part in the next round of actions now that *The Masses* had been suppressed. A number of women planned to get arrested in front of the White House and to fast once in jail as a protest against the harsh treatment to which imprisoned suffragists were being subjected. "I don't see why I shouldn't go," Dorothy responded. "I hate not to be

"The suffragists were treated as criminals and shared cells with petty thieves and prostitutes. The suffragists had recruited a large number of women from all over the United States, reflecting all classes of society, to picket with them in protest against the brutal treatment they had received."

—From Union Square to Rome

working and I don't see what else there is I can do right now." Mike took them to the terminal to catch the night bus.

The next day, November 10, a procession of nearly forty women formed at Lafayette Park, across the street from the White House. With banners in hand, each wearing a purple and gold silk sash, they walked two by two like cathedral choristers toward the White House gates. "There was a religious flavor about the silent proceeding," Dorothy wrote in *The Long Loneliness*, "and a holy light shone on the faces of the suffragists." A crowd stood by watching. "There were old women who cheered, young women whose faces glowed or were apathetic. Men were generally indignant, except the newspaper reporters, and they were enthusiastic because the suffragists were providing them with so many good stories. Some men shouted, 'Shame! In wartime too!'" Jeering boys threw stones while sailors and soldiers attempted to seize the women's banners.

Arrest quickly followed, but not jail. The judge who faced the feminists found them guilty but postponed sentence. The women immediately marched back to the White House, repeated their action, were arrested again, and the next morning won their sentences: six months for the leader of the action, fifteen days for the oldest defendant, and thirty days for the rest. Immediately, they declared themselves hunger

Suffragist arrested at White House.
(Library of Congress)

The Occoquan workhouse. (Library of Congress)

strikers, refusing to eat until imprisoned suffragists were treated not as criminals but were granted the privileges given to political prisoners in Europe: use of their own clothes, passage of letters without censorship, access to their own doctors and lawyers, and possession of books and personal papers.

It all seemed like a marvelous adventure to Dorothy until she was on the train, under police escort, watching passing lamps glowing in farmhouse windows along the route to Occoquan, a penal workhouse with a reputation for harsh treatment of prisoners. "Somehow," she told Peggy, "life and struggle seem very tawdry in the twilight. This bleak countryside makes me feel that I should struggle for my soul instead of political rights. . . . I feel peculiarly small and lonely tonight."

At the workhouse the male guards, two to each woman, seized the prisoners. The eldest was picked off the floor. Dorothy managed to bite the hand of the warden and then plant solid kicks in the shins of the guards who carried her off. "I struggled every step of the way." Finally the guards lifted her up and threw her onto an iron bench, one of them yelling, "My mother ain't no suffrager!" Dorothy was locked

Suffragist in jail.

in a cell with another prisoner who had been notably rowdy and had been handcuffed to the bars in punishment. The two went to sleep talking quietly of the novels of Joseph Conrad, of travel and the spell of the sea.

By the third day of the hunger strike, Dorothy was in deep depression. She watched the light slowly shifting in her cell and experienced "a heart-breaking conviction of the ugliness of life." She had no feeling of her own identity, no sense of future possibilities, no sense of being a hero for her act of protest. How must it be, she wondered, for those imprisoned not merely for weeks but years? She had heard of women kept for up to half a year in solitary confinement cells. More experienced prisoners talked of a whipping post for those who weren't otherwise subdued. And here she was "with thirty-seven other women—all in order that the papers might give the cause publicity and make the public think about suffrage." She wondered what good suffrage would do if it were won. No doubt many suffragists would vote for war just as men did. "I lost all consciousness of any cause. . . . I could only feel darkness and desolation all around me. That I would be free again after thirty days meant nothing to me. I would never be free again, never free when I knew that behind bars all over the world there are women and men, young girls and boys, suffering constraint, punishment, isolation and hardship for crimes of which all of us are guilty. . . . People sold themselves for jobs, for the pay check, and if they received a high enough price, they were honored. If their cheating, their theft, their lie, were of colossal proportions, if it were successful, they met with praise, not blame."

More than ever before, Dorothy felt a profound sense of identification with those whom many people view with horror and in whom they see no glimpse of themselves: "I was the mother whose child had been raped and slain. I was the mother who had borne the monster who had done it. I was even that monster, feeling in my own breast every abomination."

Her sleep was broken by nightmares. In the days she ached with dull hunger. Dorothy asked for a Bible and two days later one was given to her. It was only for literary enjoyment, she assured herself, but as she turned to the Psalms, which she had loved in childhood, she found the words revived her spirits. How reassuring it was to read:

They that sow in tears shall reap in joy.
Going, they went and wept, casting their seeds.
But coming, they shall come with joyfulness, carrying their
sheaves.

"If we had faith in what we were doing," she realized freshly, "making our protest against brutality and injustice, then we were indeed casting our seeds, and there was the promise of the harvest to come."

At the end of the sixth day of the hunger strike, the women were transferred to the prison hospital. On the eighth day, Dorothy could go on no further, accepted a crust of bread soaked in milk, but then resumed the fast. On the tenth day the fasters' demands were suddenly met. The women were given back their clothes, presented with all the mail that had accumulated, given liberty to walk the jail corridors, and served decent meals. When they had their strength back, they were transferred to the Washington City Jail where they were allowed to pick their own cells and do as they pleased, treated more as guests than convicts. Then on November 28 came the astonishing news that they were being freed at President Wilson's own order. The warden was jubilant: "A pardon signed by the President! Now you'll be home to eat Thanksgiving dinners." "We don't want a pardon," one of the women responded. "We have committed no crime to be pardoned for." "All the same," the warden said, "out you go!"

Back in New York and thrilled to be free, Dorothy initially took a job with *The Liberator*, the journal that has succeeded *The Masses*, edited by Crystal Eastman, Max Eastman's wife. Perhaps because Dorothy had been so deeply shaken by her time in jail with the suffragists, politically-driven employment was no longer as inspiring as it once had been. "I worked wherever I could, lived in one furnished room after another, moving from the Lower East Side to the Upper East Side and then down again."

As the rooms were often no warmer than ice-boxes, some-

"In spite of the fact that I was with scores of other women I felt a sense of complete solitude lying behind the bars. I felt keenly the misery of all those others in jail for criminal offenses. I was overcome by the misery of those about me."
—From Union Square to Rome

43

Top: The Provincetown Playhouse.
(Library of Congress)
Above: Playwright Eugene O'Neill.
(Library of Congress)

times Dorothy sought refuge with friends whose flats were better heated and where at least the conversation provided a kind of fireplace. She found pleasure less in work and more in hanging around in the evenings with the people involved in the Provincetown Playhouse on MacDougal Street in Greenwich Village. "No one ever wanted to go to bed," she wrote in *From Union Square to Rome.* "No one ever wanted to be alone."

Their hangout was a saloon at Sixth Avenue and West Fourth Street, the Golden Swan—a gilded swan hung over the front door—but the place was nicknamed the Hell Hole by its regulars. Some called it the Bucket of Blood. The proprietor was an Irishman and former prize-fighter, Thomas Wallace. He solved much of the problem of garbage collection by keeping a resident pig in the basement. Prohibition, less than two years away, was still only a faint gray cloud on the horizon.

Once a place known as a hangout for thugs, the Golden Swan had added bohemian writers and radicals to its community of patrons. Late in 1917 a young Dorothy Day became one of its clientele—she had turned twenty on November 8. Another patron was the playwright Eugene O'Neill. Several decades later, when The Golden Swan was no more, O'Neill used his memories of it as the setting for his play "The Iceman Cometh."

Despite the burst of recognition that had come in 1916 with the opening of his first play, "Bound East for Cardiff," O'Neill was morose and drinking heavily in the winter of 1917-18. His affair with Louise Bryant had recently ended with her departure for Russia where she joined John Reed and wrote about the Bolshevik Revolution. (The O'Neill-Bryant-Reed story is well-told cinematically in Warren Beatty's film, "Reds.")

It quickly became clear that O'Neill and Dorothy enjoyed each other's company, so much so that it seemed to friends that Dorothy was destined to fill the space left by Bryant. Though O'Neill was nine years older, the two had made some similar choices: both had dropped out of college; both had become reporters; both were attempting to make their living as writers; both were drawn to outcasts. They were both God-haunted people. Agnes Boulton, who was then sharing a Village apartment with Dorothy and who later married O'Neill, quickly realized that Dorothy was subject to "sudden and unexplainable impulses" which drew her "into any nearby Catholic church"—a religious longing similar to O'Neill's.

In her memoir, *Part of a Long Story*, Agnes Boulton recalled Dorothy joining O'Neill one night, bringing with her two seedy, tough, middle-aged men whom she had found on the icy steps of Saint Joseph's Church and brought along to thaw out while having a drink at her expense. Dorothy ordered three rye whiskeys and, sitting at the table with her half-frozen guests, proceeded to sing the ballad of "Frankie and Johnny," with its refrain, "She loved her man / but he done her wrong."

"The two men were fascinated," Boulton remembered, "but [Dorothy] paid no attention to them, stretching out her long legs and, for the moment, closing her eyes." O'Neill, she added, watched it all, "his dark eyes alive and pleased, admiring Dorothy's strange, almost staccato singing." Agnes also found Dorothy impressive. "I saw at once that this girl was a personality, an unusual one." Dorothy's face, she said, was especially attractive in candlelight, which "brought out the long classic line of her jaw and the ends of her tousled hair." She was impressed by Dorothy's clothing: "She looked and dressed like a well-bred college girl." (The essayist and literary critic Malcolm Cowley, who hadn't yet met Dorothy, would later annoy her by claiming in a memoir that she had earned the admiration of the gangsters who frequented the Golden Swan "because she could drink them under the table.")

O'Neill enjoyed reciting poetry. The poem Dorothy best loved him to repeat was Francis Thompson's "The Hound of Heaven," which described God's tireless pursuit of each person's soul:

A painting of the Golden Swan by Charles Demuth.

I fled Him, down the nights and down the days,
I fled Him, down the arches of the years;
I fled Him, down the labyrinthine ways
Of my own mind . . .

O'Neill would recite the whole of the poem, sitting across from Dorothy "looking dour and black," she remembered, "his head sunk on his chest," sighing out the words:

And now my heart is as a broken fount,
Wherein tear-drippings stagnate . . .

Her own vague longing for God sometimes drew Dorothy into the building on whose steps she had found the freezing men, nearby Saint Joseph's Church on Sixth Avenue. Here she experienced a kind of at-homeness and consolation. "Many a morning, after sitting all night in taverns or coming from balls at Webster Avenue," Dorothy wrote years later in *The Long Loneliness*, "I went to an early morning Mass at Saint Joseph's . . . [kneeling] in the back of the church, not knowing what was going on at the altar, but warmed and comforted by the lights and silence, the kneeling people and the atmosphere of worship."

(O'Neill was one of the few who understood and sympathized. Thanks to him, Dorothy said in *The Long Loneliness*, she had received "an intensification of the religious sense that was in me. . . . He brought me such a consciousness of God.")

Dorothy absorbed O'Neill into her love of the city. Together they walked in the late hours, stopping at various taverns. Sometimes she put him to bed, drunk and shaking with the terrors that often wracked him, and (as she told a friend late in her life) held him in her arms until he fell asleep. He sometimes hoped for more than motherly comfort and one night asked her, "Dorothy, do you want to surrender your virginity?" Apparently it wasn't what she wanted. What she seems to have valued in O'Neill was being with someone whose loneliness resembled her own. He was the only one in her circle of friends who shared something of the need which drove her into churches. Others around her seemed sus-

"At Mass this morning I prayed for the dead. Gene O'Neill and his black despair and tragic death; a lack of trust which would almost make him refuse to believe if he were faced with the Beatific vision."
—The Duty of Delight,
March 21, 1956

St. Joseph's Church in Greenwich Village, where Dorothy sometimes stopped to pray.

tained by anti-war or feminist convictions, by devotion to revolution, by art, by writing and reading, by social life and love affairs. For her such things were not enough. (After his death in 1953, Dorothy recognized a debt to him. "What I especially got from Eugene O'Neill was an intensification of the religious sense that was in me." She described O'Neill's "relations with his God" as warfare: "He fought with God to the end of his days." O'Neill's "black despair" was so intense that he probably would refuse to believe even "if he were faced with the Beatific vision.")

Dorothy had her own terrors to live with. Not yet twenty-one, she had left home and college, had moved from apartment to apartment in New York, walked out on her job at *The Call*, seen *The Masses* go under (and with it another job), been in jail, and now the biggest war in history was being fought in Europe. Everything seemed to be disintegrating. One night early in 1918, a death occurred which drove home to her the need for a more positive engagement. A young man she knew only slightly, Louis Holladay, discovered the woman he wanted to marry had fallen in love with someone else. Drunk and despairing at the end of what was supposed to have been a party, he took an overdose of heroin. "He died in my arms," Dorothy told Agnes Boulton and O'Neill. She was hardly able to speak through the grief she felt.

"I seemed to feel the faith of those about me and I longed for their faith. My own life was sordid and yet I had had occasional glimpses of the true and the beautiful. So I used to go in and kneel in a back pew of St. Joseph's, and perhaps I asked even then, 'God, be merciful to me, a sinner.'"

—From Union Square to Rome

47

Kings County Hospital

Kings County Hospital in Brooklyn.

With the U.S. at war, everything in New York seemed to have changed as well. Without a full-time job, Dorothy was living from freelance income, writing book reviews and articles for radical journals, but all this seemed trivial in the face of so much suffering and death in Europe. Dorothy decided to become a nurse. With so many doctors and nurses now involved in the military, local hospitals were short-handed and in desperate need.

"What good am I doing my fellow man," Dorothy wrote a friend. "They are sick and there are not enough nurses to care for them. . . . It's the poor that are suffering. I've got to care for them." In the spring of 1918, both she and her sister Della began training as nurses at Kings County Hospital in Brooklyn: changing bed pans, giving sponge baths and alcohol rubs, taking temperatures, administering injections and enemas, changing dressings, keeping charts, and dispensing medication. Making wrinkle-free beds was an especially hard-won craft, "more difficult," Dorothy decided, "than writing a book review." Her days of drinking late and sleeping late were abruptly over. The hospital's twelve-hour work day began promptly at six in the morning. In a group that had a dozen probationers at the start, Dorothy and Della were among the six to survive the exhausting first month. With an influenza epidemic raging, the burden of work got progressively worse. By October, eight to ten shaking patients arrived each day, often collapsing as they reached the ward, some dying the same day. (The pandemic lasted from March 1918 to June 1920. An estimated fifty-million people, about three percent of the world's population at the time, died of the disease.)

It had been six years since Dorothy started wheeling her baby brother into slum neighborhoods instead of parks, feeling a sense of vocation binding her to those in need. Now they were central rather than incidental to her life. Dorothy was no longer just a reporter or occasional campaigner.

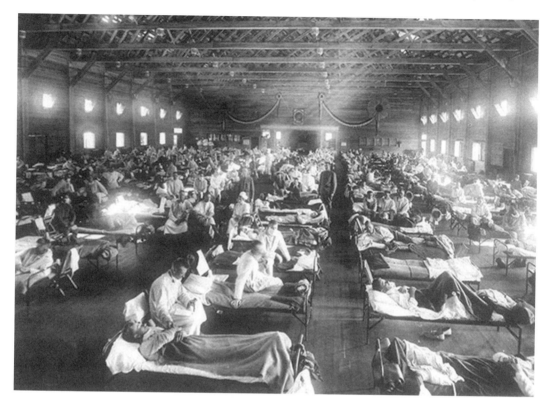

Suffering people were in her care half of each day, and she began to know them by name.

There was Mary Windsor, age fifty, who was dying slowly, "looking out of wide gray eyes, looking at the death she saw so plainly, with a dull wonder." A younger patient, Irma, was another woman facing death. "Her finely shaped mouth was always contorted with pain and there was a fierce protesting light in her eyes. The lines that agony had drawn in the ivory skin were like those of passion. She might have been clutching a lover in a last embrace, knowing that when he rose from the bed he would go out and close the door forever. There was the smell of death around her . . . and there was no one to bring her flowers to deaden it." There was a bearded woman with no breasts who spat at nurses who came within range. She was "filthy in her habits so that she constantly needed to be cleaned." Braving her fury and spit, Dorothy had to tend her daily, gritting her teeth and holding her breath.

Victims of the 1918 flu pandemic filled hospitals around the world. (Library of Congress)

49

"I liked the order of the life and the discipline. By contrast the life that I had been leading seemed disorderly and futile. . . . One of the things that this year in the hospital made me realize was that one of the hardest things in the world is to organize ourselves and discipline ourselves."

—From Union Square to Rome

Granny, age 94, furious at being bathed, screamed and clawed at the nurses who dared approach her with soap and water. It was done only out of love, one nurse explained. "Love be damned," Granny replied in defiance. Her greatest torture wasn't soap, Dorothy discovered. A hospital rule that had stripped Granny of her wig, leaving her in the ward with nothing but a cap which tended to slip over one ear, "displaying a large bald spot surrounded by a queer fringe of gray hair which was matted and awry, standing up like a field of ferns." It was a patient such as Granny who once sent Dorothy running from the ward, her uniform filthy from the bedpan that had been hurled at her. One of the senior nurses found her crying in the washroom and with great gentleness talked with Dorothy about "the responsibilities of the nurse and the dignity of her profession and 'the sacrament of duty.'"

Relief came from patients like Lora McAlister, twenty-eight years old, with auburn hair and brown eyes, who had broken her hip in a car accident. Suddenly doctors haunted her ward and the floormen weren't so hurried when doing their cleaning work. The ward became beautiful with flowers brought by visitors. Despite her injuries, Lora "powdered and primped and sewed ribbons on her night dress and sang until the ward was aglow. . . . The sixty and seventy-year-old women became conscious of their sex and were more willing to have their faces washed." They gave Dorothy money "to buy them sweet-smelling talcums and relatives appeared with dainty night dresses for them."

Dorothy found another delightful patient when she was transferred to the men's ward: Philip, a handsome, elderly man who had the gift of picking flowers that grew unseen by others in the air around his bed. With unhurried discrimination, he sniffed the blossoms and his hands touched their invisible stems, assembling a daily bouquet, presenting it to Dorothy with a courteous, grave smile when she brought him his medicine. Once she noticed him pulling at what must have been goldenrod, given its resistance. "If you try to break it, instead of tearing at it," the man in the next bed advised, "maybe you'll get it off." That worked, and Dorothy was given an armful of goldenrod.

The man who made the biggest impression on Dorothy wasn't a patient but an orderly, a big, broad-shouldered man named Lionel Calhoun Moise (pronounced Mo-ees), who worked in the men's ward to which Dorothy had been transferred. He cheerfully assisted Dorothy in such tasks as dressing and undressing longshoremen who were in no mood to wear hospital garb. During the flu epidemic, Moise carted numerous dead bodies down to the hospital morgue. At times it seemed to Dorothy that she and Moise were "the only healthy young things in the entire ward."

Moise's life, as he recounted it to Dorothy, had been adventurous enough for a Jack London story. Now twenty-nine, he had somehow avoided taking part in World War I, which had finally ended November 11, 1918. His most recent jobs had been as a cameraman with a movie crew working in Latin America, then a deckhand on a freighter working his way back to the U.S. At a saloon on the Brooklyn waterfront, he had been drugged, robbed and left unconscious under a bridge. Luckily he was noticed before he froze to death. When he woke up, he found himself in a bed in Kings County Hospital, bruised and suffering pneumonia. Once he was out of bed, he signed on as an orderly in order to work off his hospital bill.

Moise was an utterly self-possessed man with a commanding manner. His face, which bore evidence of brawls he had taken part in, reminded Dorothy of the cherished postcard she had of a broken-nosed bust of Amenemhat III, an Egyptian pharaoh who had died more than thirty-seven centuries earlier. Moise had a reputation for barroom battles, slugging cops, and throwing typewriters out of windows.

A man seemingly untroubled by self-doubt, he was confident that, despite his recent bad luck, he would make his way in the world. He had already established himself as a talented journalist. During a stretch with *The Kansas City Star*, in his home state, he had been rewrite editor for a staff that included a young Ernest Hemingway. According to a *Kansas City Star* colleague, Russel Crouse, Moise and Hemingway were "the only erudite rough and tough guys I ever knew. They could clean out a bar and then quote Shakespeare to

The bust of Amenemhat III, which Dorothy felt bore a resemblance to Lionel Moise.

A young Dorothy. (Marquette University archives)

the bartender." Friends who knew them both wondered if the rough-and-ready Moise had been not only a mentor for Hemingway, but a role model as well.

"Lionel Moise was a great rewrite man," Hemingway recalled. "He could carry four stories in his head and go to the telephone and take a fifth and then write all five at full speed to catch an edition. There would be something alive about each one. He was always the highest paid man on every paper he worked on. If any other man was getting more money he quit or had his pay raised. He never spoke to other reporters unless he had been drinking. He was tall and thick and had long arms and big hands. He was the fastest man on a typewriter that I ever knew. He drove a motor car and it was understood in the office that a woman had given it to him. One night she stabbed him in it out on the Lincoln Highway halfway to Jefferson City. He took the knife away from her and threw it out of the car."

Many women "prostrated themselves before him," Malcolm Cowley told William Miller. Cowley was bewildered by Dorothy's attraction to Moise, who "used to quote Nietzsche," Cowley recalled, "something to the effect 'goest thou to a woman and forget not thy whip.'"

Dorothy, only twenty, had never met a man she found so captivating. For the first time in her life she fell deeply and incautiously in love. Perhaps it was because Lionel Moise, unlike the idealistic men she had been close to at *The Call* and *The Masses*, was so elemental and so utterly without ideology or utopian expectations. Moise took the world as it was rather than suffer dismay with the world as it wasn't. Dorothy's was a "fatal attraction," she wrote soon after the event. She didn't hesitate to make her attraction clear. Moise, more used to being the pursuer than the pursued, assured her he wasn't the right type, but his objections, if anything, only fueled Dorothy's passion. Neither she nor Moise took distance from the other. Dorothy treasured all the time they had together and dared to imagine a future together.

Following Moise's departure from the hospital in September 1919, Dorothy took leave. How soon she did so is unknown, but shortly afterward she moved into the apartment he had rented on 35th Street in Manhattan. Moise was then earning $50 a week acting the part of a drunkard in a play that was about to open. He was pleased Dorothy had come, but accepted her on repressive terms. She wasn't to work, not even to write, but only to be "my woman." Far from objecting, Dorothy made herself at home, found ways to make the apartment more attractive, repaired Moise's clothes, darned his socks, and sewed clothing for herself, sometimes from silk remnants she bought cheaply. Cooking was the one domestic task Moise was willing to share with her.

It was not a platonic relationship, as Dorothy made clear in her autobiographical novel, *The Eleventh Virgin*. While she did not go into detail about the sexual side of their life together, it was physical and passionate. It seemed to Dorothy what she and Lionel were doing was a healthy rebellion against artificial constraints. "The life of the flesh called to me as a good and wholesome life," Dorothy wrote in *The Long Loneliness*, "regardless of man's laws, which I felt rebelliously were made for the repression of others. The strong could make their own law, live their own lives; in fact, they were beyond good and evil. What was good and what was evil? . . . The satisfied flesh has its own law."

Moise enjoyed their sexual life and also their conversations about books, but again and again reminded Dorothy that all this was temporary. "You should wait for some nice young man who will marry you and buy you a rubber tree and give you babies," Moise told Dorothy. For himself, he was dead set against marriage or anything resembling it. He didn't want a wife and, still less, children. Commitment to a woman, he explained, meant loss of freedom. He was angry at Dorothy for making him want to be with her. "Women— all I ever thought before was that you take something you need from them," Dorothy quotes the Moise-character in *The Eleventh Virgin*. "It's physically impossible for a woman to take a man. She always gives, gives herself up. And now I hate you—I don't want you because I feel everything going out of me to you. The thought of you eats into me continually." Even so, he didn't want Dorothy to leave and was intensely possessive.

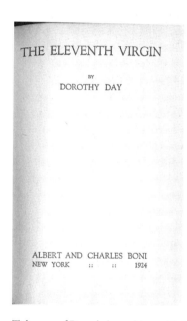

THE ELEVENTH VIRGIN

BY

DOROTHY DAY

ALBERT AND CHARLES BONI
NEW YORK   ::   ::   1924

Title page of Dorothy's autobiographical novel, *The Eleventh Virgin*.

When Dorothy renewed her friendships with Mike Gold, Peggy Baird and others, she quickly discovered Moise's capacity for volcanic jealousy. He exploded when he noticed Dorothy's hand casually resting on the shoulder of the man—was it Mike Gold?—sitting next to her in a café. Moise stormed out, saying, "I'll leave you here to embrace the gentleman on your right."

Dorothy was devastated by her sudden rejection. For days she could hardly stop weeping. Every door that opened, every phone that rang, made her hope that Moise had forgiven her. But he made no contact. Dorothy found refuge in the following days with Peggy Baird and other friends. Her despair was so profound that, while staying in a room on Greenwich Avenue, she attempted suicide, disconnecting the hose to the heater. A neighbor, Sue Brown, smelled gas coming from under her door and saved Dorothy's life. (In a 1973 letter to a young woman struggling with depression, Dorothy spoke of having twice attempted suicide.) At last Moise relented and the affair resumed, with Dorothy—now twenty-one—more desperate than ever to hold Moise. She wished that her "death would coincide" with the moment Moise stopped loving her.

Though Dorothy had been associated with publications that promoted birth control, either she and Moise made no effort to prevent conception or the method used had been ineffective. In May Dorothy realized she was pregnant and contemplated various possibilities. Given the undeclared war between her father and herself, she couldn't return home. She found signing herself into a home for unwed mothers too humiliating. She didn't dare tell Moise, certain he would leave. Abortion, though illegal, seemed to Dorothy the only course.

Dorothy tried to convince herself that it was only Moise she wanted, not a child, and that "perfect love precluded the idea of children." Lovers need only each other. And if they were no longer lovers, if he left her, how could she afford a child? How would she and her child live? Would it not be the height of selfishness to bring a child into the world without it having "a fair chance at happiness," she told her friend Peggy. Peggy didn't agree—how few children there would be if only those conceived in ideal circumstances were allowed to be born, Peggy pointed out—but she was unable to change Dorothy's mind.

Dorothy obtained the name of an abortionist but couldn't bring herself to make an appointment. In *The Eleventh Virgin*, she described herself peering at infants in baby carriages and watching children in the parks. From her apartment window, she studied two sisters playing in the yard—a five-year-old who held up her skirts and sang the Missouri Waltz and a two-year-old who occasionally turned her round face to the sky and fell "into a perfect trance of happiness."

Moise knew nothing of Dorothy's pregnancy or the turmoil she was enduring. It wasn't until September, the day he told her he had accepted a job in Caracas and would be leaving in a week, that Dorothy blurted out her desperate news. He was sorry, Moise told her, but would still be leaving. He advised her to have an abortion. Unable to argue, Dorothy wept. She felt she had fallen into an abyss.

According to the account Dorothy wrote in *The Eleventh Virgin*, the operation occurred in an apartment on the Upper East Side. (In a conversation later in life with Dan Marshall, Dorothy told him that the abortionist came to her apartment.) A surgical instrument cut the four-month-old child from the lining of her womb. For several hours there were painful contractions, one spasm every three minutes. Finally, Dorothy's child was born dead. If Dorothy's novel is as biographically accurate in the account of the abortion as it is on every other subject, Moise had promised to meet her afterward, but never showed up. At 10 P.M., Dorothy gave up waiting and went back by taxi to the apartment on 35th Street where she found no trace of Moise, only a letter in which he reminded her that millions of women had had the same experience. Advising her to forget him, he left some money with which he had intended to pay a bar bill and hoped she would get "comfortably married to a rich man."

Breaking Free

According to *The Eleventh Virgin*, following the abortion Dorothy resumed nursing work at Kings County Hospital in Brooklyn. Della had never left. It isn't clear how many months her return to nursing lasted, but in *The Long Loneliness* Dorothy describes the unpleasant experience of quitting once and for all. The superintendent of nurses wasn't surprised and sneeringly told Dorothy that it was obvious she regarded herself as "too good" for mere nursing. Her words tore into Dorothy. "I knew I loved the work and that, if it had not been for the irresistible urge to write, I would have clung to the profession of nursing as the most noble work women could aspire to."

The date is uncertain, but either in 1920 or 1921 Dorothy married Berkeley Tobey, a man sixteen years her senior who is best remembered as founder of a book club, the Literary Guild. He was one of the wealthier people in the Greenwich Village circles Dorothy was part of, with a large apartment overlooking Washington Square Park. This was Tobey's fourth marriage; after Dorothy, there would be two more. It was, as Dorothy described it, a "marriage on the

"About my marriage. . . . It lasted less than a year. I married a man on the rebound, after an unhappy love affair. He took me to Europe and when we got back I left him. I felt I had used him and was ashamed."
—To William Miller, October 8, 1975

A photo of Berkeley Tobey in the 1940s on Santa Monica Pier with Esther McCoy (one of his later wives) and Helen Dreiser.

London, 1920.

rebound." How did they meet? The most likely answer is that Tobey had been business manager of *The Masses*. They had many mutual friends and shared a love of books.

Dorothy went to Europe in 1921—it may have been her honeymoon with Tobey—and stayed for eight months. According to a letter written in June 1921 by her friend Malcolm Cowley, she was part of a group of seven leaving by ship for the "Old World." Novelists Djuna Barnes and John Dos Passos were among them, as well as Dorothy. Her time in Europe, she notes in *From Union Square to Rome*, "was spent with people who were only interested in art and literature."

In London Dorothy "walked and took bus rides and explored and thought of DeQuincey and Dickens." In Paris her imagination put her in the company of Victor Hugo, Balzac and Maupassant. But it was Italy that most delighted her and offered her more than literary associations. "The six months I spent in Capri meant that forever after, the smell of Italian cooking, the sound of buzzing flies, the loud voices of my Italian neighbors, the taste of spaghetti and polenta and the sour red wine brought me back to the months I spent beside the Mediterranean."

"In trying to write about the next few years of my life I find that there is little to say. I have never intended to write an autobiography. I have always wanted instead to tell of things that brought me to God and that reminded me of God."
—The Long Loneliness

"I spent a year writing and I cared little about the political situation, though it was a time when fascism was rising in Italy. But I was living through a time of my own personal joy and heartbreak and what happened in the world had little effect on me."

—The Long Loneliness

Cover of *The Liberator*

While in Capri, Dorothy worked on *The Eleventh Virgin*. Some elements of her early life were left out. Mother Grace remained Mother Grace. Her sister Della became Adele. Her college friend Rayna was now Regina. Mike Gold was dubbed Ivan, no doubt because of his enthusiasm for Russia. Peggy Baird became Billy Burrows. Lionel Moise had the most disguised of altered names: Dick Wemys. *The Call* was now *The Clarion* and *The Masses* was renamed *The Flame*. Much of the book was later used as a source, at times sentence-for-sentence, when Dorothy wrote *The Long Loneliness*, the autobiography published in 1952.

Even married and in Europe, Dorothy indicates that she was by no means through with Lionel Moise. "I'm still in love," she confides in *The Eleventh Virgin's* epilogue. "I thought I was a free and emancipated young woman and found out I wasn't at all, really," she reflects, despite her deep involvement with socialists, anarchists, birth control campaigners and suffragists. It seemed to her that "freedom is just a modernity gown, a new trapping that we women affect to capture the man we want. There are exceptions to the rule, of course, but they only prove it."

Later in her life, when Dwight Macdonald was interviewing Dorothy for a profile later published in *The New Yorker*, he asked her why she hadn't written anything about her marriage with Tobey. "I didn't want to write about what I was ashamed of," Dorothy responded. "The confessional dealt with that." Asked the same question late in her life by William Miller, she said no more than "the marriage lasted less than a year" and happened "after an unhappy love affair. [Berkeley Tobey] took me to Europe and when we got back I left him. I felt I had used him and was ashamed."

Moise remained a powerful magnet. Back in America and free of Tobey, Dorothy went directly to Chicago where Moise was now city editor of *The Chicago Post*. Recalling that period of her life in a journal entry made decades later, in January 1978, Dorothy wrote of having once again lived "a disorderly life" with Moise. In the same period she made her way back to the kind of people and friendships she had gravitated toward when she arrived in New York. "I was happy to be with friends again who were active in the work of changing the world."

Meanwhile, while sharing a room with a Canadian milliner who did most of her work at home, Dorothy supported herself with whatever work she could find: as a clerk at Montgomery Ward's, a copyholder to a proofreader, an auxiliary at the Public Library, a cashier at a restaurant, and a model for life drawing classes. Finally Dorothy returned to journalistic employment as secretary to Robert Minor, one of the founders of the Communist Party and editor of *The Liberator*, the publication she had worked for briefly in Manhattan and which had since moved to Chicago. Many of the editors, writers and artists of *The Liberator* had been associated with *The Masses*. Its advocacy of socialist revolution occasioned close government surveillance. "At this moment of writing," Robert Minor said repeatedly in letters that he dictated to Dorothy, "there is a man standing in the doorway across the street who has been shadowing me for the past week." Very likely it was true, but it also made good copy.

Among other locations being watched closely was a building on West Madison Street, in the skid row section of Chicago's West Side, where the Industrial Workers of the World, the Wobblies, had their national offices and a printing plant. Across the street there was a rooming house used by Wobbly visitors as well as by people in need. Occasionally Dorothy stayed there, including one night in late July 1922 when she shared a room with Mae Cramer. "We were both in love with the same man," Dorothy later wrote. Just the day before, Mae had tried to kill herself with an overdose of drugs because things were going badly between herself and Lionel Moise.

That particular night the police "Red Squad" raided the house—a roundup of radicals authorized by U.S. Attorney General A. Mitchell Palmer and his special assistant, J. Edgar Hoover, who in later years headed the Federal Bureau of Investigation. "We were undressed and getting into bed," Dorothy recalled, "when a knock came at the door and four men burst in telling us we were under arrest for being inmates of a disorderly house." A "disorderly house" was the

An IWW poster.

legal term for a place of prostitution. For Dorothy it was "an utterly terrifying experience." When she had been arrested in Washington, the event had been carried out with great dignity, as carefully and gracefully as if it were a ballet. Arrest and imprisonment had been chosen as a way to make Americans think about how undemocratic it was to exclude women from the democratic process. Now Dorothy was seized suddenly in the night, made to dress in front of armed men, and herded roughly into a police van. The presence of two single women at the IWW boarding house "meant only one thing to the men who arrested us." She thought of dime-novel covers of "a girl of the streets in revealing clothes" standing alone in a small island of light waiting to be picked up.

Far from being part of a group of well-educated and well-connected suffragists who would eventually be freed by presidential pardon, now Dorothy was treated as a whore. After two days in a crowded holding cell filled with actual prostitutes—women who made sure that Dorothy had enough to eat and a place to sleep—she was put in a cell by herself. A few days later, friends bailed her out. Soon afterward the charges against Dorothy were dismissed. But her second experience of prison, for all its brevity, impressed Dorothy even more than the first with its ugliness and brutality. "We were stripped naked. We were given prison clothes and put in cells. . . . In the cell next to me there was a drug addict who beat her head against the bars and howled like a wild animal. I have never heard such anguish, such unspeakable suffering. No woman in childbirth, no cancer patient, no one in that long year I had spent in Kings County Hospital had revealed such suffering as this." To be a thin wall away from a woman in hell made Dorothy feel as never before "the depth of the disorder of the world."

Despite the anguish she had experienced, Dorothy eventually came to regard the experience with gratitude. "I am glad indeed that I had it," she wrote in *The Long Loneliness*, because of the taste it gave her of what happened "to thousands who had worked for labor—hotel workers, miners, the textile workers—throughout the country." Workers had withheld their labor, joined picket lines at factory gates, been

"I felt a peculiar sense of disgust and shame at the position I was in, shame because I had been treated as a criminal and made to feel exactly as though I were guilty of the charge on which I had been arrested. But it was only what I could expect, I thought to myself bitterly, under the present social system, and I thought again of Debs' words: 'While there is a lower class, I am of it, and while there is a criminal element, I am of it, and while there is a soul in prison, I am not free.'"
—From Union Square to Rome

Accused radicals awaiting deportation.
(Library of Congress)

beaten and sometimes maimed and killed. They were thrown into jails by the thousands and were treated both by wardens and the press with contempt. "Every strike was an unjust strike, according to the newspapers, and every strike ended in failure, according to the same papers. The reader never took into account the slow and steady gains [shorter hours, longer breaks, safer working conditions, medical benefits and vacations], wrung reluctantly from the employer by virtue of every one of these strikes."

Following her release, Lionel Moise arranged for Dorothy to be hired as a reporter for the city news bureau of *The Chicago Post*. Her job was covering the Children's Court, the Court of Domestic Relations, and the Morals Court. In the Morals Court, a place chiefly for trying women regarded as being immoral, Dorothy must have recognized women with whom she had been in jail not long before.

Dorothy rented a room in a household that turned out to be Catholic. The three women living there, all her own age, attended Mass every Sunday as well as major holy days. For them prayer was an ordinary part of daily life. Two of the women were also in love, but weren't sleeping with the men they hoped to marry, though it was obvious to Dorothy how much they wanted to. In seeing their daily life and the role of faith in it, she began to feel "that Catholicism was something rich and real and fascinating. . . . I saw them wrestling with

"These were the days of the Palmer red raids, when no one was safe. Those were times of persecution for all radicals."
—From Union Square to Rome

moral problems, with the principles by which they lived, and this made them noble in my eyes." Seeing them at prayer, at the table and by their beds, she realized that "worship, adoration, thanksgiving, supplication—these were the noblest acts of which men were capable in this life."

"A friend of mine once said that it was the style to be Catholic in France, nowadays, but it was not the style to be one in America. It was the Irish of New England, the Italians, the Hungarians, the Lithuanians, the Poles, it was the great mass of the poor, the workers, who were the Catholics in this country and this fact in itself drew me to the Church."
—The Long Loneliness

Her own religious itch would not go away. Though nearly all her friends were militant atheists, Dorothy's affinity for the Catholic Church occasionally pulled her into the city's cathedral at lunch time. The faith of her house-mates deepened Dorothy's attraction to the Catholic Church, which she had come to see as the Church of immigrants and masses of the poor. What, she wondered, did these girls make of rudderless Dorothy, who had no religious faith? "Perhaps they did gossip about me behind my back," Dorothy write in *The Long Loneliness*, "but their behavior to me was ever kind and good to my face. I have long since come to believe that people never mean half of what they say and that it is best to disregard their talk and judge only their actions."

Another significant factor at the time was reading Joris-Karl Huysmans's novels, *The Return*, *The Cathedral*, and *The Oblate*, loaned to her by Sam Putnam, a colleague at the *Post*. "It was *The Return* which taught me the *Memorare*," Dorothy recalled in an "On Pilgrimage" column published in May 1975, "that beautiful prayer to Mary, which so impressed me that I have said it since every day of my life. . . . All I think I ever asked of her was that she should take care of me. The prayer is brief and easily remembered."

Remember, O most gracious Virgin Mary, that never was it known that anyone who fled to thy protection, implored thy help, or sought thy intercession was left unaided. Inspired by this confidence, I fly unto thee, O Virgin of virgins, my mother. To thee I come, before thee I stand, sinful and sorrowful. O Mother of the Word Incarnate, despise not my petitions, but in thy mercy hear and answer them. Amen.

Poor immigrants, many of them Catholics for whom such prayers were an integral part of daily life, were easy to find in Chicago. Taking part in workers' picnics on Sunday afternoons in various parks on the outskirts of the city, Dorothy enjoyed hearing so many languages and delighted in the multitude of national costumes and the different traditions of dancing and food. "These men and women had come to the United States to better their condition, and they became exploited in sweatshops, in the stockyards." Their hopes for themselves were meager but Dorothy saw them as part of a movement, "a slow upheaval," a seed of much needed social change, even revolution.

By now Moise had lost his charismatic appeal for Dorothy. When he left Chicago, Dorothy returned to New York. In retrospect, she regarded her most enduring debt to Moise to be her renewed interest in Dostoevsky. As a result, Dorothy "could not hear Sonya's reading the Gospel to Raskolnikov in *Crime and Punishment* without turning to it myself with love. I could not read Ippolyte's rejection of his ebbing life and defiance of God in *The Idiot* without being filled with an immense sense of gratitude to God and a desire to make some return."

Dorothy at her typewriter (1925). (Marquette University archives)

Dorothy was also on the verge of crossing a vocational border, no longer just a journalist writing at high speed to meet a deadline. The fictionalized autobiography she had written while in Europe, *The Eleventh Virgin*, had been accepted and would soon be published by Albert and Charles Boni, publishers in Greenwich Village. Eugene O'Neill, Floyd Dell, and the suffragist Mary Heaton Vorse had all agreed to a write words of praise for use on the book's jacket. With another novel nearly finished, Dorothy saw her future as a writer.

From New Orleans to Staten Island

The French Quarter in New Orleans.
(Library of Congress)

Deciding to escape winter, in December 1923 Dorothy, with her sister Della and a friend named Mary, headed south to New Orleans. After renting an apartment on Saint Peter's Street in the city's French Quarter, they were close to broke, counting themselves lucky if they had enough quarters to cook a meal. "The coin-fed gas meter was apt to run out," Dorothy recalled, "just when we had spent our last cent on a rabbit stew which took hours to boil."

Finally Dorothy got a job reporting for *The New Orleans Item* while Mary landed a job selling lingerie in a department store. Della, having been luckless in her search for employment, returned to New York.

Dorothy wrote her friend Llewellyn Jones, literary editor of *The Evening Post* in Chicago, with the news that they now had enough money to dine on fish and vegetables. One of the advantages of being in the south rather than the north, she said in the same letter, was that icy weather "was another excuse to keep drinking, and you know I never needed much excuse when the liquor flowed free as it generally did in Chicago. Fortunately we know of no place to get it here [by now Prohibition was on] and there is no one to drink with, so we never think of it." The editors of *The Item*, she told Jones, "don't mind working you like hell for very little money. However, the work is fun, and keeps me occupied so that I don't miss liquor and the bright lights." She noted she was "very tan," that there were "lots of pretty boys around," and that she was "being godly and righteous according to my lights." Instead of going out, she spent her evenings, when not on assignment, reading to the landlady and her daughter.

Dorothy's major project for *The Item* was to write a series on "taxi dancers"—dancers for hire in local night spots. "DANCE HALLS FLOODED BY DOPE, DRINK," proclaimed one of the headlines. "These dens of vice cater only to men," she wrote Jones, "and many girls are hired to dance with them.

They pay ten cents a dance, and the girl gets four of it. Working hours, from eight to twelve. I'm to investigate, under an assumed name, and disguised as a flapper, to see if this wild night life doesn't lead to vice and crime amongst our young womanhood of the South. I shall enjoy myself immensely." In fact it was a job with risks—one night Dorothy ended up with a black eye.

Across the street from their rented room was Saint Louis Cathedral where Dorothy went to pray and sometimes attended the evening Benediction service. She was pleased when her roommate Mary expressed her sympathy by giving Dorothy a rosary. "I did not know how to say the prayers [used with the rosary]," Dorothy recalled nearly half a century later, "but I kept it by me. I did not know any Catholics and would have been afraid to approach a priest or nun, for fear of their reading into such an approach some expectation which was not there."

Saint Louis Cathedral in New Orleans.

The Eleventh Virgin was published in the spring of 1924, but received few good reviews. A writer for *The New York Times* recognized that it was less a work of fiction than of autobiography and dismissed it as an example of the "truth at any cost" school of writing. "Truth is so prominent that there is practically nothing else." The book had no second printing. It didn't take long for Dorothy herself to regard *The Eleventh Virgin* as "a very bad book."

Despite its poor showing in book shops, in fact the book made money both for Dorothy and the publisher. A movie company in Hollywood bought the film rights for $5,000. While no film came of it, Dorothy's half-share of the windfall was, at the time, a small fortune. (A dollar in 1924 was the equivalent of $12.50 in 2010.)

In April, a published author with film-industry money in hand, Dorothy returned to New York where she found spring in the air and a warm welcome and hospitality from Peggy Baird. Peggy had married the essayist and literary critic Malcolm Cowley, then twenty-six and recently back in America after a three-year stay in France along with other literary members of the "Lost Generation."

Cowley was not yet well known, but the apartment he and

Peggy shared on Bank Street in Greenwich Village had become a gathering place for writers and radicals. The poet Hart Crane was one of the frequent visitors. Caroline Gordon and Allen Tate lived across the street. The makings for discussion and debate were constantly at hand. A particular conversation involving Cowley, the writer and music critic Kenneth Burke and novelist John Dos Passos lingered in Dorothy's memory "because I could not understand a word of it."

Dorothy had adopted a new look, she wrote Llewellyn Jones. "I cut off my hair like a boy's and have bleached it besides." In the same letter she confessed that her book, "now that it is in cold print, doesn't please me, but I console myself by remembering that I wrote it when I was twenty-two. Neither has it pleased my friends. I have heard much adverse criticism, and people who liked the book in manuscript, changed their minds when they saw it in print."

Peggy, worried that Dorothy's money was carelessly slipping through her fingers, suggested it would be better spent were she to buy a quiet place to write. The idea made sense to Dorothy. The two of them took the ferry to Staten Island. Before the day had ended, Dorothy had found and bought a tin-roofed fisherman's cottage on a 25-by-50-foot strip of land on a bluff fronting the beach. It was well down the Staten Island shoreline near Huguenot, between Arbutus and Huguenot Avenues.

Peggy's house-warming present to Dorothy was prophetic: a small statue of Mary. Weeks later, Peggy and Malcolm Cowley bought a small house a mile or two away, a place that had the added advantage of possessing a water heater. Dorothy made frequent use of their great luxury, a bathtub.

It was through Peggy and Malcolm that Dorothy met Lily Burke, and through Lily that she met Lily's brother, Forster Batterham. (Forster's first name, in fact, was William, but friends knew him by his middle name.) Forster was tall and lean, with a high forehead under sandy hair, a passionate lover of the outdoors. Having been born and raised in North Carolina, he had a pleasant southern accent. He was a visceral opponent of all big institutions. As Dorothy described him

(Marquette University archives)

Forster Batterham. (Marquette University archives)

in *The Long Loneliness*, Forster was "an anarchist, an Englishman by descent, and a biologist." His favorite writers were D.H. Lawrence and Aldous Huxley. Like Moise, he approved of neither marriage nor religion, but, unlike Moise, had a gentle, shy manner. Malcolm Cowley credited Forster's shyness to having had "too many sisters." Forster's major ambition, it seemed to Cowley, was to catch fish. At the time Dorothy met him, Forster was supporting himself by working in a factory making gauges. (Later, about 1934, he opened his own business, a store at 179 Broadway in Manhattan.)

Dorothy fell in love with Forster, and he with her, in the blink of an eye. In very little time, they decided to live together, though only on a part-time basis. In the first of many love letters, one dated the 3rd of April 1925, Dorothy sang the praises of her Staten Island retreat while lamenting his absence in the city: "There is plenty of room and plenty to eat, and plenty of room in the woods so you must get out. And if you don't I'll be coming back Monday. I miss you so much. I was very cold last night. Not because there weren't enough covers but because I didn't have you. Please write me, sweetheart, and I won't tear the letter up as I did the last one (but I saved the pieces) because I was mad at you. I love you muchly." She confessed in her next letter, "I . . . dream of you every night and if my dreams could affect you over long distance, I am sure they

Dorothy on Staten Island.
(Credit: *The Staten Island Advance*)

would keep you awake." (Dorothy's letters to Forster are among those recently published in *All the Way to Heaven*.)

On weekdays, the cottage was Dorothy's hermitage. She worked on her garden, pressed ahead with her novel, did occasional articles for *New Masses*, and wrote serial fiction for a newspaper syndicate. In a letter she boasted of the two gallons of dandelion wine she had made using a recipe from an old English cookbook. The area around her cottage was a kind of Eden in which she found free treasure. "This morning," she wrote Llewellyn Jones that spring, "I gathered field horse tails which like the skunk cabbage are most exotic, even phallic, in spite of their names, violets, adder's tongue, spring beauty, butter cups, arbutus, etc., so you can see what lovely months we're having."

Dorothy and Forster on Staten Island.
(Marquette University archives)

Forster returned on weekends. "When he came home," Dorothy recalled, "he would rush out to the garden with his flashlight to see how things were growing." But during the coldest weeks of winter, the uninsulated beach house being nearly impossible to heat, she took refuge in Manhattan, sharing a Greenwich Village apartment with her sister, Della.

Dorothy had begun the four most joyful years of her life, a time of love, motherhood and conversion. Dorothy's beach house was quickly furnished, she recalled in *The Long Loneliness*, "with a driftwood stove in one corner, plenty of books, comfortable chairs and couches. My writing table faced the window where I could look out at the water all day. On the walls hung the fruits of our collecting: horseshoe crabs, spider crabs, the shell of a huge sea turtle, whelks' cocoons, hanging like false curls, several mounted fish heads, boards covered with starfish, sea horses, pipe and file fish, all picked up in little pools at low tide."

Dorothy, Forster, Peggy and Malcolm often got together to swim and fish. There were occasional Saturday night social evenings at Peggy and Malcolm's. "The parties," Cowley recalled, "became rather boisterous, although Dorothy was

(Marquette University archives)

69

(Marquette University archives)

never a great drinker." Forster probably skipped the parties. In *The Long Loneliness*, Dorothy noted that he "hated social life and fled from it."

While missing Forster, Dorothy did well with her weekday solitude. She loved the sounds—the living sounds of the sea, the wind, of children playing on the beach, the singing of birds, the cries of gulls. The air, too, was a marvel—not reeking of trucks, buses and tenements, but scrubbed clean, as if it were fresh from heaven. Driftwood, free fuel for the house, was delivered by the tides. Dorothy, now an avid gardener, got a job, paid by the column inch, writing a garden column for the borough's daily newspaper, *The Staten Island Advance*. For a time, she earned $20 a week working part-time for a local real estate agent. "I am having a lot of fun," Dorothy told Jones in a letter, "showing people around bungalows and cottages and preaching the pleasures of the simple life." There were also occasional articles for *New Masses*, the latest reincarnation of *The Masses*.

Dorothy completed a second novel, *Joan Barleycorn*, about a woman who drank too much and whose teetotaler husband tries to convert his wife to sobriety by moving to a desert island, but Albert and Charles Boni turned the manuscript down with the polite suggestion that it needed more work. (*Joan Barleycorn* did, however, get into print as a newspaper serial.)

Dorothy loved her neighbors, among whom were Italians, Belgians, a family of Russian and Romanian Jews, bootleggers and fishermen. For all their differences of temperament, ethnic origins and ways of life, they got on well with each other. Events and misunderstandings that might have ignited undying enmity were excused on the grounds of nationality.

In one shack lived a beachcomber named Lefty, who slept with his crab traps and clam rakes and tried to live without money, as when he had some he only spent it drinking. "Money is bad for me, I know it," he told Dorothy. "I can trade my fish and clams for fuel and food and what else do I need?" She enjoyed watching him cook clam broth, first building a small fire in the sand banked with bricks, then steaming the clams, carefully taking them out of their shells while saving

"Later this evening the wind rose again and whistled around the house, and the noise of the sea is loud. I read now evenings until late in the night, and in my preoccupation the fire goes out, so that I have to get into bed to keep warm, clutching my books with ice cold hands."
—From Union Square to Rome

the juice, then adding water, a dash of butter, salt and pepper—the best thing for a hangover, he said. Lefty kept a special steamer chair for Dorothy's use and shared his meals gladly, not only steamed clams but coffee and at times buttered toast with fried mushrooms. It impressed Dorothy that Lefty, like many others in the neighborhood, was often penniless, yet wasn't humiliated or brutalized by poverty. Poor but not destitute, he had a place to live and managed to get by.

Sitting on the beach one day, Dorothy was reading *The Varieties of Religious Experience* by William James when, in a chapter on "The Value of Saintliness," she came upon his proposal that the only way to undo the damage done by the ideal of wealth-getting was to respect poverty: "The praises of poverty need once more to be boldly sung. We have grown literally afraid to be poor. We despise anyone who elects to be poor in order to simplify and save his inner life. If he does not join the general scramble, we deem him spiritless and lacking in ambition. We have lost the power even of imagining what the ancient realization of poverty could have meant; the liberation from material attachments, the unbribed soul."

Lefty was living proof of the text, Dorothy realized, and so was Forster, "who refused to do other than live from day to day and insisted on his freedom of body and soul." He worked, but just enough to pay for his share in their household expenses, and never spent money if he could help it.

With Forster's boundless love for the outdoors, she wrote, "he used to insist on walks no matter how cold or rainy the day, and this dragging me away from my books, from my lethargy, into the open, into the country, made me begin to breathe. If breath is life, then I was beginning to be full of it because of him."

At this point in Dorothy's life, wars, starvation, homelessness, prisons and strikes seemed light years distant from the beaches she walked while collecting driftwood, but listening to Forster read aloud from *The New York Times* over the breakfast table on weekends, Dorothy's awareness was renewed of the world beyond the beach, her books, the cottage and her neighbors. "Usually if anyone reads aloud to you," Dorothy noted, "you can listen or not, at will, but the

"We fished together, we walked every day for miles, we collected and studied together, and an entire new world opened up to me little by little. We did not talk much but 'lived together' in the fullest sense of the phrase."
—The Long Loneliness

vehemence and passion of Forster's interest and his rebellion at all injustice forced me to realize the situation with him." Forster's obsession with news, unfortunately, only seemed to confirm him in his bitterness with "the blundering of his fellow creatures," Dorothy noticed. "He loved nature with a sensuous passion and he loved birds and beasts and children because they were not men." If mankind was itself the problem, as Forster believed, the world's problems would never be solved by man, no more than an arsonist could be expected to put out fires.

Though Forster seemed to have little love for the human race in general, he loved Dorothy, even if not as unreservedly as she loved him. Long after they had separated, while writing *The Long Loneliness*, it warmed her to remember how he would come in smelling of salt air from a cold night, having dug bait at low tide in the moonlight, and "hold me close to him in silence. . . . I loved him in every way, as a wife, as a mother even. I loved him for all he knew and pitied him for all he didn't know. I loved him for the odds and ends I had to fish out of his sweater pockets and for the sand and shells he brought in with his fishing. I loved his lean and cold body as he got into bed smelling of the sea, and I loved his integrity and stubborn pride." But it pained Dorothy that Forster was so set against "the institution of family and the tyranny of love" and that he would never let her forget "that this was a comradeship rather than a marriage." At times it seemed senseless that they were together at all, "since he lived with me as though he were living alone."

An evolving sense of God's reality and immanence was gradually taking hold of her. She pitied Forster for his inability, or unwillingness, to sense the Creator in the creation he loved so wholly and desperately, the creation whose beauty impressed Dorothy as revealing God. He could not understand, share or welcome her pleasure in hearing the bells of the nearby church of Saint Joseph's as it tolled the Angelus morning and night. "Forster, the inarticulate, became garrulous only in wrath . . . caused by my absorption in the supernatural rather than the natural, the unseen rather than the seen."

Whenever Dorothy attempted to explain her sense of the

presence of God, they quarreled. Dorothy well understood Forster's angry rejection of churches and all that they claimed to represent, define and judge. Most people who rejected Christianity, she was well aware, did so not because of Christ but because of the sins of the churches which claimed to represent Christ. Dorothy also knew arguments were powerless. In any event, her own vague religious impulses were still more troubling than comforting in her own life. She belonged to no church and was ill at ease with religious doctrines. But she felt haunted by God and couldn't ban that awareness from her thoughts or silence it in her speech. "How can there be no God," she asked Forster, "when there are all these beautiful things?"

In fact, despite his atheism, it was partly thanks to Forster that Dorothy's religious life gained momentum. As she later explained, "It was because through a whole love, both physical and spiritual, I came to know God."

Dorothy in front of her first Staten Island cottage. (Marquette University archives)

Pregnancy, Faith, and Baptism

In the six years since her first pregnancy, though not a celibate, Dorothy had not conceived another child. She seems to have concluded that she was one of those women made sterile by abortion. It was a bitter thought. Living so happily with Forster, she felt the one thing still lacking was motherhood. "For a long time I had thought I could not bear a child," she wrote in *The Long Loneliness*," and the longing in my heart for a baby had been growing. My home, I felt, was not a home without one. The simple joys of the kitchen and garden brought sadness with them because I felt myself unfruitful, barren. No matter how much one was loved or one loved, that love was lonely without a child. It was incomplete."

Dorothy and Forster. (Marquette University archives)

In June 1925, Dorothy realized she was pregnant. "I will never forget my blissful joy when I was first sure." The day of certainty happened to coincide with a trip to Tottenville [in the southwest of Staten Island] to see a circus. "We brought dandelion wine and pickled eels and good home-made bread and butter. . . . I remember . . . feeling so much in love, so settled, so secure that I now had found what I was looking for."

One gets a vivid glimpse of Dorothy's exultant love of Forster, and, in several letters she sent Forster while visiting her mother in Florida that fall, a clearer image of Dorothy herself at the time.

"I had a marvelous haircut today," she reported. "They call it a pineapple bob. Next time I'll call for a coconut or an avocado bob. My ears are fully exposed but there are locks of hair before my ears so I can still look good in a hat. I am sure all this is of great interest to you—or do you love me because my legs meet together above the knees? Or because they don't? . . . Do you still want me or are you used to being without me? However, notwithstanding, cold weather is coming, so fight as you may against it you'll have to sleep with me to keep warm, and who knows in my alluring nightgown, you might be seduced into doing something besides sleep. Huh?"

Dorothy described to Forster the torment brought on by their separation: "My desire for you is a painful rather than pleasurable emotion. It is a ravishing hunger which makes me want you more than anything in the world and makes me feel as though I could barely exist until I saw you again. . . . I have never wanted you as much as I have ever since I left, from the first week on, although I've thought before that my desires were almost too strong to be borne."

She told Forster how her sister Della, with her in Florida, immediately noticed Dorothy's pregnancy "on account of the size and color of my breasts . . . and the most obvious fact of all that I can't wear a dress at all without a pad in front to keep my breasts or rather one of them from wetting everything. That's a strange symptom and I'll be glad to see a doctor when I get back to New York. Doesn't all this sound clinical?" Dorothy had an intuition she was carrying a daughter and wondered aloud about naming her Carol.

Forster was unable to share Dorothy's bliss about parenthood or even comprehend it. He didn't believe in bringing children into such a violent, toxic world. The awful responsibility of parenthood frightened him. He also sensed a child would, like God and prayer, become another barrier between himself and Dorothy. But nothing could banish Dorothy's sense that what was happening within her was marvelous, a miracle twice over. A verse from the 113th Psalm described her situation perfectly: "I found myself, a barren woman, the joyful mother of children."

Dorothy still had the rosary she had been given several years before in New Orleans. On Staten Island she began to use it during daily walks to the post office in the nearby village of Huguenot. "Maybe I did not say it correctly, but I kept on saying it because it made me happy." While walking the beach at low tide in search of driftwood for the stove, she often silently recited the words of the *Te Deum*, the ancient hymn to the Trinity that Dorothy had learned in the Episcopal church that she had attended in Chicago:

"I had known Forster a long time before we contracted our common-law relationship, and I have always felt that it was life with him that brought me natural happiness, that brought me to God."
—The Long Loneliness

We praise thee, O God; we acknowledge thee to be the Lord.
All the earth doth worship thee, the Father everlasting. . . .
Heaven and earth are full of the Majesty of thy glory. . . .
Thou art the King of Glory, O Christ.
Thou art the everlasting Son of the Father.
When thou tookest upon thee to deliver man, thou didst
humble thyself to be born of a Virgin.
When thou hadst overcome the sharpness of death, thou
didst open the Kingdom of heaven to all believers. . . .
O Lord, in thee have I trusted; let me never be confounded.

Such regal English seemed like stone that had been shaped and polished by a stream. Dorothy found each sentence beautiful to say, a joy to the tongue.

Doing housework within her cottage, her attention often drifted toward the small statue of Mary that Peggy had given her. "I found myself addressing the Blessed Virgin and turning toward her statue." She knew that some of her friends, not least Forster, regarded the religious side of her inner life a delusion. For them it was obvious, not just a tenet of Marxism, that prayer and religion were "the opiate of the people"—a source of pain relief, perhaps, a pleasant delusion, but not truth. Prayer was the numbing of consciousness rather than its sharpening, an evasion of reality, an engagement in the mentality of passivity and bondage to which so many were driven by exhaustion, injustice and sorrow. Yet the driv-

Dorothy and her sister Della.
(Marquette University archives)

ing force of prayer in her own prayer life, Dorothy realized, was gratitude and joy. "I am praying because I am happy, not because I am unhappy. I did not turn to God in unhappiness, in grief, in despair—to get consolation, to get something."

When she tried to pray on her knees, arguments against prayer and religion overwhelmed her thoughts, but whenever she set out walking—no matter what the direction, the purpose, the hour, the distance or the weather—the debate was stilled and she found it impossible not to pray. Words of praise seemed to recite themselves with each step and only ceased when she was so filled with exultation that she was beyond words and even thought. "There had been other periods of intense joy," she wrote in her journal, "but seldom had there been the quiet beauty and happiness I felt now."

Despite Forster's bewilderment and irritation, Dorothy began going to Mass on Sunday mornings. Even when audible, most of the Latin (still the language of worship throughout the Catholic Church and one that Dorothy had studied earlier in her life) was said too quickly to be comprehensible. Much of the ritual was baffling. Yet she found a mysterious peace just in being present.

Dorothy gave up worrying about her attraction to prayer and searched out books on the religious life, among them *The Imitation of Christ* by Thomas à Kempis and a life of Teresa of Avila, the sixteenth-century Spanish mystic and reformer, a saint with whom Dorothy readily identified. "Teresa liked to read novels when she was a young girl," Dorothy later explained, "and she wore a bright red dress when she entered the convent. Later she became the founder of many religious communities. When sisters in her care became melancholy, Saint Teresa responded by ordering steaks for the community meal, and on occasion took up castanets and danced." Though Teresa complained that "life is like a night spent at an uncomfortable inn," she sought to decorate the inn with reminders of heaven. She had a passionate faith, so durable and good humored that she could both argue with and tease her Creator. When thrown from a donkey while crossing a stream, she heard Christ say to her, "That is how I treat my friends." She responded, "No wonder you have so few!"

"It is so hard to say how this delight in prayer has been growing on me. Two years ago, I was saying as I planted seeds in the garden, 'I must believe in these seeds, that they fall into the earth and grow into flowers and radishes and beans. It is a miracle to me because I don't understand it. Neither do naturalists understand it. The very fact that they use glib technical phrases does not make it any the less a miracle, and a miracle we all accept. Then why not accept God's miracles?' I am going to Mass now regularly on Sunday mornings."

—From Union Square to Rome.

Now that Dorothy was settled into a house of her own and was about to become a mother, Grace Day gave her daughter some of her old high school books. Looking through the books she had studied so carefully a decade before, Dorothy found a faded slip of paper on which she had written, "Life would be utterly unbearable if we thought we were going nowhere, that we had nothing to look forward to. The greatest gift life can offer would be faith in God and a hereafter. Why don't we have it? Perhaps like all gifts it must be struggled for."

Re-reading such long forgotten reflections, Dorothy found them not embarrassing sentiments from her adolescence but more timely than the morning newspaper. She wrote in her journal: "[Since then] I have been passing through some years of fret and strife, beauty and ugliness, days and even weeks of sadness and despair, but seldom has there been the quiet beauty and happiness I have now. I thought all those years I had freedom, but now [that I am pregnant], I feel that I had neither real freedom and not even a sense of freedom."

There was an irony in the freedom she was now experiencing, as she was, due to her impending motherhood, no longer able to move about as she pleased. "No matter how much I may wish to flee from my quiet existence sometimes, I cannot, nor will I be able to for several years. I have to accept my quiet and stillness, and accepting it, I rejoice in it."

On March 4, 1926, Tamar Teresa was born. Writer that she was, Dorothy quickly found time to describe her labor and Tamar's delivery in one of her finest essays, "Having a Baby," for *The New Masses*. "I wanted to share my joy with the world," she wrote in her autobiography, "and was glad to write that joy for a workers' magazine because it was a joy all women knew, no matter what their grief at poverty, unemployment and class war. The article so appealed to my Marxist friends that the account was printed all over the world in workers' papers. Diego Rivera, when I met him some four years afterward in Mexico, greeted me as the author of it. And Mike Gold, who was at that time editor of *New Masses*, said it had been printed in many Soviet newspapers and that I had rubles awaiting me in Moscow."

"Sitting up in bed, I glance alternately at my beautiful flat stomach and out the window at tugboats and barges and the wide path of the early morning sun on the East River. The restless water is colored lavender and gold and the enchanting sky is a sentimental blue and pink. And gulls wheeling, warm gray and white against the magic of the water and the sky. Sparrows chirp on the windowsill, the baby sputters as she gets too big a mouthful, and pauses, then, a moment to look around her with satisfaction, Everybody is complacent, everybody is satisfied and everybody is happy."
—"Having a Baby," 1928

In 1943, writing about Christ's mother for *Commonweal*, Dorothy recalled entrusting her newborn daughter to the care of Mary: "You will have to be her mother. Under the best of circumstances I'm a failure as a homemaker. I'm untidy, inconsistent, undisciplined, temperamental, and I have to pray hard every day for final perseverance."

It was Tamar that occasioned Dorothy's conversion. "No human creature could receive or contain so vast a flood of love and joy as I often felt after the birth of my child. With this came the need to worship, to adore." Dorothy knew association with any church, especially the Catholic Church, would be objectionable to Forster and to nearly every friend she had. They regarded the Catholic Church as an institution that blessed injustice, practiced repression, and that had never repented its periods of torturing those suspected of heresy and burning those who were condemned. But Dorothy's attraction was based on her own experience and need, not on history or argument.

"I had heard many say that they wanted to worship God in their own way and did not need a Church in which to praise Him, nor a body of people with whom to associate themselves. But I did not agree to this. My whole experience as a radical, my whole makeup, led me to want to associate with others, with the masses, in loving and praising God. Without even looking into the claims of the Catholic Church, I was willing to admit that for me she was the one true Church. She had come down through the centuries since the time of Peter, and far from being dead, she claimed and held the allegiance of the masses of people in all the cities where I had lived. They poured in and out of her doors on Sundays and holy days, for novenas and missions."

Coming into the Church seemed the real fruit of those

Dorothy and Tamar, 1926. (Courtesy Tamar Hennessy).

Tamar Teresa. (Marquette University archives)

many long walks of joyous prayer. "What a driving power joy is! When I was unhappy and repentant in the past I turned to God, but it was my joy at having given birth to a child that made me do something definite." The Church and faith were interwoven, and she could think of nothing more precious to found her daughter's life upon than these. "I did not want my child to flounder as I had often floundered," Dorothy wrote in some notes written in later years. "I wanted to believe, and I wanted my child to believe, and if belonging to a Church would give her so inestimable a grace as faith in God, and the companionable love of the saints, then the thing to do was to have her baptized a Catholic. She would be incorporated into the Church; it was to be hoped she would grow in wisdom and grace and in following the footsteps of Jesus and have all the safeguards and helps that a universal Church would give."

When Dorothy saw a nun in her early sixties, Sister Aloysia Mary Mulhern, walking near Saint Joseph's Home, an institution for orphans and unwed mothers run by the Sisters of Charity, she didn't hesitate to approach her. "I went up to her breathlessly and asked her how I could have my child baptized. She was not at all reticent about asking questions and not at all surprised at my desires." Sister Aloysia

The beach near St. Joseph's Home, where Dorothy met Sister Aloysia.

began to visit the beach house three times each week, drilling Dorothy in memorized questions and answers about the rudiments of Catholic teaching, and challenging Dorothy to prepare herself as well as her daughter for life in the Catholic Church.

Tamar was baptized in July 1927. Forster considered the ceremony all mumbo-jumbo and wouldn't be present. His resistance to the religious direction in Dorothy's life became sharper. If he happened to be at home when Sister Aloysia dropped in, he slammed the door as he escaped with his fishing pole. Arguments and brief separations became common events, though Forster always returned to Dorothy in boyish repentance. Dorothy dreaded the prospect of life without Forster and nursed a desperate hope that he might eventually develop a toleration if not sympathy for her religious faith, and that in time he would become supportive enough so that they could formally marry. Her first marriage to Berkeley Tobey had not been a sacramental union and had no standing in the view of the Church. But the prospect of marriage in the Catholic Church, or even a civil wedding, was intolerable to Forster. He felt he would be both a liar and a hypocrite were he to take part in "any ceremony before officials of either Church or state." In the meantime, while the two continued to live together without the sanction of marriage, Dorothy's own reception into the Church had to be delayed.

Despite growing tensions between them, Tamar was a point of shared delight. Forster's earlier reservations about bringing children into the world had been swept away by the reality of his fascinating daughter. By the fall, Tamar was old enough to insist on her place in adult activities. "She gets her little hands entangled in my knitting," Dorothy noted in her journal, "or mixed up in my typewriter keys." At the time Dorothy was writing a series of articles based on interviews with workers and the unemployed. Tamar loudly protested Dorothy's long hours spent writing and reading. "She feels that I am escaping from my duty when I become absorbed in them, and she feels she must recall me to it."

Dorothy became troubled with her self-imposed exile from the slums and wondered if she weren't too contented, "nestled into this scrap of land and filled with a hideous sense of possession." Both she and Forster suffered a shared anguish in August in the days leading up to the execution of Nicola Sacco and Bartolomeo Vanzetti, Italian immigrants and anarchists who had been condemned to death for robbery and murder in Massachusetts. Despite weighty evidence of their innocence, massive demonstrations, and appeals from many countries, the governor refused to commute the death sentence to life imprisonment. (Fifty years later, a Massachusetts governor issued a proclamation declaring that Sacco and Vanzetti had been improperly tried.)

For both Dorothy and Forster, it was a ritual execution of people whose real crimes were their foreign origins, their radical beliefs, their commitment to the poor, and their indictment of the wealthy for taking so much for themselves and leaving so little for others. As Dorothy saw it, such an event was reminiscent of Christ's crucifixion. She wept in reading Vanzetti's last letter from prison.

> [Sacco] and I never brought a morsel of bread to our mouths, from our childhood to today, which was not gained by the sweat of our brows. Never. . . .
>
> [We are called thieves, assassins and doomed, yet] if it had not been for these things I might have lived out my life talking on street corners to scorning men. I might have died, unmarked, unknown, a failure.
>
> This is our career and our triumph.

"I had become convinced that I would become a Catholic, and yet I felt I was betraying the class to which I belonged, the workers, the poor of the world, the class which Christ most loved and spent His life with."
—From Union Square to Rome

Nicola Sacco and Bartolomeo Vanzetti.

Never in our full life could we hope to do such work for toler-ance, for justice, for man's understanding of man, as we now do by accident.

Our words, our lives, our pain—nothing.

The taking of our lives—lives of a good shoe maker and a poor fish peddler—all!

The last moment belongs to us—the agony is our triumph.

When news of the executions was published, the headlines were as large as those which announced the outbreak of war. "All the nation mourned," Dorothy wrote in *The Long Loneliness.* "All the nation, I mean, that is made up of the poor, the worker, the trade unionist—those who felt most keenly the sense of solidarity—that very sense of solidarity which made me gradually understand the doctrine of the Mystical Body of Christ whereby we are members of one another."

Heading in *Industrial Worker,* an IWW paper.

Forster was so stricken that for days he lived as if dead himself, barely able to eat or speak, utterly sickened by the cruelty of life and the heartlessness of those in power. No doubt it struck him that among the many institutions that stood by unprotesting while two poor men were electrocuted was the very Church to which Dorothy had attached herself.

One afternoon just after Christmas, their differences once again exploded, and again Forster stormed out the door.

No.	Name of Person Baptized	Date and Place of Birth	Date of Baptism	PARENTS	SPONSORS	PRIEST	RECORD OF MARRIAGE
	Dorothy Day	Nov. 8, 1898	Dec. 29, 1927	John Grace Saterlcey	Sister Aloysia	J U Hyland	(Died Nov 29 1980 #years) 449)

Dorothy's baptismal record from Our Lady Help of Christians in Tottenville. (The date of birth should have been 1897.)

"When he returned, as he always had, I would not let him in the house; my heart was breaking with my own determination to make an end, once and for all, to the torture that we were enduring." The same afternoon, she called the parish priest and made an appointment for her reception into the Catholic Church. On December 28, after leaving Tamar with her sister Della, Dorothy went to the church in Tottenville, Our Lady Help of Christians. She had been baptized during childhood in the Episcopal Church, but was baptized again conditionally. No friends were present except her godparent, Sister Aloysia.

The long-awaited, costly event gave Dorothy no consolation, as she contemplated the final break with Forster and its consequences for herself and Tamar. "I had no sense of peace, no joy, no conviction that what I was doing was right. It was just something that I had to do, a task to be gotten through." Participating at her first Mass as a Catholic the next day, she felt wooden, like someone going through the motions. "I felt like a hypocrite as I got down on my knees, and shuddered at the thought of anyone seeing me." Was she not betraying the oppressed and the radical movement? "Here I was, going over to the opposition, because the Church was lined up with property, with the wealthy, with capitalism, with all the forces of reaction."

It pained Dorothy to see "businesslike priests" who seemed "more like Cain than Abel," most of whom ignored the poor and never said a word about social injustice. Yet she was grateful that they offered her access to the sacraments. She took comfort in knowing that there were other priests who lived poorly and "who gave their lives daily for their fellows." Even if Christ often seemed hidden rather than revealed by the Church, still it was Christ's Church. If so many bishops and the clergy seemed unaware of the poor, the poor were in the Church.

If only, Dorothy thought, it was less a Church of charities, fine as they were, and more a Church of social justice. "I felt that charity was a word to choke over. Who wanted charity? And it was not just human pride but a strong sense of man's dignity and worth, and what was due to him in justice, that made me resent rather than feel proud of so mighty a sum of Catholic institutions." It seemed all too often that the charities were hardly better than government agencies, heavy with bureaucracy and lacking a human touch. "How I longed to make a synthesis reconciling body and soul, this world and the next."

Dorothy also longed for the restoration of her relationship with Forster, if only he would love her as she was, and if only she could convince him that marriage was not necessarily an act of surrender to an evil world that preferred law to love.

They continued to see each other, Tamar providing the occasions, but the visits were often stressful. In one letter to Forster sent early in 1928, Dorothy suggests he visit on Sunday mornings rather than Saturday nights. The implication is that, despite their frequent quarrels, evening visits make parting too painful:

> You make it much harder when you are kind to me. But we can't go on in any but a friendly relation and I suppose you will say we can't even have that. Quite aside from my religious instincts, which you refuse to recognize, we weren't getting on at all last year, as you know. We had any number of mean, ugly quarrels which are enough to corrode anyone's existence and the quarrels were not only about religion but there were resentments about the baby and about finances. . . . It is terribly hard to even mention my religious feelings to you because I am sure you do not think I am sincere. But it is not a sudden thing, but a thing which has been growing in me for years. I had impulses toward religion again and again and now when I try to order my life according to it in order to attain some sort of peace and happiness it is very hard but I must do it. Because even though it is hard, it gives me far more happiness to do it, even though it means my combating my physical feelings toward you. The strength of our physical attachment never led you to make any sacrifices or capitulations of your principles. You were always very hard about maintaining

"It was in December 1927, a most miserable day, and the trip was long from the city down to Tottenville, Staten Island. All the way on the ferry through the foggy bay I felt grimly that I was being too precipitate. . . . I doubted myself when I allowed myself to think. I hated myself for being weak and vacillating. A most consuming restlessness was upon me so that I walked around and around the deck of the ferry, almost groaning in anguish of spirit. . . ."
—From Union Square to Rome

your independence and freedom. You would never marry even when I begged you to. . . . And you always held yourself somewhat aloof from me. It is only now when I wish to give you up that you hold on to me. . . . I do not see why we can't be friends, but if you insist on not being friends with me, I'll just have to put up with it, no matter how unhappy it makes me. After all, the present unhappiness is not unbearable because I at least have the peace of knowing that I am doing what I think is best. And it's a bearable unhappiness because it has in it none of those horrible resentments I had toward you last year so often. Please do not be angry at me. You know I love you and as a matter of fact always did love you more than you loved me.

In an undated letter probably sent in the spring of 1928, Dorothy described Tamar "climbing in the window to me she gives me a good morning kiss, imitating you, and pressing her face to mine for a long time. It is too sweet. And now she insists on kissing the cat goodnight, chasing her around the room until she can grab her by the ears and plant a kiss on her nose. She is sitting in the bathtub now and I just had to jump over and rinse the soap with which she was washing her hair and which she gets in her eyes."

She guessed Forster would sneer at her for continuing to write him after having locked him out, "but I can't help wanting to keep in touch with you some way. I suppose the best thing for both of us would be if you contracted an alliance with some nice fat Jewish girl (your ideal of beauty) even though I would be racked with jealousy if you did. I dream of you every night—that I am lying in your arms and I can feel your kisses and it is torture to me, but so sweet, too. I do love you more than anything in the world, but I cannot help my religious sense, which tortures me unless I do as I believe right."

Two months later Dorothy ended a letter about Tamar with a plaintive account of a recent dream: "I dreamt the other night that you were marrying a rich widow who lived down the beach somewhere, and I thought desperately that I must have one last night with you before the wedding. You were very cold to me and kept saying, 'Well this is what you get.'"

A Marriage That Never Happened

T he five years following Dorothy's entrance into the
Catholic Church centered on her search to find
something that didn't yet exist: a way of supporting
herself and Tamar through work which linked her religious
faith, her commitment to social justice, and her vocation as a
writer. It was a journey in the dark.

Dorothy and Tamar. (Marquette
University archives)

"I do not see why we can't be friends, but if you insist on not being friends with me, I'll just have to put up with it, no matter how unhappy it makes me. After all, the present unhappiness is not unbearable because I at least have the peace of knowing that I am doing what I think is best. . . . Please do not be angry at me. You know I love you and as a matter of fact always did love you more than you loved me."

—To Forster Batterham, March 1928

She also clung to the hope that she and Forster might find enough common ground for him finally to marry her. In a letter written in March 1929, she assured Forster that she would not impose her Catholic piety on him: "I would have nothing around the house to jar upon you—no pictures and books. I am really not as obsessed as you think I am." All he would have to bear with was her going to Mass on Sundays and major feast days. There was also the matter of the religious formation of children—he would have to agree "to allow the children to be raised Catholics." And there was the problem of his submitting to a Catholic wedding—she assured him, somewhat disingenuously, that "the ceremony is as simple as that of going before a justice of the peace." She was, she admitted to Forster, struggling with depression. "I wonder how you would feel," she asked, "if one of your sisters had to go through the struggle that I do. I'm sure you would feel that marriage was a very slight concession to make and that the man was indeed a most pig-headed idiot to ruin their two lives."

With a daughter to care for, money was a more urgent problem than it had been. Dorothy made a little money providing child care for several Staten Island neighbors. She was also able to coax occasional checks from Forster.

Renting an apartment in Manhattan so that it would be easier to make a living, for a time Dorothy handled publicity for the Anti-Imperialism League, a group campaigning for the end of U.S. military intervention in Central America and raising aid and medical supplies for General Augusto Sandino, the Nicaraguan revolutionary leader. While Dorothy was at the office, Tamar was cared for at the Horatio Street Nursery at the cost of ten cents a day.

The League was a Communist-affiliated group with offices on Union Square, like so many left-wing groups. "I was so new a Catholic," Dorothy later wrote, "that I was still working for the committee some months after my baptism." She told her confessor, Father Zachary, a priest serving at her parish, Our Lady of Guadalupe Church on West 14th Street, "I am in agreement with [what the League is trying to accomplish]. We should not be sending our Marines to Nicaragua. I am in agreement with many of the social aims of Communism: from each according to his ability, to each according to his need." Father Zachary could only remind her of Lenin's insistence that "atheism is basic to Marxism." Father Zachary was, Dorothy recalled, "the gentlest of confessors with me, who, at that time, was a female counterpart of Graham Greene's *Quiet American*, wanting to do good by violence."

During the same period, she began doing part-time work from her apartment for the Metro-Goldwyn-Mayer film company, writing six-page summaries of new novels at six dollars per book. She sometimes managed to do a book a day.

Perhaps responding to Father Zachary's prodding, Dorothy began thinking about nonviolent approaches to social justice. She found a part-time job in Manhattan at the national office of the Fellowship of Reconciliation, a Christian pacifist organization which was developing nonviolent methods of struggle in the labor and civil rights movements, and whose members committed themselves to refuse any part in warfare. The Fellowship was also working for the end of Washington's "gunboat diplomacy" in Latin America. But Dorothy felt isolated as the only Catholic in an office otherwise staffed entirely by Protestants.

The seasons shaped their lives. Back in Staten Island once the weather began to warm, Dorothy found part-time work providing care for a child who was a student at the Hoffman School, several miles from her cottage. Tamar had reached the age of being eager to help with household chores—setting and clearing the table and running errands. Back in Manhattan for the winter months, Dorothy was hard hit by the flu. No neighbor seemed to notice how urgently in need of help she was, not just for herself but for Tamar—so many people crowded together yet with so little interest in each other, neighbors in name only, in reality isolated from each

Tamar in Culver City. (Marquette University archives)

other, "each afraid another would ask something from him." Warm weather brought Dorothy and Tamar back to Staten Island, where Dorothy got a summer job working as cook for priests and brothers living at the Marist House on Prince's Bay. Short of money to pay the taxes due on the cottage, Dorothy had to rent it out. Meanwhile Dorothy and Tamar stayed with the Marists, for whom it must have been startling to discover that many of Dorothy's visitors were people who, were it not for Dorothy, wouldn't be caught dead in a building full of images of Mary and Jesus.

Hollywood in the 1920s.

Then, to Dorothy's astonishment, she got a job offer to work in Hollywood writing film dialogue for the Pathé Motion Picture Company with a salary of $125 per week, big money at the time. Late in the summer of 1929, just weeks before the crash of the stock market and the beginning of the Great Depression, Dorothy and Tamar boarded the train to California. "Like all Hollywood authors," Dorothy recalled in *The Long Loneliness*, "I thought of the money I would make that would free me to live the simple life in the future and work on a novel I was always writing." Forster came to Pennsylvania Station to see them off, a tearful parting. En route to California, Dorothy wrote a short letter to him that included the words, "I do love you so much sweetheart."

Things didn't turn out in Hollywood as Dorothy had imagined. While she had a private office at the Pathé Studio and met daily with other writers, attending and discussing private screen showings, she felt isolated and saw nothing of value in what she was doing. The glamor of Hollywood left her cold. "Life in this place," she wrote Forster, "broadens the fanny and narrows the mind." She was feeling "as blue as indigo." Again she pressed him to relax his scruples against marriage: "Why don't you become reasonable or indulgent or whatever you want to call it and tell me to come back and marry you?"

In the letter that followed, she reminded Forster that she

was "not a promiscuous creature" in her love. "I've never loved anyone but you and Lionel [Moise] and that early affair seems but the dimmest adolescent crush compared to the love I have for you. But it is all so damned hopeless that I do hope I fall in love again and marry since there seems to be no possibility for a happy outcome to our love for each other. It will either be that or a single life for me from now on."

Descriptions of marital happiness were not rare in her letters to Forster: "I wish I were there to scold you and clean the house up after you and find your cap for bed. We would take a bath together so as not to waste the hot water—the bathroom could be heated easily with the oil stove which heats the water, and if the nights are cold I would keep you very warm indeed. As it is, I'm cold every night." But life in a single bed was what Dorothy got. "Young and old, even in the busiest years of our lives," she later reflected, "we women especially are victims of the long loneliness."

Dorothy's stay in Hollywood lasted only three months, as the capital of dreams was hit hard by the Great Depression. "I certainly hope the stock market won't affect your business the way it has affected the movie business," she said in a letter to Forster in November. "It is completely dead around here. No work at all. Only three writers left out of the twenty-four there were a few months ago. I'm hoping they keep me on and my hopes are based on the fact that my salary is a comparatively small one."

But her contract was not renewed. In January 1930, Dorothy and Tamar left Hollywood for Mexico in a second-hand Model T Ford. To help with expenses, she had signed a contract with an automobile club to write a monthly article on touring in Mexico. The decisive factor in her going south rather than returning to New York was her awareness of how hard it would be living so close to Forster while being divided by a wall of conflicting beliefs and expectations.

Mexico also had a positive attraction. Dorothy wanted the experience of living in a country in which Catholicism was deeply embedded in the culture. There was also the factor of being able to witness "what it was like to live [with Christians] under persecution," such as was then going on in Mexico.

Dorothy and Tamar in Mexico.
(Marquette University archives)

Dorothy on beach with Tamar.
(Marquette University archives)

"After Teresa had blessed herself with holy water and made her rather lopsided genuflection, she skipped out of the church again that she might lean over the low walls and peer into doorways at the chickens, pigs, lambs, and pigeons, not to speak of cats and dogs which shared the houses and gardens.

'These are all Mary's babies,' she said. 'The little pigs and the chickens are the boys and the girls. And these are all little baby houses, and that,' pointing to the church, 'is the mama house.'"

—Commonweal, 1930

Since 1917, the Church had been placed under the unsympathetic control of a hostile secular state. The activities and movements of clergy were restricted, convents and monasteries were banned. It was this grim reality that Graham Greene used as the backdrop for his novel of priesthood, human failure and martyrdom, *The Power and the Glory.*

Arriving in Mexico City, Dorothy rented a room from a one-armed woman whose daughter sold stockings from a pushcart at a nearby park. On the pleasant terrace outside Dorothy and Tamar's room were caged birds and potted plants.

Dorothy's fascination with the Mexican people and their faith found expression in a series of articles written for *Commonweal,* an independent Catholic journal edited by laypeople, and for *America,* a magazine edited by Jesuits. Both had their offices in New York. Her day, she reported in one article, started with Mass at the nearby Church of San Jose, and from there, along with crowds of other women, going on to the market. The drama and theater of the liturgy astonished her: churches overflowing with people, processions with life-size statues, and the deep integration of symbols of belief linking church and home. During Easter Mass, tens of thousands of flower petals showered continuously on the brightly dressed Indians packed into the church she attended. Countless small details of life were linked with religious belief. Dorothy discovered that a street called Niño Perdido was named not after a local child who had once been lost, as she had first guessed, but rather after the child Jesus, for three days separated from his parents in Jerusalem. It was obvious to Dorothy that the faith of the people thrived despite all the restrictions on religious life imposed by the government.

Hostility toward religion was a hallmark of all the radical intellectuals she met. One of these was the artist Diego Rivera, a "huge man, hearty and genial," but with no sympathy for the Catholic Church. While Dorothy agreed with some of his criticisms, she wished Rivera could glimpse the Church through the eyes of the faithful, so many of whom were the very people, "the masses," with whom he saw himself allied.

Dorothy had intended to live in Mexico for at least a few years, but half a year after arriving in Mexico, Tamar became ill with malaria. Deciding it was best to seek treatment in the U.S., Dorothy drove to her parents' home in Coral Gables, Florida. (At the time, Dorothy's father, still a sports journalist, was based in Havana, Cuba.) Tamar spent eleven days in the hospital, quickly regaining her health and weight. Apart from a brief visit with friends in New Jersey, their stay in Florida lasted

Tamar with her grandmother, Grace Day, in Coral Gables, Florida. (Marquette University archives)

through the winter. The weather was better for Tamar, Grace loved being an active grandmother, and being a guest made it easier for a freelance writer to cope financially with the Depression.

From Florida, Dorothy wrote for *Commonweal* about the nearby "colored town" of Coconut Grove with its small frame houses surrounded by an abundance of fruit trees. Toto, the woman who cleaned her parents' house, lived here in a house whose porch had been blown away by a hurricane several years before. Her eighteen-year-old daughter, Evelina, was dying of tuberculosis. Dorothy came to be with the family and their neighbors as they sat praying and singing around the bed on which Evelina was struggling for breath. Evelina kept her grip on life until her mother gave her permission to die.

With the arrival of spring in 1931, Dorothy and Tamar returned to their much-missed Staten Island cottage. In their absence, friends had taken down the crucifix, hanging in its place a crab shell. "There is no cross there," Tamar complained, "so I'll just say my prayers to the spider crab." Dorothy quickly found the crucifix in the attic and put it back in its traditional spot.

Dorothy was now thirty-four, Tamar was five. Though having to stretch each penny, Dorothy was managing to live from journalism, writing for several Catholic publications as well as doing a gardening column for *The Staten Island Advance*.

Regarding Manhattan to be better as a main base, Dorothy rented a four-room, ground-floor tenement flat in a chiefly Italian neighborhood on East 15th Street close to Avenue A. It was large enough to share with her journalist brother, John, and his pregnant wife, Tessa. Dorothy had the front room, most exposed to street noise, six-year old Tamar the next room, then the room shared by John and Tessa. Next came the kitchen, which also served as dining room, sitting room and library. In the back yard there were peach and fig trees. Having a southern exposure, the kitchen was best lit and warmest. This railway flat was soon to become the birthplace of the Catholic Worker.

Opposite: Dorothy and Tamar. (Marquette University archives)

"*I am very glad to be home again, to be cultivating my own bit of soil, to be living in my own house and to feel, for the time at least, that I am never going to leave it again. There is beauty here too, a lovely, gentle beauty of cultivated gardens and woodlands and shore. . . . Along the road we gathered sweet clover to put in the hot attic, where its fragrance will be distilled and fill the house, and Teresa sighed happily, 'Flowers and grass and things are so beautiful, they just hurt my feelings.'*"
—Commonweal, 1931

A Prayer in Washington

In 1932 the Great Depression was in its third devastating year. Economic desolation was obvious no matter which way one turned. Unemployment rose to 23.6 percent. Industrial stocks had lost 80 percent of their value. Ten thousand banks had failed. "Brother, Can You Spare a Dime" was being played on every radio. In *The Long Loneliness*, Dorothy recalled the times: "More and more people were losing their jobs, more families were being evicted, the Unemployed Councils were being formed by the Communist groups and the Workers Alliance sprang into existence. It was time for pressure groups, for direct action . . . radicalism was thriving

Unemployed waiting in a breadline. (Library of Congress)

"We were in the third year of the depression. Roosevelt had just been elected President. Every fifth adult American—twelve million in all—was unemployed. . . . In New York long, bedraggled breadlines of listless men wound along city streets. On the fringes, by the rivers almost every vacant lot was a Hooverville, a collection of jerry-built shanties where the homeless huddled in front of their fires."

—Loaves and Fishes

among all groups except Catholics. I felt out of it. There was Catholic membership in all these groups, of course, but no Catholic leadership. It was that very year that Pope Pius XI said sadly, 'The workers of the world are lost to the Church'. . . . The bitter worm of despair was eating at the human heart."

Dorothy felt she had no capacity for leadership nor even a clear idea where a leader ought to be heading. She saw herself only as a bystander, a witness, a diarist, a reporter. The strong currents that had drawn her toward the Catholic Church had not weakened, but Dorothy felt growing anguish about her own passivity. At the advice of the priest who heard her weekly confession, she gave up her custom of sleeping as late as work and parenthood allowed and began going to daily Mass. On Saturdays, besides confession, she took part in the Benediction service. She returned to the writings of Saint Teresa of Avila.

Hunger marchers in Washington, D.C. (Library of Congress)

When the warmer weather made Staten Island attractive again, she and Tamar went there, but whether at the beach cottage or on East 15th Street, Dorothy pressed on with various writing projects. Another novel was completed but found no publisher. There were occasional articles for *Commonweal* and *America*. It was for both journals that Dorothy was commissioned to report on the Hunger March, an event that proved a turning point in her life.

On November 30, Union Square, hub of so many radical events, was the departure point for about six hundred jobless men and women heading to Washington. Their rag-tag Hunger March was sponsored by the National Committee of the Unemployed Councils, which in turn was allied with the Communist Party, though few of the participants, Dorothy noted, were themselves Communists.

For most of the way, it was a march only in a figurative sense. The participants traveled in seventeen vans plus three old cars, while Dorothy followed them by public bus. The popular press treated the event as evidence of Red revolution. Little attention was given to the marchers' proposals: jobs, unemployment insurance, old age pensions, relief for mothers and children, health care and housing for those who had lost everything. Hostility along the way reached a crescendo in Wilmington, Delaware, where police hurled tear gas canisters through the windows of a Protestant church which had opened its doors to the marchers. Those escaping the gas were clubbed down and the suspected leaders were thrown into police vans and taken to jail. Despite delays and injuries, the Hunger March pressed on.

When the swelling assembly reached the edge of Washington, they found barricades had been put across the highway. The demonstrators had been barred from entering the capital. Refusing to disband, the marchers camped out for three days and nights, despite bitter weather and encirclement by heavily-armed police. Route 1 was closed to traffic.

Dorothy was struck by the contrast between what she witnessed and what was published in newspapers. Each day headlines warned of a Communist menace which bore little resemblance to the actual unarmed people who had endured insults and violence to dramatize the hardships and needs of the unemployed. "If there was not a story, the newspapers would make a story," Dorothy recalled. "The newspaper reporters were infected by their own journalism and began to beg editors to give them gas masks before they went out to interview the leaders of the unemployed marchers."

Such alarmist press reports shaped the response of the guardians of Washington. In a report written for the Jesuit weekly *America*, Dorothy described the preparations that had occurred within the city: "There were riot drills of the Marines at Quantico; guards at the White House, Capitol, Treasury, plants of the electric and gas companies, arsenals of the National Guard and the Sixth Marine Reserve." Protecting the city from the Hunger Marchers, she reported, were the police force, the National Guard, 370 firemen, even the American Legion and many volunteers. Weapons at hand included machine guns, tear gas, nauseating gas, revolvers, shot guns, night sticks and lengths of rubber hose.

On December 8, after a Washington federal court ruled in the marchers' favor, the police reluctantly removed the barricades and stood aside. In *The Long Loneliness*, Dorothy described the last leg of the march: "On a bright sunny day the ragged horde triumphantly with banners flying, with lettered

"On a bright sunny day the ragged horde triumphantly with banners flying, with lettered slogans mounted on sticks, paraded three thousand strong through the tree-flanked streets of Washington. I stood on the curb and watched them, joy and pride in the courage of this band of men and women mounting in my heart, and with a bitterness too that since I was now a Catholic, with fundamental philosophical differences, I could not be out there with them. I could write, I could protest, to arouse the conscience, but where was the Catholic leadership in the gathering of bands of men and women together, for the actual works of mercy that the comrades had always made part of their technique in reaching the workers?"
—The Long Loneliness

slogans mounted on sticks, paraded three thousand strong through the tree-flanked streets of Washington. I stood on the curb and watched them, joy and pride in the courage of this band of men and women mounting in my heart."

She felt bitterness as well. She knew the Hunger March had been organized not by Christians but by Communists and that the differences between the two groups were such that as yet she had no deep friendships with Catholics and was regarded as a traitor by many radicals she had once been close to. She had a religious faith and a social conscience, but no community. She could only watch and admire those campaigning for social justice—"I could not be out there with them."

Dorothy felt useless. "How little, how puny my work had been since becoming a Catholic, I thought. How self-centered, how ingrown, how lacking in a sense of community! My summer of quiet reading and prayer, my self-absorption seemed sinful as I watched my brothers in their struggle, not for themselves but for others. How our dear Lord must love them, I kept thinking to myself. They were His friends, His comrades, and who knows how close to His heart in their attempt to work for justice. I remembered our Lord overthrowing the money-changers' tables in the temple. . . . [What] divine courage on the part of this obscure Jew, going into the temple and with bold scorn for all the riches of this world, scattering the coins and the traffickers' gold."

The banners passed, and the marchers who had ignited such hysteria disbanded peaceably, no doubt wondering who was changed or what structures of life might be improved by their appeal and the hardship they endured along the way.

December 8 is a "holy day of obligation" for Catholics, the feast of the Immaculate Conception, celebrating Catholic belief that a special grace had touched Mary's life from the moment of her conception in her mother's womb. Before returning to her no-frills hotel room to write down her impressions of the day, Dorothy went to a church built to commemorate the event, the National Shrine of the Immaculate Conception, adjacent to the campus of Catholic University in northeast Washington. As the upper church

Sketch of the planned National Shrine of the Immaculate Conception. The upper church was still under construction in 1932.

99

The crypt in the National Shrine of the Immaculate Conception where Dorothy prayed for her vocation. In a real sense, this spot was the birthplace of the Catholic Worker. (Credit: Vicenç Feliú - Sabreur76/flickr.com)

was still under construction, she went into the crypt beneath, with its low vaulted ceilings, mosaics and dark chapels lit with the flickering of vigil candles. "There I offered up a special prayer, a prayer which came with tears and anguish, that some way would open up for me to use what talents I possessed for my fellow workers, for the poor."

Dorothy returned to New York in the late afternoon of December 9, eager to be with Tamar and to share news of the Hunger March with John and Tessa. They were all at home, but there was a stranger waiting for her as well, a man who had arrived earlier and whom Tessa had invited to stay for supper. His unpressed suit bore the wrinkles of having been slept in. He could easily have been among the marchers Dorothy had admired in Washington. His face seemed as weather-beaten as his clothing. However, the visitor wasn't down-and-out in his welcoming smile. His whole manner communicated gentleness, vitality and intellectual energy. When he spoke, his calloused hands were as lively as his thought.

"I am Peter Maurin," he said in a thick French accent. "George Schuster, editor of *Commonweal*, told me to look you up. Also, a red-haired Irish Communist in Union Square told me to see you. He says we think alike."

"Peter talked as if he were taking up a conversation where it had been left off," Dorothy recalled in *Loaves and Fishes*, her history of the Catholic Worker's first three decades. "There was a gray look about him. He had gray hair, cut short and scrubby, gray eyes, strong features, a pleasant mouth, and short-fingered, broad hands, evidently used to hard work. . . . He wore the kind of old clothes that have so lost their shape and finish that it's impossible to tell if they are clean or not."

Peter chose the occasion to recite one of his "Easy Essays," as Dorothy's brother John soon christened them—a kind of rhythmic, blank-verse poem using repeated words and phrases arranged in short lines. Aware that Dorothy had just returned from Washington, his text was a challenge to her and to all those who believe that it is the task of government to solve our problems. It began:

Peter Maurin. (Marquette University archives)

> People go to Washington
> asking the government
> to solve their economic problems,
> while the Federal government
> was never intended
> to solve men's economic problems.
> Thomas Jefferson says,
> "The less government there is,
> the better it is."
> If the less government there is,
> the better it is,
> the best kind of government
> is self-government . . .

Arguing for less government rather than more was an idea completely out of fashion with those on the Left. "When the organizers don't organize themselves," Peter continued, "nobody organizes himself, and when nobody organizes himself, nothing is organized."

Dorothy and her sister-in-law Tessa.
(Marquette University archives)

Had Tamar not been down with the measles and Dorothy not so exhausted, she probably would have defended the hunger marchers and others like them for urging the government to do more to help the homeless and jobless. Instead she turned her attention to Tamar while Peter, not at all annoyed, presented his ideas to others in the apartment—John, Tessa, a plumber who had dropped in, a man who had come to read the gas meter, and the physician who, after seeing Tamar, was attempting to leave. Having run out of attentive ears, Peter departed, promising Dorothy that he would return.

Peter was back the next day, ready to provide Dorothy with "an entirely new education." But first he needed to tell her about the three-point program he hoped she would embrace: founding a newspaper "for the clarification of thought," promoting houses of hospitality for those in need of food and shelter, and organizing farming communities so that both workers and scholars could return to the land. "I did not think," Dorothy recalled later in life, "that the second two had anything to do with me, but I did know about newspapers."

At the same time that Dorothy was beginning to glimpse the work to which she would devote the rest of her life, she abandoned her hopes that Forster would eventually agree to marry her. Her last surviving letter to him until 1968 was dated December 10, 1932, the day after returning to New York from Washington. In it she begins by responding to Forster's bewilderment about how her attitudes toward intimate relationships could have changed so dramatically in the eight years since they met each other—the Dorothy Day he had met in 1924 hadn't been slow to fall in love, nor had she been a reluctant sexual partner.

"I do indeed now feel that sex is taboo outside of marriage," Dorothy replied. "The institution of marriage has been built up by society as well as the Church to safeguard the home and children as well as people who don't know how to take care of themselves. Of course anyone who is sane and sound mentally will agree that promiscuity and looseness in sex is an ugly and inharmonious thing."

Dorothy reminded Forster of his unswerving avoidance of anything even vaguely resembling marital commitment. "You have always in the past treated me most casually, and I see no special difference between our affair and any other casual affair I have had in the past. You avoided, as you admitted yourself, all responsibility. You would not marry me then because you preferred the slight casual contact with me to any other." She also referred to an apparent lapse in her efforts to live a celibate life: "And last spring, when my love and physical desire for you overcame me, you were quite willing for the affair to go on, on a weekend basis."

She had not, Dorothy insisted, developed a longing to be a celibate. "Sex is not at all taboo with me except outside of marriage. I am as free and unsuppressed as I ever was about it. I think the human body a beautiful thing, and the joys that a healthy body have are perfectly legitimate joys. I see no immediate difference between enjoying sex and enjoying a symphony concert, but sex having such a part in life as producing children, has been restricted as society and the Church have felt best for the children. . . .

Dorothy reading to Tamar, 1932.
(Marquette University archives)

"When [in the past] I laughingly spoke [to you] about many a young girl holding out [before engaging in sex]—you should have understood what I meant. You seem to think that one should always succumb immediately to any promptings of the flesh, and you think of it as unnatural and unhealthy to restrain oneself on account of the promptings of the spirit. What I meant was that many people in the past have observed the conventions and rules, for the sake not only of convention but of principle. [But it] is hard for me to talk to you seriously [about such matters]—you despise so utterly the things which mean so much to me. . . .

"You think all this is only hard on you. But I am suffering too. The ache in my heart is intolerable at times, and sometimes for days I can feel your lips upon me, waking and sleeping. It is because I love you so much that I want you to marry me. I want to be in your arms every night, as I used to be, and be with you always. I always loved you more than you did me. That is why I made up with you so many times, and went after you after we had had some quarrel. We always differed on principle, and now that I am getting older I cannot any longer always give way to you just because flesh has such power over me. . . .

"I can understand your hatred and rebellion against my beliefs and I can't blame you. [But] I have really given up hope now, so I won't try to persuade you any more."

A Penny a Copy

As remarkable as the providence of her first encounter with Peter Maurin was Dorothy's capacity to take him seriously. To many others, Peter was just one more street-corner prophet out of touch with the real world. New York had many. Dorothy knew the type. Yet she gave him not only patient but appreciative attention.

While Peter was tireless in expounding his vision and philosophy, he was hesitant to talk about himself. It took years for Dorothy to gather together the main facts of his life. The eldest of twenty-two children, Peter had been born in 1877 into a family of peasant farmers in the French region of Languedoc, not far from Spain. He took pride in having a grandfather who lived to be ninety-four and who had still been working in the fields when he was eighty-five, after which he stayed home making baskets and praying the rosary. At sixteen, Peter entered a Catholic teaching order, the Christian Brothers, with whom he remained for nine years. In 1902, he left the order and became active in *Le Sillon* (The Furrow), a movement which advocated Christian democracy and which supported cooperatives and unions. But in 1908, with *Le Sillon* shifting from its early religious focus toward politics, Peter withdrew and soon after joined the stream of emigrants who were leaving France for Canada, where there was no military conscription and land was cheap. For two years, he homesteaded in Saskatchewan, then took whatever work he could find, first in Canada and then in the United States. By the time he met Dorothy, he had dug irrigation ditches, quarried stone, harvested wheat, cut lumber, laid railway tracks, labored in brickyards, steel mills and coal mines. He had been jailed for vagrancy and for "riding the rails"—traveling unticketed on freight cars. He had never married. In Chicago, he had supported himself by teaching French and making a good living doing so. It must have been at the end of his Chicago days that he experienced a religious

The village of Oultet, France, where Peter Maurin was born. (Francis Sicius)

Peter Maurin, living in Chicago in 1917, about thirty years old. (Marquette University archives)

awakening that reoriented his life. In the five-year period leading up to his encounter with Dorothy Day, he had been the handy-man at a Catholic boys' camp, Mount Tremper in upstate New York, in exchange for meals, use of the chaplain's library, living space in the barn (shared with a horse), and pocket money when needed.

He once confided to Dorothy that, in the rootless decade that preceded his job at the boys' camp, he had been estranged from the Catholic Church. "Why?" she asked. "Because I was not living as a Catholic should," Peter replied. "There was a finality about his answer," Dorothy commented in retelling the story in 1952, "that kept me from questioning further. I understood that his difficulties had not been intellectual but moral. . . . I could only suppose that he had been living as most men do in their youth, following their own desires."

By the time Dorothy met him, Peter had not only returned to the Catholic faith but had acquired an ascetic attitude toward both property and money: he had nearly none of either and, like Saint Francis of Assisi, rejoiced in poverty as if it were his bride. His poverty was his freedom. His unencumbered, possession-free life provided him with ample time for study, prayer and medita-tion, out of which a vision had taken form of a social order "in which it would be easier for men to be good." He sought a new weaving together of "cult, culture and cultivation," a syn-thesis he saw as being "so old that it seems like new." Cult referred to religion, the foundation of life. Culture arose from religion and meant each person becoming an artist or crafts-man in his or her field of endeavor. Cultivation meant a life rooted in the land.

As often as his work at the camp allowed, he made his way to New York City. A "flop house" hotel on the Bowery provided austere lodging for forty cents a night. His days were spent either at the New York Public Library or on the streets—often at Union Square—expounding his ideas to anyone who showed a flicker of interest. After all, he reasoned, the way to reach the man on the street is to go to the street. No doubt his accent and threadbare suit convinced many that there was no need to listen. But Peter was a born teacher, lively and good humored, and had little difficulty in finding willing listeners—not only the unemployed and radicals with time on their hands, but bankers and professors.

During the days of Tamar's recovery from measles, and for weeks afterward, Peter was nearly a full-time visitor, offering Dorothy an intensive course on the Church's role in the world. He was one of the rare Catholics who knew what recent popes had written on pressing social issues, and could even recite by heart significant passages from those encyclicals, *Rerum Novarum* and *Quadragesimo Anno*. He had studied so many authors that people who came to know Peter joked about him being a walking library.

In *House of Hospitality*, published six years after the first issue of *The Catholic Worker*, Dorothy recalled how she would get home from the library about three in the afternoon, having been hired to do some research on peace for a women's group. "Every day . . . I found Peter waiting to 'indoctrinate' me. He stayed until ten when I insisted he had to go home. He followed Tamar and me around the house, indoctrinating. If we were getting supper, washing dishes, ironing clothes or washing them, he continued his conversations. If company came, he started over again from the beginning."

Peter told Dorothy how saints, down through the centuries, had responded in radical ways to the social ills of their day. Emphasizing the "primacy of the spiritual," Peter wanted Dorothy to acquire a view of life and history that centered on sanctity—to study the past with special attention to the lives of the saints and their impact on the world around them. "It's better to know the lives of saints," Peter insisted, "than the lives of kings and generals." But studying history was also essential: "We must study history," he said, "in order to find out why things are as they are. In the light of history, we should so work today that things will be different in the future."

"Some of Peter's ideas were less readily understandable, but his verses probably helped people grasp the sense and spirit of what he had to say. He fancied himself a troubadour of God, going about the public squares and street corners indoctrinating his listeners by a singsong repetition, which certainly caught their attention. Being a born teacher, he did not hesitate to repeat his ideas over and over again."
—Loaves and Fishes

Tamar, Dorothy, and Peter in the early days of *The Catholic Worker*. (Marquette University archives)

"Peter had faith in people as well as in ideas, and he was able to make them feel his faith in them, so that they gained confidence and overcame the sense of futility that so plagues the youth of today. In fact, he gave me so great a faith in the power of his ideas that if he had said, 'Go to Madison Square Garden and speak these ideas,' I would have overcome all sense of fear and would have attempted such a folly, convinced that, though it was the 'folly of the Cross' and doomed to failure, God Himself would take this failure and turn it into victory."

—Loaves and Fishes

Peter had been praying for a collaborator and was certain Dorothy was the answer to his prayers. Her articles and what others had told him about her, as well as his own immediate impressions, convinced him that Dorothy had the potential of becoming a new Saint Catherine of Siena, the outspoken medieval reformer and peace negotiator who had counseled—and reprimanded—both popes and princes. What Saint Catherine had done in the fourteenth century, Peter believed Dorothy could do in the twentieth. She had the potential, he said, "to move mountains, and have influence on governments, temporal and spiritual."

"There is no revolution without a theory of revolution," Peter told Dorothy, quoting Lenin, but what is needed, he went on, is not a bloody "Red Revolution," such as Lenin's in Russia, built on mountains of corpses. Killing as a method of social reform only led to the cemetery. What was needed, Peter argued, was a peaceful "Green Revolution." For the theory of a Green Revolution to be made known and put into practice, a journal was needed, a radical Catholic paper that would publicize Catholic social teaching and promote the steps that could bring about the peaceful transformation of society. Dorothy, he said, should be the editor of such a publication.

Start a radical Catholic newspaper! It seemed to Dorothy that, if family roots, life experience and religious conviction had prepared her for anything, it was just such a task. It was obvious that the few Catholic publications willing to publish her writings had no revolutionary vision and no interest in reaching the down-and-out.

"But how are we to start it?" she asked. "I enunciate the principles," Peter declared. "But where do we get the money?" "In the history of the saints," Peter answered, "capital is raised by prayer. God sends you what you need when you need it. You will be able to pay the printer. Just read the lives of the saints."

Dorothy had recently read *Sorrow Built a Bridge*, a biography of Rose Hawthorne Lathrop, Nathaniel Hawthorne's daughter. At age forty, she had converted to Catholicism. Abandoning her social position, she rented a three-room tenement flat on the Lower East Side in New York and opened its door to penniless neighbors who were dying of cancer. From her hospitality to the terminally ill had sprung a religious order, the Dominican Sisters of Hawthorne, that still operates several hospices providing free palliative care for incurable cancer patients. The story of what one woman in the same neighborhood had done only a few decades earlier gave Dorothy courage.

"Why not start a newspaper in the same way?" Dorothy asked herself. "I began to look on my kitchen as an editorial office, my brother as an assistant to write heads and to help with mechanical make-up. Tamar and I could go out to sell papers on the streets!" Editing a Catholic paper that promoted a new social order was a vision Dorothy could not walk away from. "It was impossible to be with a person like Peter without sharing his simple faith that the Lord would provide what was necessary to do His work," Dorothy wrote in *House of Hospitality*.

Dorothy and Peter. (Marquette University archives)

The name Peter proposed for the paper was *The Catholic Radical*. Radical, he pointed out, came from the Latin word, *radix*, for root. The radical is someone who doesn't settle for cosmetic solutions but goes to the root of personal and social problems. Dorothy felt that the name should refer to the class of its hoped-for readers rather than the attitude of its editors and so decided to name it *The Catholic Worker*. "Man proposes and woman disposes," Peter responded meekly.

It took several months to move from vague interest to actual decision, but by the spring Dorothy was beginning to envision, then work on, the first issue. Peter knew a priest who, he thought, would allow the use of a mimeograph machine to get

"It was amazing how little [Peter and I] understood each other at first."
—The Long Loneliness

out the first issue, but nothing came of it, perhaps in part because Dorothy wanted a journal with a more enduring appearance. Through her friendship with a Paulist priest, Father Joseph McSorley, she found that the Paulist Press was willing to set type and print 2,500 copies of a letter-sized eight-page tabloid paper for $57, cash in advance. Dorothy calculated she could pay the bill with recent income from her writing and research work plus delaying payment of her gas and electric bills. "We would sell the paper, I decided, for a cent a copy," Dorothy recalled, "to make it so cheap that anyone could afford to buy." (The penny-a-copy price has never changed.)

She plunged into writing the first issue, preparing articles on labor, strikes and unemployment. Her own writing retained its usual highly personal style. In addition she selected six of Peter's "Easy Essays." These were an orator's blend of manifesto and poetry. One of them included in the first issue protested the crippling grip of wealth on the Church:

> Christ drove the money changers
> out of the Temple.
> But today nobody dares
> to drive the money lenders
> out of the Temple.
> And nobody dares
> to drive the money lenders
> out of the Temple
> because the money lenders
> have taken a mortgage
> on the Temple.

On May 1, the radicals and workers who crowded Union Square to celebrate their revolutionary hopes were the recipients of the first issue.

"My mind and heart were full of the part I had to play, self-centered creature that I was. I planned the makeup and the type, and what stories I would write to go with Peter's easy essays. I don't even think we consulted Peter as to whether he liked the title we had given to his writings in the paper, 'Easy Essays.' He was so happy over the coming incarnation of his ideas in print that he never expressed himself on the subject."

—Loaves and Fishes

Everyone's Paper

In the first issue, Peter Maurin's name—misspelled Maurain—was listed with Dorothy's as an editor, but he wasn't among those distributing the new paper at Union Square. Apart from his own Easy Essays, which filled several columns, he found the new-born *Catholic Worker* a painful disappointment and had no desire to be considered co-responsible. "It's everyone's paper," he said woefully after looking at the first issue, "and everyone's paper is no one's paper." The "everyone" he referred to was Dorothy Day. It was her voice rather than his that was dominant in the first issue, and that would remain so the rest of her life.

Peter quietly left Dorothy's apartment, where he had been an almost daily visitor for months. Several weeks passed before she saw him again. Dorothy was so caught up with the needs of the infant paper that she may have felt some relief in his absence. Mailing out sample copies to nuns and priests, editors and friends, writing letters begging for support, all the while caring for Tamar, she would not have felt an immediate need for Peter's indoctrination.

The most pressing problem was the lack of money. If help wasn't found quickly, the first issue would be the last. So pressing were her financial needs that Dorothy made a writer's most desperate sacrifice—pawning her typewriter. Fortunately, enthusiastic letters began to arrive, each with a subscription order and many with donations. The typewriter was quickly retrieved from the pawn shop.

Aware that more than a kitchen was needed, Dorothy made another leap of faith and rented office space—a former barber shop in the basement directly beneath her apartment, though this meant having to raise an additional $25 a month. Supportive friends not only gave money but made material gifts: an old desk, a filing cabinet, even additional typewriter.

Shortly after distribution of the May issue, the first of many volunteers arrived, a young woman named Dorothy

Readers of *The Catholic Worker* in Union Square on May 1, 1933. (Marquette University archives)

Weston. Twenty-one years old, she had studied journalism at Fordham, Columbia and Manhattanville College. Then there was a second volunteer, Eileen Corridan, who also had newspaper experience. Another early recruit was Stanley Vishnewski, a seventeen-year-old Lithuanian from Brooklyn. (At the end of his life, age 63 and still part of the Catholic Worker community, Stanley liked to joke that he was only a visitor, not yet sure whether or not to stay.)

While not yet living under the same roof, in the first months a community began to form. What had been a basement barber shop without furnishing quickly became an oasis of warmth and welcome. More volunteers knocked on the door. It was a rare day without visitors. In the kitchen upstairs coffee was brewed throughout the day while a pot of stew seemed always ready for whoever was hungry. "We worked," Dorothy recalled, "from early morning until midnight."

Peter returned while the second issue was being laid out. He had recovered from his initial disappointment and was ready to resume Dorothy's education. He arrived daily in the mid-afternoon, often stayed until late at night, making his "points"—jabbing the air with his right index finger, an exclamation mark in motion, while Dorothy carried on with her chores and the care of Tamar.

It became clear that Peter's objection to the first issue wasn't simply that Dorothy's voice rather than his own dominated its pages. Though Peter saw it as his role "to enunciate the principles," Dorothy noted, he was remarkably free of the need for personal recognition and he admired Dorothy's writing. What he found missing in the paper was a presentation of basic ideas and principles, a coherent strategy for a new social order, which he had hoped the paper would communicate on every page. He felt that Dorothy hadn't really understood what he had been saying all those weeks. If the first issue were pruned of his Easy Essays and the occasional quotations from the Bible and papal encyclicals, it seemed to him that most of the surviving material—stories about strikes, trials, racism, child labor and economic exploitation—could have been published in any radical publication. As Peter saw it, the first *Catholic Worker* was simply one

Peter making a point. (Marquette University archives)

more journal of protest, different from others mainly because it was edited by Catholics rather than atheists and had some specifically Christian content.

Peter was a radical out of step with other radicals. He had little interest in protest, which he believed did almost nothing to bring about real change. The old order would die from neglect rather than criticism. He had never joined a union, he told Dorothy, because he didn't want "to enlarge the proletariat." What was needed first of all, Peter was convinced, was communicating a vision of a future society alongside an easy-to-grasp program of constructive steps with which to begin realizing elements of the vision—"building a new society within the shell of the old"—in one's own life.

"'Strikes don't strike me!' Peter kept saying, stubbornly. It must have appeared to him that we were just urging the patching up of the industrial system instead of trying to rebuild society itself with a philosophy so old it seemed like new."
—Loaves and Fishes

Charlie Chaplin in "Modern Times."

"Progress" was a word that summed up for many people the popular idea that history inevitably evolves upward, but Peter, like the Russian philosopher Nikolai Berdyaev, saw too much evidence that civilization was moving downward, from the human to the subhuman, from decentralization to centralization, from freedom to slavery, from the divine to the demonic.

In "Modern Times," a film released only three years later, Charlie Chaplin converted a similar insight into the image of his silent tramp being ingested into the gears of a giant machine. It was machines that were getting better, Peter noticed, not human beings. "History has failed," he wrote. "There is no such thing as historical progress. The present is not an improvement on the past." Left-oriented political movements that described themselves as "progressive" were, in Peter's view, simply attempting to make superficial improvements to structures that were innately destructive. While sympathizing with factory workers striking for better pay and better hours, the basic structures of industrialism, Peter had

Catholic Worker artist Ade Bethune, Dorothy, Dorothy Weston, French philosopher Jacques Maritain, and Peter (1934). (Marquette University archives)

"Even now I often think, 'What an inspired attitude Peter took in his painful and patient indoctrination—and what a small part of it we accepted.' He had the simplicity of an Alyosha [in Dostoevsky's The Brothers Karamozov], a Prince Mishkin [in The Idiot]. He accepted gratefully what people offered, finding plenty of work to do, always taking the least place—and serving others."

—Loaves and Fishes

learned as a factory laborer, were hostile to human beings and to creation itself. Peter saw no point in struggling for minor concessions in places where the work was fundamentally anti-human. He considered assembly lines no less brutalizing than prisons, except that, when the whistle blew, the prisoners of the factory were sent home for the night. It is time, Peter argued, to leave behind time clocks and shift labor and "fire the bosses."

You didn't fire the bosses by briefly withholding your labor and closing factories for a week or a month. "Strikes don't strike me," Peter said. His solution to industrial ruthlessness, injustice and joblessness was summed up in one sentence: "There is no unemployment on the land." The Catholic Worker, Peter argued, should stand for a decentralized society, a society of cooperation rather than coercion, with artisans and craftsmen, with small factories that were worker-owned and worker-run. Agricultural communities would be the basic unit in which worker and scholar could both sweat and think together, developing what Peter called a "worker-scholar synthesis."

Another central concept for Peter was voluntary poverty—a poverty that he distinguished from destitution. To him, voluntary poverty did not mean having nothing. It meant living simply, with less rather than more, sharing rather than hoarding, owning only what was truly needed, "going without luxuries in order to have essentials." Voluntary poverty enabled the person "with two coats to give one of them to the person with none." Like Francis of Assisi and many other saints, Peter had been living on less rather than more for years and had found it freeing rather than limiting. He sometimes quoted a passage from Eric Gill's writings:

"The poor man, in the sense of the Gospel, in the meaning of Jesus, is not he who has been robbed but he who has not robbed others. . . . [The] poor man . . . is not he who has not been loved, but he who has loved others rather than himself."

All this, of course, struck many people as utopian—an attractive vision but not something that could happen in the real world. "Utopian" was a word that was often hurled at Peter as if no other response was necessary. Peter Maurin, his critics said, was trying to restore the medieval past. His plan also lacked details or reliance on political structures. As Dorothy noted in *The Long Loneliness*, "The trouble was that Peter never filled in the chasms, the valleys in leaping from crag to crag of noble thoughts."

But Peter had a point in noting that capitalist and communist had more in common than they liked to admit: both were looking with a similar uncritical gaze toward a horizon of smokestacks. Both communist and anti-communist were generally city people who liked to get their milk and eggs at a nearby store. Few of them aspired to the plow, the chicken coop, the dawn milking, the midnight calving, and the 365-day work year that the care of livestock and the raising of crops requires.

Following Peter's return, Dorothy became more open to his critique of assembly-line civilization and his vision of moving toward a post-industrial society. Surely there must be something more to struggle for than improved, unionized or even worker-owned industrialism. Surely community was better than mass society. Surely it was better for children to grow up with space, air, and land—where the main color was green rather than gray. Surely life on the land wasn't just for our ancestors. And would not a decentralized, farm-centered society provide a better base for a way of life that was shaped by religious faith? Surely others too were longing for a society more congenial to faith, hope and love.

Yet Dorothy's approach and Peter's were different, a difference Dorothy attributed in part to what she saw as a basic difference between man and woman. Men, Dorothy felt, tended to be preoccupied with the future and were generally more abstract, more idea driven, more idealistic, while women tended to be more centered in the present, more

Peter Maurin in front of the Mott St. headquarters of the Catholic Worker. (Marquette University archives)

"Peter, the 'green' revolutionist, had a long-term program which called for hospices, or houses of hospitality, where the works of mercy could be practiced to combat the taking over by the state of all those services which could be built up by mutual aid; and farming communes to provide land and homes for the unemployed."

—The Long Loneliness

"Young people flocked in, intent on putting their own social ideas into practice. The college students were often more disposed to discuss and argue than to work, and the old war between thinker and worker broke out at once. Peter welcomed the conflict. 'It makes for clarification of thought,' he said happily."
—Loaves and Fishes

practical and more rooted, involved as they were, as mothers and grandmothers, with solving the immediate practical problems of running a home and caring for children. Drawing on her own experience, she felt that "woman is saved by child-bearing," a role which imposes on her "a rule of life which involves others" and through which "she will be saved in spite of herself." Men didn't have to be so anchored. "Women think with their whole bodies," it seemed to Dorothy. "More than men do, women see things as a whole."

Even so, it was Dorothy, not Peter, who used ideological labels like "pacifist" and "anarchist" in describing herself. Pacifism meant for Dorothy an across-the-board rejection of war—while some wars might have more justification than others, no war was in fact good, no war was just, no war was praiseworthy, every war was a catastrophe. For her the term "anarchist" (literally, a person without a king) meant taking personal responsibility, not expecting the government to solve every problem. It's better to do things, she often remarked, "from the bottom up rather than from the top down." As she would later explain to a friend, Rosemary Bannon, her concept of anarchism was "a religious one stemming from the life of Jesus on earth, who came to serve rather than to be served."

Peter, while not disagreeing, avoided every label except Catholic and one other: "personalist." A personalist, in Peter's view, was a person seeking not to reform the state but to reform himself. Unhappy with the world? Then become yourself the person you want others to be. Do yourself what you wish others would do. "Don't criticize what is not being done," Peter said over and over again. "See what there is to do, fit yourself to do it, then do it." (The modern concept of personalism had been developed by the French philosopher, Emmanuel Mounier, whose writings Peter translated and brought into the pages of *The Catholic Worker*.)

With the second issue of *The Catholic Worker*, Peter formally withdrew his name as an editor, announcing that henceforth he was responsible only for what he signed himself, yet from that issue onward, the paper as a whole, including Dorothy's own writing, bore greater evidence of Peter's influence. This wasn't, however, at the expense of Dorothy's preoccupation with the here and now. She continued to identify with anyone who was protesting injustice and struggling for even slight improvements in the existing social order. She continued to side with strikers and union organizers and to approve of much that those on the left were doing, even if they never questioned urbanization or industrialism. But she found ways to articulate a vision of a future with fewer smokestacks and smaller cities.

In the second issue Peter described his program in more detail: his call for discussion and study groups and for the foundation of houses of hospitality and farming communes. In essence, it was a call, he cheerfully admitted, for Christian communism. "I am not afraid of the word communism," he wrote, but it was not something to be imposed on anyone—a green rather than a red communism. "I am not saying that my program is for everyone. It is for those who choose to embrace it."

Readers were invited by Peter to the first "round table discussion," an image suggesting a gathering in which all who take part have equal standing. A $3 deposit had already been paid—$7 was still owed—for a hall on East 4th Street, he announced to his readers. He must have been disappointed when only fifteen people showed up, but an enduring Catholic Worker tradition began that night. At the New York Catholic Worker, rarely has a week passed since then without a weekly public meeting, usually on Friday evenings. A similar practice is followed by many other Catholic Worker communities.

For Peter, teaching was a full-time job, not something to be done just one night a week but at every possible opportunity. By the summer of 1933, the young people drawn to the Catholic Worker began to gather at Dorothy's apartment, or in the apartment's backyard, for informal discussions with Peter. Dorothy did not always take part—by now she had a solid grounding in Peter's ideas and also had work to do preparing the next issue as well as caring for Tamar.

Those participating in these exchanges, of course, had ideas of their own, often at odds with Peter's. He listened with interest and patience to each person, but if it happened that someone came up with a thought or experience that connect-

Peter. (Marquette University archives)

ed with what he had been saying, Peter would exclaim, like a miner who had found a gold nugget, "See the point! See the point!"

Dorothy regarded Peter as a saint. "There are many saints," she wrote, "here, there and everywhere and not only the canonized saints that Rome draws to our attention." In fact saints should be common, she added, for after all, as Saint Paul had written, we are all called to be saints. Peter's patient and tireless teaching reminded her especially of Saint Paul, "who talked so much that a young man fell off the window seat, out of the open window, and was picked up for dead—Saint Paul had to revive him" (Acts 20:7-12).

By the fall, it was clear that the new paper, envisioned by Peter but edited with a firm grip by Dorothy, was meeting a real need. Few papers have experienced such rapid growth as did *The Catholic Worker* in its first year. Within the first six months, the number of copies printed rose from 2,500 to 35,000, thanks not only to many individual subscribers but also to bulk orders from parishes, schools and seminaries. Readers found a voice in *The Catholic Worker* that was unique among both religious and political journals. There were articles about principles and columns full of news. At the same time, the paper was written with a special intimacy and at-homeness, as if it were a letter between friends. The paper, rooted in a specific city and neighborhood, was full of local smells, sounds and small events that other national papers ignored, yet it appealed to readers living in distant places and different circumstances. Dorothy's intensely personal approach to journalism was a major factor in the paper's appeal. "Writing," she explained in a 1950 column, "is an act of community. It is a letter, it is comforting, consoling, helping, advising on our part as well as asking it on yours. It is part of our human association with each other. It is an expression of our love and concern for each other."

A typical example of her method as a writer appeared in the November 1933 issue: "Late fall is here. A haze hangs over the city. Fog rises on the river, and the melancholy note of the river boats is heard at night. The leaves are dropping from the fig tree in the back yard. There is the smell of chestnuts in the air, but if you buy the chestnuts, most of them are wormy. It is better to make popcorn over the fire at night. For we have fires now. The kettle sings on the range in the kitchen (the range cost eight dollars second-hand and doesn't burn much coal), and visitors to *The Catholic Worker* office are drinking much tea and coffee. And there is the smell of grapes in the air—rich, luscious Concord grapes."

Yet Dorothy's attention was never held entirely by the view from her window or the smells in the air. Against this background of rich aromas and warm fires, again and again she described the daily tragedies of her neighbors. In this case, there was the fact of winter beginning and evictions increasing. "People come in to ask for winter clothes and for help in finding apartments where relief checks will be accepted."

Her readers included many priests. In a formal sense they were poor, with little income and little personal property, but in another sense well off, living in heated rectories in which meals were prepared for them, the house kept clean, the laundry done and their clothes ironed by efficient and uncomplaining women. When one priest wrote her in 1934 suggesting that she write more about "the joys of poverty," Dorothy responded by offering a glimpse of the actual poverty she was witnessing daily: "Just yesterday I brought a doctor to a family around the corner, the mother a widow with nine children, and the five-year-old was ill. The doctor found he had tuberculosis and he had to go to the hospital at once. It was not inherited, but brought on from a winter of cold and too little to eat. Even the most saintly person, with the utmost faith in God, could find it hard under these circumstances to find anything but a sense of grim endurance under suffering in one's heart."

"By the mid-summer of 1933," Dorothy recalled, "*The Catholic Worker* ceased to be just a newspaper but had become the voice of a movement.

"Voluntary poverty means a good deal of discomfort in these houses of ours. . . It was so cold and damp and so unbelievably poverty-stricken that little children coming to see who were the young people meeting there exclaimed that this could not be a Catholic place; it was too poor. We must be Communists."
—The Long Loneliness

Ambassadors of God

The October 1933 issue of *The Catholic Worker* included an Easy Essay by Peter on houses of hospitality:

People who are in need
and are not afraid to beg
give to people not in need
the occasion to do good
for goodness' sake.
Modern society calls the beggar
bum and panhandler
and gives him the bum's rush.
But the Greeks used to say
that people in need
are ambassadors of the gods.
Although you may be called
bums and panhandlers
you are in fact
the ambassadors of God.
As God's ambassadors
you should be given
food, clothing and shelter
by those who are able to give it.
Mohammedan teachers tell us
that God commands hospitality.
And hospitality is still practiced
in Mohammedan countries.
But the duty of hospitality
is neither taught nor practiced
in Christian countries.

New York City, c. 1933. (Library of Congress)

Among Peter's heroes was Basil the Great, one of the most influential saints and theologians of the early Church. In the mid-fourth century, Saint Basil founded a "city of hos-

Dorothy (right) and the early *Catholic Worker* staff. (Credit: Henry Beck)

pitality" in Cappadocia, in the central part of what is now Turkey. Here disease was regarded in a religious light, disaster to be thought a blessing in disguise, and sympathy put to the test. Food, shelter and medical care were provided without charge. Because of its scale, Basil's astonishing "city," in which the unwelcome were made welcome, was regarded as one of the wonders of the world.

In Peter's view, what Saint Basil had done on a huge scale many Christian families could do on a small scale simply by having a room for hospitality—a "Christ Room," a phrase Peter borrowed from another saint of the early Church, Jerome, the ascetic scholar who translated the Bible into Latin.

Peter was delighted to discover that a Church Council held in the North African city of Carthage in the mid-fifth century enjoined each bishop to have a hospice (or house of hospitality) in connection with every parish—places of welcome and care ready to receive the poor, the sick, the orphaned, the old, the traveler and pilgrim, the needy of every kind. Such houses were a practical response to Jesus' identification of himself with each person in need—a tradition of welcome still practiced, if often to a more limited extent, by many monasteries. The Holy Rule of Saint Benedict obliged each monastery "to receive each guest as if the guest were Christ." This was, Peter argued, a tradi-

Dorothy and early Catholic Worker staff, William Callahan and Margaret Polk, c. 1936. (Marquette University archives)

tion that urgently needed revival at the parish level.

Self-giving love, Peter stressed, was the example Christ gave to his followers and was the consistent witness of Christians in the early Church. It was partly thanks to care of neighbors by Christians that so many of their neighbors sought baptism, despite persecution by the state that endangered every convert. Christians wholeheartedly embraced the "works of mercy" stressed by Christ in his description of the criteria of the Last Judgment: "Welcome into the kingdom prepared for you since the foundation of the world, for I was hungry and you fed me, I was thirsty and you gave me drink, I was naked and you clothed me, I was homeless and you took me in, I was sick and you cared for me, I was in prison and you visited me. I tell you solemnly, what you did to the least person, you did for me" (Matthew 25). The works of mercy, said Peter, must again become the Christian way of life.

In the Church's early years, Peter wrote, astonished bystanders noticed what Christians were doing and said, "See how they love each other," but in our own day "the poor are no longer fed, clothed and sheltered at a personal sacrifice but at the expense of the taxpayers. And because the poor are no longer fed, clothed and sheltered at a personal sacrifice, the pagans say about the Christians, 'See how they pass the buck.'" He continued:

Today we need
Houses of Hospitality
as much as they
needed them then
if not more so.

We have Parish Houses
for the priests
Parish Houses
for educational purposes
Parish Houses
for recreational purposes
But no Parish
Houses of Hospitality.

The poor are
the first children
of the Church
so the poor
should come first.
People with homes
should have a room of hospitality
so as to give shelter
to the needy members of the parish.

The remaining
needy members
of the parish
should be given shelter
in a Parish Home.

Furniture, clothing and food
should be sent
to the needy members
of the Parish
from the Parish
House of Hospitality.

"One afternoon last month we went up to
the Municipal Lodging House of the City
of New York and looked at the largest
bedroom in the world. . . . At one end of
it there were beds with little cribs by the
side of them for women with babies. . . .
Our escort told us of a family which had
come in the night before. The family had
been evicted, and the mother was so sick
she had to be carted off to the hospital. . . .
And what must have been the thoughts of
the mother lying in the hospital, wondering where her mother, her children, and
her husband were spending the night?
What but thoughts of hatred and despair
that such cruelty and inhumanity can
exist today."
—Catholic Worker, February 1934

"We need Parish Homes as well as Parish Domes," Peter concluded, demonstrating again his gift for the memorable phrase and rhyming sentence. Besides offering food, clothing and shelter, such houses of hospitality, Peter added, could serve other useful purposes—vocational training and rooms for reading, study and discussion.

In an article sent to *America* magazine in November 1933, Dorothy described the work the Catholic Worker community was doing to assist neighbors being put out on the streets. "Two or three times a week we have eviction cases. When a desperate man or woman comes in asking for help, we have to call the Home Relief to find out about get-ting a rent check. Then we have to find a landlord who will accept the [rent] voucher. Usually they won't. There is only one landlord in our entire block who will take them. Over on Avenue B there is an Irish landlord willing to cooperate. On

17th Street there is a Jew. He is a godsend because he has three houses. After we have found an apartment, we have to commandeer a truck and men to do the moving. The sixteen-year-old boys in our neighborhood have been most helpful. Then there are always unemployed men coming into the office who are eager to help." But there were others who had no rent vouchers and had nowhere to go.

Surrounded by people in need, and attracting volunteers who were excited about the ideas they discovered in *The Catholic Worker*, it was inevitable that those involved would quickly be given the chance to put the paper's writings about hospitality into practice. Dorothy's apartment on East 15th Street was the first house of hospitality, though it didn't occur to Dorothy to attach so grand a label to it as it happened in such an unpremeditated way. After her brother John got a job with a newspaper in Dobbs Ferry, he and Tessa moved out. At Dorothy's invitation, Peter plus two other men, Steve Hergenhan and an aspiring poet named Mister Minas, moved in to share the vacated room.

In a city in which evictions were happening by the hundreds every week, inevitably some of the homeless heard that there were people on East 15th Street who were concerned about people like themselves and talking about the need for houses of hospitality. On December 11, 1933, a young woman knocked on the door, came in and told Dorothy, "I understand you have a house of hospitality." Dorothy responded they had been writing about it but had not yet actually started one. The visitor explained that she and a friend had been sleeping in subways, but that her companion had, in desperation, thrown herself in front of a train. "That very afternoon," Dorothy recalled, "we rented our first apartment and named it the Teresa-Joseph Cooperative—Teresa for St. Teresa of Avila, Joseph after the foster father of Jesus. We moved in some beds and sheltered this unemployed woman." Within days other women arrived. "Since then we have always had rooms for women [as well as men]."

A few apartments elsewhere on East 15th Street were rented, one with space enough for ten women, then part of a run-down building on Jackson Square in Greenwich Village.

Next a place for men was rented on East 7th Street, just behind Saint Brigid's Church. Early in 1935, a priest told Dorothy about an old house at 144 Charles Street in Greenwich Village that was empty and for rent, with room enough for staff and guests to live in the same building plus space for the office, a meeting space, dining room, and a free clothing room. With the print run for the paper growing significantly with each issue (50,000 as 1935 began, 110,000 the following May), more and more donations were coming in, making it possible to pay the printing bill, the rent money and the expense of so much food. A supportive Catholic parish, Saint Veronica's, was nearby.

Assistance was also given to relocating neighbors being evicted for their inability to pay their rent. "We borrowed a horse and wagon and push cart," Dorothy reported in one of her early "Day After Day" columns, "and with the help of the neighborhood helped people move. We saw at first hand the actual destitution there was behind the closed doors all around us."

Dorothy was impressed not only by how many good people needed help from their neighbors but also by how many were willing to lend a hand, once they knew the need, and were even ready to turn a spare room into a "Christ Room"— a room available not only to friends and relatives but also to neighbors who were suddenly without a home. (For many people, Dorothy noted, the main impediment was not so much lack of space as an excess of fear, which in turn revealed a lack of love.)

"Every house should have a Christ Room," Dorothy wrote. "It is no use turning people away to an agency. . . . It is you yourself who must perform the works of mercy. Often you can only give the price of a meal, or a bed [in a cheap hotel]. Often you can only hope that [the money given] will be spent for that. Often you can literally take off a garment, if it be only a scarf, to warm some shivering person. But we must act *personally*, at a *personal* sacrifice . . . to combat the growing tendency to let the State take the job which Our Lord Himself gave us to do."

Catholic Worker staff on the steps of the Charles St. house. (Marquette University archives)

Early Days

Catholic Worker artist Ade Bethune.
(Marquette University archives)

"St. Joseph the Worker" by Ade Bethune.

Several artists were to play a significant role in the development of *The Catholic Worker*, and none more so than the first, a young Belgian-born woman named Ade Bethune. She was a nineteen-year-old art student at nearby Cooper Union when she first became aware of *The Catholic Worker* in the fall of 1933. The content of the paper impressed her, but she found its appearance shabby. Her response was to submit a few black-and-white illustrations that, while having elements in common with traditional religious art, were distinctly modern. The first, a linocut of Saint Joseph at work as a carpenter, was published in the March 1934 issue.

Ade Bethune's drawings had been submitted by post, but soon afterward, after collecting some clothing to donate, the artist had her first face-to-face encounter with Dorothy. "She was a tall woman with a beautiful face," Ade recalled, "with broad forehead and large eyes that pulled over to the side of her face, like those of a doe. Her jawbone was at a right angle, not slanted but square. Her short hair was turning gray. She had such a kindness to her, but at the same time she could be sarcastic and laugh at things that were funny."

Seeing the bags in Ade's arms, Dorothy assumed her young visitor, wearing a beret and a trench coat, was in need of a place to stay. She apologized for there being no free beds at the moment. "I was so shy," Ade recalled, that I stuttered, "I'm the girl who made the pictures for you, and I brought these clothes." "Oh," Dorothy responded, "you are? Fine." She took the clothing and immediately told Ade about the paper's art needs for upcoming issues, beginning with Saint Catherine of Siena for the April issue. Could she also do one of Saint Don Bosco?

Ade already had a style all her own, a fresh iconography—austere, black-and white designs. The images seemed absolutely new while at the same time linked to the tradition

CATHOLIC **THE** WORKER

| Vol. III. No. 3 | JULY-AUGUST, 1935 | Price One Cent |

of ancient Christian iconographic art, much as the Catholic Worker itself linked the early Church with the modern world. Her images tended to reveal the dignity of work by showing the saints at work. What a contrast her art made with the sentimental kitsch that characterized so much Catholic religious art at the time—saints who seemed weightless standing in rays of light, their eyes lifted wistfully to heaven while their well-washed feet hardly touched the ground. Ade was able to communicate through her work what Dorothy, Peter and others who wrote for the paper were saying in words: Christ is in our midst—not a tidy, well-scrubbed, church-on-Sunday Christ, but a Christ for weekdays, a Christ in patched clothing, a Christ of slums and flop houses, a Christ homeless and jobless, a Christ of soup lines. Over the decades, Ade made hundreds of illustrations for the paper. Mainly they were one-column linocuts of saints—images of sanctity that challenged those who saw them not to be bystanders, but to become the saints God made each of us to be: people passionate both in love of God and love of neighbor.

At Dorothy's request, Ade designed a new masthead for *The Catholic Worker*, first published in the May 1935 issue, that afterward topped the front page of every issue: a sturdy Christ standing before a cross, a worker on either side of him, one black, the other white, their hands joined in solidarity, and Christ's arms encompassing them both. (In 1985, Ade revised the design, putting a baby-carrying Latina farm worker to the left.)

One of the major interests of *The Catholic Worker* from the first issue on was bridging the racial divide, a priority made visually clear by the paper's interracial masthead, first used in the December 1933 issue. A year after the paper's

Art and masthead design by Ade Bethune. In 1985 she designed a new image, substituting a mother and child for the white worker.

"Christ the Carpenter" by Ade Bethune.

127

Julia Porcelli at *The Catholic Worker*.
(Marquette University archives)

founding, Dorothy was busy promoting attendance at a Catholic Interracial Mass Meeting. "Our paper," said Dorothy again and again, "is both for negro and white." Meetings and articles in the paper on ending racism, however, weren't enough. Peter and several volunteers decided to open a Catholic Worker center in a rented storefront on 7th Avenue in Harlem, an area of Manhattan almost solidly black. Money was so tight that, at the first meeting held there, illumination was provided exclusively by candles. The speaker on that occasion was Father John LaFarge, a Jesuit who edited *America* magazine and was well known for battling racism. "All I could see in the gloom," Father LaFarge recalled of the discussion that first candle-lit evening, "was Peter's forefinger motioning in the air as he made his points."

One of the successful programs of the Harlem storefront was a story-telling period for neighborhood children on Saturday mornings that was initiated by one of the younger volunteers, Julia Porcelli, in her last year in high school at the time. Julia also organized a class teaching sewing—making clothing for dolls was her means of teaching as only small amounts of fabric were needed. Julia quickly became one of the part-time Catholic Worker staff helping both in Harlem and downtown, then, in 1936, having at last gained her mother's approval, a full-time member of the community. "These were the people I wanted to be with," she said. "There was unity, there was brotherhood, there was family."

Selling *The Catholic Worker* on the street was, from the start, a regular activity of staff and volunteers. For those who had the knack, one person hawking the paper could sell hundreds of copies a day. Not only did their work spread the message, but also was a way of fund-raising, for many who purchased a copy gave more the one-penny asking price—a nickel, a dime, a dollar, and occasionally even five or ten dollars. Working busy corners throughout the city, the sellers also helped make the Catholic Worker better known. "In New York City you had to be housebound not to know there was a Catholic Worker movement," one of the sellers observed in 1935. The sellers, mainly men, were occasionally attacked, especially by disciples of another Catholic, Father Charles Coughlin, whose popular radio programs often featured denunciations of Jews and President Roosevelt combined with sympathy for Hitler and Mussolini.

Picketing and other forms of protest became part of Catholic Worker life beginning early on. Opposing religious persecution in Mexico, in December 1934, the Catholic Worker helped organize a picket line at the Mexican consulate in Manhattan. In the summer of 1935 there were demonstrations protesting anti-Semitism in Nazi Germany. While Peter generally advocated "*announcing, not denouncing*," he too recognized it was important for the world to know that there were Catholics opposed to religious repression, anti-Semitism and Nazi ideology. He took part in picketing both the Mexican and German consulates—at the same time taking care to pick up any leaflets that passers-by discarded so that they could be used again.

In 1936, the Depression still in high gear and the Charles Street house having become too crowded, the community moved into two tenement buildings, one in front of the other, at 115 Mott Street in Chinatown, with thirty-six rooms in all. In the confined space between the two buildings, when the weather was comfortable, Peter was able to create an open-air classroom.

Without delay, the hungry, jobless and lonely found their way to the new house. But no enlargement of the Catholic Worker could possibly find room for all those in need of a piece of bread, a bowl of soup, a cup of coffee and a bed to sleep on. Even so, a great deal was done with very little. In a letter written in December 1938 in which Dorothy explained the hospitality aspect of the Catholic Worker to New York City's Commissioner of Health, she estimated that in the past two-years, since moving to Mott Street, "The Catholic Worker has been feeding from 1,000 to 1,500 men every morning through a breadline. . . . To put it in round figures (the way charities estimate their works), we have provided 49,275 nights lodging these last three years;

> "*Do what comes to hand. Whatsoever thy hand finds to do, do it with all thy might. After all, God is with us. It shows too much conceit to trust to ourselves, to be discouraged at what we ourselves can accomplish. It is lacking in faith in God to be discouraged. After all, we are going to proceed with His help. We offer Him what we are going to do. If He wishes it to prosper, it will. We must depend solely on Him. Work as though everything depended on ourselves, and pray as though everything depended on God, as St. Ignatius says.*"
>
> —House of Hospitality

1,095,000 breakfasts of bread and jam and coffee; 131,400 lunches and suppers."

Most of the people coming in need to the Catholic Worker were men, Dorothy noted—"gray men, the color of lifeless trees and bushes and winter soil, who had in them as yet none of the green of hope, the rising sap of faith." An atmosphere of helpless resentment hung over them which occasionally exploded into fights on the line. The men came and went, most of them anonymous. Perhaps they were surprised that, in contrast with a number of Christian centers, at the Catholic Worker no one preached at them. A crucifix on the wall and statues of Mary and Joseph were the only unmistakable evidence of the faith of those who were welcoming them—volunteers who received no salary, only food, board and some pocket money.

For many people, not the least startling aspect of Catholic Worker life was that no one, including Dorothy Day, had a salary. One reader asked why, a question Dorothy replied to in the December 1935 issue. "We choose to spend the salaries we might be making if we were business-like on feeding and sharing our home with the homeless and hungry. . . . We are willing to clothe ourselves in the donations of clothes that come in, we are willing to eat the plainest and most meager of meals and to endure cold rooms and lack of privacy . . . and we feel the work gains by it."

Many visitors were unprepared for how unglamourous a life it was. Reading about it in the paper was one thing, being there quite another. "It is a wonderful work, evidently blessed by God," Catherine de Hueck commented in a letter to Dorothy soon after the move to Mott Street, "but why, since all things that belong to God are clean, orderly, and well defined, is there such a lackadaisical attitude toward those little things that matter so much?" Dorothy replied that the building was in better shape since Catherine's visit, thanks in part to the donation of a hundred dollars worth of paint and plaster from a friend. But the more serious problem, she added, couldn't be cured by brooms, mops and paint brushes—the problem of tension, sometimes conflict, within the community. The Catholic Worker household was and remained a complex mix-

Dorothy with Catherine de Hueck in the 1930s. (Marquette University archives)

ture of volunteer staff and guests, some of whom were a major challenge to live with. "I always bear in mind," Dorothy wrote, "that the devil is constantly busy around a place like this trying to set people against each other."

"People were shocked when they came down and found us living in the slums," said Julia Porcelli. "They'd come and they'd see the simple diet, the rooms, the raggedy-looking people around—very unstylish!—and they'd feel sorry for us. We wore the clothes people sent in and we didn't have salaries." Visitors who were used to greater comfort rarely stayed overnight. Just as there was distress from many visitors in encountering such austerity, there were days of discouragement for members of staff. "Whenever I got a little sad-looking," Julia recalled, "Dorothy would say somebody should take me out and buy me a steak. If someone treated me for dinner, that was the best thing."

Everyone involved understood that hospitality required not just practical help but extending a real welcome, "spiritual hospitality," as Dorothy called it in a letter to a supporter. "It is indeed very hard to extend such hospitality to everyone that comes in. It is so much easier to throw people the

Above, left: New Catholic Worker headquarters on Mott St. (Marquette University archives)
Above, right: Breadline stretching out on Mott. St. (Marquette University archives)

clothes, food or what not that they need, and so hard to sit down with them and listen patiently." The cost of spiritual hospitality was often neglect of other work, Dorothy added. "There are so many people dropping in that some days I do not sit down to the typewriter once—the work gets far behind and I have to remind myself that all those little frittering things which take up one's time are quite as important, many times more so in the sight of God, than answering letters or keeping files up to date."

Most who ate meals or got clothing at the Catholic Worker were anonymous, but those who became regulars and grew into the household were known by name—often just a first name and an adjective: Smokey Joe, Italian Mike, Saint Louis Marie, Mad Paul. These were people who had gradually come to see the Catholic Worker not just as a place to have a meal or to find a few hours of shelter from the streets, but as home. One by one, they took possession of some daily chore, staked out a particular chair or corner, and came into possession of their own bed.

The house of hospitality most often heard about in *The Catholic Worker* was Saint Joseph's in New York, where four- to five-hundred people a day were being fed in 1937, and a year later twice that number. There was a seemingly endless line of people discarded by the Depression.

A breadline on Mott Street.

From the early days, giving away clothing was an important part of the community's work. Boxes packed with used clothing were delivered by donors nearly every day of the week. There were clothing rooms for both men and women. During certain hours of the week, anyone could drop in for whatever he or she needed, from underwear to overcoats,

Men inside the Catholic Worker. Art on the wall is by Ade Bethune.
(Marquette University archives)

hats to shoes. Often the clothing was sturdily made and in good repair.

Food, though much of it was begged, also had to be purchased. Those who prepared the meals threw out what they wouldn't eat themselves and found ways to make good use of the rest. Even rock-hard bread makes excellent bread pudding. In later years, a visitor to the Catholic Worker asked a member of the staff, Tom Cornell, if there was any standard for what was purchased. "Of course," said Tom. "Nothing but the best, and the best is none too good for God's poor." This had been Dorothy's view from the Catholic Worker's first days: "What a delightful thing it is," she wrote in the 1930s, "to be boldly profligate, to ignore the price of coffee and to go on serving good coffee and the finest bread to the long line of destitute who come to us."

Striking Balances

Stanley Vishnewski hands out copies of the paper at a May Day Communist Rally. (Marquette University archives)

A recurrent aspect of Catholic Worker life from the early years was the problem of conflicting visions of what the Catholic Worker ought to be doing. There had been a divergence of emphasis and vision at the very start between Peter and Dorothy, with Peter's brief withdrawal following publication of the first issue, but it was quickly overcome following Peter's return a few weeks later.

The first major conflict occurred in 1935 when one of the volunteers, Tom Coddington, decided that the homeless, jobless and unfortunate were taking up far too much of the Catholic Worker's energy and resources. With the support of several members of the community, he advocated focusing on overcoming the structures of injustice rather than trying to assist some of the system's victims. He envisioned the Catholic Worker developing a salaried, well-structured, professional staff to develop the work, arrange conferences and make acts of protest a greater priority.

One of Coddington's complaints was that Dorothy was too dominant, "never appointing anyone to have real authority." As he saw it, both her emphasis and Peter's on the priority of the works of mercy was preventing the Catholic Worker from having greater social impact. The Catholic Worker, Dorothy insisted, was for the poor. Their needs must come first—all other work must find its place around the actual poor, no matter how unworthy or unpromising they might seem to many people, rather than around an abstract radical ideology. There was much discussion, some of it so heated and unrelenting that at one point Peter contemplated withdrawing, advising Dorothy that "it would be better to walk out and leave the dissenters [to do as they pleased] rather than continue the argument."

With Dorothy's reluctant approval, Coddington launched a group within the Catholic Worker that he christened the Campions, named in honor of Saint Edmund Campion, one of the Jesuits who had been martyred in the sixteenth century during the reign of Queen Elizabeth. So long as they had access to Catholic Worker income, the Campions continued, but the group faded and Coddington left once Dorothy decided that the Campions had to raise their own funds. In the end, Dorothy and Peter's view prevailed, but Coddington's attempt to professionalize the Catholic Worker was an exhausting ordeal for all involved. Nor would this be the last time basic challenges would arise.

It was Dorothy's conviction that the vision that she and Peter had hammered out at the start was the basis of the Catholic Worker movement and must remain so. Those who didn't think it was the right vision were free to launch other initiatives and start other groups. Clearly the Catholic Worker itself couldn't do everything that was needed. Stay if you wish to help—leave and start something else if you feel called to do so.

Coddington was right that the Catholic Worker wasn't a model of democracy, nor did Dorothy apologize for not seeing committees and voting as the way ahead. "Dorothy was an anarchist as long as she could be the anarchist," Tom Cornell later observed. "Dorothy gave us younger people lots of room and encouragement to go beyond what we thought we could. She so highly valued freedom, and yet there was no appeal from her decisions and in some cases no accounting for how she made them."

The Catholic Worker example of community, as Dorothy saw it, had much in common with the monastic model, with the abbot or abbess having the final word, but with full authority given to those who had taken on particular tasks. "A baker should have charge of the

Julia Porcelli, Dorothy, Peter, and Joe Zarella. (Marquette University archives)

Dorothy in the 1930s. (Marquette University archives)

bakery, a farmer should have charge of the fields," said Dorothy. How bread should be made and fields plowed were not matters best decided by debates and voting. Arguments were less useful than love and mutual support. As Dorothy put it, "There is only one motive that can make it possible to live in hope—love of God. If we do not live in love, we are dead indeed."

Among Dorothy's major priorities from the first issue was support of unions. One of her early trips away from New York, made in February 1936, took her south to Memphis. The invitation had come from the Southern Tenant Farmers Union, a group founded by Protestant ministers who hoped she would take a firsthand look at the plight of black tenant farmers who had been expelled from land in Arkansas for becoming active with the union. Once there, Dorothy volunteered to help in delivering flour, meal, lard, sugar, coffee and soap to them. One of the evicted black men told her of his efforts with local officials to get relief. "If we needed food, they told us to go out and kill rabbits."

Dorothy on a trip South. (Marquette University archives)

"The worst place of all was just outside of Parkin, Arkansas," Dorothy reported in an article published in the March issue of the Jesuit journal, *America*. "Along the road was a tent colony which housed 108 people, four infants among them, and God knows how many children. . . . They grow cotton but they dress in flour sacks. . . . The children can't go to school. Every child that can works in the fields." What did these union members want? Some land of their own and some help from the government the first year to buy equipment to get started. Their goal was to found cooperative farms.

Dorothy's horror at the condition of their lives and sympathy for their modest goals led her to send a telegram to Eleanor Roosevelt, the president's wife, describing what she had seen. Mrs. Roosevelt responded by contacting the governor of Arkansas, who indeed went to the camp, afterward telling reporters that these were people refusing to work who

"Most Catholics speak of Communists with the bated breath of horror. And yet those poor unfortunate ones who have not the faith to guide them are apt to stand more chance in the eyes of God than those indifferent Catholics who sit by and do nothing for 'the least of these' of whom Christ spoke."
—*Catholic Worker,* June 1934

had been stirred up by a "Catholic woman." A Memphis newspaper said the problem was outsiders "who came to criticize" but were "making fat salaries off the misery of the people."

Dorothy appealed to readers of *The Catholic Worker* to send every penny they could spare to the Southern Tenant Farmers Union so that they would have the chance to work their own land with their own tools. "We are in accord with their desire to start cooperative farming ventures where diversified farming will feed the hungry."

This was the Catholic Worker's first hands-on involvement both in the civil rights movement as well as in efforts to unionize farm workers. In the decades to come, these would remain major Catholic Worker themes.

The most powerful tool of unions was the withdrawal of labor. "Strikes don't strike me," Peter said, but they struck Dorothy. She was heart and soul with men and women who went out on strike. "When men are striking," Dorothy explained in an article in the July 1936 *Catholic Worker*, "they are following an impulse, often blind, often uninformed, but a good impulse—one could even say an inspiration of the Holy Spirit. They are trying to uphold the right to be treated not as slaves but as men. They are fighting for a share in the management, for their right to be considered partners in the enterprise in which they are engaged."

At the time this was published, Dorothy was in Pennsylvania steel towns amidst men who had shut down the mills. She was heartened that she was not the only Catholic supporter—there was a priest, Father Adalbert Kazincy, she reported in the August issue, "who stood broad and straight in the boiling sun, head held high, as he told the men, 'Do not let the Carnegie Steel Company crush you. For the sake of your wives and children, for the sake of your homes, you need a union. Remember that man does not live by bread alone. So do not let fear keep you from organizing. I am speaking to you as men, as creatures of body and soul. Remember your dignity as men.'"

In January 1937, Dorothy was present for a portion of the famous six-week "sit-down strike" at a General Motors plant in Flint, Michigan. The sit-down was a major innovation. Instead

Workers on "sit-down" strike at the General Motors plant in Flint, Michigan.

of trying to prevent strike-breakers from entering the factory by confrontational action at the factory gates, the workers took possession of the factory, making it their home, declaring themselves a community and even electing their own mayor. All doors blocked, visitors like Dorothy were hauled in through a window. It was an industrial strike that even Peter Maurin favored—he saw the workers' tactics as providing an example of nonviolence in action. General Motors signed an agreement February 11 with the recently-formed United Auto Workers union.

Waterfront branch of the Catholic Worker established to support striking seamen. (Marquette University archives)

Another early Catholic Worker engagement with labor was with striking seamen—led by Joe Curran, a boatswain and a Catholic layman—who were in conflict with what the striking men regarded as a corrupt union. During their long and difficult strikes in 1936-37, more than forty sailors were housed at Mott Street in the strike's first phase, while, during the second phase, hundreds were fed at a store rented by the Catholic Worker at 181 Tenth Avenue. The storefront's large window bore the text "Catholic Worker—Waterfront Branch." The strikers' chief opponent was Joe Ryan, head of the International Longshoremen's Union, a man more than willing to use thugs wielding baseball bats to crush union members who got out of line. When John Cort of the Catholic Worker staff approached Ryan in a search for dialogue, Ryan told him, "You go back and tell Dorothy Day that she's no lady." Partly thanks to the Catholic Worker, in 1937 the strike resulted in the seamen abandoning the International Longshoremen's Union and founding an association of their own, the National Maritime Union.

The support union members found in the Catholic Worker, Dorothy noted in a diary entry made late in 1936, "drives Peter crazy because the [seamen] are interested in wages and hours and he, being opposed to the wage system and strikes, finds it hard to start in with such elementals and

John Cort (left) with fellow Catholic Workers. Julia Porcelli and Stanley Vishnewski are on the right.

get [engaged] in this stuff. He sees history, the philosophy of labor, the long view, but he does not see immediate tactics [and] strategy."

In February 1937, the Association of Catholic Trade Unionists had its first meeting at the Catholic Worker house on Mott Street. One of the Association's prime movers was John Cort. As a student at Harvard, Cort had heard Dorothy speak and found what she had to say so compelling that soon after he moved to New York to join the Catholic Worker staff. Once there, however, he decided that Peter Maurin's agrarian approach was unrealistic. Like it or not, industrialism was here to stay, Cort argued, and thus factories, assembly lines, time clocks and the working class. For workers to defend themselves from abuse by their employers, unions were necessary and Catholics ought to play a significant role in helping build strong and healthy unions. The Association of Catholic Trade Unionists, founded by Cort, did not seek to fund itself with donations to the Catholic

Worker, as Coddington's had, but the Catholic Worker was its initial base.

Union organizing was hard and dangerous work. In May 1937, Chicago police fired into a crowd of unarmed steel workers, wounding forty and killing ten, in what infamously became known as the "Memorial Day Massacre." Dorothy was in Chicago at the time of the event. The president of Republic Steel, Tom Girdler, vowed he would close his mills and "raise apples and potatoes" before he would give in to the strikers' demands, but in the end he signed a union contract.

One of the other issues facing the Catholic Worker community, at times provoking arguments, was how best to relate to the Church's hierarchy. How independent ought the Catholic Worker to be? Not everyone was happy that Dorothy relied so much on the advice of clerics, like Father Joseph McSorley, the Paulist priest who heard Dorothy's confessions. Dorothy's stress was on being in the good graces of the local bishop and, if obedience in some matter was demanded, responding with obedience.

When the Archbishop of New York, Cardinal Patrick Hayes, contacted Dorothy with the proposal that the Catholic Worker ought to have a spiritual adviser, Dorothy welcomed the idea, suggesting McSorley take on the role. Cardinal Hayes agreed. "Father McSorley and I," Dorothy noted at the time, "are on perfectly friendly terms . . . he is the best confessor I have ever had. I would go to him with every personal problem and do exactly as he tells me. . . . But he has never tried to direct the course of the paper in the confessional." (In a column in 1974, Dorothy recalled that Father McSorley was "a man who listened" and never criticized. His advice when she asked about accepting speaking invitations was simple: "Go where you are invited.")

Eventually Monsignor James Francis McIntyre, became the intermediary between Dorothy and the archbishop, occasionally inviting her to the chancery office where, typically, he would read aloud some of the letters Cardinal Hayes had received about one or another aspect of the Catholic Worker. No demands or even suggestions were made by McIntyre. It seemed enough that Dorothy was made aware of what comments she and her work were generating, some friendly, some hostile. In a letter to Cardinal Hayes, one irate priest called for "effective police action" to close down the Catholic Worker, but not all the mail to the cardinal was from opponents. There were many bishops, priests and lay people who regarded the Catholic Worker as an answer to their prayers, "doing the work of God," as one priest wrote, "in a world desperately in need of the witness being given by the Catholic Worker." Like many other pastors, he asked that a hundred copies of each issue be sent to his parish.

No doubt part of *The Catholic Worker's* success in being distributed by so many parishes was the fact that Dorothy, always keeping a firm hand on the paper's content, did not denigrate the bishops or clergy, though it would have been easy to do so: "I do indeed keep out some of [Peter's writings] which attack the bishops," she told a priest-correspondent in 1934. "I just don't think it's politic. We differ on technique. I think that if we ask courteously for cooperation from priests we are more apt to get it than if we point out that they are not in contact with the workers and that they are not doing anything. . . . There are quite a number of priests who think Peter just quaint when he verbally attacks the clergy who would, if we printed the stuff, hold up their hands in horror."

There were also well-known Catholics who not only sent letters of gratitude and encouragement to Dorothy but came to visit. Many came back to help out and, in the case of scholars, to give helpful advice, among them the Benedictine liturgist Dom Virgil Michel, the Jesuit John LaFarge, and the French philosopher Jacques Maritain. Maritain was among those visiting the Catholic Worker when it was still centered in Dorothy's apartment on East 15th Street. (Twelve years later, having been appointed French ambassador to the Vatican, Maritain was able to give Pope Pius XII a selection of articles he had chosen from back issues of *The Catholic Worker*. Before Maritain left for Europe to take up his post at the Vatican, Dorothy gave him a pair of socks she had knitted for him.)

Despite occasional tensions regarding priorities, balances, decision-making processes and its place within the Church,

"I feel bitterly oppressed, yet confirmed in my conviction that we have to emphasize personal responsibility at all costs. It is most certainly the price of bitter suffering for myself, for I am just in the position of a dictator trying to legislate himself out of existence." —August 18, 1936

(Marquette University archives)

the Catholic Worker remained afloat. The most important indication that *The Catholic Worker* was providing a timely and influential example wasn't the number of papers printed—the print run for the fifth anniversary issue in May 1938 was 190,000—but the foundation in the first five years of more than thirty houses of hospitality in other cities, including Cleveland, Harrisburg, Boston, Milwaukee, Detroit, Chicago and San Francisco, plus one overseas, in England. Partly it was thanks to the paper, but the decisive factor in most cases was a visit by Dorothy, the talks she gave, and conversations afterward that lasted long into the night. Taking bus rides to distant places, or traveling in used cars donated by supporters, was part of the pattern of Dorothy's life until old age and failing health made her stop.

To the Land!

Peter Maurin working at Maryfarm.
(Marquette University archives)

At the heart of Peter's program was the "Green Revolution" through which he hoped society eventually would become re-centered on farms—or, as he sometimes called them, "agronomic universities," rural centers not only of agriculture but of learning, places where workers could become scholars and scholars become workers in an atmosphere of prayer. Such communities could also have workshops and even small factories.

Though Dorothy, in contrast to Peter, was city-centered and city-formed, she hadn't given up her rural beach house. She knew all too well how brutalizing the inner city could be and recognized her need for space and quiet. Ferry rides to Staten Island and long walks at the edge of the sea renewed her. She could name all the local wildflowers and was a devoted gardener. Peter's proposal of farming communities had a powerful appeal for her. She envisioned the creation of a Catholic Worker farm of ten or twenty acres organized on somewhat Benedictine monastic lines: a group of families whose buildings included a chapel, sharing daily Mass, praying, studying and laboring together, all subject to one another and accepting the benign authority of an abbot-like coordinator.

The first farm, or "garden commune" as Dorothy described it, due to its small size, was a twelve-room house with garden on a one-acre plot not far from her beach house. It was rented in the spring of 1935. Dorothy afterward remembered it as a "household of sad afflicted creatures."

The short-lived experiment was succeeded, a year later, by a more ambitious foundation in Pennsylvania, a thirty-acre farm on a hilltop outside Easton, seventy-five miles west of New York City. One of its plus points was that it had a stunning view of the Delaware River. The sum of $1,250 bought the land, a rundown five-room house, a badly rutted dirt road and a small stand of aged fruit trees. The only water supply was rain channeled into two cisterns, as Dorothy discovered

to her dismay after signing the deed; a nearby spring turned out to be on a neighbor's property. Following purchase, a community began to develop. Livestock was purchased—several pigs, two cows, chickens, a goat and three ducks. Later on, a second farm was purchased further down the hillside.

The Catholic Worker's base at Easton was a spot, Dorothy found, "of unutterable beauty," yet community life at Maryfarm, as it was named, often proved difficult and sometimes grim. "Eat what you raise and raise what you eat," said Peter Maurin, who came to live at Maryfarm. Unfortunately there were always more people interested in eating food than raising it, who preferred a discussion of theology, politics or ideology to laboring on the fields or repairing a hinge. The Easton farm, never self-sufficient, survived only by purchasing food with funds provided by St. Joseph's House in New York.

John Cort, is his memoir *Dreadful Conversions: The Making of a Catholic Socialist*, recalls what it was like living on the farm at Easton: "I expected that on our first day we would be put to work in the fields, which clearly needed help, but that was not Peter's way. This was not just a farming commune, but rather, in his words, 'an agronomic university.' One of the first objectives . . . was 'to makes scholars out of workers and workers out of scholars.' Priority went to the former. After lunch we sat around the dining room table . . . [while] Peter declaimed one Easy Essay after another, in his French

"We are making this move because we do not feel that we can talk in the paper about something we are not practicing. We believe that our words will have more weight, our writings will carry more conviction, if we ourselves are engaged in making a better life on the land."
—*Catholic Worker*, January 1936

Peter at a retreat on the Easton farm.
(Marquette University archives)

accent, for several hours." John Cort tried to make an occasional comment or raise a question, but Peter, from long debating experience at Union Square, "had learned the trick of never to breathe between sentences." What in principle was meant by Peter to be an opportunity for dialogue was often, it seemed to Cort, an opportunity for monologue. Yet as Cort came to know Peter better, irritation gave way to affection. "If you got him alone, he was a gentle, lovable soul who would listen to you patiently and give you his last pair of pants. And he rarely had more than one. . . . 'The coat that hangs in the closet belongs to the poor,' he used to say, quoting Saint Basil."

If there was more discussion in the dining room than hard labor in the fields, one great success at the Easton farm was its use in summer as a refuge for children from the city, many of whom had never seen green spaces larger than city parks. One of the children who came was Tamar, who spent entire summers at Easton, with Dorothy often present. The farm became Tamar's second home and eventually the place where she started her marriage.

For children, the farm was a kind of paradise, but for adults the Garden of Eden was nowhere in sight. "It seemed," Dorothy wrote, "that the more people there were around, the less got done." Everyone did something, she added, "but none worked hard enough." A major problem was that few had any experience of farming or even of rural life. Peter had once remarked that everyone's paper was no one's paper; at Easton one might similarly say that everyone's farm was no one's farm.

Small matters took on huge and divisive significance. A physical battle exploded one day following the disappearance of an egg one resident had set aside for lunch. Peter, who witnessed the fight, responded with a Gandhi-like vow to do without eggs and milk for the rest of the summer, thus sham-

ing the combatants into a truce. His act of self-denial animated a debate within the community as to whether justice came before love. "Those holding the view that justice came first," Dorothy observed, "were the most avid to get their share of everything, and the last to practice self-denial." While arguments flared, invisible walls rose within the community. Peter alone seemed to look after such chores as mending the road, repairing the fences, collecting the garbage, even moving rocks and breaking them up. Peter sought to set an example, and there were those who watched him with interest as he labored, but only a few seemed moved to follow his example in a determined way.

Peter preached nothing he didn't practice. His voluntary poverty had a medieval monastic quality. Bathing was a luxury. Clothes were worn until they wore out and were beyond mending. His makeshift pillow was his trousers rolled around his shoes. He lay claim to nothing. His poverty included the refusal to own enmity. No one who knew Peter recalls him arguing with anyone, condemning anyone, or holding a grudge.

Despite Peter's efforts, a split developed between the upper and lower farms. In the upper farm the men governed their families with a strict insistence on obedience, certain

Top: Tamar with a lamb at Maryfarm. *Above:* Dorothy with a calf. (Marquette University archives)

John Filliger and Arthur Sheehan at Easton. (Marquette University archives)

that it was man's God-given role to rule over women as judges, and that it fell to women to hew the wood, draw the water, till the field and clothe the family. In the upper farm, "women were forbidden to speak unless spoken to," Dorothy reported, "and were compelled to knock on the doors of even their own kitchens and dining rooms if there were men present." The men of the upper farm considered themselves "the true Catholic Workers" in contrast to Dorothy and Peter and all those associated with the lower farm.

Dorothy never made Easton her home, but visited often. Despite the many problems she encountered even at the lower farm—problems often similar to those found in Worker houses in the cities—she managed to find much needed refreshment: peaceful meals, good discussions, quiet hours of prayer, even times of forgiveness and reconciliation. One evening Dorothy wrote of the breeze sighing in the apple trees while moonlight made the fields look as if they had been washed. "There was a quiet and perfect peace and a happiness so deep and strong and thankful that even my words of prayer seemed inadequate to express my joy."

More precious than the rare moments of quiet and beauty were those visitors who seemed to bring a special grace and mystery to the table. In *The Long Loneliness*, Dorothy recalled an early guest, a Jewish working man from the Lower East Side who wore a rosary around his neck and recited the Psalms in Hebrew. "He had the gentleness of Saint Francis," she wrote. He helped in the garden, walking on the earth in his bare feet. "I can feel things growing," he said. "I look at the little plants, and I draw them up out of the earth with the power of love in my eyes." One day he sat at the table and held in his hands a piece of dark rye bread from a kosher bakery. "It is the black bread of the poor," he said. "It is Russian Jewish bread. It is the flesh of Lenin. Lenin held bread up to the people and he said, 'This is

"Every talk of Peter's about the social order led to the land. He spoke always as a peasant, but as a practical one. He knew the craving of the human heart for a toehold on the land, for a home of one's own, but he also knew how impossible it was to attain it except through community."

—The Long Loneliness

my body, broken for you.' So they worship Lenin. He brought them bread." Some at the table were shocked at what they judged a blasphemy, but Dorothy felt blessed. Certainly Lenin was no Christ and, yes, perhaps their guest was mad, but she often found it easier to see Christ in such madness than in the doctrinaire and the rigid—the "sane ones" who rarely felt the pulse of life in the earth and insisted that bread was only bread.

As would happen with several Catholic Worker farms, the one at Easton finally had to be given up, but it lasted more than a decade. Despite the many joys it brought to its guests and its residents, the farm's problems ultimately proved insoluble. Many who had come to spend the rest of their lives in community left after the first frost, discovering, Dorothy noted, "the reason for cities and relief rolls." Those who remained were often the least suited to farming and the most difficult to live with. In 1947 Dorothy severed ties with the Easton farm. The lower farm was sold to local people, while the upper farm was deeded to "the true Catholic Workers" determined to provide the world with a model of a male-ruled social order.

Dorothy lamented the contrast between the high hopes she and Peter had invested in the original Maryfarm and the events that, in the end, forced its closure. "We aimed high, too high," she said. "But at least we were able, as Peter said, 'to arouse the conscience.' . . . We might not have established a model community, but many a family got a vacation, many a sick person was nursed back to health, crowds of slum children had the run of the woods and fields for weeks, and groups of students spent happy hours discussing the green revolution."

It was through such experiences that Dorothy reluctantly came to see that the task of the Catholic Worker was not so much to establish model agrarian communities, with families and single people living a semi-monastic life with the liturgy at its hub, but mainly to provide places of refuge and welcome to the homeless and mentally battered—less farms, though farming remained a significant part of the life, than rural houses of hospitality.

Hard experience convinced Dorothy that family life, with rare exceptions, was not ideally suited to such situations. "I

"As farmers, perhaps, we were ridiculous, but Maryfarm was a happy home that summer and for many summers after. . . . In spite of our mistakes, a lot of things got done." —Loaves and Fishes

"We must contain ourselves in patience, remembering each morning that our main job is to love God, and to serve Him, and if we don't get things done due to interruptions, well, it cannot be helped, and God will take care of what we leave undone. But a tranquil spirit is important. St. Teresa says that God cannot rest in an unquiet heart. I have to remember that many times during the day."
—To Joe Zarrella, March 5, 1940

think," she wrote, "that most of the families realize this after they have gotten out of the work . . . [because] their first obligation has to be to take care of their own and not to ask others to support them." There was an inevitable tension between family needs and the austerity of Catholic Worker community life. It was "because none of us had bacon and eggs and grapefruit for breakfast," she remarked, "that we were able to feed so many on the bread line." (On the other hand, as Tom Cornell remarks, "Dorothy changed her mind every half hour." Families have been vital parts of a number of Catholic Worker farms and houses of hospitality. Much has depended not on rules-of-thumb or principles but actual persons with their particular qualities. For many years, Tom and his wife, Monica, have been the persons chiefly responsible for the Peter Maurin Farm near Marlboro, New York.)

Despite the setbacks at Easton, the hope of a viable community on the land was not abandoned. In January 1947, a new farm near the city of Newburgh was purchased for $6,000. Named the Maryfarm Retreat House, it was destined to last eight years. In this case a major function, as the new Maryfarm's expanded name made clear, was to provide a place for group and private retreats. It was only sixty miles north of Manhattan and had the advantage of being on level land, thus better suited for farming. But even a distance of sixty miles was a major obstacle for a community depending mainly on public transportation. When retreats weren't going on, the small community at Newburgh seemed stagnant to Dorothy. There was also the irritation of noise pollution, especially unwelcome during retreats, caused by aircraft taking off and landing at nearby Stewart Air Force Base.

In 1950, a farm was purchased that was much nearer at hand—a 22-acre property near the town of Pleasant Plains at the southern end of Staten Island. Its proximity to Manhattan, only a ferry and train ride away, meant a much more fluid connection between house of hospitality and farm. But purchasing the new farm had been a hard decision. Writing about the process in the September 1950 issue of *The Catholic Worker*, Dorothy described herself as an "importunate widow" who had begged God to end her irres-

olution by giving her a sign—and what Dorothy recognized as a sign was given: "It was at Mass, and I kept saying to myself, 'If I don't hear something by eleven o'clock this morning, I am going to drop the whole idea and put it out of my mind altogether.' It was a promise to the Lord. Before eleven o'clock a friend had called and offered to lend us several thousand dollars, [and] the old owners had come down in their initial payment and offered to take the mortgage themselves. I had my sign. Within another two weeks, I was able to obtain two thousand dollars more from friends, and the papers are now all signed."

Dorothy's column ended on a lyric note: "Last night coming home on the [Staten Island] ferry there was a heavy swell and a steady east wind. The taste of the salt spray was on my lips, and the sense of being upheld on the water reminded me of 'the everlasting arms' which sustain us. Gulls wheeled overhead, gray and blue against the dark sea. On the Brooklyn shore the setting sun shone red in the windows of the warehouses and piers. It was after rush hour and there were not many on the boat. It was a half hour interlude of peace and silence and refreshment. May the many who come to us on the island feel this calm and strength and healing power of the sea, and may it lift them to God as it has so often lifted me."

Above, left: Dorothy reading at the Easton Farm, c. 1937.
Above, right: Peter Maurin Farm on Staten Island. (Credit: William Carter)

The Works of Mercy
versus the Works of War

Jesus healed many and killed no one. His last miracle before his crucifixion was to heal the wound of one of the men arresting him, injured by a sword blow Peter had inflicted while trying to defend him. Jesus turned toward his friend with the command, "Put away your sword, for whoever lives by the sword shall perish by the sword." For several centuries Christians understood that Jesus was speaking not only to Peter at that moment but to all those who would seek to follow him in the centuries to come. In periods of persecution, Christians died by the thousands without defending themselves. Some were condemned to death specifically for their refusal to do military service. "I will not be a soldier of this world," Saint Maximilian told a Roman proconsul in North Africa during a brief trial, "for I am a soldier of Christ." He died saying to his executioners, "Christ lives!" Saint Martin of Tours, at the time an officer in the Roman army but preparing for baptism, gave notice he would not take part in an impending battle. "I am a soldier of Christ," he explained. "To kill is not permissible for me." (Saint Martin of Tours escaped execution, was discharged and went on to become one of the great bishops and theologians of the early Church.)

Ah, but that was a long time ago. The Catholic Church, as it was when Dorothy joined, had many centuries before accommodated itself to empires and war. There had been popes who had commanded armies and summoned Crusades. Life without weapons, the widespread practice of Christians in the early centuries, had become the exceptional witness of clerics and monks, and even they, if not using weapons, often encouraged bloodshed. Both Church and State expected ordinary men to take up arms when their rulers ordered them to go to war.

By the medieval period, a distinction had been made between Christ's "counsels of perfection," such as renouncing violence and turning the other cheek, and the "precepts of salvation" imposed on all baptized people: obeying the Ten Commandments, attending Mass on Sundays and major feasts and holy days of obligation, and fulfilling the duties of their state in life. The precepts were obligatory for all, the counsels were for the few.

Over the centuries a non-dogmatic teaching had evolved in the Catholic Church that set out criteria for recognizing a just war: war could only be declared by legitimate authority, for a just cause, using just means, and safeguarding the lives of non-combatants. But who had ever heard of any war being declared unjust or the Church forbidding its members to fight in a particular war, however manifestly unjust it was? In any event, Dorothy repeatedly asked, "How could any war today be regarded as just when it involves total destruction, obliteration bombing, and the killing of so many innocent people?"

There had been occasional efforts to revive the nonviolent witness given by Christians in the early Church. In the thirteenth century, Saint Francis of Assisi had embraced the pacifist way with remarkable impact; many thousands joined the lay order he founded, accepting an obligation neither to possess nor to use deadly weapons. In modern times, adherents to several post-Reformation "peace churches"— Quakers, Mennonites and Brethren, among others—had often refused any role in war.

St. Francis of Assisi.

But by the twentieth century, it was all but unheard of for Catholics to take such a position. On the contrary, in every country with a Catholic population, Catholics could be relied on by their governments to be part of the army—perhaps in no country more willingly than in the United States. Arriving in a land in which Protestant Christianity was dominant, Catholic immigrants encountered widespread anti-Catholic sentiment. Among other things, they were accused of being loyal to the Vatican rather than to America. Catholics responded by excelling in patriotism. Carved over the entrance to countless Catholic schools was the Latin motto, "*Pro Deo et Patria*"—for God and country. In many churches, the American flag stood near the altar.

In March 1935, many readers of *The Catholic Worker* must have been surprised to discover an article written in the form of a dialogue between Christ and an imaginary "patriot." The author was Father Paul Hanly Furfey, a sociologist teaching at The Catholic University of America. The patriot said that he loved peace as much as anyone, but he was a realist. "A strong system of national defense is our best assurance of peace. National defense is the patriotic duty of every American citizen." "All that take the sword shall perish by the sword," Jesus responded. "Yet we must be practical," the patriot pointed out. "After all, Japan and Russia are casting jealous eyes at us. Our basic policies conflict. We must arm ourselves against such nations." "You have heard that it has been said," Christ replied, "that you shall love your neighbor and hate your enemy. But I say to you, love your enemies, do good to them that hate you, and pray for those who persecute and slander you." "A noble doctrine!" answered the patriot. "Even so, common sense obliges us to be prepared to defend our own territory." "To him that strikes you on the one cheek, offer the other as well," said Jesus. "Of him who takes away your goods, ask not for their return." "But national defense," said the patriot, "isn't only to defend material rights, but is a question of life and death. Only a strong system of national defense will guarantee our personal security." "Be not afraid of those who kill the body and after that have no more that they can do." "But there is such a thing as a just war," argued the patriot, recalling familiar Church teaching. "Under certain circumstances a nation has a right to declare war." "You have heard that it has been said," Christ replied, "an eye for an eye and a tooth for a tooth, but I say to you not to resist evil."

Publication of the dialogue was the first clear indication in *The Catholic Worker* of Dorothy's conviction that following Jesus was incomplete without the renunciation of enmity, hatred, killing and participation in war. From its third year, the paper increasingly voiced this unfamiliar position, which many Catholics found disturbing and some thought might even be heretical. Dorothy described herself and the paper she edited as "pacifist" (from the Latin word for peace, pax), meaning a person for whom peace is a way of life. Given that the means determine the ends, Dorothy believed that genuine, lasting peace could only be brought about by peaceful means.

In the summer of 1936, with the outbreak of the Spanish Civil War, Dorothy's pacifism was tested against the reality of an actual war in which radicals and fascists were opposing each other. The fascist side, led by Francisco Franco, presented itself as the defender of the Catholic faith. Around the world, nearly every bishop and Catholic publication rallied behind Franco, considering only that he was pro-Catholic and anti-Communist—an enemy of atheism. To the astonishment of many readers, *The Catholic Worker* refused to support either side in the war and actively challenged Catholics to reconsider their support of Franco. Before backing Franco, Dorothy wrote, everyone should "take another look at recent events in Germany to see how much love the Catholic Church can expect" from fascists.

Failure to support Franco's side in the war brought a flood of furious letters pouring into *The Catholic Worker* office. Was Dorothy unaware that nuns were being raped and priests and monks shot, that churches were being razed by Communists and anarchists, and that only Franco could protect the Catholic Church in Spain from complete destruction?

"We all know," Dorothy replied in an editorial, "that there is frightful persecution of religion in Spain. . . . [Even so] we are opposed to the use of force as a means of settling personal, national or international disputes." Yes, there have been many priests and nuns who have been martyred. But do we honor martyrs by taking up in their name the weapons they refused to use? Ought we to kill on behalf of those who had chosen vocations that renounced all violence? To do so, Dorothy continued, "would be martyrdom wasted and blood spilled in vain." Could Christians dare to make the way of

Marjorie Crowe and Dorothy Day, c. 1940. (Marquette University archives)

155

Father Charles Coughlin.

Christ and his cross their own? "Today the whole world is in the midst of revolution. We are living through it now—all of us. And frankly, we are calling for saints." We ourselves, she continued, must be as ready as those priests and nuns in Spain to suffer and, if necessary, die in unarmed witness to our faith. "There must be a disarmament of the heart," Dorothy wrote. Only then can our love and prayer have the strength to overcome evil. Her prayers, she said, were for neither side in the war, but "for the Spanish people—all of whom are our brothers in Christ—all of them Temples of the Holy Ghost, all of them members, or potential members, of the Mystical Body of Christ."

While *The Catholic Worker*'s position regarding Franco was vindicated in later years, at the time it cost the young paper much of its support. Many individual subscriptions and most of the bundle orders were canceled. In several dioceses, bishops banned the paper from every church and parish school.

In the same period, anti-Semitism was steadily on the rise, not only in Europe but in the United States, and not least among Catholics. America's most famous anti-Semite was a priest, Father Charles Coughlin, arch-foe of President Roosevelt's "New Deal" and editor of *Social Justice* magazine, as it was called. A coast-to-coast audience of millions faithfully listened to a weekly radio program on which Coughlin ranted against Roosevelt, Jews and Communists. The Depression, he said, was due to an "international conspiracy of Jewish bankers." He also blamed Jews, not bankers in this case but Jewish radicals, for the Bolshevik Revolution in Russia. In Coughlin's view, rich banking Jews and poor Communist Jews, however opposed they seemed, were partners in a worldwide Jewish conspiracy that was bringing the world to ruin. Those selling Coughlin's paper on the streets in New York shouted "Communist" at their *Catholic Worker* counterparts, sometimes tearing *The Catholic Worker* from their hands or even knocking down those selling the paper. In May 1939 Dorothy was among the founders of the Committee of Catholics to Fight Anti-Semitism, which launched a new paper, *The Voice*, to counter Coughlin's publication. *The Voice* lasted until the U.S. entry into the war. (Coughlin was eventually ordered by his bishop to end all his political activities or be defrocked.)

Jacques Maritain, a prominent Catholic philosopher, published an essay in *The Catholic Worker* warning of the anti-Semitism that was characteristic of fascism, whether Spanish, Italian or German—"a certain religious racism," such as at earlier times had driven European Christians to murder and terrify so many Jews. Dorothy felt a similar worry for the Jews, reminding readers that Jews were "the race that Christ was part of." Peter wrote that the Jews were an "exceptional, unique and imperishable people which is protected by God, preserved as the apple of his eye."

The Catholic Worker's pacifism did not, in fact, put the movement in the camp of neutralism or those known as "America-Firsters." As early as July 1935, just two years after Hitler had become chancellor of Germany, opposition to his anti-Semitic policies had led the Catholic Worker community in New York to the docks on Manhattan's Upper West Side to join in picketing a German liner, the *Bremen*. One of the demonstrators was shot in the leg by a guard on board the ship when he climbed a mast in the attempt to remove the ship's swastika flag, which in turn led to a police attack on the crowd.

In a letter afterward to New York City's police commissioner, Dorothy expressed her distress at what she witnessed: "I was sitting on the steps of Unity Hall, a building a few doors from the station with a Catholic girl from Marquette College, Milwaukee, when two men dragged another man up the steps by the side of us, knocking me over in their haste, and in the darkness of the doorway, one man held the victim while the other began smashing his face in. I called to the policemen on the sidewalk in front of me and one rushed up the steps. When he saw

> *"As Catholics we too feel called upon to protest against the Nazi persecution of Catholics and Jews by demonstration and distribution of literature. We feel that we would be neglecting our duty as Catholics if we did not do this."*
>
> —To the New York Police Commissioner, July 1935

Dorothy and other Catholic Workers joined picketers protesting the German liner, the *Bremen*, which sailed under the Nazi flag. (Library of Congress)

what was taking place, he came down, making no attempt to interfere. The others stood there and, when I continued to protest, they merely say, 'You can't prove nothing by us. We didn't see anything.' And even as they said this, the two men administered a final blow to their screaming victim. . . . If the police do not set an example of law and order they are unwittingly aligning themselves with unchristian forces."

An appeal published in *The Catholic Worker* called on the nation to open its doors to "all Jews who wish free access to American hospitality." Similar appeals came from many quarters, but went largely unheeded. Only the exceptional—mainly scientists expelled from German universities, the fortunate, the wealthy and the well-connected—were allowed in. Most were turned away and died in the Nazi concentration camps.

But for all the evil Dorothy found in racism and in Nazi ideology, she could not accept war—an evil means sure to cause the death of vast numbers of innocent people—as a way of combating evil. It was a view she expressed both in writing and in many of the talks she gave. Remembering the heavy-handed government repression of peace movements during World War I, she expected much the same to happen again if and when the U.S. joined the war in Europe. In a letter to Stanley Vishnewski sent at the end of January 1940, she wrote: "In the world in the unsettled state it is, we may ourselves be engaged in war, the paper may be suppressed and then we would all settle quietly in concentration camps or jails."

One of Dorothy's main themes was that the works of mercy—all that we do for the most vulnerable members of society—are the polar opposite of the works of war. Why undo with your left hand what you do with your right? Clothing the naked one day—and burning them alive the next? Giving drink to the thirsty on Monday, only to destroy the water works on Tuesday? Housing the homeless, then incinerating the city? The Catholic Worker way, Dorothy said again and again, was the way of the Cross, not the way of the crucifiers. "War is the continuing passion of Christ," she wrote, "and Christ did not come down from the Cross to defend Himself."

The Second World War began in September 1939 with

"I do not see why we must accept the inevitability of war. It was only in the last century that slavery was done away with here in this country, and I suppose that everybody thought it was inevitable, something to be accepted, before that time. If we are working toward peace, we must look with hope that in a future generation we will do away with war. You know with how great suffering and how great prayer we are trying to hold up these ideas."

—To Bob Walsh, May 3, 1940

the German invasion of Poland and rapidly expanded. With war underway in Europe and with the prospect of U.S. entry a growing likelihood, Dorothy was concerned that conscription legislation under discussion in Congress would make provision for conscientious objectors only if they belonged to the small "historic peace churches" (Quakers, Mennonites, the Church of the Brethren).

In July 1940, Dorothy went to Washington to testify at hearings before the Military Affairs Committee of Congress, which was discussing adoption of the Compulsory Military Training Law. She pointed out that the proposed law failed to protect conscientious objectors who might take the position that this war failed to meet the criteria for a just war or who were opposed to taking part in any war. If such an unjust law were passed, Dorothy warned, the Catholic Worker movement would regard it as its duty to resist. (When the revised bill was passed in August, it recognized conscientious objectors from any church, but only if the objector was, for religious reasons, opposed to participation in all wars; no provision was made for "selective conscientious objectors"—objectors to a particular war.)

The following month, Dorothy sent an open letter plus a handbook on conscientious objection to all Catholic Worker communities. In it she urged those houses which could not identify with the pacifist position not to dissent publicly—as the Seattle community had done when it burned one issue of *The Catholic Worker*—or break their connection with the Catholic Worker movement. Dorothy wrote:

"We know that there are those who are members of Catholic Worker groups throughout the country who do not stand with us on this issue. We have not been able to change their views through what we have written in the paper, in letters, or personal conversation. They wish still to be associated with us, to perform the corporal works of mercy. In such cases they will still distribute the paper (and, since they are called Catholic Worker groups, it is their duty to do so). In other cases, they take it upon themselves to suppress the paper and hinder its circulation. In these cases, we feel it to be necessary that they disassociate themselves from the

From Ade Bethune's series of woodcuts of the Works of Mercy.

159

Catholic Worker movement and not use the name of a movement with which they now are in such fundamental disagreement.

"Our workers have taken it upon themselves to try to follow the counsels of perfection. They accept the assistance of others and their cooperation in so far as they can give it. Many can only go part of the way, what with family obligations, health consideration, even a different point of view. If they wish to work with us, we are glad and thankful to have them, but they cannot be said to be representing the Catholic Worker position.

"Sometimes there are only one or two at a house of hospitality who follow the position of the paper. Perhaps in some cases there are none, but as a group are associated together to feed the hungry, clothe the naked, shelter the harborless in a house of hospitality. Perhaps it would be better in these cases for the houses to disassociate themselves from the Catholic Worker movement. They can continue as settlements for the works of mercy, but not as Catholic Worker units."

Seventeen months later, on December 8, 1941, the day after the Japanese attack on Pearl Harbor, the U.S. Congress declared war on Japan, then three days later on Germany and its allies. Dorothy's commitment to a Christ-like nonviolent life was unshaken. A headline spread across the front page of the January 1942 issue of *The Catholic Worker* declared:

Dorothy in the late 1930s. (Marquette University archives)

Our Country Passes from Undeclared War to Declared War
We Continue Our Christian Pacifist Stand

"Because of our refusal to assist in the prosecution of war and our insistence that our collaboration be one for peace, we may find ourselves in difficulties. But we trust in the generosity and understanding of our government and our friends, to permit us to continue, to use our paper to 'preach Christ crucified.'"

—Catholic Worker, January 1942

"We will print the words of Christ who is with us always," Dorothy wrote in an editorial, "even to the end of the world. 'Love your enemies, do good to those who hate you, and pray for those who persecute and calumniate you, so that you may be children of your Father in Heaven, who makes His sun to rise on the good and the evil, and sends rain on the just and the unjust.' . . . We are still pacifists. Our manifesto is the Sermon on the Mount, which means that we will try to be peacemakers. Speaking for many of our conscientious objectors, we will not participate in armed warfare or in making munitions, or by buying government bonds to prosecute the war, or in urging others to these efforts."

Opposition to the war, she went on, had nothing to do with sympathy for America's opponents in the war. "We love our country. . . . We have been the only country in the world where men and women of all nations have taken refuge from oppression." But the means of action the Catholic Worker movement supported were "the works of mercy rather than the works of war. . . . I would urge our friends and associates to care for the sick and the wounded, to the growing of food for the hungry, to the continuance of all our works of mercy in our houses and on our farms."

Many in the Catholic Worker movement could not agree with Dorothy. They could see no other effective means apart from war to combat Hitler and his rapidly expanding Third Reich. Neither could they accept that Dorothy's personal convictions on such an issue should be presented as the position of the entire movement, in which hundreds were active in houses of hospitality all over the country.

Dorothy appealed to friends and co-workers for mutual charity and patience, but faced with the war, many of the Catholic Worker's young men decided it was a time for battle rather than patience. They felt obliged to leave their communities in order to enter the armed forces, as indeed did many of the men who previously had been on line waiting their turn for a bowl of soup. Lines at Catholic Worker houses rapidly shrank as the army and the war industry absorbed millions who had been out of work.

Fifteen houses of hospitality closed in the months following the U.S. entry into the war. "The reason for the closing was lack of workers rather than lack of need for the houses," Dorothy noted in her column in *The Catholic Worker*. "There are always the poor, as our Lord reminded us. There are always the lame, the halt and the blind, people being discharged from hospitals, unemployables, vagrants. There are always these, 'our least brethren,' in whom we may see Christ as he told us to. And the harder it is to see him under dirt and drink and vermin, the more we are exercising our faith. 'Love

"I will not register for conscription, if conscription comes for women. . . . I shall not register because I believe modern war to be murder, incompatible with a religion of love. I shall not register because registration is the first step toward conscription, and I agree with Cardinal Gasparri, that the only way to do away with war is to do away with conscription."
—*Catholic Worker*, January 1943

is surrender,' we had been told . . . 'Give yourself to God in the poor.' And how else can we show our love for God?"

John Cogley, a member of the Chicago Catholic Worker community and later in life an editor of *Commonweal*, wrote Dorothy to say that he considered the Catholic Worker movement had died. "Now there is a group of pacifists defending their positions by calling attention to their good works and another group of diehards like myself who leave gracelessly. Peace! Peace! And there is no peace!"

In a letter to Dorothy, a member of the Worker community in Milwaukee wrote of the conflict within her household, mourning the passage of tranquility and order that had held them together in the past. "Damn war!" she wrote. "Damn pacifism and stands! . . . How I wish you weren't a heretic. And sometimes how I wish that I were one too."

Following the big subscription losses during the Spanish Civil War, the movement had gained new support, with *The Catholic Worker* printing 75,000 copies every month, but the pacifist position that the paper took after Pearl Harbor brought in a new wave of cancellations. Some argued theology, others politics. The gentler letters asked such questions as what Dorothy would do if an armed maniac threatened her daughter. "How many times have I heard this?" Dorothy responded. "Restrain him, of course, but not kill him. Confine him, if necessary. But perfect love casts out fear and love overcomes hatred. All this sounds trite, I know, but experience is not trite."

Despite closed houses, division among co-workers, and lost subscriptions, Dorothy's view—shared by many—prevailed. Partly this was due to Dorothy's determination. She simply wouldn't budge. She continued to edit *The Catholic Worker* and every issue reaffirmed her understanding of the way Christians were summoned to live. Issues of the journal that appeared during the war included a simple design, Saint Francis standing beside a wolf he had tamed, accompanied by the words, "Peace without victory."

At the New York house, an Association for Catholic Conscientious Objectors (ACCO) was founded to encourage and assist young Catholic men of draft age who held paci-

"In listing houses of hospitality that have been closed, I should state that the reason for the closing was lack of workers rather than lack of need for the houses. There are always the poor, as our Lord reminded us. There are always the lame, the halt and the blind, people being discharged from hospitals, unemployables, vagrants. There are always these, our least brethren, in whom we may see Christ as he told us to. And the harder it is to see him under dirt and drink and vermin, the more we are exercising our faith."
—*Catholic Worker*, January 1943

fist views. Among the committee's projects was publication of a newspaper, *The Catholic Conscientious Objector*. Those who were draft-eligible, and who identified with the Catholic Worker movement during the war, generally spent much of that four-year period either in prison or working in hospitals, while others did unarmed military service as medics. For five months, in 1942-43, the ACCO managed to sponsor a rural Civilian Public Service camp, mainly populated by Catholic conscientious objectors, near Warner, New Hampshire. Those involved in the camp's brief life found it a purgatory-like experience. Not all the inmates were Catholic Worker-style pacifists—some were there because they would not fight in a war in which the United States was allied with Soviet Russia's atheist regime. (The story of Camp Simon, named after the man who helped Christ carry his cross, is told by one of its participants, Gordon Zahn, in *Another Part of the War*.)

Half the Catholic Worker houses of hospitality remained open during the war, despite smaller staffs and fewer people in need. Apart from a half-year retreat taken during the war, Dorothy traveled from house to house and spoke in public wherever there was a willingness to hear her. Even in the midst of war, many invitations were offered.

Civil Public Service camp sponsored by the Association of Conscientious Objectors. (Marquette University archives)

The Catholic Worker's pacifist witness seemed traitorous to the ultra-patriotic and embarrassing to many bishops. When an article in *The Catholic Worker* urged young men not to register for the draft, Dorothy was summoned to the chancery office of the New York Archdiocese where a representative of Cardinal Francis Spellman told her she had gone too far. On reflection, she agreed. "I realized that one should not tell another what to do in such circumstances. We have to follow our own consciences."

Even in correcting herself, as she did in the paper's next issue, Dorothy's cry against war, and her protest of Church complicity in it, was never muted. Wartime, she insisted, does not exempt us from the commandment to love our enemies and do good to those who curse us, for the Gospel never changes. "Our rule of life," she said repeatedly, "is the works of mercy."

A Lonely Single Parent

Dorothy visiting the Maryknoll seminary in the 1940s. (Marquette University archives)

At the center of the Catholic Worker movement, with its houses of hospitality, its controversies, quarrels and protest actions, stood Dorothy Day. Within a few years of the Catholic Worker's founding, she had become well known, enjoying the respect and esteem of a great many people. There was a column by her in every issue of *The Catholic Worker* and she was often writing for other publications. She was someone taken seriously by the hierarchy and a person of interest to non-Catholics as well. Even in wartime, the work she led received encouragement and financial support from a number of bishops. Through Dorothy and the movement she was leading, many people found a new direction in life and saw Christianity as the bearer of a radical message. Dorothy had become a missionary, not so much to the heathen as to her fellow Catholics, drawing them to a deeper engagement in a faith many thought was already theirs by virtue of birth or weekly attendance at Mass.

Dorothy was also controversial—some of the talk her name generated was malicious. In a letter to her friend Catherine de Hueck in December 1936, she had summed up the current gossip about herself: "I'm supposed to be an immoral woman, with illegitimate children, a drunkard, a racketeer, running an expensive apartment on the side, with money in several banks, owning property, in the pay of Moscow, etc." In part to set the record straight, in 1938 she wrote her first autobiography, *From Union Square to Rome*, a book, one reviewer noted, that "would have created a sensation if it had been written in the form of a novel."

Dorothy was often on the road, traveling far and wide among the scattered Catholic Worker communities and speaking at churches, colleges, seminaries and union halls. Writing from Spokane, Washington, in late January 1940, she told Stanley Vishnewski, "There are meetings every morning, afternoon and evening. This morning I speak at the Good

Shepherd House at nine, then catch a ten thirty bus and go out to Pullman where Washington State College is, get there at twelve-thirty, get back here at seven-thirty to speak again. Tomorrow four meetings—I'll take the train for Seattle at ten, spend two days there and go on to Portland again for four days and then to California. Surely it is my duty to visit the other [Catholic Worker] houses [on the way back to New York] . . . at St. Louis, Chicago, Milwaukee, Minneapolis, Detroit, Akron, Cleveland, Toledo, Pittsburgh, Buffalo, Rochester, Troy, etc. [Assuming I make all these stops,] it will be quite a time before I get back. After all, they are our Catholic Worker houses, and it is up to us to get around and visit them. I can scarcely consider Mott Street my home any more."

For many people, hearing Dorothy speak was a memorable, even life-changing event. Jack English provides a vivid account of his first encounter with Dorothy in 1935. He had missed a talk Dorothy had given at his college, but the next day found an animated discussion about her going on in the cafeteria. "They were talking about how beautiful she was. She had talked the entire lecture with a cigarette hanging out of the corner of her mouth, with a beret on, and someone said it looked as if she needed her neck washed." Jack was so intrigued that he decided to attend a meeting Dorothy was addressing that night in a nearby town. He found her amazing. "What impressed me so much was that she said, 'You can do this work wherever you are.'" In a brief conversation with Dorothy afterward, she urged him to read *The Catholic Worker*. "That was the beginning of it. Something happened in my life. It wasn't a profound thing at the moment. She was not the kind of person that had been described to me that morning in the coffee room. I had read some of the lives of holy people and saints, but I had the feeling—I hate to use the word—of *holiness* about Dorothy." (Jack ended up joining the Catholic Worker's New York staff, later took part in World War II, became a prisoner of war, and, following the war, became a Trappist monk.)

Dorothy's audiences found in her an example of what could be done by ordinary people, and by lay women, in a Church governed by men who, in those days, rarely consult-

"I feel assured that though we know nothing of the results of such constant speaking engagements, that even though the CW may never see them, countless people are aroused in new ideas, a sense of responsibility, to new works, to renewed effort, because of hearing about the CW and the basic ideas of our work. At so many of the meetings there are groups of people who have heard me speak time and again. . . . We have to do the work most needed, that's all. Try to adjust ourselves to it, take it as happily as possible, etc. I'm afraid I'm not very good at bearing my fatigue. . . . And I've been told I look snappish at people when they throng around me telling me how wonderful the books, the work is. I've got to learn to smile sweetly and love my neighbor."
—To Joe Zarrella, March 14, 1940

Dorothy in the 1930s. (Marquette University archives)

ed the non-ordained and still less sought the advice or collaboration of women. Talking informally, usually without notes, often with a cigarette in hand, Dorothy impressed her listeners with her conviction that the world would be remarkably improved if Christians were willing to search for the face of Christ in others, especially the poor and the condemned, the people so many of us tend to avoid. "Those who cannot see Christ in the poor," Dorothy often said, "are atheists indeed."

Yet for all the conversions and new communities that Dorothy had inspired, and all the food and caring that had poured out of these communities, she still suffered a very private "long loneliness." Her not-quite marriage with Forster, which had ended when Tamar was a child not yet two, remained an unhealed wound. "A home and a companion is just about the nearest one gets to happiness in this world," she told one of her correspondents, Donald Powell, in 1938. "I'm all for appreciating the natural joys." When writing *The Long Loneliness* nearly twenty years after her separation from Forster, the same anguish was still with her: "A woman does not feel whole without a man and, for a woman who has known the joys of marriage, yes, it was hard. It was years before I awakened without the longing for a face pressed against my breast, an arm about my shoulder. The sense of loss was there." Following her conversion, many years had to pass before Dorothy fully abandoned the hope that Forster would at last change his mind about marriage, with the happy result that a shared life could resume.

Not only had Dorothy failed in her attempts to change Forster's mind about marriage, but she often felt she was failing in her role as mother. The demands of the Catholic Worker on Dorothy were such that, once the newspaper began turning into a movement, the time she had for her daughter was greatly reduced. Apart from weekends and holidays, Tamar spent much of her childhood at a Catholic residential boarding school, Saint Patrick's, on Staten Island. Even during the times Tamar was with her, Dorothy's attention was often deflected by the urgent needs of others.

"There were plenty," Dorothy noted, "who laid claim to my sympathy and loving care to the extent of forgetting that I had personal family obligations." Some of the Catholic Worker guests were jealous of Tamar's place in Dorothy's life. One guest took Tamar's clothing and destroyed her collection of bird nests, egg cocoons and other natural specimens she had carefully gathered. At the Catholic Worker farm in Easton, an adobe village Tamar was building was wrecked by a guest resentful of the time Dorothy gave to her daughter. These were ordeals for Dorothy as much as for Tamar, an awful consequence of being a single parent with competing responsibilities.

It was about this time that a priest told Dorothy that her views on many topics would be more moderate if she were a family woman. "I was going through a difficult time," she recalled. "I was thirty-eight, wishing I were married and living the ordinary naturally happy life and had not come under the dynamic influence of Peter Maurin." But as she considered the priest's criticism, she realized that his perception of her—indeed her own perception of herself—was incomplete: "I am a woman of family. I have had a husband and home life—I have a daughter and she presents problems for me right now."

A rare photo of Dorothy in her chain-smoking days. (Marquette University archives)

In the summer of 1936, Dorothy wrote in her journal about Tamar's problems of the day. She had suffered a nosebleed, a headache and stomach pain. Dorothy was distressed at "the little time I have with her, being constantly on the go, having to leave her in the care of others, sending her away to school so that she can lead a regular life and not be subject to the moods and vagaries of the crowd of us! This is probably the cruelest hardship of all. She is happy, she does not feel torn constantly as I do. And then the doubt arises, probably she too feels I am failing her. . . . Never before have I had such a complete sense of failure, of utter misery."

But there were also many times of shared joy for mother and daughter. These included occasional trips together to Florida to be with Tamar's grandmother, Grace, who became a widow in 1939. (John Day died May 17, an event Dorothy

Tamar on the beach. (Courtesy Tamar Hennessy)

mentioned with extreme brevity in her diary. Following his instructions, John's ashes were spread over Hialeah Race Track, near Miami, Florida. To the end of his life, he had regarded Dorothy as "the nut of the family," though he had related well with Tamar and his great-grandchildren. "Dorothy clashed with him," his great-granddaughter Martha Hennessy told me, "perhaps because they were similar in their headstrong ways.")

Writing from Florida in early December 1939, Dorothy told Joe Zarrella, office manager of Saint Joseph's House, of her mother Grace's weakening health and also described Tamar's adventures that day with her cousin Kate: "Tamar is over on the island, which is a dream of quiet and beauty. Calm, deserted tropical beach. Plenty of fishing. There are raccoons, turtles, land crabs, snakes, but no birds, which is strange." Dorothy decided to extend their Florida stay through Christmas.

But weeks would pass when Dorothy and Tamar were far apart. In April 1940, writing from Los Angeles while on a lecture trip, Dorothy noted plaintively, "I miss Tamar terribly— it's like a toothache." A diary entry that July struck a similar note: "It took me hours to get to sleep. I miss Tamar terribly, unhappily at night, but in the day not sadly. My nights are always in sadness and desolation and it seems as though, as soon as I lie down, I am on a rack of bitterness and pain."

All the while, Tamar was growing up. In 1941, now fifteen, Tamar began to take a lively interest in the bright, attractive men who were coming as volunteers to the Catholic Worker. Tamar was now also impatient with the boarding school she had been attending. Dorothy responded with a search for a school offering courses more in line with Tamar's interests. That fall, Tamar was enrolled in a boarding school in Canada, the *Ecole Manegere*, which taught domestic and agricultural crafts, including spinning and weaving.

When Tamar returned to the Catholic Worker farm at Easton the next summer, she and one of the new volunteers, David Hennessy, not only fell in love but decided they wanted to marry, start a farm together, and raise a family. Dorothy responded by doing all she could to keep Tamar and David apart, bringing Tamar from Easton to New York as often as possible. A major factor in Dorothy's opposition to marriage was the fact that Tamar was only sixteen while David was twenty-nine.

In the fall, Dorothy arranged for Tamar to stay in Rhode Island to study crafts and calligraphy with Ade Bethune, the artist who played so important a role in the pages of *The Catholic Worker*. In a letter Dorothy sent to Tamar while she was staying with Ade, Dorothy referred to an agreement she had wrung out of her reluctant daughter to go a year without contact with David: "I trust you not to write to Dave and to return his letters, if he writes any to you, unopened." It's not a promise one can assume Tamar kept. Neither distance nor maternal pressure dampened her intention to marry David. Nor was David open to Dorothy's efforts to point him in another direction. He returned letters Dorothy sent him unopened.

In her daughter's struggle for independence and a stable home of her own, no doubt Dorothy was reminded of her own early flight from home, her bohemian past, and also of her inability to provide Tamar with the kind of rooted family life Tamar longed for. But Dorothy was far from certain that David was the man Tamar saw in him. She worried that Tamar would experience some of the bitter disappointments with men that she had known. Dorothy hoped she might convince Tamar to go slow, using time apart from David to acquire useful skills and experience a time of independence before undertaking marriage.

There was also the fact that it was immensely difficult to let go of her only child and the person dearest to her. "I was always having to be parted from her," Dorothy wrote. Again and again she had been forced to give up those she loved: mother, younger brother, husband, and now daughter. It seemed no matter how many times she had to submit to such separations, "I had to do it over again."

"I remember one time we were walking together down Mott Street," Dorothy later wrote in an essay on marriage. "Tamar was walking close to my arm, clinging to me as she often did, and I warned her that she must learn to be self-reliant, to depend on herself, to learn to stand alone. I probably

Tamar on her wedding day at Maryfarm, in Easton. (Courtesy Tamar Hennessy)

Right: The cabin at Maryfarm where Tamar and David lived following their marriage.
Below: Dorothy and her granddaughter Rebecca, 1946. (Marquette University archives)

hurt her by so saying. We are always hurting those we love."

Tamar was her mother's match in stubbornness. Refusing to give up her plans to marry David Hennessy, in 1943 Dorothy was finally forced to give way, only winning the agreement that the wedding would be delayed until next spring, when Tamar turned eighteen. In the meantime Tamar studied at the State School of Applied Agriculture in Farmingdale, Long Island, while Dorothy, having arranged a leave from the Catholic Worker, lived nearby.

The marriage took place April 19, 1944, six weeks after Tamar's eighteenth birthday, at Saint Bernard's Church in Easton. A wedding breakfast followed at Maryfarm. In the austere circumstances of the Catholic Worker community, there had been neither bathtub nor mirror for Tamar's use as she prepared for her wedding. "She bathed in a pail the night before," Dorothy remembered, "and never did she know how lovely she looked in her wedding dress."

Peter, his mind now failing, used the celebration that followed the wedding to speak out against raising pigs for profit, though Tamar and David had no intention of raising pigs. "We all laughed," Dorothy recalled, "but we all had to listen too. After all, it would not have been a Catholic Worker wedding without a speech from Peter."

Tamar and David moved to the farm at Easton where they were given use of a cabin. The next spring, Dorothy held in her arms her first grandchild, Rebecca. Eight more were born in the following years.

Retreats

An ordinary day began for Dorothy with early Mass and ended about midnight. She pushed herself hard and was often tired, beset by the tensions within the Catholic Worker communities and her sense of inadequacy both as a mother and leader of a movement. She felt ill equipped for the task. She found herself too impatient, too judgmental, too distant, too severe.

Apart from periods of prayer, there were seldom times of rest and peace, and when they came she tended to feel guilty about them. The Worker way of life seemed to be one of permanent crisis, not only because it was turned toward injustice and violence in the neighborhood and in the larger world, but because of daily collisions with human need and brokenness within the house: fights on the line, injuries, sickness, mental breakdowns, hysterical or despairing individuals, drunkenness, clashing personalities, ideological combat, empty bank accounts, theft or destruction of property, fires, evictions, demands from the city for costly alterations of buildings, withdrawal of co-workers to other places, and the interventions of death. A day without at least one crisis was rare.

One way or another, Dorothy was often required to respond, and not only within the New York community. Through letters and visits, the needs and difficulties of other houses were brought to her. Sometimes reluctantly, other times of necessity, she was often the final arbiter of conflict within the Catholic Worker movement.

Describing in her journal what was happening at Saint Joseph's House in the summer of 1940, she commented that she was "often shocked at the positive venom" directed toward her by some of those she lived with. At the time there was a young man enraged with her for failing to get him back into the seminary from which he had been expelled. Another man, lately released from a mental hospital after making an attempt on his brother's life, was outraged that Dorothy

"Always when I come down to the farm there are so many problems, so much unrest which seems to center around me since everyone wishes me to settle something, that I need some time alone for prayer and reading so that I can attain some proper perspective and peace of spirit to deal with myself and others. I need to overcome a sense of my own impotence, my own failure, and an impatience with others that goes with it. I must remember not to judge myself, as St. Paul says. Such a sense of defeat comes from expecting too much of one's self, also from a sense of pride. More and more I realize how good God is to me to send me discouragements, failures, antagonisms. The only way to proceed is to remember that God's ways are not our ways."
—August 27, 1940

"To Father Roy the spiritual and the material gifts were inseparable. He went on to talk not about the social order but about love and holiness, without which man cannot see God."

—Loaves and Fishes

wouldn't arrange a private room for him at the Easton farm. Dorothy felt the spiritual life she was leading, though many might regard it with admiration, was inadequate for the task of living in such a volcano.

There had been one occasion in the Catholic Worker's first years when Dorothy went to a contemplative monastery in Manhattan for what she had intended to be a prolonged retreat, but that experiment quickly proved a bad fit. The nuns lived an "enclosed life"—voluntary confinement behind grills that reminded Dorothy of prison bars. The idea of a cloistered life centered on prayer impressed Dorothy, but she found she lacked the temperament for it. "It was a hard time," she recalled. "When I left, I felt as if I was suddenly able to breathe again." She returned to the turbulent Catholic Worker household much readier to appreciate its highly unrarified atmosphere. She preferred reading the writings of contemplative saints—Saint Therese of Lisieux was one of these—to seeking out places similar to those in which they had lived. Yet she continued to sense an incompleteness in her spiritual life.

In 1939, Providence intervened with the visit to Saint Joseph's House of a French-Canadian priest, Father Pacifique Roy. His work at the time was in Baltimore. Probably he had hitch-hiked to New York, as that was his usual way of traveling. He loved hitch-hiking as it provided an opportunity to chat with strangers. Father Roy was so possessed by his faith that, despite his basic shyness, he could readily talk about the stories and sayings of Jesus, doing so in a way that captivated rather than irritated his drivers. He did the same at the Catholic Worker house in Manhattan, holding everyone spellbound. Hours passed, people arrived and left, the phone rang, but Father Roy continued to talk with the eager community that had gathered around him.

"He spoke with such enthusiasm, with such joy," Dorothy remembered, and it was always so with him. "It was like the story in the Gospels, when the two apostles were talking on the way to Emmaus, grieving and fearful and lamenting over the death of their leader. Suddenly a fellow traveler came along and began to explain the Scriptures, going so far as the town with them and even going to an inn to break bread with them. They knew Him in the breaking of bread. They had to say to each other, 'Was not our heart burning within us, while he spoke on the way?'"

In Father Roy, Dorothy at last had found a priest who heard in the Gospel a call to a way of life which was revolutionary and who recognized in the Catholic Worker movement a faithful response to that call. He was also someone with a gift for inspiring a deeper, more passionate spiritual life. Though each day's headlines bore appalling news—expanding war in Europe, Hitler's growing empire, the doors of the United States and many other countries locked against so many Jews and others who were begging for refuge—the Catholic Worker staff was preserved from despair and hope was given back, in part thanks to the timely arrival of Father Roy. The day-to-day work of a house of hospitality struggling with so many needs and its own limitations—this too was transformed. "We saw all things new," wrote Dorothy. "There was a freshness about everything as though we were in love, as indeed we were."

At the time it would have been unsurprising to hear one's parish priest explain that you needn't measure your life against the Sermon on the Mount—that sort of thing was for monks and nuns and the odd would-be saint. For everyone else, it was enough simply to be loyal, practicing Catholics, baptized and confirmed, going to confession, attending Mass, observing the marriage laws, raising one's children as Catholics, and giving financial support to the Church. The minimum was enough. Conformity was enough.

Like Dorothy, Father Roy was unable to see the Gospel as a two-tiered book, the harder part of its contents aimed for those living under the vows of poverty, chastity and obedi-

Fr. Pacifique Roy in his later years. (Marquette University archives)

"[Fr. Pacifique Roy] *convinced us that God loved us and had so loved us that He gave His own Son, Who by His life and death sent forth a stream of grace that made us His brothers in grace, closer than blood brothers to Him and to each other. He made us know what love meant, and what the inevitable suffering of love meant. . . He made us feel the power of love, he made us keep our faith in the power of love.*"

—Loaves and Fishes

Retreat at Easton, c. 1945. Dorothy, Fr. Roy, and Peter Maurin are among those who are standing. (Marquette University archives)

ence in officially-sanctioned religious communities. For Father Roy, like Dorothy and Peter, the Gospel was for all Christians. Its message was that everything we do should be infused with God's love, for we are saved by love, not by keeping in line. "Love is the measure by which we shall be judged," Dorothy said repeatedly, quoting Saint John of the Cross.

A large part of Dorothy's debt to Peter Maurin was his passionate conviction that the followers of Jesus should not ignore the more demanding aspects of the Gospel—the "hard sayings" of Christ. "To give and not to take," Peter often said, "that is what makes man human." Love, Father Roy said, is what makes us want to give. Giving is the essence of religious life: giving time and attention, giving prayer, giving possessions and money, giving space in one's life and home, giving a welcome, giving forgiveness, giving love, even giving one's life. Don't save. Don't store up "treasure which moth and rust attack." Live by the rule of giving.

"Suppose," Father Roy said, "you want to go to California

and it costs a hundred dollars. You have fifteen. It is not enough. So give it away. Give it to the poor. Then you suddenly have twenty-five, and that is not enough and so the only thing to do is to give it away too. Even seventy-five. That is not enough. Tell the Lord you need more. Throw it away recklessly. You will get it back a hundredfold. Maybe it will cover your spiritual needs, and not just your physical. But sow, sow! And as you sow, so shall you reap. He who sows sparingly, reaps sparingly." And what if you never get the hundred? Then stay where you are. "The good Lord knows what you need. Maybe you shouldn't go to California!" His voice rang out with delight. Such teaching rang bells for Dorothy. She began to take part in "days of recollection" that Father Roy occasionally led in Baltimore.

Late in the summer of 1940, Dorothy wrote in her diary: "Turn off your radio. Put away your daily paper. Read one review of events a week and spend [more] time reading . . . [titles mentioned included *The Power and the Glory* by Graham Greene and Sigrid Undset's novel of life in fourteenth-century Norway, *Kristin Lavransdatter*] . . . [Such books] make us realize that all times are perilous, that men live in a dangerous world, in peril constantly of losing or maiming soul and body. We get some sense of perspective reading such books. Renewed courage and faith and even joy to live. And man cannot live long without joy, without some vestige of happiness to light up his days."

Realizing that Father Roy would have a similar impact on others, Dorothy wrote a letter to all the Catholic Worker communities—thirty houses of hospitality and eleven farms at the time—urging all who could come to spend Labor Day weekend participating in a retreat with Father Roy. More than an invitation, Dorothy's letter was an introduction to a deepened spiritual life she hoped would become rooted in all those associated with the Catholic Worker movement. She recalled a saying of Saint Catherine of Siena: "All the way to heaven is heaven, because Jesus said, 'I am the way.'" It was also true, Dorothy added, "that all the way to hell is hell." Heaven and hell are not simply ultimate destinations reached only after death. Each can touch us in any moment of life.

"What are we trying to do? We are trying to get to heaven, all of us. We are trying to lead a good life. We are trying to talk about and write about the Sermon on the Mount, the Beatitudes, the social principles of the Church, and it is most astounding, the things that happen when you start trying to live this way. . . . Peter Maurin emphasized the primacy of the spiritual, the correlation of the spiritual and the material, translating these ideas into actual living today. . . . With these war years we have come to emphasize more our opposition to the use of force, the necessity of sanctity, of aiming at perfection, at a spiritual renewal while undertaking the making of a new social order." —Letter of January 1948

Peter Maurin at a retreat at Easton.
(Marquette University archives)

When we turn our backs on the urgent needs of others, failing to recognize Jesus in the least person, we are in hell at that moment, for hell is not to love. To glimpse Christ in another, to love and care for another, is already to be in heaven. Life lived in awareness of the presence of God is a foretaste of heaven. Those who carry that awareness with them in their daily lives are saints, which ought not to be a rare thing. The world is in desperate need of saints.

In response to Dorothy's letter, representatives of nearly all the Worker communities came together at Easton. More retreats followed in succeeding years. These were the center points in a process in which Dorothy's need to give new vitality to her own spiritual life came to involve nearly everyone who identified with the Catholic Worker movement, as the retreats not only affected those who took part but also influenced the content of the newspaper and the climate of every household in the Catholic Worker movement.

Most of the retreats in the war years were led not by Father Roy but another priest whom he had recommended to Dorothy, Father John Hugo of Pittsburgh. Like Peter, Father Hugo often recited a quotation from G.K. Chesterton: "Christianity has not been tried and found wanting. It has been found difficult and left untried. Even watered down, Christianity is still hot enough to boil the modern world to rags."

A writer as well as a retreat leader, Father Hugo's essays often appeared in *The Catholic Worker*. *The Catholic Worker* also published two books by Hugo: *Applied Christianity* and *The Gospel of Peace*. The latter presented a theology of peacemaking such as had been embraced by Dorothy. Remarkably, both texts received an *imprimatur*—official sanction for its publication—from Cardinal Spellman, Archbishop of New York and Military Vicar for the Armed Services. Both were issued in 1944, while World War II was still raging.

Father Hugo, Dorothy recalled in 1978, "was young and preached so thrillingly a doctrine of 'putting off' the world and 'putting on' Christ." In retreats and writing, he emphasized Christ's command that we forgive others, not sparingly but "seventy times seven times," taking Christ at his word, never withholding forgiveness from any who sought it. He emphasized Christ's most challenging teaching, the love of enemies. The Christian under attack is called, like the martyrs of the early Church, not to answer violence with violence, but to respond to violence with love.

Echoing the Gospel, Hugo stressed renunciation—"the best thing to do with the best of things is to give them up," a phrase Dorothy often repeated. Don't use what you don't need, he said—and have as little as possible. The coat hanging in your closet on a winter day belongs to someone who is freezing without it. Give it away. Do without. Do it for the love of others, especially for the poor, for Christ has hidden himself among the hungry and thirsty, the naked and homeless, the sick and imprisoned. Try to live as much as possible at a higher level, the level of the spirit, the level of love. "Natural" actions would bring only a natural reward and would be buried with you in your grave. Those who seek and obtain rewards, Jesus said in the Sermon on the Mount, "have their reward already." Supernatural action, action free of all selfishness and fear, was the only kind of action that brought with it an eternal reward.

"This was what I was looking for in the way of an explanation of Christian life," Dorothy exulted during a retreat with Father Hugo. "I saw things as a whole for the first time with a delight, a joy, an excitement which is hard to describe. This is what I expected when I became a Catholic." Father Hugo's constant preoccupation was the Gospel, even if his critics saw him as reading it in too rigorous a way. Dorothy lamented the fact that most Catholics are far less likely to hear the Gospel preached at Sunday Mass than to hear a sermon on the preacher's pet peeve or an appeal for money. "I think to myself with a touch of bitterness," Dorothy noted, "that the ordinary man does not hear the word of God. The poor do not have the Gospel preached to them. Never have I heard it as I hear it now, each year in retreat, and with the sureness that it is indeed the Gospel. . . . The shepherds are not feeding their sheep."

Partly at Father Hugo's urging, in the fall of 1943 Dorothy took temporary leave from the Catholic Worker in order to begin a period of extended retreat. A community of

Fr. John Hugo. (Marquette University archives)

sisters in Farmingdale, Long Island offered her a vacant room formerly used for cooking classes. Making the plan known via her column in the September 1943 issue, Dorothy linked the decision to an experience of prayer that summer: "I was kneeling before a statue of the Blessed Mother," she wrote, "when suddenly I began to think of how beautifully hidden and quiet a life was hers."

In a diary entry written in July, Dorothy spoke of motives she made less public, a sense that perhaps God was calling her to entrust *The Catholic Worker* to others: "I always felt God would indicate his will for me by some exterior act—by the paper being suppressed, by the Archbishop suggesting that I leave. Now it suddenly comes to me, Why do I not just hand the paper over to Peter and Arthur, Dave and Father Duffy, and leave? I no longer feel I can save my soul by this work." In the same entry, Dorothy worried that she was in danger of neglecting her family. "The world is too much with me in the Catholic Worker," she wrote. "The world is suffering and dying. I am not suffering and dying in the CW, I am writing and talking about it."

In a letter to a priest sent shortly before her retreat began, Dorothy brushed off the warning that, without her, the Catholic Worker movement would fold: "I know that they are all wrong, that they know very little about the work or the people concerned. It is filled with little saints, hidden saints, who have been keeping it going with their hard work and their prayers. It is of tremendous importance and immensely blessed by God. . . . [I am well aware that ours] is the only Catholic paper crying 'Peace, Peace.' The only one which calls for the works of mercy—the Folly of the Cross—as a program. It is because it is doing so much, and because it means so much that God has called upon me to prune it and to prune it that it may bear much fruit. And that pruning takes me out of it—only to work more actively, in prayer, to hold up its arms . . . by my prayers."

Dorothy's retreat began in October. Its timing was as good as it would ever be. During the war years, Catholic Worker houses throughout the county were fewer and were caring for smaller numbers of people. Many of the men who had once lined up by the hundreds for a bowl of soup or other assis-

"For a long time now I have talked about the fathers of the Desert. For a long time I have threatened to get away and be one. This retreat has confirmed me in my conviction to seek God in prayer and poverty and work, leaving the Catholic Worker and its manifold activities to the very competent staff hereabouts."
—To Fellow Catholic Workers, July 28, 1943

tance were now either in the army or had jobs in factories.

Amid stoves and sinks, Dorothy made herself at home in her former classroom, joining the sisters for daily Mass, praying privately in the convent chapel, and taking long walks. She had been able to arrange her retreat location so that it put her near the school Tamar, still unmarried, was now attending. Dorothy and Tamar often had lunch or an afternoon cup of hot chocolate together. Once a week Dorothy went by train to visit her mother, Grace Day, now living on Long Island. But most of the time, she was alone, struggling in her aloneness to go further in spiritual growth than had been possible in brief retreats. Her main work was prayer, which at times came with "joy and delight," but more often in a state of utter boredom, her prayer only an act of will.

It was early in this period of withdrawal that Bishop (later Cardinal) McIntyre called Dorothy into the New York chancery office. "He asked me," Dorothy recalled two decades later in a letter to Thomas Merton, "where I would be during the coming year and told me that they would hold me responsible for the work then as well as any other time. This I took as a mandate to continue—a very indirect one."

One of the issues Dorothy struggled with during her months living alone at Farmingdale was how far she was from actual poverty: "I sit here on a clear cold winter's afternoon down on Long Island surrounded by a snow-covered countryside and listen to the Philharmonic Symphony," she wrote in her diary in February 1944. "At the same time I darn stockings, three pairs, all I possess, heavy cotton, gray, tan, and one brown wool, and reflect that these come to me from the cancerous poor, entering a hospital to die. For ten years I have worn stockings which an old lady, a dear friend, who is spending her declining years in this hospital, has collected for me and carefully darned and patched. Often these have come to me soiled, or with that heavy hospital smell which never seemed to leave them even after many washings. And the wearing of these stockings and other second-hand clothes has saved me much money to use for the running of our houses of hospitality and the publishing of a paper. But the fact remains that I have stockings to cover me when others go cold and naked."

Dorothy in the late 1940s. (Marquette University archives)

"What I must do is cultivate a joyful silence and not criticize others for criticizing: to confess my sins in confession and not to explain or justify myself. Let others accuse, criticize as they will, I must maintain a cheerful silence. I feel sick? I must keep silent. I am sad? I must keep silent. I have had bad news? I must keep silent."—February 1944.

179

The same month Dorothy wrote about what an uphill climb prayer can be: "My mind like an idiot wanders, converses, debates, argues, flounders. If [in a day] I get in fifteen minutes of honest to God praying, I'm doing well."

Dorothy had meant to keep her retreat for a full year, but in the end six months was all she could stand. As had happened during her brief stay in a New York monastery years earlier, it became clear that, as much as she admired the solitary life, it was not for her. "Man is not meant to live alone," she wrote with conviction afterward. "To cook for one's self, to eat by one's self, to sew, wash, clean for one's self is a sterile joy. Community, whether of family, or convent, or boarding house, is absolutely necessary."

Father Hugo was not only Dorothy's spiritual director in this period, but was an influential figure in the Catholic Worker movement as a whole—though not without his critics, many of whom regarded his approach as excessively austere. All through World War II, Father Hugo led retreats, published articles, and in every possible way maintained close ties with the Catholic Worker—remarkable considering how out-of-step he was with many Catholic bishops and theologians at the time. Only after the war did he come under real attack. The bishop of Pittsburgh ordered him to stop giving retreats and to cease publishing. He meekly accepted the order, quoting to friends the text, "Unless the seed fall into the ground and die, it remains alone, but when it dies, it bears much fruit."

At the chancery office of the New York Archdiocese, Dorothy was advised of the silencing and told that she should not again publish Father Hugo's work. It was a painful experience for her, but she complied, perhaps comforted by the thought that what he had done for her and for the Catholic Worker movement could not be undone. Meanwhile, there was no problem about maintaining her own ties with Father Hugo. (She made her last retreat with him in 1976, four years before her own death and nine years before his, by which time Father Hugo had been permitted to resume his retreat ministry. By this time, his rigorism had softened.)

"Love is a commandment," Dorothy recalled, in summing

"What we would like to do is change the world—make it a little simpler for people to feed, clothe, and shelter themselves as God intended them to do. And to a certain extent, by fighting for better conditions, by crying out unceasingly for the rights of the workers, of the poor, of the destitute . . . we can to a certain extent change the world; we can work for the oasis, the little cell of joy and peace in a harried world. We can throw our pebble in the pond and be confident that its ever-widening circle will reach around the world. We repeat, there is nothing that we can do but love, and dear God— please enlarge our hearts to love each other, to love our neighbor, to love our enemy as well as our friend."
—Catholic Worker, June 1946

up what she had learned from Father Hugo. "It is a choice, a preference. If we love God with our whole hearts, how much heart have we left? If we love with our whole mind and soul and strength, how much mind and soul and strength have we left? We must live this life now. Death changes nothing. If we do not learn to enjoy God now, we never

will. If we do not learn to praise Him and thank Him and rejoice in Him now, we never will."

Fr. Clarence Duffy leads prayers before a meal at Peter Maurin farm. Stanley Vishnewski is across the table from Dorothy. (Credit: © Vivian Cherry)

The major benefit of Dorothy's half-year retreat was that, when it ended, she felt renewed confidence in returning to the work she had begun in 1933. "How fearful a work this is," she wrote in her diary eleven months later, in March 1945. "I wonder at my presumption and yet I have to go on. I pray for love—that I may learn to love God."

Community life was often a trial by fire. "When . . . accusations begin to rain down upon me, I can see all too clearly that though immediately and specifically not applicable, they are generally true, of the past if not of the present. . . . I can see how I have been guilty and am suffering only for my sins, past and present."

It would have been easy to choose a different, less lonely, less stressful path. The strains within the Catholic Worker movement were at times, if not outright hellish, then certainly purgatorial. "I am surrounded by such human hatred and dislike that all natural love and companionship is taken from me," she noted in the same diary entry. "Certainly all the joy one has in loving others is taken from me. . . . I can only comfort myself by remembering that vines must be pruned to bear fruit."

Breathing in the Dead

Atomic bomb over Nagasaki. (Library of Congress)

In May 1945, Germany surrendered in Europe. Three months later the war ended in the Pacific. Though the bloodshed was finally over, Dorothy was incapable of celebration. Many millions had perished. Whole cities been destroyed. Hitler was dead and Hirohito had surrendered, but militarism had not only survived but was better equipped than ever before— and fascism, with its concept of the all-powerful state, was only in hiding, disguised by new labels. The war had brought into existence tools of mass destruction, including the atom bomb, such as no general in earlier times could have imagined. In a pair of blinding flashes, Hiroshima and Nagasaki—cities of minor industrial importance, one of them the center of Catholicism in Japan—had all but disappeared. Using hurricanes of more conventional bombs, the same had been done with Dresden, Berlin, Tokyo and other cities. The word "firestorm" had been added to the vocabulary of the gods of war. For Dorothy, it seemed that the real victor in 1945 wasn't the Allies but death, and that now death was armed with weapons capable of causing human extinction.

Reading the first reports of Hiroshima's destruction on August 6, Dorothy learned that President Truman was "jubilant." She thought about his name: *"True man."* How strange a name it was, she realized, when regarded as two words. "We refer to Jesus Christ as true God and true Man," she wrote in the September 1945 *Catholic Worker*. "Truman is a true man of his time in that he was jubilant about destruction. He was not a son of God, brother of Christ, brother of the Japanese, jubilating as he did." She thought of those who had been so close to the explosion that they were instantly vaporized, so like the dead who had been converted to smoke at Nazi concentration camps, "men, women and babies, scattered to the four winds over the seven seas. Perhaps we will breathe their dust into our nostrils, feel them on our faces in the fog of New York, feel them in the rain on the hills of Easton."

"The great ones of the earth are conferring. The very scientists that brought forth the atomic bomb are the most afraid of what is to come. What do to? We can only suggest one thing—destroy the two billion dollars' worth of equipment that was built to make the atomic bomb; destroy all the formulas; put on sackcloth and ashes, weep and repent. And God will not forget to show mercy."
—Catholic Worker, November 1945

The press was full of news about the basic principles behind the bomb's construction, the scientists and universities that played a part, at what secret, remote places the work had been carried on. It was "a miracle of science." Even God was given some of the credit. Press photos showed the large chapel beside the plant at Oak Ridge, Tennessee, where the fissionable material for the bomb had been processed. It was reported that scientists had prayed just before the first nuclear weapon was tested at Alamogordo, New Mexico. With an ironic nod toward the Creator of life and being, the trial explosion of the doomsday device had been code-named Trinity.

"But God is not mocked," Dorothy reflected. "We are held in God's hands, all of us, and President Truman, too. God holds our life and our happiness, our sanity and our health. Our lives are in His hands. He is our creator." The True Man, Christ, came not to destroy but to save. He said, "What you did to the least person, you did to me."

Death touched Dorothy's life not only in dust, fog and rain, but in the loss of her mother in October, just three months after the war's end. For years they had been seeing a great deal of each other, especially following John Day's death, after which Grace moved to Long Island. In the last weeks of Grace's life, Dorothy was at her bedside every day. "Do not pray that I live longer," she asked Dorothy. "I have been through two world wars, the San Francisco earthquake and a Florida hurricane, and I have had enough!"

While religious faith had never been a meeting point for Dorothy with her mother or any other member of the family, as Grace neared death, she asked Dorothy, "What about a future life?" Dorothy said she could no more imagine life beyond the grave than a blind man could imagine colors, but she pointed to a bouquet of violets near the bed. Flowers are like a promise from God, she said, "and God keeps His promises." She pointed to the trees outside the window, maples that had recently been blazing with color but now were being stripped of their leaves, seemingly dead. In just a few months these

"How good God was to me, to let me be there [with my mother]. I had prayed so constantly that I would be beside her when she died. For years, I had offered up that prayer. And God granted it quite literally."
—*Catholic Worker*, November 1945

Grace Satterlee Day.

bare maple trees would be clothed anew in bright green leaves, another sign of a promise, said Dorothy. After a while Grace said, "I can only pray the Our Father and the Creed. Is that enough?" Yes, Dorothy assured her. "It was like being present at a birth," said Dorothy, "to sit by a dying person and see her intentness on what was happening to her. . . . One is absorbed in a struggle, a fearful, grim, physical struggle, to breathe, to swallow, to live."

Before Grace's death, all traces of bitterness and fear seemed gone from her. "She sat up in bed," Dorothy recalled, "and, sipping on a cup of tea, remarked how comforting it was. She had taken up the little bouquet of violets, her favorite flower, and holding it to her face, smiled with happiness." She died the same day, October 24.

Peter Maurin's life was also in its last phase. Visiting the farm at Easton at the end of her six-month retreat in 1944, Dorothy had been distressed to discover how much Peter had aged in her absence. His voice lacked its usual vitality. He spoke slowly and had difficulty remembering names. His last talk, as Dorothy recalled, was his oration against raising pigs for profit given at Tamar and David's wedding that April. By the end of the year Peter could no longer recite any of his Easy Essays, texts so familiar to the staff that they could sing them out antiphonally with him as if they were Psalms. He gave his last manuscript to Arthur Sheehan, a member of the community who later wrote the first biography of Peter, saying he had "done enough, now it is up to the younger people." Within a few months his memory was gone. "He could no longer 'think,' as he tried to tell us sadly," Dorothy wrote.

On the advice of a doctor, in 1946 Peter received the last rites, the sacrament the Catholic Church offers to those close to death, but in his peasant sturdiness, Peter lived on. In 1947 he wandered off and for several days couldn't be found. Afterward notes with his name and address were put in his pockets. When the new farm and retreat center was purchased that spring in Newburgh, New York, it became Peter's new home. His room was a former chicken coop with a concrete floor, chosen for Peter as it was one of the farm's warmer structures. Occasionally Peter's memory returned

Peter Maurin late in life. (Marquette University archives)

"Yes, Peter has lost his memory—his mind. . . . We all have to die—if we don't put off the old man to put on the new, it is done for us. That is a consolation at least—that God will purify us in spite of ourselves."
—To Claude McKay, February 8, 1947

briefly and he could think and make his "points" again.

Leaving New York in early January 1948, Dorothy took another extended break from her usual work, staying several months with Tamar and David and their growing family at their no-frills farm twelve miles from Berkeley Springs, West Virginia.

Dorothy with Peter Maurin, a year before his death, reading the May 1948 issue of *The Catholic Worker*. (Marquette University archives)

"There is great joy in being on the job, doing good works, performing the works of mercy," Dorothy explained to her readers. "But when you get right down to it, a work which is started personally often ends up by being paper work—writing letters, seeing visitors, speaking about the work while others do it. One can become a veritable Mrs. Jellyby [a character in Dickens's novel, *Bleak House*, for whom family was far less a priority than various causes], looking after the world and neglecting one's own who are struggling with poverty and hard work and leading, as such families with small children do these days, ascetic lives." The headline event of her stay was the birth February 20 of a new member of the family, a boy named Eric (in honor of Eric Gill, a Catholic artist, writer and communitarian from England much admired by Peter Maurin).

Back in New York in December, Dorothy found Peter was enjoying a brief remission from his inability to discuss the world around him. He was impressed by reports of priests working in factories in post-war France among those who wouldn't dream of attending Mass. Peter saw the existence of "worker priests" as a significant effort to make openings in the wall dividing the Church from the working class—the kind of thing he had meant in proposing a "worker-scholar synthesis." Discussing the current state of the labor movement, Peter remarked that people are too preoccupied with

"When [Peter's] great brain failed, he became silent. . . . For the last five years of his life he was this way, suffering, silent, dragging himself around, watched by us all for fear he would get lost. . . . The fact was he had been stripped of all. He had stripped himself throughout life; he had put off the old man in order to put on the new. . . . He loved people; he saw in them what God meant them to be, as he saw the world as God meant it to be, and loved it. He had stripped himself, but there remained work for God to do. We are to be pruned as the vine is pruned so that it can bear fruit, and this we cannot do ourselves. God did it for him. He took from him his mind."
—*Catholic Worker*, June 1949

"[Peter] was a man of sincerity and peace, and yet one letter came to us recently, accusing him of having a holier-than-thou attitude. Yes, Peter pointed out that it was a precept that we should love God with our whole heart and soul and mind and strength, and not just a counsel, and he taught us all what it meant to be children of God, and restored to us our sense of responsibility in a chaotic world. Yes, he was 'holier than thou,' holier than anyone we ever knew."
—Catholic Worker, June 1949

this world. "If we were more preoccupied about the next world," he commented, "maybe we would solve the problems of this world too."

But Peter's inability to find words soon returned. His mouth often hung open. Friends sensed in him a painful struggle to comprehend what was going on. He died quietly in his room May 15, 1949, six days after his seventy-second birthday. The funeral Mass in New York City two days later was loud and triumphant, crowded not only with friends, Dorothy felt, but with angels and saints. In death as in life, Peter was dressed in castoff clothing contributed to the Catholic Worker. His burial plot was also donated. The undertaker tried to sell Dorothy artificial grass with which to cover the "unsightly grave." She refused, recalling how Peter loved the earth and enjoyed working it with his hands. His death was reported in the Vatican newspaper, *L'Osservatore Romano*, the editor aware that perhaps it was a saint who had died. Even *Time* magazine noted the passage of a joyful Christian who had embraced poverty and the poor while trying to build up a society in which it was easier "for people to be good."

In the final years of his life, Peter had lost touch with world events. While he had been aware that the U.S.-Soviet alliance against Hitler had culminated jubilantly in the meeting of the victorious armies at the Elbe River in Germany on April 25, 1945, he had not been able to follow the process of world polarization known as "the Cold War" that soon began to unfold.

Early in 1946, while visiting the United States, Winston Churchill called for a post-war alliance against Soviet Communism, which had drawn an "iron curtain" dividing Europe. Before the year was over, a new western military alliance was formed: the North Atlantic Treaty Organization. In 1948, the United States initiated a massive program to aid and strengthen non-Communist Europe—the Marshall Plan. The years 1948-1949 were also the dramatic period of the Berlin Airlift: eleven months of American flights delivering food and basic supplies to the people of West Berlin when road and rail routes were closed by the Soviet Union. In 1949, Communists took power in China.

More and more of the world was under Communist rule.

But no post-war event shocked Americans so much as the successful explosion of an atom bomb by the Soviet Union in August 1949. Congressman (later President) Richard Nixon, a member of the House Committee on Un-American Activities, was among the first to blame the Soviet achievement on "Red spies" in the United States. In February 1950, Senator Joseph McCarthy told a Women's Republican Club in West Virginia that he had in his possession a list of Communists employed by the State Department. Though he refused to reveal any of the names on the list, his speech was front-page news across America. The McCarthy Era was suddenly underway, a long and nasty season of suspicion, accusations and fear. ("I'm afraid I have not kept this spirit of respect towards Senator McCarthy," Dorothy recorded confessionally in a 1953 journal entry. "There is no room for contempt of others in the Christian life.")

J. Edgar Hoover, director of the Federal Bureau of Investigation, initiated a nationwide spy hunt for those who, he charged, had "betrayed American secrets to the Kremlin." In the summer of 1950 Julius and Ethel Rosenberg, two Communists living in New York, were arrested and accused of passing on atom bomb secrets to the Soviet Union.

For years "the enemy within" was a major theme in American political life. The Communist Party was outlawed, its members regarded as agents of a foreign power. A Communist was defined not simply as a person belonging to the Communist Party, but as anyone whose political views resembled to some degree those held by the Communist Party. Those who advocated peace or disarmament, who protested racial segregation or criticized capitalism, were likely to be called, if not Communists, then "reds," "pinkos" or "fellow travelers." Actual and suspected Communists were purged from leadership roles in labor unions. Teachers and civil servants were required to sign "loyalty oaths." The mere suspicion of Communist sympathies or a Communist past cost many people their jobs. Nor was the Communist Party the only target. The Attorney General drew up a list of "Communist-front" organizations—groups that were judged

Senator Joseph McCarthy.

A Cold War comic book depicts the Communist peril for America.

to be significantly influenced by the Communist Party. "Better dead than red," ran a popular American slogan of the 1950s. Another proclaimed, "The only good red is a dead red."

The clergy were often as fervent as politicians and editorial writers in denouncing Communism, but perhaps no major Christian church was so renowned for its anti-Communism as the Catholic Church. Pope Pius XII—though he had been among those who appealed to President Eisenhower to spare the Rosenbergs' lives—declared that any Catholic collaborating with Communists was automatically excommunicated.

Many hands reached out to welcome and reward those who repented of their radical past, so long as their repentance was demonstrated by a readiness to prove their opposition to Communism by "naming names"—to testify against those who had been, still were or seemed to be Communists.

Dorothy Day was often accused of being a Communist. Though she had never joined the Communist Party, she occasionally spoke of herself as having once been a communist (in the generic sense of the word) when she was a young adult. She was among the speakers at a Carnegie Hall event in 1952 where two of the most repressive Cold War laws passed by the U.S. Congress—the McCarran Act and the Smith Act—were denounced. (The McCarran Act required the registration of Communist organizations with the Attorney General and established the Subversive Activities Control Board to investigate persons suspected of engaging in seditious activities. Members of such groups were barred from becoming citizens and could be prevented from entering or leaving the country. The Smith Act made it a felony to publish or circulate "any written or printed matter advocating, advising, or teaching the duty, necessity, desirability, or propriety of overthrowing or destroying any government in the United States by force or violence, or attempts to do so.")

Even some of those who knew Dorothy was no disciple of Marx, Lenin and Stalin were disturbed by her still unbroken friendships with Mike Gold and Elizabeth Gurley Flynn, both prominent Communists. Far from disowning them, Dorothy was among the few who spoke up for Flynn and ten other leading Communists when they were arrested and charged with "conspiring to advocate the overthrow of the United States government by force and violence." As only lawyers tended to notice, none of those arrested were accused of acts of violence or even the advocacy of violence. It was entirely a conspiracy indictment. They were accused of "conspiring to advocate" revolutionary actions to occur at some time in the indefinite future. As one former Communist later put it, "We were part of a movement with a lot of cloak but no dagger." When Dorothy protested that the jailed Communists should be allowed freedom on bail while they prepared their defense, *The Catholic Worker* received a wave of angry letters and subscription cancellations.

Far from backing off, Dorothy replied with a column emphasizing her debt to Communists friends: "I can say with warmth that I loved the Communists I worked with and learned much from them. They helped me to find God in His poor, in His abandoned ones, as I had not found Him in the Christian churches. . . . My radical associates were the ones who were in the forefront of the struggle for a better social order where there would not be so many poor." Christianity has points in common with Communism, Dorothy pointed out. It was a Christian ideal that Marxists had borrowed in advocating "from each according to his ability, to each according to his need." Dorothy shared Marx's hope that the state would eventually wither away. Of course she disagreed with Communists about violence being an acceptable method of reforming society, but in this, she added, she disagreed with Republicans and Democrats as well, and with many Christians, so many of whom endorsed violence and war when other political methods failed. "If only," Dorothy reflected, "we who follow Christ had the zeal for the exploited workers and the poor that one regularly finds among Communists!"

The identification of Communists with unions, protests and calls for social justice was so automatic in the post-war years that when a small union of grave-diggers went on strike against the Archdiocese of New York in 1949, Cardinal Spellman told the press that the striking men were under Communist influence. He refused to meet with them and

"We are in favor of life. We are trying to work here and now for the brotherhood of man, with those minorities, those small groups of 'willful men' who believe that even the few can cry out against injustice, against the man-made suffering in the world, in behalf of those who are hungry and homeless and without work, in behalf of those who are dying."
—*Catholic Worker, April 1952*

189

ordered seminarians—some of whom were the sons of men out on strike—to dig graves until the strike was crushed. The strikers responded with an oath that their only motive was their economic problems and that Communism had nothing to do with it.

Though Dorothy had always emphasized her respect for the bishops, and for Cardinal Spellman personally, she quickly came to the side of the grave-diggers, expressing her regret for the cardinal's "show of force" in turning seminarians into strike-breakers. She took part in the union's picket line in front of the cardinal's office behind Saint Patrick's Cathedral on Madison Avenue and wrote of the striking men in her column as "victims of that most awful of all wars, the war between clergy and laity." In a letter to Cardinal Spellman, she begged him to realize that the strikers were not only seeking better wages and working conditions but "their dignity as men." Dorothy urged him, as "a prince of the Church, and a great man in the eyes of the world," to meet personally with the strikers and open himself to their appeal. "They want to talk to you, and, oh, I do beg you so with all my heart to go to them." There was no response either to Dorothy or to the grave-diggers. The strike was defeated within a month.

Dorothy's public criticism of the cardinal's response to the strike and her participation in what was surely the first picket line of devout Catholics in front of any bishop's chancery, plus her failure to disown the Communists she knew personally, were sure to be long remembered by Cardinal Spellman, a man outspoken in his views on the "Red menace" and a strict believer in obedience and conformity within the Church. Two years later, in March 1951, Dorothy received a request from a member of his staff, Monsignor Edward Gaffney, to come to the chancery office. "He told me," Dorothy recalled, "that we would have to cease publication or change our name."

Monsignor Gaffney, no doubt acting on orders from Cardinal Spellman, had every reason to expect Dorothy's compliance. She had often said that, if she had to make the choice, she would put obedience to her bishop above continuation of her newspaper. "We recognize and accept the authority of the Church as we do that of Christ himself,"

Cardinal Francis Spellman of New York.

(Credit: Ed Lettau)

Dorothy had written at the time of the grave-diggers' strike. But she had never committed herself to instant compliance. She told Monsignor Gaffney that she needed to give this matter more thought and, after all, it wasn't only for her to decide. She must consult with those in the community who shared responsibility for *The Catholic Worker.*

A few days later she responded by letter, reaffirming her "love and respectful obedience to the Church, and our gratitude to this Archdiocese, which has so often and so generously defended us from the many who attack us." She did not, however, wish to take advantage of such kindness, "nor count on the official protection which the name Catholic brings us." Therefore she was personally willing to change the paper's name rather than to cease publication. However, she added, others involved in editing the paper were opposed to making such a change. "All feel that *The Catholic Worker* has

"The Last Supper" by Fritz Eichenberg.

been in existence for eighteen years . . . under that name, and that this is no time to change it." After all, Dorothy pointed out, an independent lay group like Catholic War Veterans was under no pressure to change its name. Should not the Catholic War Veterans and *The Catholic Worker* be equally free to express their points of view without being held as representing the official views of the Archdiocese or the Catholic Church as a whole? She appealed for dialogue instead of suppression. "We are all ready to receive respectfully and give practical heed and application to all scientific, scholarly criticism and correction of mistakes . . . and to all theological or spiritual censures of theological or spiritual errors."

Dorothy added that "we cannot simply cease the publication of a review which has been built up, with its worldwide circulation of 63,000. . . . This would be a grave scandal to our readers and would put into the hands of our enemies, the enemies of the Church, a formidable weapon." She regretted that she had not herself given more time to her editorial responsibility and promised to take a firmer hand. "Whether or not I am at fault," she went on, "I and my associates have spent years" trying to publish a journal which encourages its readers to build up "a new society within the shell of the old . . . [a] cooperative order as opposed to the corporate state." She pointed out that Catholics were not by definition capitalists or committed to capitalism and that the Vatican's own newspaper, *L'Osservatore Romano*, had criticized both the Soviet and American economic systems. Both were deeply flawed, and *The Catholic Worker* was flawed too. She promised to "try to be less dogmatic, more persuasive, less irritating, more winning."

Dorothy did not say no. She only set out reasons that the paper ought to continue and that its name should remain as it was. Apparently her argument was persuasive—the request (it had never reached the point of becoming an order) from the Archdiocese was quietly dropped. A change of heart in the chancery office? A tactical withdrawal? Perhaps a little of both? As for the content of *The Catholic Worker* following Dorothy's letter, one finds no change.

Dorothy's own position was significantly strengthened the following year, in January 1952 when her autobiography, *The*

Long Loneliness, was published and well received. The title was a phrase borrowed from the writings of Blessed Mary Ward, an English nun, born in 1585, in the later years of the reign of Queen Elizabeth I. "I think, dear child, the trouble and the long loneliness you hear me speak of is not far from me, when-soever it is, happy success will follow," Ward had written in a letter. "The pain is great, but very endurable, because He who lays on the burden also carries it." Ward was a controversial woman in her day because the order she founded was not one of contemplatives hidden from public sight, but women work-ing in the world as educators. At the time not only was enclo-sure the norm for all nuns, but it was a papal requirement. Dorothy felt that, like Blessed Mary Ward, she had a pro-found experience of the long loneliness.

On another occasion, Dorothy credited Tamar with play-ing a role in the book's title: "When I was beginning it," Dorothy wrote, "[Tamar] was writing me about how alone a mother of a young child always is. I had also just heard from an elderly woman who had lived a long and full life, and she too spoke of her loneliness. I thought again, 'The only answer in this life, to the loneliness we are all bound to feel, is com-munity, the living together, working together, sharing togeth-er, loving God and loving our brother, and living close to him in community so we can show our love for him.'" (In an "On Pilgrimage" column in 1959, Dorothy gave still another expla-nation for the book's title: "I called [it] *The Long Loneliness* because I tried to point out, with St. Augustine, that no mat-ter how crowded life was with activity and joy, family and work, the human heart was never satisfied until it rested in God, the absolute Good, absolute Beauty, absolute Love.")

One of the attractions of *The Long Loneliness* was its beauty, thanks to the graphic artist Fritz Eichenberg, who did a wood engraving for the book's cover plus engravings for each of the book's three main sections. Dorothy had met Fritz in 1949, thirteen years after he fled to the United States from Nazi Germany. "Dorothy loved Dostoevsky," Fritz recalled, "and knew me for my illustrations for *Crime and Punishment* and *The Brothers Karamazov*. I think she shared with Dostoevsky the conviction that beauty will save the

Illustration by Fritz Eichenberg for *The Long Loneliness*.

world. She had such an intense love of beauty, for art of any kind." As soon as they met, Dorothy asked Fritz if he might occasionally contribute some art work to *The Catholic Worker*. In the years that followed, his work was often featured on the front page. Not every subscriber had the education to read the articles, but even the most unlettered person could understand what the paper stood for thanks to the art of Fritz Eichenberg and Ade Bethune.

The Long Loneliness sold well, was translated into many languages, and has never gone out of print. Reviewers immediately compared the book to Saint Augustine's *Confessions*, rightly predicting Dorothy's book would also become a classic of religious autobiography. *The Long Loneliness* also inspired Dwight Macdonald to write a long and admiring two-part profile of Dorothy for the distinguished weekly magazine, *The New Yorker*. Dorothy suddenly found herself facing the problem of being widely admired, even regarded as a living saint, and not only by many Catholics.

Now that she was so much in the public eye, it would have been understandable if Dorothy had prudently withdrawn from any public expressions of sympathy for Communists in order that the paper be "less irritating, more winning." But she was deeply and publicly troubled about the arrest of the Rosenbergs and appealed—unsuccessfully—to Cardinal Spellman to oppose their execution, as the Pope had done.

One of Dorothy's more memorable essays for *The Catholic Worker* was her "Meditation on the Death of the Rosenbergs," published in the issue following their execution on June 19, 1953. That evening she bathed one of her grandchildren, Nickie, while praying for the condemned couple: "God, let them be strong, take away all fear from them, let them be spared this suffering, at least this suffering of fear and trembling." She recalled Dostoevsky, who had been sentenced to death and then was spared at the last moment, and she continued to hope against hope that there might still be a reprieve. She thought of Albert Einstein and Harold Urey, both of whom had declared their belief in the innocence of the Rosenbergs. (Early in the war, Einstein had written to President Roosevelt to suggest the possibility of producing an atomic device, while Urey was one of the scientists who actually developed the bomb.)

But what if the Rosenbergs were guilty, Dorothy wondered? "Even so, what should be the attitude of the Christian but one of love and great yearning for salvation?" Soon after Nickie's bath was over, the jazz music on the radio was interrupted to give the bulletin reporting the Rosenbergs' deaths in the electric chair at Sing Sing, a prison on the Hudson River not many miles north of Manhattan. In the morning, Dorothy carefully read the detailed account of the execution in *The New York Times*: "A rabbi who had attended them to the last said that they had been his parishioners for two years. He followed them to the execution chamber reading from the psalms, the 23rd, the 15th, the 31st. Those same psalms Cardinal Spellman reads every week as he reads his breviary."

Convicted "atom-spies" Julius and Ethel Rosenberg. (Library of Congress)

"How mixed up religion can become," Dorothy wrote. How little our activities are shaped by the holy words we know by heart. Christian prelates "sprinkle holy water on scrap metal to be used for obliteration bombing, and name bombers for the Holy Innocents or for Our Lady of Mercy . . . [and] bless a man about to press a button which releases death on fifty thousand human beings."

She noted that the Rosenbergs had gone to their deaths firmly and quietly, expressing their love for their two sons and professing their innocence. "At the last Ethel turned to one of the two police matrons who accompanied her and, clasping her by the hand, pulled her toward her and kissed her warmly. Her last gesture was one of love."

The One-Man Revolution

Late in 1949, the year of Peter Maurin's death, a cross-country speaking trip brought Dorothy to Phoenix, Arizona. Welcoming her at the bus station was a lanky man a few years her senior named Ammon Hennacy. Dorothy had briefly met him once before, in 1937. From 1941 onward, she occasionally published Ammon's writings in *The Catholic Worker*, while he became one of the most committed distributors of the paper, hawking it outside local Catholic churches after Sunday Mass. It must have puzzled church-goers, as Ammon never took part in Mass himself. The Catholic Church wasn't for him, he explained, but the Catholic Worker was. Following his Phoenix meeting with Dorothy, Ammon began to engage himself more deeply in the Catholic Worker movement, forgiving it for being Catholic and becoming one of its more legendary figures.

Ammon—born in 1893 in rural Ohio—was tall, with a jutting chin, eagle nose, piercing blue eyes, and long, dense hair that seemed suitable for a lion's mane. Like Peter, he was a man of radical ideas who was nowhere more at home than in street-corner debates. But Ammon's temperament was quite different from Peter's. Peter agreed with some of the de-centralist anarchist writers, especially Kropotkin, but preferred to call himself a "personalist"—a less confrontational word for describing his refusal to conform to a money-driven social order, to place civil law higher than God's law, or to shirk personal responsibility. Ammon, though in action as nonviolent as Gandhi, enjoyed using words that went off like hand grenades. He identified himself as an anarchist, which he defined as someone "who doesn't need a cop to make him behave." The way to change the world, Ammon said, was not by casting an occasional vote but by living each day of your life the way that you wanted others to live. Each person could cause a revolution, a "one-man revolution," by self-transformation. For this you didn't have to wait for election day, cast a ballot, and hope your side won.

During the First World War, Ammon had refused to register for the draft, for which he spent two years in a federal penitentiary. Reading the Bible again and again while behind bars, he had come to a personal, un-churched Christian faith that was anchored in the Sermon on the Mount. "The opposite of the Sermon on the Mount," he realized, "was what the whole world had been practicing, in prison and out of prison; and hate piled on hate had brought on hate and revenge. It was plain that this system did not work." He decided to use the Sermon on the Mount as the basis for his own life. Freed from prison after the war, he began a career in professional social work, but, when World War II began, gave it up rather than pay taxes—he wasn't willing to pay for others to fight a war he wouldn't fight himself.

In 1943 he began "a life at hard labor," as he called it, doing farm work for cash wages from which no taxes were deducted. He found twelve-hour days in the field a challenge. He had, Dorothy wrote, "tremendous strength and endurance." In one of his occasional articles for *The Catholic Worker*—a piece reminiscent of Dorothy's "poverty squad" reporting in her early days as a journalist—Ammon gave an account of how he lived on ten dollars a month, itemizing his expenses: whole wheat flour, 25 lbs, $1.25; shortening, 3 lbs, 68 cents; corn meal, 5 lbs, 46 cents; margarine, 2 lbs, 38 cents; raisins, 2 lbs, 23 cents.

Ammon was the only contributor to *The Catholic Worker* who was not only outside the Church but didn't even like Catholicism. He objected to the Church's hierarchical structure, its rituals, its near silence regarding social injustice, its acceptance of war, its wealth, its stress on obedience, and its apparent indifference to individual conscience. His animosity toward Catholicism was expressed with such a fierce conviction and rigidity that some at the Catholic Worker called him "Father Hennacy," teasing him for being so dogmatic. "You are much more dogmatic than I," Dorothy noted in a letter to Ammon in 1951. "The example you set is tremendous, but I do not feel you have a right to judge as you do. Everyone is so different. The great job is to judge ourselves, to know ourselves, to change ourselves."

Perhaps the fact that Dorothy wasn't intimidated by

Top: Ammon selling *The Catholic Worker* on the streets of New York. (Credit: © Vivian Cherry)
Above: Ammon picketing during his annual fast.

Ammon picketing at the Atomic Energy Commission in Las Vegas, 1957. (Marquette University archives)

Ammon made him take her seriously. "I didn't believe in the Church," he admitted, "but I believed in Dorothy." And Dorothy was deeply impressed with Ammon. After their 1949 meeting, she described him in her column as someone who wasn't just talking and protesting and refusing to take part in war but who was "trying to change the conditions that bring about war." Though without benefit of the sacraments, she added, he was "doing the things we Catholics should be doing."

During Easter 1950, Ammon paid his first visit to the Worker house in New York. He soon announced his reservations about the hospitality aspect—the community shouldn't waste its time "feeding bums," he said. Yet he found it hard to leave. In 1952 he returned for a stay that lasted eight years.

Ammon's respect for Dorothy and her commitment to the Catholic Church was such that, to her joy and astonishment, he became a Catholic himself in November 1952. He explained to friends that Dorothy's example had been the decisive factor to him—he mentioned how she had kneeled rather than stood when the Star Spangled Banner was played at a church she visited. Ammon's conversion did not, however, make him less critical of the hierarchy. There was, for example, the occasion when, having been invited by the Ladies' Altar Society of a certain parish to speak to the group about the Catholic Worker and its work with the poor, he was asked what he thought of Pope Pius XII. His response was: "Just another Italian gangster!" (When Dorothy heard about this, she was furious.)

Yet, important as she was in his decision to join the Catholic Church, it wasn't only due to Dorothy. In *The Autobiography of a Catholic Anarchist*, published in 1954, Ammon wrote with embarrassment about the anti-Catholic remarks he had often made earlier in his life and how important and strengthening Mass had become for him. "This was not being priest-ridden," he said. "It was a means of spiritual growth."

But had Dorothy not lived a life so centered on the Mass, it's unlikely Ammon would have been drawn in that direction. Ammon's attraction was not only to the radical ideas that those engaged in the *Catholic Worker* were trying to live out, but to Dorothy personally. For years he was ardently in love with her. He left the New York house only when he was drawn to another member of the community, but while his love of Dorothy lasted, he poured it out to her in frequent notes and letters, even while expressing—one senses with reluctance—his admiration for Dorothy's determined celibacy. (One of the section headings Dorothy had considered using in *The Long Loneliness* was "The Unwilling Celibate.")

Dorothy's feelings about Ammon are obscure. She was now a grandmother. The loneliness she had lived with since her separation from Forster remained acute, and was only made more intense by the admiration so many had for her. It may well be that she was grateful that Ammon not only found her a praiseworthy human being but an attractive woman. But when it became clear to her just how womanly he found her, she sought to make clear to Ammon that what she was looking for was a friendship, not romance and marriage. "For one thing you are sixty nearly and I am 55," she wrote him in March 1953, "a mature age, when calm affection and friendship, deep and sincere, can be respected, but romantic love not. There is something quite sane in this. Such love is associated with youth and the time of mating, and the idea of procreation . . . [but] the idea of sexual love is out of place at our age." (Dorothy once showed me Ammon's many letters to her. Along with Peter Maurin's handwritten manuscripts, they were filed in an unlocked file cabinet on the porch at the Catholic Worker farm on Staten Island. Now they are part of the Catholic Worker Archive at Marquette University.)

Dorothy's published writings about Ammon were quite dry-eyed. He had a tendency, she wrote, to fall in love with women and had told her he couldn't remember a time when he wasn't in love with someone, and yet, Dorothy noted, "he often spoke of women scornfully, insisting that they held men back in their radical careers." More troubling to her was Ammon's tendency to make "hasty judgments of others and his inability to see himself as ever in the wrong." He was the sort of person, irksome in his self-sufficiency and self-recognized perfection, who "knows how to work, how to eat, to fast, to sleep, to meet each and every problem of the day." Ammon looked in the mirror and saw *Saint* Ammon. But

"Dear God, I want to pray now for Ammon, that you give him light to come with humility to the baptism font. . . . How much he would learn to bring strength and comfort to others, to turn from the world and turn to You, to love You and their brothers for love of You. I am very hopeless and pessimistic about asking this, so forgive this too, in me, my unbelief, my lack of faith. I am so surrounded by the poor in interior and exterior goods, they are so gaunt, I can see their faults clearly. So I don't expect too much from them. I know too that only You know the heart. I don't know how good or bad people are. How much vanity, willfulness, pride there may be. . . . But I do know that I want with a great longing that Ammon become a Catholic, and I ask You this now, here on the eve of the feast of your mother's Immaculate Heart. To soften his heart and convert him now. Still, not as I will but as You will, be it done."
—Diary entry, August 21, 1952

when she saw what he did rather than what he said, Dorothy was deeply moved. "When an extra bed was needed, he gave up his own over and over"—to the very "bums" about whom he had been complaining only moments before.

Dorothy was grateful for the energy and enthusiasm Ammon brought to the Catholic Worker. He had Peter's devotion to finding people where they were rather than waiting for them to walk through the door. Yet, once Ammon found them, he was more a man of monologue than dialogue. Conversations with him tended to be one-sided and thick with one-liners. (If asked if he believed in free love, his stock response was, "Do you believe in bought love?")

A large part of Ammon's ordinary day was given over to standing on the streets selling *The Catholic Worker*. In the course of each week he made his way from Wall Street in lower Manhattan to the Fordham University campus uptown in the Bronx. Over the years thousands came to recognize him. Among his regular partners in friendly debate were bankers and professors. Some became admirers and friends. One of them, a popular humorist, song writer and television host, Steve Allen, wrote the introduction to Ammon's self-published autobiography, *The Book of Ammon*, an updated version of *The Autobiography of a Catholic Anarchist*.

"Ammon," Allen wrote, "has experienced—not just read about—atheism, socialism, anarchism, pacifism, communism, anti-communism, violence, poverty, civil disobedience, Christianity, Protestantism, Catholicism, Mormonism, picket lines, freedom rides, imprisonment, hunger, manual labor, farming, vegetarianism, despair, faith, hope and love." This was far from a complete list, he added, but at least it indicated Ammon's "zest for bare, natural, principled life. . . . Even if Ammon were mistaken on every one of his fundamental beliefs and assumptions—which is true of no one—we could still learn something from him because of his love of the world."

Ammon was nothing if not an activist. He made and carried many a picket sign proclaiming his convictions. Every year he fasted publicly to commemorate the anniversaries of the atom bombings of Hiroshima and Nagasaki, a sign in hand explaining to passers-by why, on such death-shadowed days, a penitential fast made more sense than eating as usual. It was Ammon who, beginning in the fifties, inspired the Catholic Worker to engage in more public protest activity than it had since the thirties.

Fifteen years after becoming Catholic, then living in Salt Lake City, he withdrew from the Church in outrage after the local Catholic bishop failed to speak out against the pending execution of two men on Utah's Death Row. He had become a Catholic, Ammon explained, because of Dorothy Day—if she had been a Mormon and had edited *The Mormon Worker*, he would have become a Mormon.

Ammon Hennacy with Dorothy and seven of her grandchildren. (Marquette University archives)

Ammon renounced the Church, but remained linked to the Catholic Worker. Though alienated from Catholicism, he had been converted to the bums. After leaving the New York house in 1961, he founded a house of hospitality in Salt Lake City. It remained his home until he died in 1970. The center was named in honor of one of Ammon's personal saints, Joe Hill, the labor organizer and songwriter whose life had been ended by a Utah firing squad. Joe Hill's best known song, often heard on picket lines and in union halls. was a parody of a religious hymn. Ammon loved its irreverent refrain: "Work and pray, live on hay—you'll get pie in the sky when you die."

"Dorothy admired Ammon," Tom Cornell points out, "because he was reliable and responsible and for his deep faith in God as Truth and Love revealed in Jesus. If not a model Catholic, he was a genuine Christian." "Don't listen to what Ammon says," Dorothy had often counseled. "See what he does. Go and do likewise!"

It is often recalled that Ammon was arrested more than fifty times for acts of civil disobedience. Less remarked on or noticed were his countless small deeds to benefit the world around him. If he found garbage strewn on the pavement, he would pause and put it in a trash bin.

Laughter in the Park

Top: Ruins of the Catholic cathedral in Nagasaki, destroyed by an atom bomb on August 9, 1945.
Above: Civil Defense Poster.

In 1945 two Japanese cities had been destroyed by American atom bombs. Four years later the Soviet Union exploded its first nuclear weapon. In 1952, the US successfully exploded the first hydrogen bomb, a weapon far more powerful than the atom bomb, over an island in the Pacific Ocean. While it took three years for the USSR to test a similar device, it was clear the event was inevitable. As time passed, ever more powerful nuclear weapons were tested by both sides, the explosions carried out in the open air with the highly toxic radioactive waste carried far and wide by the four winds. The annihilation of civilization was no longer a far-fetched theme in the domain of science fiction writers. To anyone paying attention, nuclear war, with millions of casualties and the destruction of hundreds of cities, seemed an event that was bound to happen. For many Americans, making preparations to survive a nuclear war was the order of the day and "civil defense" the phrase coined to describe it. Thousands of families built shelters in their basements or—more costly—underground in their back yards.

In the spring of 1955, the New York press reported that a state-wide civil defense drill, "Operation Alert," was scheduled for June 15. The news came with a warning: anyone refusing to take shelter—going into subways or basements, crouching in designated hallways or under desks in schoolrooms—risked up to a year in prison plus a $500 fine. The message underlying the drill was that, should nuclear war occur, if the right steps were taken beforehand, many could survive. A national shelter industry sprang to life despite warnings from those familiar with the effects of nuclear explosions that all the average buyer could reasonably hope to obtain for his investment was a larger-than-average coffin, while those who did survive underground confinement would find themselves in a radioactive wasteland better suited to insect than human life. One peace group, the Fellowship of Reconciliation,

responded by launching a "Shelters for the Shelterless" campaign, as a result of which thousands of small houses were built for homeless people in India. The same group printed a sign which families brave enough to risk being called "Communist dupes" put on their front doors:

THIS HOUSE HAS NO FALLOUT SHELTER
Peace is our only protection.

News of preparations for New York City's first air raid drill caught Ammon Hennacy's eye. He proposed to those at the Catholic Worker house and to other pacifists in New York that this was a foolish law that was well worth breaking. On June 15, Dorothy, Ammon and twenty-seven others met in the park in front of City Hall in lower Manhattan. "In the name of Jesus, who is God, who is Love, we will not obey this order to pretend, to evacuate, to hide," a Catholic Worker leaflet declared. "We will not be drilled into fear. We do not have faith in God if we depend upon the Atom Bomb." When the air raid sirens began to wail, cars and buses pulled to the

Above: An empty Times Square during the civil defense drill on June 15, 1955.

Below: Dorothy, Ammon, and other pacifists protest the City's civil defense drill. (Credit: Robert Lax)

"On June 15, when there was supposed to be a nationwide air raid drill, 28 of us refused to obey orders and sat out in City Hall Park. It was our usual group. . . . We were all arrested, and from 2 p.m. on we went from jail to jail, Elizabeth Street, Thirtieth Street, Center Street, and finally we women ended in the Women's House of Detention on Greenwich Avenue. It was a most wonderful experience of performing the work of mercy of visiting the prisoner, by being ourselves one of them. When I knelt down in that little cell in the women's prison, I thought, this is the closest I shall ever get to a Carmelite monastery."

—To Jack English, June 24, 1955

Above: Dorothy carrying picket sign. (Marquette University archives)

Opposite: Dorothy under arrest while protesting civil defense drill. (Credit: Robert Lax)

curb and New Yorkers drained into cellars and subway stations. Within minutes, New York, playing war rather than business, seemed like a ghost town—except at City Hall Park, where Dorothy and the other pacifists (not only from the Catholic Worker but from the War Resisters League and the Fellowship of Reconciliation) stayed where they were, looking more like picnickers than protesters. While cameras filmed their quiet witness, police escorted the lawbreakers into vans and drove them off.

"As 679 warning sirens wailed," *The New York Sun* reported the next day, "millions of New Yorkers took shelter in the city's greatest air raid drill—an exercise marred only by 29 arrests and, in spots, by errors, lethargy and defiance, but hailed nonetheless as a 'complete success' by authorities. An imaginary H-bomb fell at the corner of N. 7th St. and Kent Ave. in Brooklyn, 'wiping out' vast areas of the city and claiming 2,991,185 'fatalities.' Another 1,776,899 men, women and children were listed as 'injured' as imaginary flames roared through the area. Robert Condon, [New York] City Civil Defense Director, called the drill 'a complete success as far as public reaction goes.'"

To most Americans, the handful of people who had openly refused to take shelter must have seemed out of touch with reality. Not only is the law the law, but surely such drills were only for everyone's ultimate safety? The Russians were ruthless atheists, people with no principles and no respect for human life, and now they were armed with nuclear weapons. Was it not common sense to try to save as many lives as possible in the event of war?

This was not Dorothy's view of what was going on. She saw such rehearsals as making nuclear war seem survivable and winnable and therefore not an option to be rejected. For her, refusing to take shelter was also "an act of penance" undertaken by an American whose country "had been the first to drop the atom bomb and to make the hydrogen bomb."

At eleven o'clock that night those who had been arrested appeared in night court. One of them, the actress Judith Malina, laughed out loud in the courtroom as the bailiff mispronounced prisoners' names. When the judge summoned

her to the bench for making the distur-
bance, Judith explained that she was
giddy because she hadn't had anything
to eat all day. He asked if she had ever
been in a mental institution. "No," she
replied, "have you?" Those in the courtroom laughed, but not the judge, who
ordered that Judith be taken for obser-
vation at the Bellevue psychiatric ward.
For the others he set $1,500 bail, a sum
associated with crimes far more serious
than sitting quietly on park benches.
("Well, it was a serious crime," said one
member of the Catholic Worker community. "We were defying the White House.
We were defying the Pentagon. We were
defying the governor. We were defying
the national mood. We were defying the
habit of war. We were refusing to get
ready for war.")

Dorothy and the others refused to
provide bail, but after twenty-four
hours were sent home without sentence or fine by a friendlier
judge. "All we got was a slap on the wrist," one of them said.
But even a day in jail had given Dorothy time to kneel on the
floor of her cell—"a bare, stark cell that would outdo the
Carmelites in austerity"—and "thank God for the opportunity to be there, to be so stripped of all that the earth holds
dear, to share in some way the life of prisoners, guilty and
innocent, all over the world."

A year later, the drill was repeated, as was the protest, this
time in Washington Square Park. On this occasion the
demonstrators were ordered to pay a fine or serve five days in
jail. (One of those who opted for the fine was David Caplan,
a physicist, who tried to convince the judge that civil defense
preparations in a prime-target city like New York were dis-
honest: one would need to be far deeper—not in a subway
tunnel just under the street—to have any hope of survival.)

Dorothy chose jail. The poor couldn't pay fines, she said,

*"So many in these days have taken vio-
lent steps to gain the things of this
world—war to achieve peace; coercion to
achieve freedom; striving to gain what
slips through the fingers. We might as
well give up our great desires, at least our
hopes of doing great things toward achiev-
ing them, right at the beginning. In a way
it is like the paradox of the Gospel, of giving up one's life in order to save it. That,
in effect, is what we did when we went to
jail. It was part of it. We were setting our
faces against the world, against things as
they are, the terrible injustice of our capitalist industrial system which lives by war
and by preparing for war. . . . We made
our gesture; we disobeyed a law."*
—September 1957

Dorothy under arrest. (Credit: Robert Lax)

which was one of the reasons the jails were full of the poor. Also, Jesus had said, "I was a prisoner and you came to be with me."

Dorothy was jailed again in 1957. By then her disobedience seemed a kind of annual urban ritual, like painting a green stripe down Fifth Avenue on Saint Patrick's Day. In a leaflet, Dorothy sought to explain the Catholic Worker's small act of witness: "We know what we are in for, the risk we run in openly setting ourselves against this most powerful country in the world. It is a tiny Christian gesture, the gesture of a David against a Goliath in an infinitesimal way. We do not wish to be defiant, we do not wish to antagonize. We love our country and are only saddened to see its great virtues matched by equally great faults. We are a part of it, we are responsible too. With this small gesture we want to atone in some small measure for what we did in Hiroshima, and what we are still doing by the manufacture and testing of such weapons."

The press, in greater numbers than ever, came to watch the pacifists get loaded into paddy wagons, not at City Hall Park this time but on Chrystie Street, the Catholic Worker's own neighborhood. The judge, a Catholic, advised Dorothy to read the Bible and said that those who disobeyed the civil defense laws were a "heartless bunch of individuals who breathe contempt." He imposed a thirty-day sentence.

Putting Dorothy Day in jail was akin to throwing a rabbit into the briar patch. "It is good to be here, Lord," Dorothy wrote from her cell in the Women's House of Detention in Greenwich Village, not far from the saloon where, in earlier times, she had spent many an hour with Eugene O'Neill. "We were, frankly, hoping for jail," Dorothy admitted to readers of *The Catholic Worker*. Being in jail, one could come closer to real poverty. "Then we would not be running a house of hospitality, we would not be dispensing food and clothing, we would not be ministering to the destitute, but we would be truly one of them."

Her month-long jail stay was a shocking, grinding experience—"crushing, numbing and painful at the same time." It wasn't just the abrasive, sack-like clothing, the constant assault of the mind by noise, the small and crowded cells, or the sexual harassment being suffered by so many of the younger inmates. What was most difficult was the deep sadness and despair that filled the prison. So many prisoners could look toward the future only with dread.

Dorothy left prison in a state of mental, physical and even spiritual exhaustion, she told her readers, yet grateful for the experience and ready to face the same consequences again next year. "It is a gesture, perhaps, but a necessary one. Silence means consent, and we cannot consent to the militarization of our country without protest. Since we believe that air raid drills are part of a calculated plan to inspire fear of the enemy, instead of the love which Jesus Christ told us we should feel, we must protest these drills. It is an opportunity to show we mean what we write when we repeat over and over that we are put here on this earth to love God and our neighbor."

The longer jail term made Dorothy think again of the need for a completely different response from society to those convicted of crimes. She had witnessed the ways in which prisons damage those who live or work in them, making many inmates only more angry and dangerous than they were before, while reducing others to an awful, passive brokenness, and harming the guards as well. Would not much more be accomplished in small, more homelike settings in which prisoners were recognized as persons of value and promise? In prison, staff was mainly hired to guard inmates, "not to love them." She envisioned rural centers at which the inmates raised much of their own food, baked their own bread, milked cows, tended chickens, engaged in creative activity and shared responsibility for the institution so that it wasn't a static environment but was, "in its own way, a community." Prison as it exists, she found, was the opposite of community. The prisoner is simply an object which can be stripped and searched in the crudest possible ways—in the case of women prisoners, "even to the tearing of tissues so that bleeding results."

Why, she asked, were Christians so blind to Christ's presence in the people it locked away and regarded without compassion? "Christ is with us today, not only in the Blessed Sacrament and where two or three are gathered together in

Catholic Worker cover for the July-August 1955 issue with illustration by Fritz Eichenberg.

"Next week we demonstrate again, stick our necks out, protest, say no, carry out into the street some of the Pope's words . . . such as 'War is murder and suicide.' (It would naturally follow from that that it is forbidden us.) We will be arrested again, in jail again, maybe for a day, maybe for a month, or six months. It is not easy. I just have to remember that I am visiting the prisoner, the last work of mercy and the hardest to perform. Do pray for us."
—To Donald Powell, April 9, 1959

(Marquette University archives)

His Name, but also in the poor. And who could be poorer and more destitute in body and soul than these companions of ours in prison?"

In 1958, Dorothy and Ammon, with seven others, again stayed above ground as an imaginary nuclear explosion occurred above New York. This time the judge suspended sentence. In 1959 there were fourteen. Ammon, Dorothy, and her friend and co-worker Deane Mowrer were sentenced to fifteen days in jail. The judge was a kindly man, but found that they were failing to render to Caesar the things that are Caesar's. "Caesar has been getting too much around here," Ammon replied. "Someone has to stand up for God."

For Dorothy, among the benefits of taking part in an act of civil disobedience was the opportunity it gave for practicing one of the most neglected of the works of mercy, visiting the prisoner, and doing so not just for a short time but for days on end, and not as a visitor but as a fellow-prisoner.

In the diary entries she kept while back at the Women's House of Detention that spring, Dorothy reflected on the struggle it is "trying to see Christ in our sisters and loving them in their suffering. . . . [In doing so,] we are not oblivious to their faults, their sins. This is true love because primarily we love them because Jesus loved them—He came to call sinners, to find the lost sheep. . . . [Many of them] are beautiful, young, tall, of good carriage, strong, graceful, etc. [Here in jail they] are also sober. Outside, stupefied with drugs or ugly with drink, they would be hard to love. They showed [Deane Mowrer and me] pictures of their children and their faces were alive with love and longing. Afterwards, they lay sorrowful on their beds. But many times too they were triggered by some affront or injustice, screaming or flaring into temper or foul language, and their rage was such that others kept silent until their mutterings died down like the thunder of a summer storm. Arguments, shouting, cursing, laughter. Some nights the arguments on the ward were hideous, sometimes there was wild gaiety, and most vulgar humor."

Imprisonment confronted Dorothy not only with the clandestine sexual activity that occurred among her fellow prisoners in the shadows of jail, but made her reflect on her own sexual past. "I felt myself assaulted by memories of my own sex life, my life with Forster, of the sins of my past life," she wrote "I suddenly realized that this was in the air and if I, a woman of 61, felt this at a time of life where . . . temptations are of the mind more than of the flesh, how much more so in these young ones, whose flesh must cry out fiercely for consummation and fruition."

One of the early hints that the sixties were going to be very different than the fifties was the crowd that gathered with Dorothy in front of City Hall on May 3, 1960. When the air raid sirens howled, five hundred stood in the park and another five hundred on the sidewalks across the street. Laughter greeted police orders to take shelter. In the arrests that followed, it seemed obvious they were under orders not to arrest Dorothy Day. The twenty-five who were arrested were punished with five-day sentences. This time the demonstrators were no longer a subject for editorial ridicule. The *New York World Telegram* said that the war drills were "an exercise in futility." Civil defense would work, the paper added, only if "the enemy's plan is to drop marshmallow puffs." An article in the *New York Post* was headlined, "Laughter in the Park." Clearly the politicians were increasingly uncomfortable with this annual spectacle. Being scolded is one thing, being laughed at another.

The following spring a good two thousand people gathered in cheerful disobedience at City Hall Park. The police arrested a symbolic forty. The protest was not only in front of the mayor's office. All over New York there were individuals and groups refusing to take shelter. The air raid sirens

"One of the greatest evils of the day is the sense of futility. Young people say, 'What can one person do? What is the sense of our small effort?' They cannot see that we can only lay one brick at a time, take one step at a time; we can be responsible only for the one action of the present moment. But we can beg for an increase of love in our hearts that will vitalize and transform these actions, and know that God will take them and multiply them, as Jesus multiplied the loaves and fishes."
—*Catholic Worker*, September 1957

seemed to call people onto the streets rather than underneath them. For Civil Defense officials and politicians, it was a stunning defeat. Not only in New York but elsewhere in America, there were no more compulsory drills. (It happened that Dorothy missed the final round; at the time she was traveling in the Southwest on a speaking trip.)

While the New York press gathered annually to watch Dorothy and others sitting quietly on park benches during air raid drills, no journalist had been present to witness an act of unauthorized sitting on a bus in Montgomery, Alabama. On December 1, 1955, Mrs. Rosa Parks, a seamstress and a devout Christian much respected in Montgomery's black community, declined to give up her seat to a white man in a segregated bus in which blacks were required to sit in the back. Tired from her day of work and tired of all the rituals of racism, she stayed where she was. The driver summoned a policeman, a man who seemed embarrassed at the job which had come to him. "Why didn't you stand up?" he asked Mrs. Parks. "I don't think I should have to," she replied. "Why do you push us around?" "I don't know," said the policeman, "but the law's the law, and you are under arrest." He drove Mrs. Parks to the jail, where she was then locked up. "I don't recall being extremely frightened," she said afterward, "but I felt very much annoyed and inconvenienced because I had hoped to go home and get my dinner, and do whatever else I had to do for the evening. But now here I was sitting in jail and couldn't get home."

Rosa Parks. (Library of Congress)

Her quiet act of self-respect awakened a new will among Montgomery blacks to resist segregation. Some had been waiting for just such a moment, among them a young pastor who had only recently come to Montgomery, Dr. Martin Luther King, Jr. He was a Georgian, and among the rare Christians in America who had a special interest in Gandhi. Four days after Mrs. Parks's arrest, Dr. King was elected president of a new organization, the Montgomery Improvement Association, and a boycott of the city buses began. Black people would rather walk than return to segregated buses, Dr. King announced. Mrs. Parks had been "anchored to that seat," he said, "by the accumulated indignities of days gone by and the boundless aspirations of generations yet unborn."

Almost unnoticed in the boycott's first days, "an experiment in the power of unarmed truth" had begun in Alabama which did much to bring into existence a new, revitalized national civil rights movement. In just over a year, despite much violence against blacks in Montgomery and the bombing of Dr. King's home, the city buses were peacefully integrated.

Dorothy was elated. At last America was taking seriously a method of struggle which sought conversion rather than defeat of opponents, a *nonviolent* way to overcome injustice. "Nonviolence" was suddenly a word in American usage. The nonviolent way of life that Dorothy had long seen in the Gospels was being practiced by increasing numbers of ordinary people, some of whom had been beaten and imprisoned, and others murdered

Civil Rights march. (Maryknoll archives)

Dorothy's special interest in community had long made her aware of Koinonia, a Christian agricultural community at Americus in rural Georgia, where blacks and whites had been quietly living together since 1942. Koinonia (the Greek word for community) had been founded by Clarence and Florence Jordan, local people well aware of the anger many felt toward any who ignored racial segregation. Clarence Jordan, a white Baptist pastor, was a biblical scholar. In his spare time he translated the ancient Greek New Testament into the language of rural Georgia—"the cotton patch translation," as he called it. In sermons and conversations, he was able to say hard things in a comic way. He liked to tell the story of a minister who boasted about how his congregation had raised ten thousand dollars to put a gilded cross on top of the church's steeple. "You got cheated!" Clarence replied. "Times were when Christians could get crosses for free."

The bus boycott in Montgomery, and the Supreme Court decision overturning segregation in education, outraged those committed to racial separation. Tensions rose in Americus as they did in many towns and cities, and some local people began to think it would be a good thing if there was no more Koinonia. Early in 1956, soon after the house of the King family had been bombed in Montgomery, members of the Koinonia community began receiving threatening phone calls. Local people who had been buying eggs and other produce from the community farm canceled their orders. Sales started dropping at their roadside farm stand. Then store owners in Americus refused to sell anything to Koinonia. Just after the U.S. Supreme Court decided that segregation of city buses was unconstitutional, shots were fired at the community farm stand, and a month later—July 1956—the stand was demolished with a dynamite blast. In November, a refrigerated meat case the community owned was destroyed by gunfire. The day after Christmas, the community fuel pump was shot to ruins. In January one of the Koinonia houses was hit by machine-gun fire. In February other houses were targets. The Ku Klux Klan members burned crosses on community land.

The same month Dorothy, who had been following the news closely, decided to spend some days at Koinonia, wanting to meet those she knew only by name, and to keep Lent by sharing in their trials and hopes. She arrived in Americus after a day and night of bus travel from New York and immediately got a taste of local anger. Driving with Florence Jordan to towns in the area, she saw that no one was willing to sell seed to anyone from Koinonia.

In a letter to the community of Saint Joseph's House in New York, she reported on what had happened in the nearby town of Smithfield: "A man dressed in a business suit came out of a store screaming incoherently and followed Florence into the store. She had time to learn that the owner of the store was in Florida and left at once, while the man

Opposite: Dorothy in front of the Chrystie St. Catholic Worker house. (Credit: Robert Lax)

212

"Last night I was shot at for the first time in my life. Elizabeth and I watched from 12 to 3 a.m., she with her accordion, to while away the night watches with hymns, and me with my breviary, remembering the Trappists rising at two. At one thirty we were sitting in the first and second seats of a station wagon, under a floodlight, under a huge oak tree, and a car slowed up as it passed and peppered the car with shot. . . . There was no other sound from the slowed down car which gathered speed and disappeared down the road. The black silence, the sound of shots, so crackling in the still night. These things are ominous. We continued our watch until three but nothing else happened."

—Catholic Worker, May 1957

went on raging . . . . He called us dirty Communist whores and nigger lovers . . . and said that he would see to it that no one would sell to us. He shouted that we should be driven out of town. We left quickly, of course, before a crowd could gather—not that you ever see any evidences of a crowd in these little southern towns."

Refusing the advice of her hosts, Dorothy insisted on joining one of the community members for the midnight-to-three shift at the sentry post set up by a large oak tree at the entrance to Koinonia. The two sat side by side, "Elizabeth with her accordion, to while away the night watches with hymns, and me with my breviary, remembering the Trappists rising at two." Noticing an approaching vehicle had reduced its speed, an intuition of danger led them to duck just as their car was peppered with gunshots. Neither woman was hurt but both were deeply shaken. "Last night I was shot at for the first time in my life," she wrote in her "On Pilgrimage" column for the May 1957 issue, adding that she had "not yet resisted unto blood." (Recalling the event ten years later, Dorothy remarked: "It is strange how the fear always comes afterward, your bones turn to water, and your whole body seems to melt away with fear.")

The drama in Americus was far from over, but Koinonia survived its siege and today lives on friendly terms with its neighbors.

Bonds That Never Break

News came in 1950 that the house on Mott Street, which had served as the base of the New York Catholic Worker since 1936, was to be sold by the owners. New quarters had to be found. At the same time, Dorothy was coming to the decision that a farm closer at hand would be a real benefit—Maryfarm in Newburgh was not only too distant but was not ideal for retreats because of aircraft taking off and landing day and night at nearby Stewart Air Force Base.

Peter Maurin Farm on Staten Island.
(Drawing by Jim Forest)

Before the year was over the Catholic Worker community bought two new properties. The first, twenty-two acres on Staten Island that had a house in reasonably good condition plus a good-sized barn and pond, was christened the Peter Maurin Farm. The other—the new Saint Joseph's House—was a handsome and sizable brick structure at 223 Chrystie Street, a block east of the Bowery, nowadays a gentrified avenue, but in the fifties a grim area notorious for its population of alcoholics and the down-and-out.

Having a farm on nearby Staten Island rather than ninety miles up the Hudson River meant that staff, guests and visitors could get there quickly and cheaply, with a refreshing five-cent ferry ride across New York Harbor en route. Dorothy paid the thousand-dollar down payment using her advance from Harpers for *The Long Loneliness*. (Fourteen years later, with Staten Island becoming more and more citified, the farm was relocated to Tivoli, New York, about an hour's drive north of Manhattan. Dorothy loved the Tivoli farm's sweeping view of the Hudson River.)

The new Saint Joseph's House on Chrystie Street had space within for a large kitchen, dining room, clothing rooms,

"Martyrdom is not gallantly standing before a firing squad. Usually it is the losing of a job because of not taking a loyalty oath, or buying a war bond, or paying a tax. Martyrdom is small, hidden, misunderstood. Or if it is a bloody martyrdom, it is the cry in the dark, the terror, the shame, the loneliness, nobody to hear, nobody to suffer with, let alone to save. Oh, the loneliness of all of us in these days, in all the great moments of our lives, this dying which we do, by little and by little, over a short space of time or over the years."

—Catholic Worker, January 1951

The Catholic Worker dining room on Chrystie St. (Marquette University archives)

offices, library, bathrooms and bedrooms—plus two basements—all for $30,000. It was two buildings made into one, with a central wall in the middle and staircases on either side so that the house could be equally divided, men on one side, women on the other. It was a good fit, the main problem being that the building turned out not to measure up to city housing standards. Inspectors descended on Saint Joseph's House in 1955, compiling a list of code violations, the main one being that it had no sprinkler system in case of fire. Dorothy was brought to court and charged with being a slum landlord: someone putting the residents of a building at risk and doing so for her own profit.

In court Dorothy was confronted with a judge who had no idea who she was and had never heard of the Catholic Worker. "The judge was aggressive," Dorothy reported in the October 1955 issue, "acting as though I were an exploiter of labor. He asked me if the Catholic Worker were a charitable agency, then ruling we were not, determined we were a private enterprise running for profit. . . . He wanted to know if we had a license to solicit funds, [and] who did all the work? When I said we had volunteer labor, he stated that if a man did any work for us and was paid by a meal, we were responsible for any injuries to him while he was with us. . . . His questions were put in such a way that I had a hard time answering before he cut me short with another question. I was put under oath and everything I said was taken down by a stenographer on his little machine. The final words of the judge were that I had better consult a lawyer or I would find myself in a great deal of trouble."

Such experiences impressed on Dorothy "the sad fact that a man was a criminal if he begged, a criminal if he tried to earn his living by selling on the streets without a license, [and] a criminal if he helped his brother in need without being an accredited charitable organization." She felt like a character in Franz Kafka's novel, *The Trial*.

Fortunately, as the weeks passed, *The New York Times* and other newspapers and magazines took an interest in the case, dispatching journalists and photographers to Chrystie Street to interview Dorothy and see what a house of hospitality looked like at close range. Not all the opportunities to make the Catholic Worker and its needs better known attracted Dorothy— she turned down an invitation to appear on a popular television program, "Strike It Rich," but W.H. Auden did it for her. "He was very good and not at all undignified," Dorothy noted in her diary. "They asked him questions about Franz Werfel, Galileo, and had him iden-

The loft at Spring St. (Marquette University archives)

tify the 'Blue Danube Waltz.'" He won $315 for the Catholic Worker and also asked each person in the program's audience to send a dollar to the Catholic Worker.

One consequence of all the media attention was that the judge discovered Dorothy Day wasn't a slum landlord or an abuser of labor. She wasn't jailed and the fine he had imposed was withdrawn. She was also given time to bring the Chrystie Street building up to what the city regarded as necessary safety standards. Donations poured in, often from people who had heard of Dorothy Day and the Catholic Worker only because of all the publicity that the court proceedings had occasioned. It took more than two years, but the building on Chrystie Street was at last able to pass inspection.

The repairs were hardly completed, however, before the City of New York decided that plans for a new subway line would require the demolition of 223 Chrystie Street. In March 1957, the community received an order to vacate. On December 30, 1957, the house was closed.

The only viable solution at the time was far from ideal. A loft was rented on nearby Spring Street in the heart of Little Italy. Dorothy missed the old building but for the moment the loft at 39 Spring Street was the only affordable option in the area adjacent to the Bowery. The space was large enough to absorb guests for free meals without having them wait in line outside, but it had the handicap of being one flight up, accessible only by climbing a steep staircase. As no one could live here, a number of $25-a-month cold-water flats were rented in the neighborhood for

"'Precarity,' or precariousness, is an essential element in true voluntary poverty, a saintly priest from Martinique has written us. 'True poverty is rare,' he writes. 'Nowadays religious communities are good, I am sure, but they are mistaken about poverty. They accept, admit, poverty on principle, but everything must be good and strong, buildings must be fireproof. Precarity is everywhere rejected, and precarity is an essential element of poverty. . . . Precarity enables us better to help the poor. When a community is always building, enlarging, and embellishing, there is nothing left over for the poor. We have no right to do so as long as there are slums and breadlines somewhere.'"
—Catholic Worker, May 1952

David Hennessy, Della Spier (Dorothy's sister), Dorothy, Tamar, and grandchildren. Stanley Vishnewski is in the foreground, left. (Courtesy Tamar Hennessy)

"We are the rich country of the world, like Dives at the feast. We must try hard, we must study to be poor like Lazarus at the gate, who was taken into Abraham's bosom. The Gospel doesn't tell us anything about Lazarus's virtues. He just sat there and let the dogs lick his sores. He would be classed by any social worker of today as a mental case. But again, poverty, and in this case destitution, like hospitality, is so esteemed by God, it is something to be sought after, worked for, the pearl of great price."

—Catholic Worker, July-August 1953

staff plus those who had become part of "the family." Responding to rumors in the press that the closing of the Chrystie Street meant the Catholic Worker was discontinuing its hospitality work, Dorothy wrote in the April 1958 issue of *The Catholic Worker*, "While there are slums, we must live in them, to share the condition of the poor. . . . As for myself I would rather live in an Italian neighborhood where there is such basic Catholicism that the ancient virtue of hospitality is understood."

In fact hospitality to the unwashed proved to be a problem. Many of those living in the vicinity were dismayed to discover that the Catholic Worker attracted a steady flow of people who normally stayed a few blocks to the east, centering their lives on the Bowery. In her journal, Dorothy noted a conversation with a Mr. Guiddoti, a local undertaker who was annoyed that "our Bowery men" were loitering in doorways, drinking, smashing bottles, urinating on walls and in alleys, blocking the sidewalk and "horrifying and frightening his customers." The Catholic Worker breadline was, he said, ruining the neighborhood. "Couldn't we just ask [guests] to walk on the other side of the street? Couldn't we station a watchman at the door to make the men cross the street and not pass his undertaking establishment?"

It took two years before a better location was found—a three-storey structure in poor repair at 175 Chrystie Street, a little south of the old address and not the old building's equal by any measure. The ground floor became a dining room and kitchen, the second floor was used for a social area plus clothing room, while the third floor served as the office. Like the loft on Spring Street, there was no living space. "We have found a landlord who will put up with us," Dorothy noted in her journal. "We have signed a two-year lease at $250 a month." (In 1968, Saint Joseph's House moved to a larger and better building a few blocks to the north, at 36 East First Street, where it remains to this day.)

The problems of finding and maintaining a house of hospitality were huge, with the financial considerations not the hardest part. The most demanding aspect was the frustration and exhaustion of living with people, both guests and co-workers, whose needs were overwhelming—nor, for them, was Dorothy the easiest person to work with. In a 1953 journal entry, Dorothy wrote: "Yesterday was so desperately hard. I had to come down here [to Staten Island] last night . . . to hold myself together. Cannot sleep. Nerves and fatigue. [I feel like] an empty cistern. I must rest here quietly spending hours in the chapel—beyond the sound of human voices." In a journal entry made the next year, Dorothy remarked on the failure to "pay enough attention to each other because of tremendous pressure of visitors, house, breadline, mail, etc. I am conscious daily of erring in this regard."

Admirers of the Catholic Worker might look on from a distance at what they imagined was happening in a house of hospitality, seeing it in the warm light of sentimentality, but sentiment does not sustain participating in such work year after year. More than anything, Dorothy often pointed out, hospitality and life in community are acts of will. "Love in action," she said so often, quoting a line from Dostoevsky's novel, *The Brothers Karamazov*, "is a harsh and dreadful thing compared to love in dreams." Staff members found much to argue about, disagreeing with each other and with Dorothy on issues that ranged from religion and ideology to who should receive the occasional small donations of such luxury food items as eggs and butter. It was no rare event for a member of staff to leave abruptly, worn out from the work, infuriated with someone else on staff, and sometimes disillusioned with Dorothy. But there were others who came for years, even decades, and who died within the community.

In the same period the marriage of Tamar and David Hennessy was coming undone. There had been difficulties for years. In a 1952 letter to Tamar, Dorothy wrote that she been praying "to [G.K.] Chesterton and Eric Gill [both people David greatly admired] to find David better and more satisfying work and to take special care of him. . . . I think you are a wonder and growing all the time, through troubles and vicissitudes too. It is always hard when the babies are all small. You can do so much and have so much too, so many interests."

Dorothy with one of her grandchildren.
(Courtesy Tamar Hennessy)

"While I was in Mexico I talked with a saintly old priest, 80, and all he talked about was the need for suffering, the joy in suffering, and how we had to bear our share, and I just burst into tears, and I told him I found it very hard to take, just to think of all the suffering that might happen to Tamar and the family, for instance. . . . If we could only learn that the only important thing is love, and that we will be judged on love—to keep on loving, and showing that love, and expressing that love, over and over, whether we feel it or not, seventy times seven, to mother-in-law, to husbands, to children—and to be oblivious of insult, or hurt, or injury. It is a hard, hard doctrine. Where there is no love, put love and you will take out love, St. John of the Cross says. I am preaching to myself too."
—To Dorothy Gauchat,
February 11, 1958

In a letter written six years later, Dorothy notes that David was again unable to find a job and that Tamar was struggling with loneliness—"there are no young neighbors with children; her ambitions to farm, to garden, to keep animals are constantly thwarted by lack of money." What money they had often came from Dorothy, a sharing of income from her writings plus occasional checks from speaking.

She had "been worrying so much about Tamar and David and their attitudes," Dorothy noted in her diary October 22, 1959. Even so, she was doggedly optimistic: "They see each other's faults and are solidly Catholic so they'll stick together and work it out." She was reassured in reflecting that the children took good care of each other. David's efforts to make a living had never been successful. A home-based mail-order business he had started, the Distributist Book Stall, lost more income than it generated. Toward the end, Dorothy received letters from customers complaining about having paid for books they never received. Jobs off the farm were necessary but hard to find, and, once found, proved short-lived.

In a January 1960 diary entry, Dorothy noted that David "is overcome by a sense of futility." A diary entry a few months later referred to a "psychologist who says David must learn to drive." In August 1961, she recorded that David had entered a Vermont mental hospital. By the end of the year, he was out of the hospital, but had moved to Washington, D.C. His marriage with Tamar ended in permanent separation. "No one knows his address in Washington," Dorothy wrote to Fritz Eichenberg in 1964. "One of our friends ran into him, and he told him he was dishwashing and living in a furnished room. The psychiatrist said it was anxiety and fear of responsibility and so on that led to his collapse. We pray for him that he get a job in a bookshop which might be the beginning of his healing. It is horrible for men to have work to do that they loathe." While a great deal of Dorothy's life made its way into her monthly columns, the marital struggles Tamar and David faced were not included, only reports of her visits with them and the joy she took in her grandchildren.

One other important event was unmentioned. While readers of *The Long Loneliness* were left with the impression that Dorothy's association with Forster Batterham had ended with the breakup that followed Tamar's birth in 1927, in fact they remained in touch throughout Dorothy's life. Two years after their separation, Forster found a new partner, Nanette, with whom he lived for the next three decades, sharing a bungalow on Staten Island. In September 1959, Forster contacted Dorothy to tell her Nanette was dying of cancer and to ask if Dorothy could find time to help care for her. Dorothy said yes. Two other women also assisted: Lily Burke, Forster's sister, and Jean Walsh, a nurse who belonged to the Catholic Worker community. "Nanette was a sweet, sweet woman, beautiful and childlike," Jean Walsh recalled in an inter-

Dorothy reading to her grandchildren. (Marquette University archives)

view with Rosalie Riegle, "so innocent and so uninhibited. I remember one day Nanette was all excited, telling me that when she got well, she was going to give all her clothes away and her jewelry and live like Dorothy did, like Jesus."

Many of Dorothy's journal entries in that period have to do with the last months of Nanette's life. "Forster awakened me early, weeping that Nanette could not get up, so I rushed down," Dorothy noted in October 1959. "She was dizzy, felt bilious, could eat nothing. When the nurse came she told her to drink more liquids, she tried eating some soup."

In November, Dorothy brought Nanette a relic of Saint Therese of Lisieux, noting that Nanette had "been having a very hard time . . . pain all through her. She lay there and cried pitifully today. There is so little one can do, except just be there and say nothing. . . . I told her how hard it was to comfort her, one could only keep silence in the face of suffer-

Tamar and Forster. (Courtesy Tamar Hennessy)

"Nanette has been having a very hard time. There is so little one can do, except just be there and say nothing. I tried to talk to her—telling her the history of Ammon to distract her. I told her how hard it was to comfort her, one could only keep silence in the face of suffering, and she cried bitterly, 'Yes, the silence of death.' I told her I would pray the Rosary for her."

—November 25, 1959

ing, and she said bitterly, 'Yes, the silence of death.' I told her I would pray the rosary for her."

By December Nanette's decline had reached the point of her wanting to commit suicide. Forster was in a state of almost constant grief, to the point Dorothy was irritated with his tears. "I get so impatient at him and his constant fleeing from her, his self-pity, his weeping," Dorothy noted the day after Christmas, "that I feel hard and must fight to overcome it. Such fear of sickness and death. I think it was Father Faber who said, 'Do not add one straw to the burden another is carrying.'"

As 1960 began, Nanette "cried out [that] she was losing her mind and screamed continually," Dorothy noted. "Nanette cannot believe she has cancer since the doctor refused to tell her or let others tell her. 'If it were malignant why don't they use radium? If it is a high infection why don't they use antibiotics? Why don't they give something for the nerves?' And she screams out that he has been lying to her, everyone has been lying to her. It is inexpressibly painful to hear her despairing. And Forster keeps running away. He would like to go in a coma and escape it all."

On January 7, the eve of her death, Nanette asked to be baptized. "[Jean Walsh and I] said the rosary together and at eleven, Lucille baptized her. [Nanette] had said many times she was sorry for her sins, had asked God's mercy, had kissed [an image of Jesus], [and] had venerated the relic of the Little Flower."

"The Cross was not as hard as this," Nanette told Dorothy in her last hours. "People in concentration camps suffered like this, she said, showing her arms. She died peacefully, after a hemorrhage. She had a slight smile, calm and peaceful."

Concordances, Not Differences

Soon after the death of Pope Pius XII on October 9, 1958, the College of Cardinals elected his successor: Angelo Roncalli, the seventy-six year old Metropolitan of Venice. It was a choice that surprised observers. Journalists reporting from the Vatican saw him as a "compromise candidate" and a "transitional pope." They assumed that the Catholic Church would experience a few quiet years under the gentle care of an elderly traditionalist who would not rock the boat. Roncalli chose the name John (unused by Bishops of Rome since the fourteenth century) and in his first message following election quoted from the Gospel of John: "My children, love one another. Love one another because this is the greatest commandment of the Lord."

Far from being a pope-between-popes, this large, homely Italian, though most orthodox and pious, proved to be a quiet revolutionary. The duty of the Pope, he explained, was not only to guard the treasure of faith but to devote himself, "with joy and without fear to the work of giving this ancient and eternal doctrine a relevancy corresponding to the conditions of our era." He summed up his program in a single Italian word, *aggiornamento* ("bringing up to date"), that quickly became part of the world's vocabulary. The Church was not a museum, John announced. The time had come to open the windows and let in some fresh air.

Popes have often seemed remote, legalistic and condemning. John XXIII impressed the world as a man of compassion, enthusiasm, hospitality and renewal. The contrast with his immediate predecessor was startling. Pius XII had excommunicated Catholics who cooperated with Communists, while John appealed to Catholics not to allow any political and religious divisions—even between Marxism and Christianity—to impede cooperation in the service of peace and the common good. Granting a private audience to the son-in-law of the Soviet premier, Nikita Khrushchev,

Pope John XXIII. (Maryknoll archives)

"Immediately following his election as pope [John XXIII] went to visit the prison in Rome—'You could not come to see me, so I came to see you,' he told the prisoners. Every day of his long priestly life he had prayed at the third hour of the office, 'Let our love be set aflame by the fire of Your love and its heat in turn enkindle love in our neighbors.' God had so answered his prayer that his own love kindled a fire which is sweeping over the world, and the whole Church is enkindled."
—"Reflections During Advent," Ave Maria Magazine, December 17, 1966

Pope John gave an unprecedented example of Christian-Marxist encounter. At least in the papal apartments, doors in Rome that had long been locked were suddenly opening.

John had been pope barely three months when he surprised the world and astonished the cardinals by announcing his intention to convene a council, only the second such event in four hundred years. It had been nearly a century since the First Vatican Council, an event cut short by the military occupation of Rome and the fall of the Papal States. That council's only memorable accomplishment had been its proclamation that, in matters of faith and morals, the Roman Pontiff could speak with infallibility. It was a dogma that had occasioned a schism and widened the distance between Catholics and other Christians. A century later, it remained a point of controversy even within the Catholic Church.

This new council, said John, would declare no dogmas, issue no condemnations or excommunications, and do nothing to inflame hostility or sanction enmity. It would be a "pastoral" council helping to restore "the simple and pure lines that the face of the Church of Jesus had at its birth."

"We must seek concordances, not differences," said John, words Dorothy often repeated in the years that followed. It was advice summarizing her long-standing commitment to seek areas of agreement and cooperation with those whom Catholics had so often regarded as enemies to be met only in combat.

The same month that Pope John announced his plan for a Council—January 1959—a revolution led by a young, radical lawyer, Fidel Castro, achieved victory in the Catholic country of Cuba, just ninety miles from Florida. The regime of Fulgencio Batista had been defeated—"one of the most bloody and repressive dictatorships in the long history of Latin American repression," in the words of President John Kennedy.

Many Americans were alarmed by the revolution in nearby Cuba. The U.S. Central Intelligence Agency began to explore means of bringing about the collapse of Castro's regime. But Dorothy was one of those who greeted the changes in Cuba with hope. Here was a situation in which we should be seeking, she said, "concordances, not differences." The possibility of visiting Cuba haunted her.

On April 17, 1961, twelve hundred anti-Castro Cuban exiles landed at the Bay of Pigs on the southwestern coast of Cuba. They had been trained and supplied by the Central Intelligence Agency, which anticipated that the landing would spark a country-wide counter-revolution. In fact the invasion only unified the country and strengthened support for Castro. Most of the invaders were captured alive—more than a thousand—and were later returned to the United States in exchange for food and medicine.

One of the few *Catholic Worker* readers in Cuba, Mario Gonzalez, wrote to Dorothy in 1962 appealing for help. He wondered if it would not be possible for some Catholic bishops from the United States to come to Cuba on "a journey of reconciliation" to demonstrate that "the Church is really interested in uniting all Christians under one banner of humility and love." Perhaps even "the new, healthy Pope" would come and make an appeal from Cuba, asking Americans "to give up hatred." The bishops in Cuba, he

Che Guevara, center, and Fidel Castro, left, celebrate the victory of the Cuban Revolution. (Maryknoll archives)

"We are certainly not Marxist socialists, nor do we believe in violent revolution. Yet we do believe that it is better to revolt, to fight, as Castro did with his handful of men, than to do nothing. . . . God bless the priests and people of Cuba. God bless Castro and all those who are seeing Christ in the poor. God bless all those who are seeking the brotherhood of man because in loving their brothers they love God, even though they deny Him."

—*Catholic Worker*, July-August 1961

Fidel Castro. (Maryknoll archives)

"Man needs work and the opportunity to work, the tools, the strength, the will to work. And when we see Castro dealing with the problem of unemployment and poverty and illiteracy, we can only say, 'We will see this good in him, that which is God in every man,' and we will pray for him and for his country daily."

—Catholic Worker, December 1961

added, had been close to the former corrupt government. Under Batista, they had enjoyed much power and wealth. They needed a "lesson in humility" that would inspire them to stop living like royalty and to turn their estates into houses of hospitality, schools and hospitals.

Rather than urge any bishop to make such a journey, Dorothy decided to go herself, successfully applying for visas both from the U.S. State Department and its Cuban counterpart. "I go to see Christ in my brother the Cuban, and that means Christ in the revolutionary, [and] Christ in the counter-revolutionary," she wrote in her diary, "but to both sides, being violently partisan, such an attitude will be considered reasonable by neither." For eighty dollars she bought a tourist class ticket for a round-trip voyage from Jersey City to Havana, one of the last commercial tickets to Cuba sold in the United States in that decade, as it turned out. After weeks of daily tutoring in Spanish at the Berlitz School in New York, Dorothy sailed aboard the *Guadalupe*, a Spanish ship on which Mass was celebrated daily.

After three days at sea, Dorothy arrived in Havana on September 8. She checked into a small hotel, then delivered several cartons of medical supplies to the National Hospital. She managed to hear Castro speak at a rally in Havana's Chaplin Theater and to interview a Dr. Ortega, a physician who had been educated in New York and practiced medicine there for years before returning to Cuba. "He is heart and soul in the revolution." Dorothy noted, but also "against euthanasia, abortion, and birth control." Ortega described the urgent effort underway to set up free medical clinics throughout the country and to launch programs for the prevention of common illnesses, one of which was to provide shoes for all children so that such parasites as hookworms could not enter the body.

After a few days Dorothy obtained press credentials, but these were almost immediately cancelled—all credentials issued to American journalists were withdrawn by the Cuban government in light of the rapidly deteriorating relations between the two countries. However, before the courier brought the cancellation order to her hotel, Dorothy had checked out and was on her suitcase "in a long line in the bus station, in a mob of soldiers, campesinos, and their wives and children." At about four in the morning, Dorothy began the eighteen-hour passage to Oriente Province, the eastern tip of Cuba, on the first of the many overcrowded buses that carried her little by little around the island.

Dorothy's plan was to have an unguided and unmonitored look at ordinary Cubans and their country. She was not interested in political reporting, but in offering her readers what Thomas Merton had called insights into "the human dimension," a level beneath politics. "I am here to write, not to embarrass governments," Dorothy wrote in her diary.

In her diary, published over several months in *The Catholic Worker*, Dorothy described her encounters with ordinary people ignored by the mass media. She told of families living in dirt-floor houses in areas still without electricity where old and young gathered around oil lamps at night to learn to read. She took note of what she found on the shelves in village shops: tins of evaporated milk, pencils, paper and books. Everywhere she noticed schools and clinics being opened. Despite the hardship and shortages, it seemed to her that the people were animated by hope. In earlier times the land had either belonged to powerful American companies or to a few wealthy Cuban families—now it was theirs. Poverty remained, but serfdom was finished. Literacy and books were finding their way into every family.

The American press at the time was emphasizing the exodus of many priests from Cuba and the tensions between the Church and the young Communist government. Dorothy emphasized that, no matter where she went, she was able to participate in Mass each day, and that everywhere she found people involved in the Church and willing to talk about both the inspirations and the problems they, as believers, found in

Cover of *The Catholic Worker* with Dorothy's account of her Cuba pilgrimage.

"I must confess that righteous wrath as well as any kind of wrath wearies me. Rebellion, too, I find exhausting. To grow in love, to rejoice, to be happy and thankful even, that we are living in such parlous times and not just benefiting unwittingly by the toil and suffering of others—rejoicing even that there is every sign that we are going to be give a chance to expiate here and now for our sins of omission and commission—and so to help the revolution and convert the revolutionaries. This is a dream worth dreaming."
—*Catholic Worker*, July-August 1962

227

Dorothy in the Catholic Worker office with Charles Butterworth and Ed Turner. (Marquette University archives)

"Several of our old editors have accused us of giving up our pacifism. What nonsense. We are unalterably opposed to armed resistance and armed revolt from the admittedly intolerable conditions all through Latin America as we ever were. . . . No one expects that Fidel will become another Martin of Tours or Ignatius and lay down his arms. But we pray the grace of God will grow in him and that with a better social order, grace will build on the natural good, and the Church will be free to function, giving us the Sacraments and the preaching and teaching of the Man of Peace, Jesus."
—Catholic Worker, September 1962

revolutionary Cuba. Some of them found it very difficult.

One mother asked Dorothy, "How can we send our children to schools where Marxism-Leninism is taught? How can we take part in groups that are led by Marxists? How can we cooperate in such a society?" Dorothy responded by describing the children of American black families who were insulted and jeered for entering schools that had previously been all white. One must be ready to withstand abuse and contempt, she said, and always be ready "to find concordances, as our Holy Father has urged, rather than to seek out heresies, to work as far as one can with the revolution, and always to be ready to give a reason for the faith that is in us." She carried with her two Catholic catechisms recently published on Cuban government presses, one for beginners, the other for more advanced students. Such booklets, she said, suggested that the government was seeking to fulfill its commitment to respect religious belief and the rights of the Church.

Wherever she went, Dorothy spoke about the Catholic Worker movement, its philosophy of work and its life of community with the poor and the oppressed. There had been no equivalent movement in Cuba, she realized. If only, she said, the Church had been less concerned with its own privileges and the comfort of the clergy and more concerned about the poor. So many priests "wear their lives away building ever bigger buildings and institutions while the family and the poor are left to the state to care for." Whenever religion ignores the urgent needs of the poor, offering them nothing but assurances of happiness after death, "then that religion is suspect." But Dorothy, disturbed about the arrest of priests who were charged with opposing the revolution, sent a telegram to Castro appealing for their release.

Dorothy's Cuban diary disturbed a number of her readers, some of them former co-workers. While respecting her wish to see events from the bottom, many regarded her as naive about the fate of the Church in Cuba. Others wondered how she could be so uncritical of a revolution that had been brought about by violent means. "Several of our old editors have accused us of giving up our pacifism," Dorothy noted. "What nonsense." She reaffirmed her opposition to violence, whether in war, revolution or the treatment of prisoners. "We are certainly not Marxist socialists nor do we believe in violent revolution. Yet we believe it is better to revolt, to fight as Castro did with his handful of men, than to do nothing." Nonetheless, she insisted, her own path remained the nonviolent way of the Cross. Not the least part of her own suffering, she said, was the recognition "that so much suffering is unnecessary" and that so many who represent the Church "are shouting 'Lord, Lord' and yet denying Him in his poor, denying Him in their acceptance of the armies of the State." She pointed out that one of the unfortunate points of concordance existing between Marxists and most Catholics is that "both believe that there is nothing nobler for a young man than to bear arms for his country."

Dorothy's month-long stay in Cuba ended October 11, 1962, the very day the first session of the Second Vatican Council was convened in Saint Peter's Basilica in Rome, the vast church barely large enough to contain the flood of bishops, theologians, observers and journalists. But within several days world attention abruptly shifted from the Vatican to Cuba. American spy planes had discovered that Soviet medium-range missiles capable of carrying nuclear weapons were being based in Cuba. Castro admitted it, saying they were there to deter further U.S. invasions. On October 22, the U.S. government announced that it had placed Cuba under "naval quarantine." The United States demanded that the Soviets withdraw the missiles. American armed forces were put on alert, ready for war should the demand be ignored. A nuclear war between the superpowers suddenly became an immediate possibility.

The fact that there was no war, it was learned only years later, was partly thanks to Pope John's personal intermediary role—carried on despite his losing struggle with cancer—with both Kennedy and Khrushchev. It was an extraordinary effort to find points of agreement and compromise when accord seemed impossible and the smell of World War III was in the air. In less than a week, a bargain was struck: Soviet missiles would be withdrawn from Cuba and the missile bases dismantled—an apparent "backing down" of the Russians before U.S. threats. Unseen by the world public was a parallel

Protest of Women Strike for Peace during the Cuban Missile Crisis.

Dorothy in Rome with members of a pilgrimage of "Mothers for Peace." (Marquette University archives)

withdrawal of U.S. nuclear-armed missiles based near the Soviet border in Turkey. At the same time, the United States made a secret pledge not to undertake or assist any further invasions of Cuba.

One of the least visible figures at the Vatican Council was the Pope himself. John followed the proceedings by closed-circuit television from his private apartment overlooking Saint Peter's Square. Despite his end-of-life battle with stomach cancer, he managed to carry on with his various responsibilities, speaking to huge public audiences at least once a week.

Perhaps Pope John's most enduring undertaking in his final year was writing an encyclical letter addressed not only to his fellow Catholics, the usual audience for such papal documents, but to "every person of good will." *Pacem in Terris* (Peace on Earth) was signed and made public on Holy Thursday, April 11, 1963. Stressing that the most basic human right of all was the right to live, Pope John spoke eloquently of the "urgent demand that the arms race should cease," for the greatest threat to life was war. Peace between East and West, John said, was not only possible but essential. Nuclear weapons, being the worst of the weapons of mass destruction, should be entirely banned. States should enter into binding agreements to bring about the elimination of all weapons of mass destruction whether atomic, chemical or biological. For centuries the Church had tolerated wars while trying to mitigate their worst consequences. John now declared that developments in weaponry were such that it had become "irrational to argue that war can be considered a fit means to restore violated rights."

Nor did the Pope agree that the work of peacemaking should be entrusted only to the powerful and prominent—it was everyone's responsibility. "There is an immense task incumbent on every person of good will, namely the task of restoring the relations of the human family in truth, in justice, in love, and in freedom." While recognizing that at present those "endeavoring to restore the relations of social life are not many," he pleaded with them to persevere. He found comfort in the hope "that their number will increase, especially among those who believe." Engagement in peacemaking is not for an isolated minority but for everyone; it "is an imperative duty; it is a requirement of love."

Pacem in Terris, whose spirit and principles had long been anticipated by Dorothy, was still in the headlines when she sailed for Rome as one of fifty "Mothers for Peace." This was, she said, "a true pilgrimage to the Holy City of Rome, to the head of the Church on earth . . . to present ourselves as though the first fruit of his great encyclical, *Pacem in Terris*, to thank him, to pledge ourselves to the work for peace, and to ask, too, for a more radical condemnation of the instruments of modern warfare." The mothers came from many countries and reflected the diversity of belief, religious and non-religious, found among those working for peace. A few were friends of Dorothy, including Hildegard Goss-Mayr from Vienna, secretary of the International Fellowship of Reconciliation, and Hermene Evans and Marguerite Harris, both Americans, who together had provided for Dorothy's ticket and travel expenses.

"We will meditate on [Pope John's] words to us all, because he said he was addressing all men of good will, and we will know, too, as we have known in the past, how difficult it is to apply these words to individual situations. We need all the gifts of the Holy Spirit for our work; we need all the help of our guardian angels."

—Catholic Worker, June 1963

The group had hoped that, despite Pope John's illness, a private audience with him might be possible. Hildegard, Marguerite and Dorothy drafted a letter proposing such a meeting, explaining the group's purpose. It was given to one of the Pope's secretaries, but there was no response. Other meetings did occur, however, including a long discussion with Cardinal Augustin Bea, head of the Vatican's Secretariat for Christian Unity, a close friend of Pope John's and a leading figure in the Council. After the women had abandoned any hope for more personal contact with the Pope, they were invited to be among those participating in his weekly public audience.

John was late in arriving, Dorothy wrote in *The Catholic Worker*. "Finally there was a surge in the vast mob within

"At three o'clock that afternoon someone came in with news of the Pope's death. It had been a long agony, and daily I had prayed the Eastern Rite prayer for 'a death without pain' for this most beloved Father to all the world. But I am afraid he left us with the suffering which is an inevitable part of love, and he left us with fear too, if the reports of his last words are correct, fear that his children, as he called all of us in the world, were not listening to his cries for pacem in terris."

—Catholic Worker, June 1963

Saint Peter's Basilica and a sudden silence followed by almost a roar of greeting. Borne aloft on his chair, the procession proceeded around the columns and then the Pope, blessing all, was conducted up to his throne where he sat while a list of all the pilgrim groups was read aloud.... And our pilgrimage was not even mentioned!" She imagined that no one had even made the Pope aware of the one pilgrimage group that had come in response to his peace encyclical. "But then the Pope began to speak and the words seemed directed to us." He expressed his gratitude and encouragement to the "Pilgrims for Peace." He thanked them for their message, said it brought comfort to his heart, blessed them and asked them to continue in their labors for peace. The women, wearing their large "Mothers for Peace" buttons, immediately became the attention point for others in the basilica. "It seemed too good to be true," Dorothy wrote, "and if those around us had not kept assuring us he was speaking to us, I would have considered it but a coincidence that he spoke as he did. Our message had reached him, impossible though it seemed."

Dorothy saw Pope John once again, May 22, the day before her departure. He was too weak to leave his apartment (in earlier times these were rooms for servants of the papal household), but stood at a window, leading the crowd in the recitation of the Angelus prayer. It was his next-to-last public appearance. He died June 3, just after Dorothy's arrival back in New York. For a huge part of humanity, not only for Catholics, it was a death in the family.

Pope John's final days had been painful, Dorothy wrote in The Catholic Worker, and these sufferings, he made known, were offered by him as a prayer for the Council and for world peace. "He had said, almost cheerfully," Dorothy continued, "that his bags were packed, and that he was ready to go, and that, after all, death was the beginning of a new life."

Angelo Roncalli—John—had been Pope only fifty-six months, but it was long enough. "He left us closer to God," one of the cardinals said when the council resumed, "and the world a better place to live." Certainly neither the Church nor the world was quite the same, which enraged those who opposed the Council, but moved far more to gratitude.

That fall, Dorothy was in Europe once again. In England to speak at the annual meeting of the Pax Association, a Catholic peace group, Dorothy took time to go to London's Highgate Cemetery to visit the grave of Karl Marx. "The grave stands out because of its huge iron bust of Marx," Dorothy wrote her sister Della. She described the mist, a crucifix standing opposite, the birds singing, and the fresh red roses someone had left on Marx's grave—also confessing that, despite all the followers of Marx she had known, she had never read anything Marx wrote. Dorothy prayed for Marx's wife, Jenny, who for years had almost nothing but bread and potatoes to feed her family in their two-room Soho apartment. Several of their children had died of the consequences of destitution. Dorothy recalled how Jenny sought frantically for loans in order to buy a coffin for one daughter. While Marx wrote his books, his wife suffered several nervous breakdowns.

Grave of Karl Marx at Highgate Cemetery in London. (Credit: Robert Ellsberg)

Dorothy's days in London included a boat ride up the Thames to Greenwich and a visit with Muriel Lester, in whose house of hospitality in the East End of London Gandhi had stayed in 1931. Dorothy had a day with the Benedictine nuns at Stanbrook Abbey and another day in the university town of Cambridge. A particular joy of her time in England was meeting Donald Attwater, much of whose scholarly work had been devoted to writings on the history of Christianity and the lives of the saints, East and West.

There was a refreshing stay with the Taena Community near Gloucester. Here twelve adults, twenty-three children, thirty-five cows, forty-five sheep and eighty chickens shared one hundred and thirty acres. Dorothy stayed in a stone farmhouse that stood on sixteenth-century foundations "with, God forbid, no central heating." In her column, she described an animated discussion with the children of the family about the annual bonfires which consume the effigy of Guy Fawkes, executed centuries earlier on the charge of having tried to blow up Parliament. Days before the annual bonfire, Dorothy found the straw-stuffed figure at home in the living room, man-sized, with a clown face, lolling comfortably in an easy chair. "Rebecca sits on his lap and Rachael wags his

The Second Vatican Council.
(Maryknoll archives)

"These pains which went with the fast seemed to reach into my very bones, and I could only feel that I had been given some little intimation of the hunger of the world. God help us, living as we do, in the richest country in the world and so far from approaching the voluntary poverty we esteem and reach toward."
—*Catholic Worker*, November 1965

head, but he will not be treated so kindly next week . . . It occurred to me to be shocked by all this, and I suggested that the children have a trial and pardon the dynamiter, but they will have none of it."

Dorothy made two more trips to Rome. In September 1965 she sailed with Eileen Egan, a close friend who directed the work of Catholic Relief Services in South Asia and who also was a founder of the American branch of Pax (later the U.S. section of Pax Christi International). They brought with them several hundred copies of a special issue of *The Catholic Worker* on "The Council and the Bomb." The third and final session of the Vatican Council was about to get underway. Its agenda included completion of a text, passages of which had aroused active opposition from the American military establishment. Schema 13, as it was called in the drafting stage, finally was published as the Pastoral Constitution on the Church in the Modern World, *Gaudium et Spes.*

Once again Dorothy was part of a community of women, this time only twenty and all Catholics. They had committed themselves to a rigorous ten-day fast expressing, Dorothy said, "our prayer and our hope" that the Council would issue "a clear statement, 'Put away thy sword.'" The fasters hoped the council would endorse active nonviolence as an appropriate means of struggle for social justice, condemn weapons of mass destruction, and express support for those who refused to do military service.

After several days of meeting with bishops and others active in the council, Dorothy enjoyed an evening meal at Il Scoglio, a noted Roman restaurant. "I felt rather guilty at prefacing a penitential fast in this way," she confessed to readers of her column, "but Eileen reminded me that, after all, Lent was prefaced by carnivale." The next morning, after an Eastern-rite Mass at Saint Peter's, Dorothy made her way to the Cenacle on Piazza Priscilla at the edge of Rome where the women would be lodged during their fast. Each day that followed began with an early Mass. Times of common prayer, reading and conversation were scattered through the day. There was a daily lecture. At 6 P.M. a doctor visited to be sure of each faster's well-being. The only nourishment taken was water.

Dorothy had fasted before and expected hunger, headaches and nausea, but instead experienced a deeper and different suffering than she had ever known in the past. "I had offered my fast in part for the victims of famine all over the world, and it seemed to me that I had very special pains . . . a kind I had never known before which seemed to pierce to the very marrow of my bones as I lay down at night." She was sixty-seven and as accustomed as she could manage to arthritic pain which, she said in letters, "one accepts as part of age." In such pains she found "an intimation of the hunger of the world." Rest eluded her at night. In the day she was refreshed by knitting, reading, and conversation with visitors—some of them bishops and abbots—who had learned of the fast despite the fasters' avoidance of publicity.

On the night of October 10, the fast ended, as it had begun, with prayer. Hard though it had been for Dorothy, she regarded it as a "widow's mite, a few loaves and fishes. May we try harder to do more in the future."

Dorothy made no claim that this almost invisible act of witness had significant influence on the bishops taking part in the Council, or that it had been more important than the public exhibition on nonviolence and peacemaking that had been set up for the bishops by the organizers of the fast, the Community of the Ark, a European movement founded by Lanza del Vasto, a Catholic disciple of Gandhi. But she was convinced that prayer and fasting had a power that even believers rarely imagine. In a hidden but significant way, the fasting women had contributed to the work of the Council.

Dorothy had reason to rejoice in December when, on the next-to-last day of the Council, the Constitution on the Church in the Modern World was made public, complete with many controversial passages. The text included the only specific condemnation produced by the Second Vatican Council:

Lanza del Vasto, founder of the Community of the Ark. (Credit: Jim Forest)

Every act of war directed to the indiscriminate destruction of whole cities or vast areas with their inhabitants is a crime against God and humanity, which merits firm and unequivocal condemnation.

Dorothy reading galleys, 1962. (Credit: Mottke Weissman)

"As Pope John told the pilgrimage of women, Mothers for Peace, the seventy-five of us who went over to Rome to thank him for his encyclical Pacem in Terris, just the month before his death, 'The beginnings of peace are in your own hearts, in your own families, schoolrooms, offices, parishes, and neighborhoods.' It is working from the ground up, from the poverty of the stable, in works as at Nazareth, and also in going from town to town, as in the public life of Jesus two thousand years ago. And since a thousand years are as one day, and Christianity but two days old, let us take heart and start over."—December 1965

Emphasizing the role of conscience, the bishops called on states to make legal provision for those "who, for reasons of conscience, refuse to bear arms, provided that they agree to serve the human community in some other way." Those who renounce violence altogether, seeking a more just and compassionate society by nonviolent means, were honored:

We cannot fail to praise those who renounce the use of violence in vindication of their rights and who resort to methods of defense which are otherwise available to weaker parties too, provided this can be done without injury to the rights and duties of others or to the community itself.

Those who, in the name of obedience, obey commands which condemn the innocent and defenseless were described as "criminal," while those who disobey such corrupt commands merit "supreme commendation."

Though the final document contained numerous indications of compromise, the Council text was a ringing vindication for Dorothy and the Catholic Worker movement.

When Dorothy was next in Rome, for the International Congress of the Laity in October 1967, she was an honored and well-cared-for guest. Of the Americans present, she was one of two—the other was an astronaut—invited to receive Communion from the hands of Pope Paul VI during the final Mass of the Congress in Saint Peter's Basilica. What had she felt about this privilege, a journalist asked. "I could think nothing, feel nothing," she responded, "but only to say a most heartfelt prayer for Pope Paul, who had been ill and who looked that morning as though he were under a great strain." She prayed for others as well, she said, including "all those nonviolent ones who are in prison today, for their conscientious objection to this terrible Vietnam war in which we are now engaged."

A Time of Burning Children

The sixties was both a decade of many sad and terrible events—invasions, wars, assassinations, the murder of civil rights workers—as well as of extraordinary breakthroughs, including publication of Pope John XXIII's *Pacem in Terris*, the Second Vatican Council, and the passage by the U.S. Congress of the Civil Rights Act in 1964 and the Voting Rights Act of 1965 which gave it teeth. It was also a period of immense social dislocation and experiments in new life styles, ranging from a wide range of attempts in community life to the use of psychedelic drugs. In San Francisco, a rundown section called Haight-Ashbury became a colorful mecca for "flower children," while the Catholic Worker's neighborhood in New York—now christened the East Village—acquired a similar reputation. Thousands of young people, whose parents had been models of hard work, good behavior, success and patriotism, found themselves radically estranged from America's political, economic and cultural structures—a division that was tagged the "generation gap."

The sixties hit the Catholic Worker with hurricane force. Some of those who helped invent and define the counter-culture of the sixties were drawn to the New York Catholic

Dorothy with *Catholic Worker* editors Charles Butterworth, Ed Turner, Judith Gregory, Walter Kerell, 1962.

(Marquette University archives)

"One of the things which bothers me mightily is the bitterness and criticism of angry young men. Do pray for them and all such. Sometimes I try to tell myself, finding myself too critical, 'they are prophets crying out in this time.' But there are too many of them. Around a place like the Catholic Worker there are always too many, too much of the rebellious spirit. . . . All this rebellion makes me long for obedience, hunger and thirst for it. . . ."

—To Thomas Merton,
October 10, 1960

Worker, staying as long as Dorothy's welcome lasted—and sometimes longer..

In the case of the New York house, while some joined after asking Dorothy if they might become part of the staff, in fact her permission wasn't essential or always sought. There was no formal entrance procedure—no forms to fill out, no tests, no interviews, no letters of reference, no agreed-upon commitments, no training program, no novitiate. You arrived and began to help. You either rented your own apartment—in 1961, $25 a month was enough to get a room or even two—or some member of the staff, whose rent was paid by the community, would offer use of a spare bed or a mattress on the floor. Your work might mean collecting food, assisting in cooking meals, washing up afterward, cleaning the house, helping distribute clothing, or, more than likely, all of the above. If you became a fixed part of the community and Dorothy valued your involvement, at some point your name might be added to *The Catholic Worker* masthead, the paper's list of assistant editors.

In the thirties, forties and fifties, most of those drawn to the Catholic Worker were in fact practicing Catholics who came because they were excited by the vision the newspaper promoted and wanted to help put it into practice. But in the sixties and afterward, the attraction for some volunteers was that the Catholic Worker represented an alternative way of life in which there were no rules, or at least none that were enforced. Many communities, including the one in New York, had to struggle with what it meant to be Catholic.

For Dorothy, it was a particularly trying period. When Thomas Merton sent a letter to her in April 1962 acknowledging that the Catholic Worker, "along with the Beats," stood among those on society's margins who were "challenging the culture of death," Dorothy responded by stressing how unbeat the core staff was. "I do assure you that we are not 'beats.' Charles Butterworth [the community business manager at the time] is a Harvard Law School graduate and a convert. He formerly practiced law in Philadelphia. . . . Ed Forand is a former Marine, reconverted [to Catholicism] by Fr. Hugo when he was in a veterans' hospital. . . . Walter Kerrell is a convert, a lover of music and painting. Judy Gregory is a Radcliffe graduate. . . . She is getting her Ph.D. on Simone Weil and Personalism. Anne Marie Stokes works with non-government agencies at the U.N., teaches French to support herself, and uses her apartment to take care of some of our worst problems in an emergency. Bob Steed supports himself by a night watchman's job and helps edit the paper . . . and so on and so on. I say all this because in your letters you associate us with 'beats,' of whom there have been, thank God, but a few and they a fly-by-night crew who despised and ignored the poor around us and scandalized them by their dress and morals. I am afraid I am uncharitable about the intellectual who shoulders his way in to eat before the men on the line who have done the hard work of the world, and who moves in on the few men in one of the apartments and tries to edge them out with their beer parties and women. They can sleep on park benches as far as I am concerned. Unfortunately we are left with the women who are pregnant for whom I beg your prayers. We have two girls with babies, and three expecting, on the farm now. As far as I am concerned, I must look on these things as a woman, and therefore much concerned with

"'The corruption of the best is the worst' and these young people come from good families, have good education, and have been given every advantage. Sometimes I don't wonder the Communists wipe out the so-called intellectuals and Lenin had to write to Rosa Luxemberg of the bourgeois morality of the young. This whole crowd goes to extremes in sex and drugs and then flatter themselves they are at least not perverts. . . . This is not reverence for life, this certainly is not natural love for family, for husband and wife, for child. It is a great denial and is more resembling nihilism than the revolution which they think they are furthering."
—Letter to a friend, dated
April 9, 1962

239

"They have shown hatred, contempt for the very sources of life itself, and have defaced in every way the creativity within them, a blasphemy and a horror from which one can only recoil with fear and disgust at this breath of evil among us."
—Diary entry, March 2, 1962

the flesh and with what goes to sustain it. Sin is sin and the sentimental makes a mystique of it."

One incident that had especially outraged Dorothy centered on Ed Sanders, a student at Columbia University who was drawn to the writings and poetry of such Beat writers as Allen Ginsberg (himself an occasional guest speaker at the Catholic Worker) and Jack Kerouac. Sanders was not himself a member of the community but was close to several people who were. He was also deeply engaged in local anti-war activity, side by side with several Catholic Workers. His interest in the Catholic Worker was mainly social; he regarded Catholic teaching in general as absurd if not, when it came to sex, harmful. He enjoyed being outrageous. When he launched a mimeographed poetry journal, he named it "Fuck You: A Magazine of the Arts." The first issue included the claim— meant by him only as a joke—that it had been produced at the Catholic Worker. The only actual link was that several of the poets represented in the journal's first issue were younger members of the Catholic Worker staff.

When a copy reached Dorothy's hands, she was irate. No doubt it crossed her mind that, should a copy find its way into the hands of Cardinal Spellman, he would demand that the Catholic Worker no longer describe itself or its publication as Catholic. Explaining to him that this was an ill-considered prank that had nothing to do with the Catholic Worker movement was not likely to make him change his mind. The scandal would be ruinous. Decades of work by herself and others would be discredited. (Fortunately, so far as is known, Ed Sanders's journal was never seen by the cardinal.) Dorothy's response was a demand that anyone involved with Sanders's magazine leave immediately. They were not welcome at the house on Chrystie Street nor would their rents be paid by the community.

In this case, the several people involved withdrew, but in later years, similar demands from Dorothy—especially to some of the people living at the Catholic Worker Farm, once it had moved to Tivoli in 1964 and had room for up to seventy inhabitants—were sometimes ignored. After all, they knew Dorothy would not summon the police. Such people became, in effect, squatters insisting on their right to live at the Catholic Worker, which, after all, claimed to be a place of hospitality. If they lived in a way which Dorothy regarded as scandalous (drinking heavily, smoking marijuana, using other drugs, engaging in non-marital sexual relationships, etc.), that was her problem, not theirs.

It was a quandary that, during Dorothy's life, never resolved itself. She never resorted to police intervention. These people too, she acknowledged, were among the wounded. Periodically, she admonished herself not to judge them. "Two things we have to learn," she wrote in her journal in March 1962, "not to judge others and not to mind others judging us. To endure conflict between charity and common good, authority [and] freedom, state versus personal responsibility."

"But Dorothy didn't tolerate unmanageable situations indefinitely," Tom Cornell points out. "In the case of the Easton farm, in the end she simply handed it to its occupants and, in the case of the farm at Tivoli, when the squatters refused to leave, finally she sold the place out from under them." In recent years the New York Catholic Worker finally resorted to legal intervention in "last resort" situations, in 2005 evicting a woman who refused to leave Maryhouse and, in 2010, doing the same to a disruptive guest who had had been asked to leave the Peter Maurin Farm. But, in almost all cases, sooner or later ultra-trouble-some guests simply move on.

A friend asked Dorothy, "Why does this movement attract all the crazy ones?" She agreed that "We do have a goodly share of wan-dering monks." Her wish was that, if they wished to be pilgrims, their stays at the Catholic Worker would be shorter rather than longer. "But my attitude should be," she added, "if people are slightly mad, how much more attractive it is that they should be mad for God."

In a letter sent in the spring of 1962 to the parents of one young person who for a brief time had been part of the staff

Dorothy speaks at a rally in Union Square to support five young men burning their draft cards, November 1965. (Credit: Jim Forest)

With pacifist A.J. Muste watching, five men (including *Catholic Worker* Tom Cornell on left) burn their draft cards in Union Square.

"So often one is overcome with a tragic sense of the meaninglessness of our lives—patience, patience, and the very word means suffering. Endurance, perseverance, sacrament of the present moment, the sacrament of duty. One must keep on reassuring oneself of these things. And repeat acts of faith, 'Lord, I believe, help my unbelief.' We are placed here; why? To know Him, and so love Him, serve Him, by serving others and so attain to eternal life and joy, understanding, etc."—Diary entry, July 2, 1962

but had since been drawn deeply into the counter-culture, Dorothy wrote to tell them what was happening in their daughter's life since her departure from the Catholic Worker. "I realize," she concluded, "that you must be very unhappy, just as I was when I saw Tamar so set on marrying at eighteen someone that was not capable of supporting her and who has finally cracked up under the strain, and has left her and is living near his family. I know you can't stop [your daughter] any more than I could stop her. Parents have to let their children find their way, and God brings good out of evil. We grow by pruning and it hurts."

Hospitality, whether to some of the more beat or hippie-minded young volunteers or to battered veterans of the streets, had rarely been easy. Many of the people who came to the Catholic Worker, whether to help or simply to find food and shelter, had serious problems—addictions, madness, threatening behavior, etc. But even in the most difficult cases, the goal was always to help them as much as possible, if only by providing meals and paying them into one of the nearby flophouse hotels which charged about a dollar a night.

At times Dorothy noted in her diary what a failure the Catholic Worker was even in its efforts to practice hospitality, with her explosive, judgmental self the chief failure. As she put it in a 1968 entry, "I have no power to judge or forgive, considering my own past. I cannot help people by condemning them, by my cold disapproval, my silence."

Meanwhile, as the decade unfolded, the Catholic Worker was confronted with the problem of living in a militaristic society that was inching its way into a major war in Southeast Asia. When the sixties began, there had been relatively small numbers of U.S. military advisors in South Vietnam, an almost invisible involvement that Graham Greene had described in his novel, *The Quiet American*. In 1965, full-scale Americanization of the war began with U.S. bombing of North Vietnam and the landing of 3,500 Marine combat troops in South Vietnam at Danang. Within three years, the number of U.S. troops climbed to 510,000. The war would drag on, with heavy casualties, vast destruction and wide-spread environmental ruin, until U.S. withdrawal in 1975.

At a time when the majority of Americans were unaware of Vietnam, the Catholic Worker initiated the first demonstration solely against U.S. participation in the Vietnam War. On July 16, 1963, near the entrance to a building in midtown Manhattan where the United Nations Observer from the Republic of South Vietnam Nations resided, two Catholic Workers, Tom Cornell and Chris Kearns, carried signs reading "The Catholic Worker Protests U.S. Military Support of Diem Tyranny." (Diem was, at the time, the leader of the South Vietnamese government.) Announcing they would be there for an hour at noon each day for the next nine days, they invited members of the various peace groups in New York City to join them on the tenth day. About 250 people turned out on July 26. It was the first nationally televised demonstration against the Vietnam War.

While the war raged, to many it seemed that a daily battle was being fought between David and Goliath, as defenseless hamlets were destroyed by jets, helicopters and foot-soldiers, yet the guerilla forces emerged again and again from their tunnels to take the offensive. For every insurgent Vietnamese soldier killed, it was estimated that ten to twenty ordinary civilians died, most often children and the aged, those least quick, able or skilled in finding shelter. Among the "anti-personnel" weapons developed during the war was a type of bomb that implanted fragments of razor-edged metal or plastic in its victims. Bombs filled with napalm was widely used: gasoline chemically treated so that, while burning, it clung to the skin

Napalm bombs explode in a Vietnamese village.

like glue. Vietnam, wrote the Jesuit priest and poet Daniel Berrigan, had become "the land of burning children."

Dorothy had only recently returned from her fast in Rome during the Council's final session when a death by burning occurred within the Catholic Worker community. At 5:20 A.M., November 9, 1965, Roger LaPorte sat in the street before the United States Mission to the United Nations, two miles north of the Catholic Worker house, poured gasoline on himself, struck a match, and became a pillar of fire in the darkness of night. "I am a Catholic Worker," he said before lapsing into a coma at a nearby hospital. "I did this as a religious action. I am anti-war, all wars." Before his death thirty-three hours later, he regained consciousness. "I want to live," he told a Carmelite priest who heard his last confession. "He made the most devout act of contrition I have ever heard," the priest said afterward. "His voice was strong and he meant every word."

Only three days earlier, Roger had been present with other young volunteers from the Catholic Worker for a rally at Union Square where five pacifists burned their draft registration cards as an act of civil disobedience for which they faced up to five years of imprisonment. One of them was

Tom Cornell, a former managing editor of *The Catholic Worker* who had become co-secretary of the Catholic Peace Fellowship. Dorothy was one of several speakers at the event.

"I speak today as one who is old," said Dorothy, "and who must endorse the courage of the young who themselves are willing to give up their freedom. I speak as one who is old, and whose whole lifetime has seen the cruelty and hysteria of war in this last half century . . . I wish to . . . show my solidarity with these young men, and to point out that we too are break-ing the law, committing civil disobedience, in advocating and trying to encourage all those who are conscripted—to inform their consciences, to heed the still, small voice of conscience, and to refuse to participate in the immorality of war." Meanwhile, across the street, counter-demonstrators chanted "Moscow Mary! Give us joy. Bomb Hanoi!" When the five small draft cards were ignited, their chant became, "Burn yourselves, not your draft cards!"

Roger LaPorte burned himself.

"It has always been the teaching of the Catholic Church," Dorothy wrote in the days following Roger's death, "that suicide is a sin, but mercy and loving-kindness dictate another judgment." She noted that normally those who take their own lives are temporarily unbalanced, possibly insane, and thus can be absolved from their guilt. But no one had noticed any indication of mental illness in Roger. He had been an honor student who had entered the seminary and then tried the monastic life before coming to the Catholic Worker in 1963, where he had devoted himself wholeheartedly to the poor and sick while still carrying on his studies. What he did "must be spoken of in a far deeper context [than despair or mental illness]. It is not only that many youth and students throughout the country are deeply sensitive to the sufferings of the world. They have a keen sense that they must be responsible and make a profession of their faith that things do not have to go on as they always

Dorothy speaks with A.J. Muste, chair-man of the Committee for Nonviolent Action, at draft card burning. (Credit: Jim Forest)

have—that men are capable of laying down their lives for others."

Dorothy recalled the revolutionary hero in Ignazio Silone's novel, *Bread and Wine*, who risked capture and execution by leaving his hiding place at night to write slogans of dissent on public walls in fascist Italy. Someone scolded him for endangering himself in order to make such insignificant gestures. The dissenter responds, "The Land of Propaganda is built on unanimity. If anyone says, 'No,' the spell is broken and the public order is endangered."

Roger had used his own flesh as a wall to bear that message, to cry a "No" that might be heard throughout America. "In forty-eight hours last week," Dorothy reminded her readers, "there were six massive air strikes in Vietnam. There were more killed on both sides last week than at any time since the war began." While the young and innocent died, others living in safety grew wealthy from the war. She cited a headline she had noticed a few days earlier in *The Wall Street Journal*:

VIETNAM SPURS PLANNING FOR BIG RISE IN OUTLAYS
FOR MILITARY HARDWARE
SPENDING ON TANKS, COPTERS, OTHER GEAR MAY DOUBLE

The *Journal* article seemed to rejoice in the recent U.S. commitment to a more active combat role in Vietnam. This promised to give "added zip for the nation's economy," the *Journal* predicted, by funneling "billions into pocketbooks in many parts of the country."

"There is something satanic about this kind of writing," said Dorothy. "On the other hand, witness Roger LaPorte. He embraced voluntary poverty and came to the Catholic Worker because he did not wish to profit in this booming economy of which *The Wall Street Journal* speaks so gloatingly. He was giving himself to the poor and the destitute, serving tables, serving the sick. . . . And now he is dead—dead by his own hand, everyone will say, a suicide." But Dorothy saw Roger as a "victim soul" who had been constantly searching for ways to offer his life for others, trying to take to himself "the sufferings that we as a nation are inflicting upon a small

"In view of the terrible things that are happening—the accidental bombing of friendly villagers, the spraying with napalm of our own troops yesterday, there is bound to be increased protest. I am glad that there are so many now. The Catholic Worker has borne the burden for 33 years—protesting wars, Chinese-Japanese, Ethiopian, Spanish, World War II, Korean, Algerian, and now this."
—To Thomas Merton,
November 15, 1965

country and its people." He was not driven by despair or the hatred of life but rather by compassion and an anguished awareness of those who were being burned, far from our sight, in the villages of Vietnam. Yes, it was a "sad and terrible act, but all of us around the Catholic Worker know that Roger's intent was to love God and his brother."

Confronted by a war in which the typical victim was an unarmed civilian and in which America's allies in Vietnam were far from inspiring, those subject to conscription sought ways to evade the draft—some by obtaining student deferments, some by hiding, and some by leaving the country. Many others became conscientious objectors, a legal option for those of religious or philosophical motivation who

Bombs being released over Vietnam.

were opposed in principle to all war. If officially recognized, they did two years of alternative service, usually assisting in hospitals. A smaller number who often would have qualified as conscientious objectors refused to seek any special recognition or exemption from the draft boards and often spent two or three years in prison. (Dorothy was close to people in both groups, though her heart was especially with the draft resisters. Draft-age men in the Catholic Worker movement during the Vietnam war tended to end up in prison.)

Hundreds of thousands of people took part in demonstrations, teach-ins, vigils, picket lines and other acts of protest. Never in American history had so many been engaged in public opposition to their own country's military activities.

In 1965, the Catholic Worker, in combination with the Fellowship of Reconciliation, gave birth to the Catholic Peace

Fellowship, which concentrated on educational work directed at Catholic students, educators and pastors. One of its major tools was a booklet, "Catholics and Conscientious Objection." Partly thanks to having obtained an *imprimatur* from Cardinal Spellman (his official declaration that the text contained no moral or theological errors), the booklet went through many printings—150,000 copies were distributed during the Vietnam war. By the latter sixties, the Catholic Peace Fellowship was often counseling, in person or by letter, fifty conscientious objectors and draft resisters a week.

Tom Cornell and Jim Forest in the offices of the Catholic Peace Fellowship.

Many found that the refusal to do military service was only a first step and looked for ways to impede the war by active, nonviolent resistance. Some of the actions that emerged were intentionally shocking and controversial, even within the peace movement itself. "Let us burn paper instead of children," Daniel Berrigan advised. Catholic Workers such as Chris Kearns, Jim Wilson, David Miller and Tom Cornell had burned their own draft cards. Then in April 1968, nine Catholics, including Daniel and Philip Berrigan, entered the draft board offices in the town of Catonsville, Maryland, took out the files of those classified as draft eligible, and burned the papers in an adjacent parking lot with homemade napalm. In the early fall, a group of fourteen, including myself and several others associated with the Catholic Worker movement, took similar records from all nine draft boards of the city of Milwaukee, burning them in a park while reading from the Gospel and praying until they were put under arrest.

"It is mid-October and the weather is still warm," Dorothy wrote soon after the Milwaukee action. "The maples and the oaks and the sumac are brilliant. . . . If only there were not the radio! The news of bloody death and destruction at the other end of the world, in the name of defense. . . . It is in the light of this anguish that one can understand the attempt made by the Catonsville Nine and the Milwaukee Fourteen, amongst whom so many are our friends, to suffer with these fellow human beings so devastated by war and famine. These men—priests and laymen—have offered themselves as a living sacrifice, as hostages. They have offered the most precious gift apart from life itself, their freedom, as well as the prayer and fasting they have done behind bars, for these others"—both the Vietnamese and the young Americans "being enslaved in our immoral wars."

Despite her support for those imprisoned for such acts of protest, Dorothy found the destruction of property a troubling issue. While she agreed that Jesus had given a similar example in overturning the stands of the money-changers in the Temple in Jerusalem, she also said that we ought not do to others what we would not have them do to us. She worried too that less dramatic efforts to end the war would be denigrated and judged less valuable than actions that risked long prison sentences. Early in 1969, she reminded her readers that peacemaking most often took quite ordinary forms. "The thing is to recognize that not all are called, not all have the vocation, to demonstrate in this way, to fast, to endure the pain and the long drawn out, nerve-wracking suffering of prison life. We do what we can, and the whole field of the works of mercy is open to us. . . . All work, whether building, increasing food production, running credit unions, working in factories that produce for human needs, working in the handicrafts—all these things can come under the heading of the works of mercy, which are the opposite of the works of war."

The dimension of penance was essential to any work of social healing, Dorothy emphasized, but penance isn't only found in the deprivations of prison. "It is a penance to work, to give oneself to others, to endure the pinpricks of commu-

"I wrote the life of St. Therese because she exemplified the 'little way.' We know how powerless we are, all of us, against the power of wealth and government and industry and science. The powers of this world are overwhelming. Yet it is hoping against hope and believing, in spite of 'unbelief,' crying by prayer and by sacrifice, daily, small, constant sacrificing of one's own comfort and cravings—these are the things that count. . . . I am convinced that prayer and austerity, prayer and self-sacrifice, prayer and fasting, prayer, vigils, and prayer and marches, are the indispensable means. . . . And love. All these means are useless unless animated by love."
—To Mike Cullen, February 1970

Dorothy with Jesuit Father Daniel Berrigan at a meeting at the Catholic Worker. (Marquette University archives)

"Thank God, you are truly bearing the Cross, giving your life for others, as Father Phil is in cramped cell and enforced idleness, away from all he must crave day and night to do, surrounded by suffering, enduring the clamor of hell itself—he too is giving his life for others. I cannot tell you how I love you both, and see more clearly how God is using you, reaching the prisoners and reaching the young. They all call you 'Dan' and 'Phil,' but I call you Father Dan and Father Phil because always you are to me priests and prophets."

—To Daniel Berrigan,
Catholic Worker, December 1972

nity life. One could certainly say on many occasions, 'Give me a thorough, frank, outgoing war, rather than the sneak attacks, stabs in the back, sparring, detracting, defaming, hand-to-hand jockeying for position that goes on in offices and "good works" of all kinds, another and miserable petty kind of war.' ... So let us rejoice in our own petty sufferings and thank God we have a little penance to offer."

Yet there were those who were called to acts of resistance that could result in prison and even injury and death. She compared Daniel Berrigan to an earlier Jesuit, Saint Edmund Campion, who had been an underground priest when Catholicism was outlawed in England and later, during the reign of the first Queen Elizabeth, had been tortured to death. She thought too of Martin Luther King, "a man of the deepest and most profound spiritual insights," who had often been jailed, whose home had been repeatedly bombed, who had almost died of a knife wound, and who was finally shot down in Memphis on the eve of Good Friday, 1968.

Those who gave up their freedom and risked their lives, Dorothy argued, were not disobedient. They were obedient to the way of the Cross. They were obedient to the commandment not to kill. It was not they who should be accused. "I accuse," wrote Dorothy, "the government itself, and all of us, of these mass murders in Vietnam, this destruction of villages, this wiping out of peoples, the kidnapping, torture, rape and killings that have been disclosed to us.... Reparation is needed. We must do penance for what we have done to our brothers.... But meanwhile in this hushed room there is prayer, for strength to know and to love and to find out what to do and set our hands to useful work that will contribute to peace, not to war."

Dorothy also challenged the American bishops over their role in the Vietnam War which, in its early years, mainly ranged from passive to active support. The most outspoken supporter was Cardinal Spellman who, while visiting U.S. troops in Vietnam, told them they were engaged in a struggle for civilization.

"I sit in the presence of the Blessed Sacrament," Dorothy wrote from the chapel at the Catholic Worker farm, "and wrestle for peace in the bitterness of my soul . . . ." She noted that the hardest people to love are usually not far away but close at hand, even in one's own religious community, one's Church. She wondered if "these princes of the Church" are not blinded to Christ's presence in "the enemy" because of their terror of the enemy. In Cardinal Spellman, she noted genuine courage in his annual Christmas visits to American troops, not only in Vietnam but in other far-flung locations. "But oh God, what are all these Americans, so many of them Christians, doing all over the world, so far from their own shores?" (In 1967, the year she asked this question, one of the soldiers in Vietnam was her grandson Eric.)

Dorothy recalled that Cardinal Spellman, ignoring papal appeals for a negotiated peace, had called for total victory in the war. "Words are strong and powerful as bombs," she commented, "powerful as napalm. How much the government counts on those words, pays for those words to exalt our own way of life, to build up fear of the enemy. . . . Love casts out fear, but we have to get over the fear in order to get close enough to love those we fear." She wished that everyone would read the Book of Hosea, which is so emphatic about God's steadfast love not only for the Jews, the chosen people, but for everyone. "We are all one, all one body, Chinese, Russians, Vietnamese, and He has commanded us to love one another."

"There is plenty to do, for each one of us, working on our own hearts, changing our own attitudes, in our own neighborhoods. If the just man falls seven times daily, we each one of us fall more than that in thought, word and deed. Prayer and fasting, taking up our own cross daily and following Him, doing penance, these are the hard words of the Gospel. As to the Church, where else shall we go, except to the Bride of Christ, our flesh with Christ? Though she is a harlot at times, she is our Mother."

—*Catholic Worker*, January 1967

Viva la Huelga!

Cesar Chavez. (Maryknoll archives)

The first *Catholic Worker* article on the plight of farm workers appeared in 1934, hardly surprising given the special interest Dorothy had in unions and Peter in farms. For more than a decade beginning in 1965, it was a rare issue which failed to speak about the farm workers' struggle to unionize themselves. All attempts in earlier years had been crushed so effectively that farm workers were considered the best example of a labor strata that could not be organized: farm workers moved with the crops, had no community roots, had no influence with legislators, and were almost invisible to the press and public. Growers had easily crushed the strikes that had been organized in the past.

In 1962, Cesar Chavez, a Mexican-American who had grown up on the fields, decided a fresh effort had to be made and founded the National Farm Workers Association. His initial economic base was the $1,200 in his savings account. By 1964, he had signed up a thousand members and been joined by several co-workers. In 1965, the union won a pay raise for grape workers on one California ranch. In the fall, a strike—*huelga*—by grape workers on other ranches sought to extend the first small victory. In 1966, union members had a real victory to celebrate—a major wine-producing corporation, Schenley Industries, not only agreed to a pay raise but signed a contract, the first ever negotiated in the history of American farm labor. Rejoicing over the Schenley contract, one farm worker wrote to Dorothy, "Now we have rest rooms and a place to wash our hands."

By this time, a nationwide network had been built up which appealed effectively for consumer boycotts. Year by year, a series of boycotts had removed iceberg lettuce, table grapes, raisins and (among other labels) Gallo wine from hundreds of thousands of homes, institutions and retail stores. Picket lines—the participants singing such hymns as "*De Colores*"—were a common sight across the United States.

Tightly focused boycotts proved to be an effective weapon in winning better pay and safer working conditions for those who labored in the fields.

While Dorothy was supportive of any effort to improve the lot of working people, Cesar was of special importance to her because of his emphasis on religious faith (one of the union's main symbols was the image of Our Lady of Guadalupe) and his commitment to nonviolence. "We have recognized," Dorothy wrote in an "On Pilgrimage" column in 1967, "that the problem of agriculture is insoluble without tapping the deep religious instincts for patience and perseverance of the people."

In April 1966, Cesar came to visit Dorothy and to meet the Catholic Worker community in New York. "He looks just like his pictures," Dorothy noted, "perhaps even younger, with straight black hair, face browned by the sun, and brown as an Indian's is brown." They shared a deep devotion to Mary, the mother of Jesus. "When he saw the picture of Our Lady of Guadalupe, which has been hanging on our walls for so long that it is dark with age, he immediately left his seat at the table and stood before it a few moments before we began to talk." Cesar told Dorothy about the truckloads of food and clothing being sent down regularly by the Catholic Worker community in San Francisco.

"When finally farm workers are organized in one small town after another," Dorothy wrote about their common vision, "and all together begin to feel their strength in the largest of all United States' industries, agriculture, they may begin to have a vision of the kind of society where the workers will be owners—of their own homes, a few acres, and eventually of large holdings in the form of cooperatives." She suggested to Cesar that Israel's *kibbutzim* might be models for agricultural development in the United States.

In May 1969, Dorothy went west by bus on a speaking trip that brought her to Delano, a town in the San Joaquin Valley in central California, then the headquarters of the farm worker campaign. "My shoes are covered with dust and I am down at the heels indeed," she wrote back to New York. A priest met her at the Delano bus terminal and took her to

"Dear Pope John—please, yourself a campesino, watch over the United Farm Workers. Raise up more and more leader-servants through the country to stand with Cesar Chavez in this nonviolent struggle with Mammon. . . . Help make a new order wherein justice flourishes, and, as Peter Maurin, himself a peasant, said so simply, 'where it is easier to be good.'"
—Catholic Worker, September 1973

Cesar and Helen Chavez's small house. Once inside the door she found a picture of Gandhi on the wall identical to one at the Catholic Worker's First Street house in New York—and, of course, an icon of Our Lady of Guadalupe. It was in this house that Cesar had fasted for twenty-five days in 1968, an act of penance for episodes of striker violence. His fast renewed the union's commitment to nonviolence.

The day after her arrival, Dorothy took part in a memorial Mass for Robert Kennedy, a strong supporter of the farm workers who had been murdered while running for President. "It was the first anniversary of his assassination," she wrote, "and Chavez will always remember that Kennedy came and broke bread with him as he ended his fast. He considered him a *compañero* in a very deep sense." Cesar asked Dorothy to read the Epistle, and after the Mass called on her to speak. "The best thing about this," she said, "was that it gave me a view of the packed hall with the beautiful dark faces of the Filipinos and the Mexicans, men, women and children, the seats all filled, and the aisles, yet no one restless. They broke out now and then in a crescendo of applause which became faster and faster clapping of hands and stamping of feet which died down as suddenly as it flared up. And there were the shouts of '*Viva la huelga, viva la causa*' [long live the strike, long live the cause] over and over again."

Taking part in the dawn picketing of one of the fields, Dorothy was nearly run down when a car, in a sudden burst of speed, swerved toward her. Despite her age and arthritis, she was agile enough to leap back to safety. The tire tracks were shown to a sheriff, who had previously been taking down the name of a striker who had ventured into the grape field to talk to the pickers. "The sheriff was perfunctory about both complaints," Dorothy wrote. The driver wasn't arrested.

It was a beautiful morning, with singing birds offering "such a paean of praise to their Maker." But the fierce heat was quick in coming. "There was no breeze and such a dust haze that one could not see the mountains though they were nearby." Dorothy watched the workers—strike-breakers—in the field, thinning leaves, tossing aside defective grapes, putting bunches of good grapes in paper-lined boxes. "I saw children in the field helping their parents." The pay, one of the strikers told her, was $1.10 an hour, with a penny extra for each vine thinned. A good worker, doing a six-day week, could thin three hundred vines. But the striker recalled trying to collect the extra three dollars one week and instead being threatened by the grower with a rifle.

Dorothy noted the many strikers who were not simply endangered but had been injured in attacks. One striker had been cut on his face with grape scissors, another kicked in the ribs and beaten by a grower, and still another kicked in the face and body by a foreman. Dorothy wrote their names and the details of what had happened to them, quoting a proverb of the strikers: "We have to sacrifice to deserve."

"Remember these things," Dorothy asked readers of *The Catholic Worker*, "you whose mouth waters for table grapes. Remember the boycott and help the strikers. . . . Their struggle has gone on for years now. It is the first breakthrough to achieve some measure of justice for these poorest and most beloved of God's children."

Late in 1971, after a stay with the Catholic Worker community in Los Angeles, Dorothy was with Cesar again. The threats on his life were such that the union had put a high wire fence around his house. Cesar was accompanied by two German shep-

(Marquette University archives)

herds (Boycott and Huelga) wherever he went, plus an unarmed bodyguard. Though head of the union, he continued to receive the same pay provided every worker on the union staff: room and board, travel money when needed, and $5 a week. Dorothy and Cesar renewed their conversation about long-range visions, when workers would no longer be "hired hands" but would have a share in the land they worked. In their discussion of the violence the union was

Dorothy just before her arrest for picketing with striking farmworkers. (Credit: © Bob Fitch)

experiencing daily from its opponents, it impressed Dorothy that Cesar never spoke of "enemies" but only of "adversaries." He had refused to dehumanize the growers.

In the column describing her 1971 stay with the farm workers, Dorothy tried to respond to several critical letters that had been received from contributors who wanted to be sure that their gifts would be used to feed the hungry and not to publish "propaganda" and social criticism. "Why," a reader asked Dorothy, "do you give so much attention in *The Catholic Worker* to such matters as the condition of workers, unions, boycotts?"

"Let me say," Dorothy replied, "that the sight of a line of men waiting for food, dirty, ragged, obviously sleeping out in empty buildings, is something that I will never get used to. It is a deep hurt and suffering that food is often all we have to give. Our houses will not hold any more men and women, nor do we have workers to care for them. Nor are there enough alternatives or services to care for them. They are the wounded of the class struggle, men who have built the railroads, worked in the mines, on ships, and steel mills. They are men—and women too—from prison and mental hospitals. They are often simply the unemployed. But bread lines are not enough, hospices are not enough. I know that we will always have men on the road. But we need communities of work, land for the landless, true farming communes, cooperatives and credit unions. There is much that is wild, prophetic and holy about our work.... The heart hungers for the new social order wherein justice dwelleth."

It was this marrow-deep longing for such a new social order that drew Dorothy toward Cesar Chavez. It was because of this, she explained, that the Catholic Worker would never limit itself to caring for the victims of the existing social order without trying to help create a society that didn't throw people away like used Kleenex. "Our problems," Dorothy had once said, "stem from our acceptance of this filthy, rotten system."

Dorothy's sense of identification with the farm worker struggle resulted in her last arrest. In the summer of 1973, Joan Baez invited Dorothy to spend a week with the Institute for the Study of Nonviolence in California. By the time Dorothy arrived, however, a California judge had forbidden all farm worker picket lines. "My path was clear," Dorothy wrote. She decided to take part in the prohibited picket lines. On August 1, after rising at 2 A.M., she picketed through the day at several vineyards, facing lines of police armed with clubs and guns. She occasionally rested on her folding chair-cane, a much used item in her later years when the pain of arthritis slowed her movements. "We talked to the police," she wrote, "pleading with them to lay down their weapons." She told them she planned to return on the following day and would read aloud the Sermon on the Mount.

The next day, after a night with the nurses at one of the farm worker clinics that the union had opened, she was up at 4 A.M. and at a meeting before dawn where Cesar spoke about the latest arrests. "We set out in cars to picket the area where the big and small growers had united to get the injunction," Dorothy wrote. "Three police buses arrived some time later and we were warned to disperse. When we refused, we were ushered into buses and brought to this 'industrial farm' (which they do not like us to call a jail or prison, though we are under lock and key and our barracks surrounded by barbed wire). Here we are, ninety-nine women and fifty men, including thirty nuns and two priests." They were charged with "remaining present at the place of a riot, rout and unlawful assembly" from which they refused to disperse despite lawful warning.

Bob Fitch's photo of Dorothy, sitting on her chair-cane, in calm conversation with armed police, is probably the photo of

"The strike was widespread and mass arrests were continuing. My path was clear: the U.F.W. has everything that belongs to a new social order. Since I had come to picket where an injunction was prohibiting picketing, it appears that I would spend my weeks in California in jail. . . . I was glad I had my folding chair-cane so I could rest occasionally during picketing, and sit there before the police to talk to them."
—Catholic Worker, September 1973

Dorothy that has been most widely published. She looks like a grandmother patiently admonishing children about war toys.

While negotiations involving the farm workers' union went on through the night, the nuns jailed with Dorothy organized a prayer vigil with two-hour shifts. The Mexican women prayed the rosary with their arms outstretched, as if to unite themselves with Christ on the cross. "Our barracks were alive with prayer," Dorothy reported. During the days, there were also seminars. Dorothy led one on labor history. Another prisoner, a great lover of Saints Thomas Aquinas and Augustine, taught about rhetoric. "I tried to understand what rhetoric really means," Dorothy admitted, "and she explained, but I cannot remember now." On August 8, Daniel Ellsberg and Joan Baez came to visit. "Joan sang to us a most poignant prison song, which tore your heart."

While held captive, Dorothy wrote a letter addressed to all the Catholic bishops of California:

"I trust you will not think this letter an affront. Call it brain damage from bumping my head every time I sit up in this lower berth of one of 24 double-decker beds where I lie . . . [one of] 99 women in two barracks, 30 of them Sisters. . . . A group of Mexican women, most of them young mothers, are playing jacks. . . . The Sisters from various religious orders around the country are fasting. . . .

"Here in our women's barracks I've never been with a more beautiful crowd of women and girls. Warm and loving, pure and clean of life and speech. They are women of great dignity and recognize in the struggle of the United Farm Workers against agribusiness the importance of *La Causa*. . . . They realize the long fight there is ahead. They may seem to be losing or to have lost, but the strike goes on against growers, corporation farms, child labor, poisonous insecticides. . . .

"I saw men sitting in the vineyards with rifles the other day. Each day on the picket lines we were faced by rows of police with long clubs and guns in their holsters, and a new kind of handcuff I never saw before made of plastic. Some of the strikers said they saw cans of mace, a horrible weapon to use against the weaponless. . . .

"This morning here in a grassy yard the bishops of El Paso

"I must copy down the charges made against me (we were listed in groups of ten): 'The said defendants, on or about August 2, were persons remaining present at the place of a riot, rout, and unlawful assembly, who did willfully and unlawfully fail, refuse, and neglect after the same had been lawfully warned to disperse.'"
—*Catholic Worker*, September 1973

offered the Mass and several hundred received communion. But where are the other bishops of California? We want their pastoral visits. Visiting the prisoner is a corporal work of mercy commanded by Jesus in Matthew 25 as of vital importance. 'Inasmuch as you did not visit the prisoners, you did not visit me.' Surely the farm workers—Filipino, Mexican, Arab, Chinese—are 'the least of these, His brethren.'

"But the bishops will lose the support of the growers, it is said. How wonderful it would be for you to embrace holy poverty by having wealth taken from you! It is hard to know how to go about divesting oneself when there are a dozen consultors, priests and laymen in a diocese who might not agree to selling your superfluous holdings and giving to the poor. . . . You certainly would quicken the process of acquiring voluntary poverty by visiting the striker or non-striker prisoner and taking the consequences. . . .

"Cesar Chavez is leading the way in building a new social order in the United States. Renewal is coming from the bottom up, not from the top down . . . by cooperatives and credit unions, by decentralization and regionalism, by land trusts. The church could provide the means for these beginnings. . . .

Dorothy wearing her prison smock.
(Credit: Stanley Vishnewski)

"Forgive me for being presumptuous but Christ's words are so clear—'Sell what you have and give to the poor.' Your Father knows you have need of these things.' 'If you sow sparingly you will reap sparingly.' The trouble is—after every revolution the Church starts getting her own back again.

"This has been a strange jail experience. Mass every evening at seven. This going to jail had none of the suffering of [myself and other women who protested the air raid drills]. There were no humiliating rectal and vaginal searches for drugs, no dispossessing us of books, suitcases, clothes. My only complaint is the complete lack of privacy—fifty women in one long room, and five [uncloseted] toilets, ranged along the wash room. Very inhibiting. But I am forgetting I am writing to bishops about most serious affairs. They are our dear fathers who in turn ordain other fathers who provide us with the sacraments— the water of salvation, the 'knowledge of salvation through forgiveness of our sins'—the bread of life, and shall we not, through them as through Him, receive all good things?

On the back of this photo, Dorothy wrote: "*This was my prison uniform, signed all over by my fellow prisoners. It was like a Retreat. The Mexicans prayed the rosary arms outstretched. Cesar Chavez and family are wonderful people. He and his wife were received by Pope Paul. Truly poor and prayerful.*" (Credit: Stanley Vishnewski)

"I see empty convents, institutions, academies, novitiates and [recall that] Jesus said 'Sell what you have and give alms.' 'Feed the hungry, house the homeless, visit the sick and the prisoner.' You will reap a hundredfold."

On August 13, after nearly two weeks on the prison farm, all charges were dropped and the prisoners freed. Dorothy surprised the warden by refusing to return her sack-like prison dress. In their gratitude for her presence with them, the others arrested with her had signed it and made it a gift. "This is state property, Miss Day," the warden said. "You can't keep it." "My friends have written their names on it," she replied. "They gave it to me and I won't give it up." Dorothy kept the dress.

In Fresno that night, in a park across from the courthouse, the farm workers celebrated Mass. They rightly felt that a small victory had been won, though it was another two years before state laws were passed that allowed farm workers to freely choose their own union representation in secret-ballot elections. The great majority chose the United Farm Workers, though it wasn't until 1978 that the union was secure enough to retire its major weapon, the consumer boycott. By then the union was a secure national structure representing farm workers from California to Florida, though even then still only a minor percentage of farm workers were union members.

"The human cost in personal and family life of establishing the United Farm Workers union was an incalculable price paid by the legions of dedicated, idealistic and sometimes driven people who made the union a reality," the lead article in the February 1978 *Catholic Worker* commented. The writer, Dr. Marion Moses (also Dorothy's physician), expressed her hope that the UFW would never lose its original values and become just one more selfish labor bureaucracy. There were still hundreds of thousands of unorganized farm workers in need of a union "hungering and thirsting after justice," she noted. The fight by growers to prevent agriculture unions was far from over.

Further Travels

In January 15, 1970 Dorothy received the news that Ammon Hennacy had died that day in Salt Lake City, Utah—heart failure while recovering from a heart attack a week earlier. The news came not only from those who shared the work of Joe Hill House, founded by Ammon nine years earlier, but also from a monsignor at Salt Lake City's Catholic cathedral. He wanted Dorothy to know that the chaplain at Holy Cross Hospital, a Father Winteret, had often talked with Ammon during his last week, including a conversation the night before his death, when it seemed Ammon was recovering. Following the second heart attack, Ammon had received the last rites of the Church, he said, while "still alive and surrounded by nurses and doctors." How aware was Ammon of what was happening? No one knew. "But the sense of hearing is the last one to leave," the chaplain had pointed out.

Ammon Hennacy. (Marquette University archives)

On her way to Salt Lake City to attend Ammon's funeral, Dorothy recalled the words from Saint Paul's letter to the Romans that had been especially important in his life: "All things work together for good for those who love God." If Ammon had been put in charge of editing the New Testament, substantial parts of Paul's writings would have been left out, but not this sentence. Dorothy had no doubt that the world had been made a better place and many people's lives made less fearful thanks to Ammon's "one man revolution"—the revolution of living the way you wished other people would live.

Writing a final article about Ammon for the February issue, Dorothy recalled that, for Ammon, "obedience was a bad word." Occasionally she pointed out to him how obedient he was in so many contexts. Doing hard labor on farms, Ammon did as he was told, "accepting the authority of those who were authorities and knew what they were doing and how to do it." Ammon, she went on, "knew much labor history but very little about Church history." There was a sympathetic priest, she recalled, who said that Ammon had received

"One of Ammon's favorite quotations from Scripture was: 'Let him who is without sin cast the first stone.' But I must admit that Ammon was a great one to judge when it came to priests and bishops and his words were coarse on many an occasion, so that it was hurtful to me to hear him, loving the church as I do. But there's that love-hate business in all of us, and Ammon wanted so much to see priests and bishops and popes stand out strong and courageous against the sins and the horrors and the cruelty of the powers of this world. But we cannot judge him, knowing so well his own strong and courageous will to fight the corruption of the world around him."

—*Catholic Worker*, February 1970

"so great a light during that first jail sentence of his in Atlanta Penitentiary [during World War I] that it had blinded him." By the time he was released, Dorothy continued, "he had become a Bible Christian, not in the sense of [belonging to] a sect, but of one who accepted the word and did his best to live that word no matter how inconvenient it might be." When it came to hard work and voluntary poverty, it was Dorothy's opinion that Ammon "outshone everyone." If anyone had need of his bed, he "could be trusted to relinquish it immediately. He claimed nothing as his own "but the clothes on his back, and when he gave up his bed, he slept on the floor in the big living room where we had our meetings. He slept side by side with all the Bowery men whom [members of the staff] brought in on cold winter nights."

Though Ammon had eventually become a Catholic, Dorothy wrote, "his instruction had been slight." There was a long period when Ammon went to Mass every morning and, after communion, prayed for all the people—he carefully kept a list—who had sought his intercession. (Even after announcing he had left the Church in 1965, he still sometimes went to Mass and received communion. The rupture in practice was less absolute than it was presented in his writings.)

Ammon agreed with the motto "Wars will cease when men refuse to fight them" and was scandalized that this message was almost never preached at Mass. "He would have liked to give his life," wrote Dorothy, "for the obliteration of wars and all injustice from the face of the earth. He would have welcomed being shot just as Joe Hill was, that labor martyr after whom he named his house of hospitality in Salt Lake City. But Ammon's death was a triumph just the same"—his first heart attack came while he was on his way to protest the impending execution of two men on death row.

His funeral took place at the Church of St. Joan of Arc, a warrior like Ammon. Had he changed his mind about his many objections to the Catholic Church? Surely no one at the funeral could imagine that. But perhaps, as breath slipped away, Ammon embraced what the Church is called to be—an icon of Christ—rather than what it so often is, an institution revealing human ambition and hearts of stone.

From Utah, Dorothy went on to Florida and Georgia before reaching Michigan. Lou Murphy, one of the staff of the Detroit Catholic Worker community, noticed Dorothy was having difficulty breathing and took her to a nearby hospital. "This is a case of heart failure," Dorothy wrote in her journal that night. "Water in my lungs, hardening of arteries, enlarged heart and so on were responsible for the pains in my chest and shortness of breath, which makes me sit gasping for five minutes after I walk a block or have to hurry or am oppressed by haste, urgency, etc." The hospital visit went unmentioned in her "On Pilgrimage" column.

Dorothy pondered the implications of her failing heart in a journal entry made on February 28: "Does God mean, by my present troubles or rather illness, to indicate that I should give up the projected trip around the world . . . projected and to be paid for by Australian priests? . . . I am afraid it does mean just this. [But] this does not mean I will not take occasional speaking engagements. This is a necessity in our work. One engagement paid for a new boiler at the farm. A new roof is needed there too, before ceilings begin to fall down and the house to disintegrate."

Despite the cautionary news, Dorothy pressed on to Boston before returning home, then later in the year decided, after all, to risk a round-the-world journey. It started in Australia and went on from there to Hong Kong, India, Tanzania, a brief pause in Rome, and finally to England. Her traveling companion was her long-time friend, Eileen Egan.

At the airport in Calcutta, Mother Teresa (since her death recognized as Blessed Teresa in the Catholic Church) met the pair and garlanded them with flowers before taking them to the Missionaries of Charity hospice for the dying in the heart of the city. During her days with the community, Dorothy had an opportunity to speak to the novices, stressing a theme central to both their order and to the Catholic Worker movement: "Christ remains with us not only through the Mass but in the 'distressing disguise' of the poor. To live with the poor is a contemplative vocation, for it is to live in the constant presence of Jesus." Though the novices were astonished at Dorothy's accounts of her arrests and times in jail, "they understood going to prison

Dorothy in Australia.

"One does a lot of praying on a trip like this, where the power of man is so manifest in conquering the earth and the air—when space and time mean nothing. One travels from Hong Kong to Calcutta in 4½ hours flight time. But the power and the peace of God! 'All that may be known of God by men lies plain before their eyes, etc.' He has given them the senses to see, the mind to discern and understand, and yet how much baffles him."

—August 29, 1970

Dorothy with granddaughter Susie Hennessy. (Courtesy Tamar Hennessy)

"I owe great thanks to God that he gave me an appreciation of his beauty so young. . . . I have never gotten over my love for the sound of water, little waves lapping on the beach, retreating through the heaps of small stones and shells. . . . I am sure that it is because the Church is so alert to Man, as body and soul, because she believes in the resurrection of the body and life-ever-lasting, that I became strongly attracted to her when I began to catch glimpses of her later."
—Diary entry, November 3, 1970

for truth and liberation, as Gandhi had done," wrote Eileen, an old friend of Mother Teresa. "Now they were hearing it in a specifically Christian context, that of the work of mercy of visiting the prisoner by entering prison."

After Dorothy's talk, Mother Teresa pinned on Dorothy's dress the black cross with the figure of Christ worn by professed members of the order, in effect recognizing Dorothy as an honorary member. No one else had been honored by Mother Teresa in this way, yet it was another event about which Dorothy was silent in her column, though she did mention having been caught in a flood in Calcutta and coming down with dysentery in New Delhi and Bombay.

Arriving at Dar-es-Salaam in Tanzania, Dorothy and Eileen were met by members of the Maryknoll missionary congregation who had invited them. From the air, Dorothy was thrilled to see the great mountain, Kilimanjaro, highest point in Africa, but what impressed her most was the effort going on in Tanzania to develop a "gentle socialism" that respected village life. She noted that Tanzania was the first state in Africa to provide exemption for conscientious objectors to military service.

Details of her brief stopover in Rome went unmentioned in her journal. While in England she addressed a conference of War Resisters International and spent time with her old friend Donald Attwater, now losing his sight. He had devoted much of his life to writing biographies of the saints, for which Dorothy was profoundly grateful. "Peter Maurin," Dorothy recalled in her journal entry, "used to say we should study history by studying the lives of the saints."

The following year, 1971, Dorothy had an invitation from her friend Nina Polcyn in Chicago to join her in going to Eastern Europe with a tour group led by a professor of theology from Yale. A benefactor would take care of the cost. Dorothy attempted to be prudent. "I need to conserve my strength or rebuild it after my last year's travels," she wrote Nina. "After all, born in 1897, I've seen a lot of this world, and I'm not much longer in it . . . unless I take pains to conserve my energy, sit in the sun, walk a little instead of being propelled everywhere. I would like to have ten more years to write, to live the life of a hermit, here in community." But by the time the group set off in July, Dorothy had signed on. She found she couldn't say no.

The stops included Poland, Bulgaria and Hungary, but the main part was in Russia—or rather "Holy Mother Russia," as Dorothy invariably put it even during the Soviet era—the Russia whose authors, icons and exiles had mattered so much in shaping her Christian faith. Another Russian influence was her friend Helene Iswolsky, whose father had been the last ambassador of the tsar to France. Helene had taught Russian language, literature, history and spirituality at Fordham University and was also the founder of the Third Hour, a group promoting dialogue among Orthodox, Catholic, and Protestant intellectuals. Its core group of participants included both Dorothy and W.H. Auden. (Late in her life, Helene made the Catholic Worker farm at Tivoli her home, living in a room in which she was surrounded by icons.)

Having arrived in Saint Petersburg (still Leningrad at the time), the most important stop for Dorothy was the Saint Alexander Nevsky Monastery. In the monastery cemetery, she prayed at the grave of her beloved Dostoevsky, so many of whose characters she spoke of with the familiarity of friendship and whose fictional Father Zosima in *The Brothers Karamazov* was as real to Dorothy as any living friend.

Also within the monastery walls was an Orthodox seminary and a "working church" (in contrast to a museum church). "It was in the middle of the week," Dorothy wrote, "so

Dorothy in Red Square. (Marquette University archives)

we did not expect a service, or even that the church would be open. But as we passed the rear of the church in our exploration of the grounds, we saw seated on some boxes a row of little old ladies, drably dressed and with shawls over their heads, murmuring together like a row of birds." A Russian-speaking friend who was with Dorothy asked a nun if there would be any services that day. "Yes, at five Vespers would start and the church door would be opened. So we too sat and waited, and it was good to sit. It was a long service, but there was a good choir of mixed voices and some beautiful singing."

Dorothy was ashamed that, due to her arthritis, she had to sit part of the time on her cane-chair. She recalled that, in pre-revolutionary times, even the tsar was expected to stand throughout the liturgy. During the service, Dorothy noted that the old were joined by the young, including parents with children in their arms. "We left before the service was over and by that time the church was full of lighted candles and the smoke of incense. We too venerated the icons and went away happy that we had had the opportunity to praise God."

In reporting on her trip in *The Catholic Worker*, Dorothy recalled the great suffering that Russian believers have experienced since the revolution, the times of "awful desecration of churches and icons trampled underfoot, acts expressing the hatred of religion when it collaborated so closely with the government." But even after decades of atheism, church destruction, many martyrs and unimaginable suffering, "the life of the spirit goes on," Dorothy wrote. She reminded her readers that a third of the population of Leningrad, a million people, had died of starvation, illness and the cold in the city's 872-day siege during the Second World War. "Now you see a religious revival among the young, many of whom are being baptized and bringing their friends to belief with them."

Dorothy occasionally provided challenging moments for the government officials and guest-minders present at arranged meetings. While expressing gratitude for the care being given to icons and the few surviving churches, as well as the rarity of "crude expressions of atheism" in the post-Stalin Soviet Union, she was distressed at the official denunciations of Alexander Solzhenitsyn, author of *The Gulag Archipelago* and *The Cancer Ward*. Dorothy compared him to Dostoevsky and Tolstoy. "Perhaps," Dorothy commented, "it was my tribute and my expressions of regret at the treatment of this great Russian that caused the meeting to break up."

In Moscow, Dorothy prayed the psalms each day while looking out a window that offered a view of four churches whose brilliantly colored onion domes were shining in the

"Today was lovely. Mass at the American Embassy. Only one Roman Mass in the city. Fine young priest. Then a museum to see some of the most famous ikons, etc. etc. Every museum is full of people, but no music, no concerts. I've walked my legs off and rested all evening, while poor Nina had to spend it in a seminar. In no time at all I'll be home and at my typewriter, disentangling my copious notes. I miss the home folks very much."—To Frank Donovan, July 1971

summer sky. The most exuberant church in view, dominating Red Square, was Saint Basil's Cathedral. While she knew that it was at the time only a museum, she saw it even in this capacity as an invitation to faith. "Who knows," Dorothy reflected, "what the effect will be on millions of children who are guided through such churches, even the ones that are museums today?' The world will be saved by beauty.'" The phrase from Dostoevsky's novel *The Idiot* was one Dorothy's most often-repeated sentences.

Rublev's "Old Testament" Holy Trinity Icon.

Next to the Kremlin wall on the same square was Lenin's Tomb, a building as grim as Saint Basil's was festive. Here people from every corner of the Soviet Union came each day, no matter what the weather, waiting patiently in line before entering. Dorothy too joined the line, at last finding herself in a room illuminated by a soft blue light where Lenin's chemically-preserved body lay on a stone slab. "The silence was rather awesome," she said. Though everyone on line was supposed to keep moving, Dorothy "stopped a moment to make the sign of the Cross and to say a prayer for this man who brought such upheaval into the world." By the Kremlin wall, she prayed as well at the grave of Jack Reed, whom she had known when they both worked for *The Masses*.

Dorothy prayed again at the Tretyakov Gallery, a museum housing many of the treasures of Russian art. Most beloved for Dorothy were the Holy Trinity icon, made by Saint Andrei Rublev, and the ancient Vladimir icon of the Mother of God. Dorothy stood before the latter image—the face of the infant Jesus pressed gently against his mother's anxious face, a work legend attributes to Saint Luke—and thanked God that "the Russians are not following the example of the West, where we seem to be trying to obliterate devotion to Our Lady."

"These icons," Dorothy told the community at Tivoli when she was home in August, "have such tenderness and beauty. They make you think of all mothers, all children. They help us to overcome all violence and hatred."

A Strange Beauty

During her world-circling trip in 1970, Dorothy's plane had passed directly over Vietnam. From so high an altitude, Dorothy could only imagine the war going on beneath her, claiming so many Vietnamese and American lives, while sending many in the Catholic Worker movement to prison.

It was not until after the Vietnam War ended in 1975 that the Catholic Worker community became fully aware of how much attention its many years of antiwar activities had generated in the Federal Bureau of Investigation. Following an application made by Catholic Worker staff member Robert Ellsberg under the terms of the Freedom of Information Act,

Vespers at St. Joseph House. (Credit: Jon Erikson)

sections of the FBI files were received packet-by-packet in the latter 1970s. Altogether 575 pages were delivered, many of them heavily censored. Many other pages were withheld "for reasons of national security." The FBI investigation stretched from the Second World War to the war in Vietnam. The file was started in 1940 when the Bureau received a tip about "a radical front" in New York which was described by the informer as "The Dorothy Day Art Studio." In due course the FBI became aware that the art studio was in fact a soup kitchen and also a base of protest and the dissemination of radical ideas. It was decided that Dorothy Day was worth keeping an eye on. On April 3, 1941, eight months before U.S. entry into the war, J. Edgar Hoover filed a memorandum with the Special Defense Unit of the Justice Department recommending that Dorothy Day

Dorothy praying. (Credit: © Bob Fitch)

"be considered for custodial detention in the event of national emergency." (Thousands of Japanese living in the United States, as well as U.S.-born citizens of Japanese descent, were put in "custodial detention" camps during World War II, but tentative plans to do the same to people regarded as radicals were not realized.)

The last major entry in the file concerned Dorothy's speech at Union Square in 1965 in support of Tom Cornell and others who burned their draft cards to protest military conscription and the war in Vietnam. By this time thoughts of detaining her had cooled, though it was clear Dorothy was liable for prosecution for having advocated violation of the Selective Service Act.

Even more than the FBI, the government agency most fascinated by the Catholic Worker during the Vietnam War was the Internal Revenue Service, the nation's tax collector—and, from the Catholic Worker point of view, chief fund-raiser for war. The IRS found the Catholic Worker a peculiar object. No one, including Dorothy Day, received a salary, yet it couldn't be regarded as a convent or monastery—no one wore special clothes or took any vows. Nor had it ever sought recognition from the IRS as a "charity"— what was given away, Dorothy always stressed, was more a work of justice than charity. In any event, what charity engaged in protest, often had staff members in jail for acts of protest, or advocated nonviolent revolution? (On the other hand, the Catholic Worker has been registered with the New York State Bureau of Charities since its founding and each year submits a report to officials in Albany.)

In April 1972, during a period of military escalation in Vietnam, an IRS letter addressed to the Catholic Worker demanded payment of $296,359—"unpaid taxes" plus fines and interest. Dorothy wondered whether this was the beginning of a process that would effectively suppress the paper and put her back to prison, this time for a much longer stay. Still more likely would be confiscation of the Catholic Worker house on First Street and the farm at Tivoli plus whatever money happened to be in the community's bank account.

Dorothy struggled to imagine what could be done, if worse came to worst, for the forty adults and twelve children then in residence at Tivoli, plus another crowd of adults in New York who were packed "like sardines" into the First Street house. "I can only trust that this crisis will pass," Dorothy wrote in the May issue, "that some way will be found to avert the disaster, or for us to continue to care for our old, sick, helpless, hungry and homeless if it happens."

She was aware that the Catholic Worker movement's longstanding opposition to paying war taxes was an incite-

"Dorothy Day has been described as a very erratic and irresponsible person. . . . She has engaged in activities which strongly suggest that she is consciously or unconsciously being used by Communist groups. From past experience with her it is obvious she maintains a very hostile and belligerent attitude towards the [FBI] and makes every effort to castigate the Bureau whenever she feels so inclined."

—J. Edgar Hoover, in the FBI file on Dorothy Day

St. Joseph House at 36 E. First St.
(Credit: Ed Lettau)

ment for the IRS to take up such an action. "One of the most costly protests against war, in the long run," Dorothy wrote, "a protest involving enduring personal sacrifice, is to refuse to pay income taxes for war." Dorothy was aware that if the Catholic Worker redefined itself in such a way that it would be eligible for recognition as a tax-exempt charity, the present demand would probably be withdrawn, and also that, with tax exempt status, many more people would be inclined to make contributions, for they could then deduct such gifts from their taxable income. But she could not in conscience apply for any such special recognition.

Dorothy begged her readers' prayers and understanding. "I'm sure that many will think me a fool indeed, almost criminally negligent, for not taking more care to safeguard . . . the welfare of the lame, halt and blind—deserving and undeserving—that come to us. . . . We are told by Jesus Christ to practice the works of mercy, not the works of war. And we do not see why it is necessary to ask the government for permission to practice the works of mercy, which are the opposite of the works of war."

News editors recognized an ant-and-elephant story. A report appeared in *The New York Times* under a four-column headline. An editorial in the same paper, titled "Imagination,

Please," wondered if the IRS did not have more useful things to do than to close down a house of hospitality and silence a newspaper. Many papers took up the story, and supportive letters flooded the Worker's First Street house.

A September date was set for Dorothy to appear in federal court to explain the Catholic Worker's refusal to pay taxes or "structure itself" so as to become tax-exempt. "We are afraid of that word, 'structure.' We refuse to become a corporation," Dorothy wrote in her June column. "It is not only that we must follow our conscience in opposing the government in war," she explained. "We believe that the government has no right to legislate as to who can or who are to perform the Works of Mercy."

She apologized to her readers for the anxiety she felt. "I would like to say . . . that I am not at all worried about this mishmash and the outcome. But of course one becomes intimidated in the awesome presence of a judge, not to speak of stenographers, and swearing to tell the truth, the whole truth, and nothing but the truth, so help me God, and then not being allowed to finish a sentence, or to explain. Anyone who writes as much as I do is not a woman of few words!"

"We are not tax evaders," she explained to readers who thought she was opposed to all taxes. She pointed out that the Catholic Worker quite willingly paid local property taxes, both in New York and Tivoli, and made no attempt to avoid these on religious or charitable grounds. Dorothy said she had much praying to do and was finding consolation in reading Tolstoy's *War and Peace*.

In July, the IRS withdrew its claim—a kind of "absolution," Dorothy wrote with relief. She was relieved as well not to have to stand before another judge. The IRS had no doubt been impressed by the support of the press as well as many religious and political figures who had raised their voices on behalf of the Catholic Worker and Dorothy Day. By then, she had lived long enough to be seen as venerable and prophetic rather than written off as a religious crank.

On Dorothy's seventy-fifth birthday in November, the Jesuit magazine *America* did a special issue about her, finding her the individual who best symbolized "the aspiration and action of the American Catholic community during the past forty years." Notre Dame University honored her with its highest award, the Laetare Medal. The text that came with the medal bore the simple message that Dorothy Day had "comforted the afflicted and afflicted the comfortable virtually all her life." Mother Teresa sent Dorothy a birthday letter from Calcutta: "So much love—so much sacrifice—all for Him alone. You have been such a beautiful branch on the Vine, Jesus, and allowed his Father, the Vine-dresser, to prune you so often and so much. You have accepted all with great love."

Dorothy was embarrassed by admiration, most of all from those whom she herself admired. She felt that she was far from being the person others imagined her to be. "I am a mean impatient soul," she wrote in her diary in May 1973. How many times had she sought forgiveness for being too judgmental, too irritable? And the battle was far from over. (During Lent in 1973, she wrote to "beg forgiveness" of a former member of the Catholic Worker staff, myself, toward whom she felt she had been too harsh. "I want to apologize for my critical attitudes and to promise to amend my life— or attempt to by 'mortifying my critical faculties.'")

A major area of distress for her in the 1970s was what seemed to her the erosion occurring in the spiritual life of her fellow Catholics, including many in the Catholic Worker movement. To her joy, more than ever Catholics seemed attentive to social issues, but so many were alienated from the Church and increasingly neglectful of disciplines of Church life that were fundamental to her. "Penance seems ruled out today," she noted repeatedly. It pained her to notice co-workers skipping Mass and not taking the time for prayer. "With prayer, one can go on cheerfully and even happily, while without prayer, how grim is the journey," she commented. "Prayer is as necessary to life as breathing. It is drink and food."

"Without the sacraments of the church, primarily the Eucharist, the Lord's Supper as it is sometimes called, I certainly do not think that I could go on," Dorothy wrote in her journal in November 1970. "I do not always approach it from need, or with joy and thanksgiving. After thirty-eight years of

"What I feel about the institutional church. . . . For me it is the place in the slum, in our neighborhood, where it is possible to be alone, to be silent, to wait on the Lord. . . . No matter how corrupt the Church may become, it carries within it the seeds of its own regeneration."
—To Karl Meyer, August 3, 1971

"As a convert, I never expected much of the bishops. In all history popes and bishops and father abbots seem to have been blind and power-loving and greedy. I never expected leadership from them. It is the saints that keep appearing all thru history who keep things going. What I do expect is the bread of life and down thru the ages there is that continuity."
—To Gordon Zahn, October 29, 1968

almost daily communion, one can confess to a routine, but it is like a routine of taking daily food." "The sacraments mean much to me," she wrote Karl Meyer in August, 1971. "The daily bread we ask for is there."

"You cannot imagine how hard it is to live at the Ammon Hennacy House here [in Los Angeles]," she confided in a December 1971 letter to Frank Donovan, a key staff member of the New York house. "No prayer, no Mass-going, not even on Sundays—a terrible bitterness . . . against Cardinal McIntyre and the 'institutional' church. Just six people in the house, and not a practicing Catholic among them."

She mourned the widespread abandonment of the rosary as a tool of prayer and meditation. She insisted on calling priests "Father" and nuns "Sister" and was annoyed with those who preferred, even demanded, informality. She wished that priests and nuns would retain the traditional clothing which made their vocations visible to strangers. Casual sex outside of marriage dismayed her. She was horrified with the growing acceptance of abortion in the larger society: "I say make room for the children. Don't do away with them."

She was irked by those who wanted her to say "person" rather than "man." "When I write 'men,'" she commented testily in one column, "I mean 'people.'" Though a strong woman who had stood up to many men in her life, she resisted identifying herself as a feminist—a word that for many implied promotion of abortion—or to be called one by others.

She was saddened by the frequent expressions of contempt toward the Pope and bishops—though she granted that there had been popes, bishops and priests who reminded her more of vultures than doves. She confessed that she found great pleasure in her tattered, out-of-date English-Latin Mass books, and treasured "their short, precious accounts of the saints." Her gratitude for Pope John XXIII was undiminished; she regarded him as a saint and, in one of her columns, published a prayer begging his intercession for the farm workers. But she felt that many were, in the name of Pope John's renewal, vandalizing the Church. This grieved her. At times she felt bitter.

"It is the young ones, their new morality, their religious justification of it, their conviction that we will just have to accept, that makes one feel that these surroundings are not right for us now. Or not right for them. Life on the land should have its discipline, its hard work, so that people sleep instead of staying up making music all night."
—To William Miller, October 5, 1971

Dorothy walking at Tivoli. (Credit: © Bob Fitch)

"We feel so powerless. We do so little, giving out soup. But at last we are facing problems daily. Hunger, homelessness, greed, loneliness. Greatest concern of the Bible is injustice, bloodshed. So we share what we have, we work for peace."
—Diary entry, June 19, 1973

Maryhouse at 55 E. Third St. (Credit: Jim Forest)

Her sense of duty was undiminished. Despite the speed with which exhaustion came, she pressed on with travels—in the summer of 1973 going to California, and that winter, in obedience to a request from Mother Teresa, flying to England and Northern Ireland to visit houses of hospitality associated with the Simon Community. Early in 1974 she went to Boston to accept the Isaac Hecker Award from the Paulists. After that she went south by bus, with stops in Washington, Charlottesville, Danville, Atlanta and Tallahassee, among others. From Florida she hurried back to New York in order to speak at Vassar College at Poughkeepsie, not far from the Catholic Worker farm at Tivoli.

But increasingly she had to face her physical limitations. She began to mention "my sick, weak heart" in her columns and to complain about her failing memory. Sometimes she discovered she had answered the same letter twice.

Dorothy was far from absent-minded about homeless women, who were becoming more numerous in New York. In her column in the March 1974 *Catholic Worker*, she described the overcrowding at Saint Joseph's House on First Street in Manhattan. "I came back from a short speaking trip to see one woman sleeping on a chair just inside the door, her head on two telephone books resting against a heavy stone statue of Saint Joseph which is on the window sill. On still another row of chairs against the wall, another is prone, covered with her coat. Upstairs in the mailing room, there is another young woman, stark upright but with a heavy scarf covering her head and face. If I climb the stairs to the third floor, where seven women with all their belongings fill our limited space, I may find another woman lying against the wall in the hall." Thanks to the financial support of Dom John Eudes Bamberger, abbot of the Trappist Abbey of the Genesee in western New York State, a building on East Third Street was purchased in June 1974 and given the name Maryhouse. A former music school, it was spacious—three houses joined into one. It was ideal, not only for much hospitality for women but a better environment for Friday night public meetings "for the clarification of thought," a principle central to Peter Maurin. However, first a great deal of work

Dorothy with Eileen Egan, leaving Mass at Nativity Church on 2nd Ave. (Credit: Bill Barrett)

was needed—it took nearly two years—before the city issued a certificate of occupancy.

In the meantime, the house on First Street had to meet every need. It seemed to Dorothy more "like a railroad or bus station" than a community. "I'm afraid we are still individual-istic, not communitarian." Dorothy admitted to times of depression. At least "we are getting a lot of work done, and hundreds of meals are put on the table daily." There was also the healing smell of fresh bread baking in the ovens of the Worker kitchen, but even that reminded her of all those for whom there was no welcome and no bread—the millions of homeless people facing starvation.

Reading continued to be part of the basic structure of each day. As she had commented in a journal entry in June 1972, "No matter how old I get . . . no matter how feeble, short of breath, incapable of walking more than a few blocks, what with heart murmurs, heart failures, emphysema per-haps, arthritis in feet and knees, with all these symptoms of age and decrepitude, my heart can still leap for joy as I read and suddenly assent to some great truth enunciated by some great mind and heart."

"How little I can do these days but suffer patiently the innumerable small difficul-ties of aging. And always Prayer which is a joy. Psalms are always the joyful ones on Thursday, in honor of the Last Supper. Where else would we have room save at Tivoli Farm for so much joy and suffering?"
—Diary entry, September 2, 1976

Paper work, cleaning the house, dealing with the innumerable visitors who come all through the day, answering the phone, keeping patience and acting intelligently, which is to find some meaning in all that happens—these things, too, are the works of peace, and often seem like a very little way.
—Dorothy Day, *Catholic Worker,*
December 1965

In February 1973, she copied into her journal one such "great truth," a passage by William James that she had come upon in a collection of his letters:

I am against bigness and greatness in all their forms, and with the invisible molecular moral forces that work from individual to individual, stealing in through the crannies of the world like so many soft rootlets, or like the capillary oozing of water, and yet rending the hardest monuments of man's pride, if you give them time. The bigger the unit you deal with, the hollower, the more brutal, the more mendacious is the life displayed. So I am against all big organizations as such, national ones first and foremost; against all big successes and big results; and in favor of the eternal forces of truth which always work in the individual and immediately unsuccessful way, underdogs always, till history comes, after they are long dead, and puts them on top.

Dorothy was also rescued from bleak periods by her lifelong gift of seeing beauty where others only noticed ugliness. She noted in her "On Pilgrimage" column for September 1974:

The world will be saved by beauty, Dostoevsky wrote, and Solzhenitsyn quoted it in his talk when he accepted the Nobel Prize for Literature. I look back on my childhood and remember beauty. The smell of sweet clover in a vacant lot, a hopeful clump of grass growing up through the cracks of a city pavement. A feather dropped from some pigeon. A stalking cat. Ruskin wrote of "the duty of delight" and told us to lift up our heads and see the cloud formations in the sky. I have seen sunrises at the foot of a New York street, coming up over the East River. I have always found a strange beauty in the suffering faces which surround us in the city. Black, brown and gray heads bent over those bowls of food, that so necessary food which is always there at St. Joseph's House. . . . We all enter into the act of hospitality, one way or another. So many of those who come in to eat return to serve, to become part of the "family."

The View from the Window

"I now have 11 great-grandchildren," Dorothy reported exultantly in a February 1975 letter to Karl Meyer. So large a family! In her column that month, she had quoted the Psalm, "Bless the Lord, O my soul, let all that is within me bless His holy name."

Many of her grandchildren, it pleased Dorothy to note, were farmers, including a granddaughter who had joined several Catholic Worker families and "gone back to the land" in West Virginia. "They haven't founded 'houses of hospitality on the land,' as some of our farms have been called," Dorothy said when accepting the Gandhi Award at a church in New York, "nor are they farming 'communes' or 'agronomic universities,' as other Catholic Worker people have called such ventures. All those high-sounding titles we used to give our little bits of land! These are more like villages, with families living close together, sharing and cooperating in all those many ways that used to be common to any small village. This is happening in the Catholic Worker movement and many other groups working for peace and keeping the nonviolent

Dorothy with grandchildren.
(Marquette University archives)

Above, top: The dining room at the Tivoli farm.
Above, bottom: Testifying at a meeting for bishops preparing for the bicentennial, 1975.
(Marquette University archives)

way. . . . There's a strong, strong work going on within the peace movement, with all the joy of youth and the strength of youth, living the normal life of the family—making clothes, raising food, and having babies. So it's a healthy movement, living in the midst of these appalling, murderous times."

Crediting an "upsurge of strength," Dorothy was able to go to West Virginia that year to visit inmates at the Federal Prison for Women at Alderson and to see a nearby Catholic Worker house of hospitality that assisted the inmates' families, but her age and frailties were impossible to ignore.

In the March issue of *The Catholic Worker,* Dorothy announced her retirement from day-to-day responsibilities. She cited the Buddhist teaching that life was divided into three stages: the first for growing up and basic education, the second for marriage and family and work, and the third for detachment. "The third period is the time for withdrawal from responsibility, letting go of the things of this life, letting God take over." From now on, she said, everything was in the care of "our generous crowd of young people" who put out the paper, take care of the house, and who "perform in truth all the works of mercy."

In the same column, Dorothy stressed the role of the Catholic Worker as a place in which young volunteers who came to help often discovered their direction in life: "People ask what is the Catholic Worker Movement all about. It is, in a way, a school, a work camp, to which large-hearted, socially-conscious, young people come to find their vocation. After some months or years, many know most definitely what they want to do with their lives. Some go into medicine, nursing, law, teaching, farming, writing and publishing. They learn not only to love, with compassion, but to overcome fear, that dangerous emotion that precipitates violence. They may go on feeling fear, but they know the means, they have grown in faith, to overcome it. 'Lord, deliver us from the fear of our enemies'—not *from* our enemies, but from the *fear* of them."

Writing for the July issue, she recalled a Russian proverb: "In a field where a poisonous weed is found, there is also found the antidote." The times were full of toxic weeds, she said, even though the war in Vietnam had finally ended. "For me, the Jesus Prayer, used by the Russian pilgrim, is the remedy growing in the field." It is the simple prayer, "Lord Jesus Christ, Son of God, have mercy on me, a sinner." She had read *The Way of the Pilgrim*, a classic book of Russian Orthodox spirituality in which an anonymous seeker relates his search for someone who could teach him how to pray without ceasing.

In September Dorothy recommended frequent use of the Our Father. "Often I am tempted to depression, thinking that I have scarcely begun the spiritual life, or even to live the life we all profess to, that of voluntary poverty and manual labor. It is a great cleanser of conscience, this living in community, with so many poor and suffering. That harsh saying, 'You love God as much as the one you love the least,' often comes to mind. But just to say over again that one prayer, the Our Father, is to revive, to return to a sense of joy." (Some months later, she wrote with sympathy of a young woman who said to her, "The word 'Father' means nothing to me. It brings me no comfort. I had a drunken father who abused my mother and beat his children." In so many cases, Dorothy commented, "we can do nothing with words. So we are driven to prayer by our helplessness. God takes over.")

After so many years of activity and travel, Dorothy was daily reminded of her own weakness, helplessness and growing immobility. In December, she wrote of "the last enemy, death." But in the spring of 1976, with work on Maryhouse at last completed and an occupancy certificate issued by the city, Dorothy felt renewed strength. With Stanley Vishnewski, she drove to Vermont to see her daughter. A pilgrim again, she remembered a song she sang to her baby brother John when he was teething: "I'm a pilgrim, I'm a stranger! I can tarry, I can tarry but an hour!"

Dorothy's last public lecture occurred a few months later, in August. Both she and Mother Teresa had been invited to

Walking in the woods at Tivoli.
(Courtesy Tamar Hennessy)

"To embrace a faith is to 'kiss a leper,' to make a leap, as over a chasm, from one world into another, or to plunge into an abyss—'underneath are the everlasting arms.'"—December 29, 1975

Dorothy reading at her desk. (Credit: Jon Erikson)

address the Eucharistic Congress, a major event involving Catholics from all over the world. This year it was to be held in the United States in the city of Philadelphia. By chance, the date chosen for Dorothy's speech was August 6—the Feast of the Transfiguration and also the thirty-first anniversary of the destruction of Hiroshima by the first atom bomb used in war. For weeks beforehand, Dorothy had been in a state of nervous dread about giving the talk. "It is almost easier to stand before a judge than to stand before you," she confessed to her audience when the moment came. She had been welcomed with a standing ovation.

Dorothy recalled the events that had led her to the Church and the Eucharist—how the material world "began to speak to my heart of the love of God." The way of the spirit begins with the physical, Dorothy said. "It was also the physical aspect of the Church which first attracted me"—the bread and wine, the oil and water, the incense. In the Church she had learned, however, that among the gifts one brings to the altar is our reconciliation with others. "Penance comes before the Eucharist," she said. After citing the several holocausts of the twentieth century, she noted, "It is a fearful thought that unless we do penance, we will perish. Our Creator gave us life, and the Eucharist to sustain our life. But we have given the world instruments of death of inconceivable magnitude."

This was one of the rare talks that Dorothy had written out beforehand, though she often strayed from the text as she stood in the congress hall. One departure toward the end was an appeal: "Let's all try to be poorer. My mother used to say, 'Everyone take less, and there will be room for one more.'

There was always room for one more at our table."

Following the Congress, Dorothy went to Pittsburgh in order to take part in a week-long retreat led by Father John Hugo, who had been so important an influence in her life in earlier years. But the two events were a major strain. The next month, back at Tivoli, Dorothy found herself suffering pains in her chest and arms and with a gasping need of fresh air—another heart attack. After electrocardiograms and x-rays at a nearby hospital, she was sent back to her room at the Tivoli farm with orders to rest for at least a month. "Thank goodness," she noted in a letter, "[the doctor] did not put me in the hospital intensive care. He believes in home care." From her bed, she pondered the Psalm, "Be still and know that I am God."

"Unto old age and gray hairs, O Lord, forsake me not," Dorothy wrote in *The Catholic Worker*'s forty-third anniversary issue in May 1976. Dorothy continued writing her "On Pilgrimage" column, but her pilgrimages now were mainly inner ones—no bus, car, ship or plane was required. The news she reported month by month was of reading, prayer, visitors, opera on the radio, plays and films on television, the view from the window, the changing seasons. She wrote about her memories, often from the nineteen-thirties. She often recalled her brief journey to Russia. She wrote of her continuing struggles with impatience and irritation, her sadness over uprooted trees that she had come to know and love via her window, and her distress with estrangement from the Church that she noted in some of the young volunteers. But she also gave thanks for the "utterly reliable people" who carried on the active work. Maryhouse on East Third Street and Saint Joseph's House on East First Street were carrying on. The paper was thriving. "We print 94,000 copies," she noted in 1976, "and everyone joins in the job [of helping get out the mailing]."

Often Dorothy wrote about death. "When saying the Hail Mary this morning," she wrote in the June 1977 issue, "it suddenly occurred to me how good it is to end our prayer to Mary with 'now and at the hour of our death.' I don't think I had ever realized before how often we pray for the hour of our death, that it would be a good one. It is good, certainly, to have a long period of 'ill health' . . . nothing specific, mild but

Dorothy's cottage on Staten Island. (Marquette University archives)

"I had a mild heart attack in September, pains in my chest and arms and a gasping need of fresh air. It is certainly frightening not to be able to breathe. One line of a psalm is: 'Be still and know that I am God.' You hear things in your own silences. The beauty of nature, including the sound of waves, the sound of insects, the cicadas in the tress—all were part of my joy in nature that brought me to the Church."

—Catholic Worker,
October-November 1976

"'In the beginning God created heaven and earth.' Looking out over the bay, the gulls, the 'paths in the sea,' the tiny ripples stirring a patch of water here and there, the reflections of clouds on the surface—how beautiful it all is. Alone all day. A sudden storm in the night. Vast, dark clouds and a glaring, lightning flash with thunder."

—*Catholic Worker,* July-August 1977

frightening pains in the heart, and sickness, ebb-tide, the ebbing of life, and then some days of strength and creativity." She rejoiced that, during her ebb-tide, she was "surrounded by loving kindness. Tulips, a rose, a picture, food. Tender, loving care! We all need it, sick or well."

Dorothy didn't mellow with old age, but continued to speak firmly about values that mattered in her life. "I wish colleges would stop offering me honorary degrees which I must in conscience refuse," she said in a 1976 letter to the president of a Catholic college, "but wish to refuse with all respect and gratitude. Whoever is responsible for making such an offer to me certainly knows nothing of the philosophy of the Catholic Worker movement." Why should a school honor a pacifist like herself when, at the same time, it hosts a government-funded military program? In the same letter she pointed out that "love of country is not synonymous with love of governments." She was ready to acknowledge that the word "anarchist," which she often had used in describing her political philosophy, might be confusing to others. "I am coming to the conclusion that 'personalist' is a better word than 'anarchist'" as a term of self-description. (In the last decade or two of her life, Dorothy turned down at least fifteen invitations from Catholic colleges to be awarded an honorary degree. In each case she cited her distress at the subversion of education by the military.)

Remembering various Jewish friends, Dorothy often wrote about the Jews, especially Mike Gold, who had died in 1967. She wondered if his book, *Jews Without Money,* was still in print. She discovered and recommended the novels of Chaim Potok—*My Name Is Asher Lev, The Chosen, The Promise.* These were "a joy to read," she said, "full of a sense of the sacramentality of life." She and Potok had memories that almost overlapped. "These books are about Brooklyn. Having grown up there, the first seven years, it was intensely interesting to get this picture of the Williamsburg section, where the Hasidic Jews are settled, and to learn about the Hasidim of today, this movement of Jews filled with the fervor and joy of a Saint Francis, the men dancing and singing at celebrations." A few months later, writing about her love

of the Bible, she quoted a question from a Potok novel: "I wonder if Gentiles clasp Holy Scripture in their arms and dance with it, as we Jews do?" "Well," she responded, "I've often seen people kiss the Book before and after reading it, and I do myself."

She recalled her encounters with anti-Semitism in the early years of the Catholic Worker. There had been many collisions with the supporters of the then much admired anti-Semite, Father Coughlin. "Our papers were torn from our hands and thrown back into our faces, and when I tried to protest, 'But our Lord Jesus Christ was a Jew,' the people coming from one [Coughlin] meeting shouted at me, 'But He's a long time dead!'" She remembered an article about anti-Semitism that she had submitted to *America* magazine, a prominent Catholic journal. "I was advised," Dorothy wrote, "to stick to my 'delightful, informal essays.'" (It would have pleased Dorothy that, in 2010, *America* published the once-rejected article.)

Her contemplative eye for the ordinary wonders of the natural world was undiminished. Writing from the beach house on Staten Island for the July 1977 issue, she described the doleful sounds of the mourning dove in a nearby mimosa tree. She was enchanted with the mimosa. "No matter how small the seedlings are, they close up their fernlike leaves if you touch them."

Tiring easily, she felt unable to deal with the needs and problems that people brought to her. "I cannot tell you the state of nervous exhaustion I've been through," she confided in a letter to Deane Mowrer in May 1977. "It's been like a constant trembling of my nerves, a need for solitude and no responsibility. With everyone else taking responsibility and have been taking it for so long, bearing so much, I feel like an utter failure—wrung dry. But I am beginning to recover from the miserable state of depression, this sense of a nervous breakdown." In a letter to her sister, Della, sent that September, Dorothy confessed to enduring dark nights of the soul in recent months: "I have had a period of melancholy too. Declining years, I guess. Eighty my next birthday."

Her eyes still took in a great deal, though they tired easily,

"'I have sinned exceedingly in my life,' Tolstoy said to Maxim Gorki once. This phrase comes to mind when fulsome praise comes my way. . . . My loose life as a young woman was like that of so many young women today, only there was no 'drug scene' then. We drank; we were the flaming youth of the 20s, portrayed by Hemingway and Malcolm Cowley. In my book The Long Loneliness *I tried to write only of those things which brought about my conversion to the faith—a happy love affair, a love of nature, a truly good life in the natural sense."*

—Diary entry, November 1976

especially when she tried to read small print. Nonetheless, she continued to read. That summer her main book was Pasternak's *Doctor Zhivago*, with his vivid account of revolution and civil war in Russia, a portrait of events so different than Jack Reed's *Ten Days That Shook the World*. In November she described herself as not so much "housebound" on East Third Street as traveling, via the printed word, across Siberia with Anton Chekhov to a prison on Sakhalin Island. A few months later, having finished Tolstoy's *Anna Karenina*, she pressed on with his novel *Resurrection*.

From October 1977 until the following February, Dorothy was too weak to leave her room at Maryhouse. The March 1978 issue contained her glad report that she had at last been able to go downstairs and sit in on a Friday night meeting—former staff member Bob Gilliam had spoken on the Church and tradition, major topics for Dorothy. She added, however, that she still lacked "the strength or ambition" to deal with all the papers that were piled high on her desk.

Dorothy at Maryhouse, 1979. (Credit: Bill Barrett)

Again and again, she was grateful for the volunteers that kept coming to carry on the exhausting, sometimes abrasive labor of a house of hospitality, though she noted how few found a long-term vocation in such work. She quoted one of Stanley Vishnewski's funny but accurate comments: "Some come, saying they have found their life work, and remain a few months. Others, more tentative, speak of a visit and stay forever."

Dorothy's window was a reliable friend, always worth looking through, never accusing her, never making demands. "Across the street I can see a sycamore tree with a few little seed balls hanging from it. When I first get up and sit by the window, the rising sun at the foot of the street has made it a golden tree, and during the heavy snows, a tree gold and white—a joy to survey."

Her friendship with Forster Batterham, Tamar's father, had become stronger in recent years. As a young man, he had been opposed to bringing a child into a world of such violence and injustice, but once Tamar had been born he was glad to be her father—and then a grandfather and now a great-grandfather. Dorothy expressed remorse for having pushed him away in the course of her conversion half a century earlier. "In becoming a Catholic I deprived him of a child whom he loved the first two years of her life and he felt her loss keenly," she confided to her friend Dixie MacMaster in February 1976.

"Tamar drove down, or rather was driven down, with Nicky and one of his friends Sunday afternoon," she told Forster in a letter written in September 1976, "and was on time for the baptism of your latest great-grandchild, Charlotte Rose. We run to girls you notice. In case you forget your grandchildren are Becky, Susie, Eric, Nickie, Mary, Maggie, Martha, Hilaire, and Katy. Nine in all. And great-grandchildren: Lara and Justin, Tanya, Kachina, and Charlotte Rose, Shawn Patrick, Sheila, Joshua, Jude, and another due this month . . . thirteen great-grandchildren. All these are your progeny!"

As 1978 began, in a letter to Nina Polcyn, Dorothy provided a glimpse of her life at the start of her ninth decade: "Tamar is spending some weeks with me and doing a lot of knitting for her grandchildren, who are beauties. Her father, Forster, calls me almost every day and Stanley makes my illness an excuse to abandon the rural life for a time and be a gallant amongst all the young lady volunteers around here. He and Tamar go for walks, exploring bookshops, and bring me back presents. This week it is a wonderful book on China. We have Mass twice weekly here at the house. The Little Brothers of Charles de Foucauld are around the corner and come and inspire us."

With the spring of 1978, Dorothy was strong enough to come downstairs more regularly, for the evening meal and the twice-weekly Mass. But she felt a captive of her frail body. Reporting on the arrest of community members Robert Ellsberg and Brian Terrell at a nuclear weapons plant in Colorado, she mourned her inability to take part in such actions

"Pray for Forster, Tamar's father, who has had one cancer operation after another and gone through a long agony. He always calls me for visits when he goes to the hospital. But he hangs on to life. He is 80."
—To Dixie MacMaster,
February 15, 1976

herself. "I am confined in another way than prison, by weakness and age, but truly I can pray with fervor for those on active duty."

In May and June, she was able to return to Staten Island, but still complained of her sense of confinement. "Patience! Patience!" she wrote in her July column. "The very word patience means suffering." She was glad for her years of studying Latin while a student. "Being a journalist, I use many words, and I like to get at the root of them." But patience was harder than etymology. She had wanted to take part in the sit-ins that had just occurred at consulates of the nuclear-weapon states. Among those arrested were twenty members of the Catholic Worker community.

Dorothy was often impatient with her memory. She was haunted by lines of poetry but at times could not recall the authors. "'Doth it not irk me that upon the beach, the tides monotonous run? Shall I not teach the sea some new speech?' Who wrote it? Those lines came to mind when I woke up this morning." It puzzled her that she should suddenly remember this particular text, as she had no complaint about the speech of the tides. "I love it here."

The Catholic Worker farm at Tivoli.
(Courtesy Johannah Turner)

Among notes about the flowers that were blooming by the back door and her need for two blankets at night if the window was open, she briefly mentioned a visit from Cardinal Cooke, Archbishop of New York, "to bring me [eightieth birthday] greetings from Pope Paul! I was overwhelmed by this. How one dreads such honors when inactive. . . . One feels like a figurehead!"

Visiting Staten Island with Tamar and Stanley, Dorothy collected beautiful stones on the beach. Dorothy never tired of Stanley's jokes. "The Catholic Worker is made up of saints and martyrs," he was famous for saying. "You have to be a martyr to put up with the saints."

"Every day, I am promising to walk a little more, to get my strength back." But strength evaded her. In the September issue, she wrote that her column would better be named "On

Dorothy and Eileen Egan at Maryhouse. (Credit: Bill Barrett)

"My birthday. Party in the dining room and many flowers. Eileen Egan gave me warm stockings for the coming winter."
—Diary entry, November 8, 1978

the Shelf" rather than "On Pilgrimage." She mentioned how tremulous her handwriting had become. It was nearly impossible to write letters.

In August she mourned Pope Paul's death but was excited to learn that his successor, John Paul I, was the son of a socialist who had worked in a glass factory. More than many popes, he would know at close range how dehumanizing factory work could be. Just thirty-three days later, she grieved the same pope's sudden death but was pleased with the election of the first non-Italian pope in many centuries, John Paul II from Poland. "I sat at the TV set from the early hours until it was time for our Sunday Mass here at Maryhouse, watching the Inauguration Mass in Rome."

In the fall she wrote about the irritation she had felt with a prayer book using the term, "Ordinary Time," a term referring to periods on the calendar that weren't linked to major feasts. "To me," she wrote, "no times are 'ordinary.'" At the time, the Catholic Worker was having one of its more extraordinary times, selling its farm at Tivoli. "Within a month or two," Deane Mowrer wrote in her column from the farm, "this place will be closed, this community dispersed. I could dwell on the problems, difficulties, defeats, failures, and complain with Ecclesiastes that all is vexation and vanity. I know, however, that most of us in time will remember the joys, friendships, beauty, fulfillment, love, peace, and prayer we have sometimes known here." She pointed out that "the Catholic Worker is not a place, but a way of life."

In November 1978, on her eighty-first birthday, Dorothy found that one of the members of the Maryhouse community had put on the wall of her room a huge painting of a pink-robed, orange-haired guardian angel carrying an armload of lilies—"wildly decorative," Dorothy commented in her December column. From Tamar she received a beautifully embroidered pillowcase. Among other gifts she noted were books by Isaac Bashevis Singer, Dostoevsky, and a profusely-illustrated history of Judaism, *Wanderings*, by Chaim Potok. Following a special Mass, there was a party in the Maryhouse dining room.

Peggy Scherer and other members of the Catholic

Worker staff had been visiting Central America, a subject featured in many issues of the paper and much in Dorothy's thoughts as well. She was reminded of the committee she had worked for briefly before meeting Peter Maurin that sent medical supplies to Sandino's movement in the Nicaraguan mountains and campaigned for the withdrawal of the U.S. Marines. John Nevin Sayre of the Fellowship of Reconciliation, she remembered, had in those years courageously traveled on mule-back in remote parts of Nicaragua in his efforts to bring about peace.

While Dorothy often complained of her memory, in fact much of the time it was reliable and vivid. "I am steeped in memories," she wrote, thinking of the Tivoli farm and the events that had happened there. "I am overcome with nostalgia for the past." But her eyes and thoughts were on the present as well. She took pleasure in updating her readers on the view from her window: "At exactly 8:05 A.M., the morning sun gilds the upper floors of the buildings across the street, creeping from the gray one to the red brick one. A lovely sight. Pigeons fly from the roofs. Looking up, I see squirrels on the roof edge. The sycamore tree stirs in the cold, east wind. The sky is a cloudless blue. And now one side of the tree, reaching the third floor of those tenements, is all gilded, as the sun spreads rapidly around. Young people are on their way to work, but the children are not yet on their way to school. 'My' tree is now radiant with sun!"

The television she had been given provided another window. Dorothy watched Eugene O'Neill's plays on television and remembered the Golden Swan saloon on Sixth Avenue where they had spent so many evenings together. She recalled a line of poetry by Max Bodenheim, one of the others who was often there, recited one night in the saloon's back room: "I know not ugliness, it is a mood which has forsaken me."

Dorothy admonished herself to forsake all attachments, to cultivate "holy indifference"—the grateful acceptance of powerlessness. "I should rejoice that I am 'just an old woman,' as the little boy said at dinner in the Rochester House of Hospitality long ago. He said, 'All day long they said "Dorothy Day is coming," and now she's here and she's just an old woman!'"

"My brain, my memory is like a rag bag. I reach in and pull out of it the scraps that make up these columns."
—Diary entry, January 18, 1978

The Mules Are Packed

"My resolution for the new year," Dorothy wrote in the January 1979 *Catholic Worker*, "is to get out and walk more." She still felt herself a captive in her room, which at times she compared to a room Dostoevsky had described in his short story, "The Honest Thief": less a room than a corner. She felt cornered. "Sometimes I feel like a relic," she confided in a letter to Nina Polcyn. "Everyone is always giving me things of beauty so I sometimes think that in addition to running a library I am in a museum."

Some of those close to her during her last few years sensed that her loneliness deepened with the stripping away of her immense physical strength. She was rarely able to take part in the decision-making process of the house or even in deciding the content of the paper. "She made of her loneliness monastic solitude," Tom Cornell recalls.

Her disciplined spiritual life continued. She spent at least half an hour in preparation for receiving communion, which Frank Donovan brought each day from the house chapel, and half an hour in thanksgiving afterward. The rest of the day was punctuated by reading the Psalms and other parts of the monastic office, times for silent prayer and the rosary, reading, meals, radio and television. "It was close to a monastic life," remarked Dan Mauk, a former Franciscan seminarian who was part of the community in that period. There were many for whom she prayed each day, among them various people who had committed suicide. She prayed that those who had taken their own lives would have the grace of final repentance. That her prayers occurred long after their deaths was of no matter, she said, "because there is no time with God."

Tragedy struck in the first weeks of 1979 with the death of her great-grandson, Justin, hit by a car in Vermont. "I feel prostrated," Dorothy wrote in her diary. "Grief is numbing."

Dorothy took note of those members of the Catholic

(Credit: Larry Hales)

"Woke up with two lines haunting me. 'Duty of delight.' And 'Joyous I lay waste the day."—Diary entry, January 6, 1979

Worker staff who often experienced death on a daily basis through their work at Saint Rose's Home, a hospice near the East River for indigent New Yorkers dying of cancer. When she met Peter Maurin, Dorothy remembered, she was reading *Sorrow Built a Bridge*, a biography of Rose Hawthorne, founder of the order responsible for establishing this hospice and several others.

Dorothy's sense of humor was still with her. In a letter to Nina Polcyn written on May Day 1979, the 46th anniversary of the Catholic Worker's founding, she noted that Frank Donovan, the staff member who brought her the daily mail every morning, "grabs the 'loot' [the donations enclosed with letters] to keep me from going out and living 'riotously'!" She rejoiced in how many people were sending her letters: "What a privileged life I've had, to meet so many great people!"

Dorothy recalled how disappointed Peter had been with the first issue of *The Catholic Worker*, which he had expected would be full of his own essays. "Peter certainly got to the roots of our acquisitive society," she went on. His vision had centered on the works of mercy. "But we are so busy with the corporal works of mercy that we often neglect the spiritual ones—converting the sinner, instructing the ignorant, counseling the doubtful, comforting the sorrowful, bearing wrongs patiently, forgiving injuries, and praying for the living and the dead."

One of the corporal works of mercy was to feed the hungry, but at times Dorothy longed for better cooks to do it. "We had hard baked potatoes for supper, and overcooked cabbage. I'm in favor of becoming a vegetarian only if the vegetables are cooked right." At another meal, she discovered chopped onions, herbs and spices in the fruit salad. "A sacrilege to treat food this way. Food should be treated with respect, since Our Lord left Himself to us in the guise of food. His disciples knew Him in the breaking of bread." She envied Stanley's ability to eat everything with enthusiasm— a gift he attributed to the fact that he was still a "growing boy." She reminded herself that cooking at the Catholic Worker is a hard job and that "the human warmth in the dining room covers up a multitude of [culinary] sins."

A few months later Dorothy was rejoicing over a fruit salad brought to her by her godchild, Jean Kennedy, though she had a slightly guilty conscience. "I ate it all! How sensual I am. A glutton. Was it Saint Catherine of Siena or Saint Angela Foligno who wanted to tie a baked chicken around her neck and run through the streets shouting, 'I am a glutton'?"

The following week she noted her forgetfulness and also that her hearing wasn't what it had been. "My memory is so bad—old age is certainly trying. Also I am getting deaf. When Joan Walsh and Tamar are talking quietly in the room by the windows, I cannot hear them."

Dorothy's appetite for books remained huge. Among the titles she mentioned in 1979 and 1980 were Solzhenitsyn's *The First Circle*, Tolstoy's *War and Peace*, *The Third Man* by Graham Greene, *All the King's Men* by Robert Penn Warren, and two classics of the spiritual life, *The Little Flowers of Saint Francis* and *The Imitation of Christ*. Dostoevsky remained indispensable—she reread *The Idiot*, *The Possessed*, and *Crime and Punishment*. Increasingly, however, she turned to

"One of my birthday presents last November was a subscription to the National Geographic. I love it not only for its texts (I can still be 'on pilgrimage' while reading it) but also its pictures. I woke up this morning with a tune running thru my head—'He has the whole world in His hands, He has the whole wide world, in His hands.' So why worry? Why lament? 'Rejoice,' the Psalmist writes, 'and again I say Rejoice!'"
—Diary entry, February 5, 1979

Dorothy and Mother Teresa, during a visit to Maryhouse. (Credit: Bill Barrett)

television. Films she watched included *Wuthering Heights, Gone with the Wind*, and *The African Queen*. Radio and television broadcasts of opera were, as always, a particular joy. Wagner was her favorite composer. She recalled that, many years earlier, a couple associated with the Catholic Worker farm at Easton had been scandalized to discover that Dorothy had gone to the Metropolitan Opera House to see Richard Strauss's "Salome."

Dorothy was sometimes touched, other times distressed, at the care given her by the community around her. She felt "treasured and pampered and 'spoiled rotten,' as my mother used to say," she said in a letter to Nina Polcyn that March.

In April 1979, she was heartened with the news that her book, *Therese*, was being reprinted by Templegate Press in Illinois. Saint Therese of Lisieux, with her stress on "the little way" and the significance of small actions, had been a source of inspiration for decades.

That Easter, Cesar Chavez—one of Dorothy's living heroes—came to see her.

In June, Mother Teresa arrived at Maryhouse for what proved to be her last visit with Dorothy.

"Remember Julian of Norwich, 'All will be well, all manner of things will be well!' I'm a feeble creature these days. Too much celebration here at the house. Our house is packed and I enjoy getting down to dinner at night and getting acquainted with all the women. What a variety. . . What a privileged life I've had, to meet so many great people."
—To Nina Polcyn, May Day 1979

"'God wills that all men be saved.' 'Thy will be done.' The story of Lallah's son who committed suicide and how a priest at Our Lady of Guadalupe told me, 'There is no time with God.' All the prayer you will say for him will have given him the grace to turn to God at the last moment. A rich reader in Milwaukee who heard this story wrote how sorry he was that I have no time for God and sent me a weighty book on theology to study."

—Diary entry, September 16, 1979

Dorothy's window never ceased to provide her with a pleasing view. "Little patches of green pushing out thru cracks in the sidewalk," she wrote in June. "The sturdy ailanthus tree! My one large tree which just reaches to the third floor of the beautiful old building across the street. Fire windows on each floor, arched and pillared and decorated most beautifully, one greenstone with two red brick structures, six stories high. Beautiful little children live in the one opposite— they look Korean or Vietnamese or Chinese, I cannot tell which. The fire escapes serve as porches for the little ones!"

That summer and the next, her weakened condition prevented a stay at the beach house on Staten Island. In her July column, Dorothy shared with readers a letter from her sister-in-law, Tina de Aragon Feldman, who had just learned that she was suffering from cancer of the spinal cord: "I was given the verdict at Saint Vincent's Hospital," Tina wrote. "For two hours, I was in mortal terror. Then, a thought came to me. Not an experience, just a thought out of the writings of Saint Teresa [of Avila] about her wanderings along the roads of Spain. 'The mules are packed, they are kicking, the road will be rocky, but the destination is sure.' Saint Teresa encourages familiarity with God. This descendant of converts, very female, very stormy, very valiant, does not want us to fall back from the quest in awe of greatness. She asks that we join her in all our failing humanity, since there is nothing to disturb or afright us except, perhaps, vermin in uncomfortable inns." Tina's illness, Dorothy later noted, had "brought about the reconciliation of sisters" and that this had made Tina regard her suffering as "worth it."

Dorothy felt that her own mules were also packed. "The paper is in the hands of young people," she said to Robert Ellsberg during a visit, "and the houses are strong. My prayer is, 'Now let thy servant depart in peace.'"

In November, Stanley Vishnewski died. Joking to the end, he said to those at his bedside, "It must have been the soup." He had been forty-five years with the Catholic Worker, though he still reminded staff and visitors that he hadn't yet decided whether or not to stay. He was a man of great spiritual depth and, at the same time, the court jester of the

Catholic Worker—which he often called the Catholic *Shirker* movement. He had become the Worker's resident historian, but his book about the movement's early years, *Wings of the Dawn*, hadn't found a publisher when he died. "I can truthfully say," he told his co-workers, "that I have been rejected by some of the best publishers in America." (His book was at last published in 1984 by the Catholic Worker, which sold it, Catholic Worker fashion, for whatever the buyer offered, from nothing on up. Stanley would have approved. "Here we practice the economics of the Kingdom of Heaven," he had pointed out more than once. "Everything is free. It is also already broken in. I have a suit that was test-worn for eight years before I agreed to accept delivery.")

There was no "On Pilgrimage" that month, but in December Dorothy wrote Stanley's obituary, "A Knight for a Day." It was her last actual article, though her column continued with short entries from her diary. She remembered Stanley's arrival as a seventeen-year-old Lithuanian from Brooklyn, and how in the early years he had once rescued her when she was pinned against a wall by a police horse being used against a picket line, and how in later years he rescued her from a demented veteran who had nearly crushed her one day at the Tivoli farm. "Stanley used to come in these recent years," Dorothy wrote, "and have dinner with me, and we watched television."

"On Pilgrimage" was again missing in the January 1980 issue, but in February a series of one and two sentence notes from Dorothy's diary appeared. She was enjoying a Dorothy Sayers mystery novel, *Gaudy Night*, had heard Wagner's "Siegfried" on the radio, and seen "How Green Was My Valley" on television. She noted that Deane Mowrer and others from the Catholic Worker community in New York were off to Washington for a week-long vigil at the Pentagon. There was but a hint of frustration at her being unable to go along: "It would be ungrateful," the column ended, "not to find enjoyment in my inactivity, not to 'rejoice always,' as the psalmist says. Was it Ruskin who wrote about 'the duty of delight'? What a nice phrase!"

In her diary for March, Dorothy recalled the saying so

"Things ('phrases') to remember. 'Duty of Delight' (Ruskin?). 'Jesu, Joy of Man's Desiring.' Lovely title for music. 'Romeo and Juliet'—beautiful music, tho not as beautiful as Wagner's 'Tristan and Isolde.'"
—Diary entry, February 25, 1980

Dorothy on the stairway at
Maryhouse, 1979. (Credit: Bill Barrett)

often repeated in *The Catholic Worker*: "The less you have of
Caesar's, the less you have to render to Caesar." She had listened to Wagner's "Parsifal" on the radio.

In April, Dorothy's sister Della died. They had been constant friends throughout their lives. In earlier years, Della's
death would have brought forth a long essay in the paper.
Now Dorothy wrote simply: "My most dear sister Della died

yesterday." On May 1, noting in her diary that it was *The Catholic Worker's* forty-seventh anniversary, she recalled the distribution of the first issue on Union Square, mentioned the special Mass and dinner at Maryhouse, then added, "How one misses a sister!"

She was reading Dorothy Sayers's *Five Red Herrings* and had heard more Wagner on the radio.

In June Dorothy wrote in her diary that "I am in my second childhood." Too weak to receive visitors, she was praying, watching television and listening to the radio. Communion was brought daily to her room.

In her July diary, she noted Ammon Hennacy's birthday on the 24th. "He would have been eighty-seven years old today." She was rereading Mike Gold's autobiographical novel, *Jews Without Money*.

In August, on the feast of Saint Augustine, she copied down a favorite passage from Augustine's *Confessions*: "What is it that I love when I love my God? It is a certain light that I love and melody and fragrance and embrace that I love when I love my God—a light, melody, fragrance, food, embrace of the God-within, where, for my soul, that shines which space does not contain; that sounds which time does not sweep away; that is fragrant which the breeze does not dispel; and that tastes sweet which, fed upon, is not diminished; and that clings close which no satiety divides—this is what I love when I love my God."

Dorothy's last "On Pilgrimage" column appeared in the October issue. It began with praise for televised Masses—"wonderful for shut-ins." She was watchful of signs of life outside her window: "The morning glories are up to the third floor of Maryhouse. I can see them grow each day!" Continuing with Dorothy Sayers, Dorothy was now reading short stories that featured Lord Peter Wimsey. She mentioned watching Kenneth Clarke's "Civilization" series on television, which reminded her of something that Peter Maurin had said: "The thirteenth was the greatest of centuries."

Once again, she wrote about Eugene O'Neill and Mike Gold. "I still have a beautiful postcard from Mike when he was visiting Russia when the Catholic Worker was still on

"Mike Harank has planted morning glories in front of Maryhouse again. The strings for them to climb on go up to the third floor. Beauty!"
—Diary entry, May 27, 1980

"Frank brought me up Communion this a.m. I walked a little in the hall—getting my 'sea legs' under me, a family saying. My mother's forebears in Marlboro and Poughkeepsie were whalers."
  —Diary entry, October 5, 1980

"My birthday. 83 years old."
  —Diary entry, November 8, 1980

"Taken to hospital. Carried on chair downstairs."
  —Diary entry, November 11, 1980

"Home. Stanley Vishnewski first anniversary. We still miss him."
  —Diary entry, November 14, 1980

Chrystie Street." Dorothy was looking forward to watching a play based on Dostoevsky's *Crime and Punishment*. She had been able to walk a little in the hall one day, "getting my 'sea-legs' under me." After all, she noted, she was a descendant of seagoing people—whalers.

She was grateful to Father Lyle Young, one of the priests most involved with the Catholic Worker household, for the copies of *The New Yorker* he passed on to her. She recalled something her sister Della used to say: "Had I foreseen what was to befall me, I would have rued the day." She missed traveling, especially by bus. "You feel you are really seeing the country, as you speed along the highway, over plain and mountain." Her final words in the column were about the "beautiful statue of the Madonna behind the altar in the Maryhouse chapel, which Tina de Aragon, my sister-in-law, carved for us from *lignum vitae*."

"Losing my mind," she wrote in her diary November 27. "Wake up not knowing what day it is until Frank brings in mail and [*The New York*] *Times*."

On November 29, on the eve of the First Sunday of Advent, Dorothy talked with Eileen Egan on the telephone. She had been watching a news report about the survivors of an earthquake in southern Italy who were struggling to keep themselves alive in mountain snows. "Her voice was strong with compassion," Eileen recalls. "She asked me what was being done for them by Catholic Relief Services and was relieved to hear about the emergency air shipment of blankets, food and medicine. Dorothy suggested that the blankets could also be made to serve as tents."

Later in the afternoon, Tamar came to visit. During the visit, Dorothy asked for a cup of tea and remarked how good life can be at certain moments. She held Tamar's hand.

At 5:30 P.M., Dorothy's tired heart stopped beating. It was a death as quiet as the turning of a page.

Deo Gratias

Dorothy's body, clothed in a blue-and-white checker dress, was placed in a plain, unvarnished pine coffin that was set, top open, on top of the altar in the Maryhouse chapel, adorned with a single long-stemmed rose. A *prie-dieu* was placed in front of it, its red plush worn thin

by years of kneeling. Above the coffin was a cross made of two pieces of driftwood such as Dorothy had often collected on the beach at Staten Island. Tina de Aragon's statue of the Madonna stood close by. "Dorothy looked so thin, so old and fragile and shrunken," Tom Cornell wrote me a few days later, "but still beautiful and strong. Her cheekbones and her chin and her mouth were as ever, and there was a look of peace in her face."

Funeral procession on Third St.
(Credit: Tom Lewis-Borbely)

The day following her death and long into the night, visitors came to the wake to pay their respects and share their memories. Many knelt in prayer before the coffin, at times praying in tears. Some kissed her forehead or touched her face lightly. In death as in life, Dorothy was surrounded by unlikely friends and companions, ranging from those "living rough" on the streets to well-known writers, editors and teachers. Some were distinguished in the Christian community, while others were distinguished for their troubles in that same community. The Christians predominated but they could not claim a monopoly on Dorothy. There was a wide variety of believers, some atheists too, and some who were a bit of both. There were those who either had no unusual political convictions or were convinced of views far to the right or left of Dorothy. Some were there simply because they had found in the Catholic Worker a channel through which their donations actually reached the poor. In a room adjacent to the chapel, many stories were told over coffee and tea. There were moments of laughter, and others of silence and tears.

In the morning, Dorothy's grandchildren carried the coffin to the Church of the Nativity, half a block away, the parish in which Dorothy and others in the Catholic Worker community had often shared in the Mass. At the entrance to the church, Cardinal Cooke blessed Dorothy's coffin. A huge crowd had turned out, as diverse a mixture as could be found in any New York City subway car. Some had traveled thousands of miles. Among the mourners was Forster Batterham, whom Dorothy had always referred to as her husband. Nothing would have astonished Dorothy more than seeing Forster among those waiting in line to receive communion.

Many reporters were present. When asked what had impressed him most about Dorothy Day, Dan Berrigan responded, "She lived as though the truth were actually true." One journalist asked Peggy Scherer, editor of The Catholic Worker at the time, whether the movement could continue without its founder. "We have lost Dorothy," she replied, "but we still have the Gospel."

Dorothy was buried at Resurrection Cemetery on Staten Island—a grassy meadow overlooking the ocean within

"In the face of world events, in the face of the mystery of suffering, of evil in the world, it is a good time to read the Book of Job, and then to go on reading the Psalms, looking for comfort—that is, strength to endure. Also to remember the importunate widow, the importunate friend. Both are stories which Jesus told. Then to pray without ceasing, as Paul urged. And just as there was that interpolation in Job—that triumphant cry— 'I know that my Redeemer liveth,' so we, too, can know that help will come, that even from evil, God can bring great good, that indeed the good will triumph. Bitter though it is today with ice and sleet, the sap will soon be rising in those bare trees down the street from us."
—Catholic Worker, February 1971

walking distance of the beach house where Dorothy's conversion had occurred. A small stone was set over the grave, ornamented with a loaves-and-fishes design by Ade Bethune that had often been used in *The Catholic Worker*. The stone's text, its two Latin words chosen by Dorothy, was brief:

"In the joys and sorrows of this life, we can pray as they do in the Russian liturgy for a death 'without blame or pain.' May our passing be a rejoicing."
—Catholic Worker,
October-November 1973

Dorothy Day
November 8, 1897—November 29, 1980
Deo Gratias

Thanks be to God.

Postscript: Saint Dorothy?

Icon by Nicholas Tsai.

ong before her death, many people spoke of Dorothy
Day as a saint. It made Dorothy uncomfortable and
sometimes irritable. If people knew her better, she
insisted, they would see her in a far more critical light. She
staunchly resisted being regarded as a model Christian. She
famously said, "Don't call me a saint—I don't want to be dismissed so easily." On the other hand she aspired to sanctity
and was impatient with those who regarded saints as a breed
apart. "We are all called to be saints," she often said, para-
phrasing Saint Paul's Letter to the Romans. Sanctity isn't for
the few but for the many, not for the exceptional but for the
ordinary. But no sane person looks in a mirror and sees a
halo. One certain indication of someone being far from sanctity is imagining themselves being portrayed on a holy card.
Actual saints seek recognition only as great sinners.

What Dorothy could not see in herself, many others,
including people who knew her well, perceived. In September
1983, the Claretians, a Catholic religious order active in sixty
countries, took the first step in promoting recognition of
Dorothy Day as a saint. Their campaign was launched with
the publication of an article by Father Henry Fehren in a
Claretian journal, *Salt*. Canonization would, Fehren argued,
make Dorothy's life known to generations to come with the
result that "more people would learn about her and be
inspired and strengthened by her. Saint Augustine said that
funeral customs were more for the living than for the dead;
and canonization also is not to benefit the dead but the living."

What impressed him most about Dorothy Day, he wrote,
"was her perseverance—year after year living an austere life
in the grimmest of conditions, being jailed again and again,
never giving up doing the works of mercy, never getting cyn-
ical, never letting her love of God and people dissolve.
Anyone can be saintly for a week or two, or even a year, but

to persevere from youth through old age, to remain on the cross until death—that is a mark of true holiness."

The Church calendar, he continued, needed more lay people, women especially. "Most of the canonized saints . . . are nuns, brothers, priests, and bishops; yet the Church is almost entirely made up of lay people, and the emphasis in our time is on the work and responsibility of the lay people in the Church. . . . Dorothy Day did not ask Church officials for permission to do her works of mercy. . . . Nor did she found a religious order, as so many holy women of strong character had in the past. . . . 'How to love,' she wrote in one issue of *The Catholic Worker*, 'that is the question.' She answered that question by her life."

The Claretians solicited prayers and testimonials and also printed cards with a drawing of Dorothy Day on one side and a prayer on the reverse: "Merciful God, you called your servant Dorothy Day to show us the face of Jesus in the poor and forsaken. By constant practice of the works of mercy, she embraced poverty and witnessed steadfastly to justice and peace. Count her among your saints and lead us to become friends of the poor ones of the earth and to recognize you in them." Over the years, tens of thousands of the cards, plus similar posters, have been distributed—the Claretians have lost count of how many. Part of their website is devoted to Dorothy Day.

In 1997, seventeen years after Dorothy's death, Cardinal John O'Connor, Archbishop of New York, took the first steps in launching the actual process of canonization. For those who recalled the military dimension of O'Connor's background, it must have come as a surprise. In 1952, seven years after his ordination as a priest, O'Connor joined the U.S. Navy as a chaplain. He often entered combat zones, first in Korea, later in Vietnam, to say Mass and administer last rites to the wounded. In 1975, he was appointed Chief of Navy Chaplains with the rank of rear admiral. In all, he spent twenty-seven years with the military before he was appointed Bishop of Scranton in 1983 and then, the following year, Archbishop of New York.

A bishop who is also an admiral, one might have imag-

"There are, of course, the lives of the saints, but they are too often written as though they were not in this world. We have seldom been given the saints as they really were, as they affected the lives of their times—unless it is in their own writings. But instead of that strong meat we are generally given the pap of hagiography. Too little has been stressed the idea that all are called. . . . Where are our saints to call the masses to God? Personalists first, we must put the question to ourselves. Communitarians, we will find Christ in our brothers and sisters."
—Catholic Worker, May 1948

Forster Batterham and Tamar at a memorial service for Dorothy in 1980.

Dorothy in later years.

ined, is an unlikely candidate to seek the canonization of a woman who had spent much of her life encouraging people not to go to war. On the other hand, someone who has seen the reality of combat would not be last in line to appreciate Dorothy's hatred of war. "No priest can watch the blood pouring from the wounds of the dying, be they American or Vietnamese of the North or South, without anguish and a sense of desperate frustration and futility," he wrote. "The clergy back home, the academicians in their universities, the protesters on their marches are not the only ones who cry out, 'Why?'"

As a bishop, O'Connor not only opposed abortion but capital punishment, and was also outspoken in his critique of war and militarization. In the 1980s, he condemned U.S. support of counter-revolutionary guerrilla forces in Central America, opposed America's mining of the waters off Nicaragua, questioned spending vast sums on new weapon systems, and in general advocated caution in regard to American military actions around the world. In 1998, he questioned whether U.S. missile strikes on Afghanistan and Sudan were morally justifiable, and, in 1999, during the

Kosovo War, declared that NATO's bombing campaign of Yugoslavia did not meet the Church's criteria for a just war. "Does the relentless bombing of Yugoslavia," O'Connor asked, "prove the power of the Western world or its weakness?" He was also known as strongly pro-labor. Had she lived to know Cardinal O'Connor, Dorothy would have applauded his stands on many issues, no doubt recalling how uncritical of American military actions Cardinal Francis Spellman had been.

In a homily given at Mass in Saint Patrick's Cathedral in New York on November 9, 1997, a day after the hundredth anniversary of Dorothy's birth, O'Connor said he was considering proposing Dorothy Day for canonization and invited responses to this idea from any interested persons. She was, he said, "a truly remarkable woman" who had combined a deep faith and love for the Church with a passionate commitment to serving the poor and to saving

lives. He would soon be meeting with persons knowledgeable about Dorothy's life, he announced, including some who were present as his invited guests at Mass that day.

O'Connor acknowledged that some might object to his taking up the cause of Dorothy Day because "she was a protester against some things that people confuse with Americanism itself," but this was a view he completely rejected. Others, he said, might argue that she was already widely recognized as a living saint and therefore formal canonization is not needed. "Perhaps," O'Connor said, "but why does the Church canonize saints? In part, so that their person, their works and their lives will become that much better known, and that they will encourage others to follow in their footsteps—and so the Church may say, 'This is sanctity, this is

"We are all called to be saints, St. Paul says, and we might as well get over our bourgeois fear of the name. We might also get used to recognizing the fact that there is some of the saint in all of us. Inasmuch as we are growing, putting off the old man and putting on Christ, there is some of the saint, the holy, the divine right there. . . . We are all called to be saints. Sometimes we don't see them around us, sometimes their sanctity is obscured by the human, but they are there nonetheless."—The Third Hour, 1949

Dorothy serving soup to Franciscans in Detroit, c. 1955. (Marquette University archives)

"Like Lord Jim, in Conrad's story, we are all waiting for great opportunities to show heroism, letting countless opportunities go by to enlarge our hearts, increase our faith, and show our love for our fellows, and so for Him."

—*Catholic Worker*, January 1951

the road to eternal life.'" Dorothy was, he said, someone who believed that a person is "a temple of God, sacred, made in the image and likeness of God, infinitely more important in its own way than any building. . . . To Dorothy Day, everyone was a cathedral."

Dorothy Day, he continued, "saw the world at large turned into a huge commercial marketplace where money means more than anything else. She saw people turned into tools of commerce. She saw the family treated as a marketplace. She reminded us frequently enough that the Church herself could become simply a marketplace. She loved the Church, and she was immensely faithful to the Church. She had no time for those who attacked the Church as such, the Body of Christ. She loved the Holy Father. But she recognized that we poor, weak human beings—people like you, people like me—could turn the Church into nothing but a marketplace." The more reading he had done about Dorothy Day, he said, "the more saintly a woman she seems to be."

He noted that Dorothy had often been severely criticized. "She suffered in many, many ways. Some of the sufferings, she herself would say, she brought on herself. Others came from enemies. Most of her suffering came from seeing the sufferings of Christ in the poor."

Praising Dorothy for all she had done to draw attention to Saint Therese of Lisieux, he read aloud the final paragraphs of Dorothy's book about "the Little Flower":

So many books have been written about Saint Therese, books of all kinds, too, so why, I ask myself again, have I written one more? There are popular lives, lives written for children, trav-

elogue lives following her footsteps, lives for the extrovert, the introvert, the contemplative, the activist, the scholar and the theologian.

Yet it was the "worker," the common man, who first spread her fame by word of mouth. It was the masses who first proclaimed her a saint. It was the "people."

When we think of the masses, we think of waves of the sea, of forests, of fields of wheat, all moved by the spirit which blows where it listeth. When we think of the people we think of the child at school, the housewife at her dishpan, the mother working, the mother sick, the man traveling, the migrant worker, the craftsman, the factory worker, the soldier, the rich, the bourgeois, the poor in tenements, the destitute man in the street. To a great extent she has made her appeal to all of these.

What was there about her to make such an appeal? Perhaps because she was so much like the rest of us in her ordinariness. In her lifetime there are no miracles recounted, she was just good. . . .

Dorothy with Fr. Daniel Berrigan.
(Credit: Jon Erikson)

What did she do? She practiced the presence of God and she did all things—all the little things that make up our daily life and contact with others—for His honor and glory. She did not need much time to expound what she herself called "her little way," which she said was for all. She wrote her story, and God did the rest. God and the people. God chose for the people to clamor for her canonization.

Noting that, prior to her religious conversion, Dorothy had aborted her first child, O'Connor said, "I wish every woman who has ever suffered an abortion, including perhaps someone or several in this church, would come to know Dorothy Day. Her story was so typical. Made pregnant by a man who insisted she have an abortion, who then abandoned her anyway, she suffered terribly for what she had done, and later pleaded with others not to do the same. But later, too, after becoming a Catholic, she learned the love and mercy of the Lord, and knew she never had to worry about His forgiveness. This is why I have never condemned a woman who has had an abortion; I weep with her and ask her to remember Dorothy Day's sorrow but to know always God's loving mercy and forgiveness."

Dorothy's gratitude for the Church, despite every human shortcoming and sin, warranted O'Connor's admiration: "Her respect for and commitment and obedience to Church teaching were unswerving. Indeed, those of us who grew up knowing her recognized early in the game that she was a radical precisely because she was a believer, a believer and a practitioner. She, in fact, chided those who wanted to join her in her works of social justice, but who, in her judgment, didn't take the Church seriously enough, and didn't bother about getting to Mass."

The approach of Dorothy's hundredth birthday, he said, had inspired a number of people to send him letters urging her canonization. O'Connor read several of them aloud, including one written several years earlier by Robert Coles, a physician on the faculty of the Harvard Medical School who had come to know Dorothy when he was a medical student:

> *Fourteen years ago my wife started getting some numbness in her left side. I took her to a prominent doctor, who, after a diagnostic work-up, told us that she had a brain tumor and she had six months to live. The doctors were absolutely definite about it. . . . I wrote to Dorothy; I told her. And I started getting a letter or a postcard a day from her with her prayers and her messages. She didn't contradict the doctors, but her letters were different in nature—full of encouragement and love. After the months turned into years, the doctors started talking about a "miraculous recovery." They said that my wife somehow had "made it." . . . The only one who didn't tell me my wife was going to die in six months was Dorothy Day.*

"I wish I had known Dorothy Day personally," O'Connor concluded. "I feel that I know her because of her goodness.

"I do know that my nature is such that gratitude alone, gratitude for the faith, that most splendid gift, a gift not earned by me, a gratuitous gift, is enough to bind me in holy obedience to Holy Mother Church and her commands. . . . My gratitude for this sureness in my heart is such that I can only say, I believe, help Thou my unbelief. I believe and I obey."—Diary entry, December 1967

But surely, if any woman ever loved God and her neighbor, it was Dorothy Day! Pray that we do what we should do."

O'Connor's decision to formally begin the process quickly followed. On February 5, 1998, he invited various people who had known Dorothy well (among them Tom and Monica Cornell, Eileen Egan, Robert Ellsberg, Jane Sammon, Frank Donovan and Pat and Kathleen Jordan) to come to his office for an unhurried discussion that started at 4 P.M. and lasted until 6:30. O'Connor sat on the couch for the meeting, Tom Cornell recalled, "joking about how a cardinal should sit higher not lower." Thanks to the notes taken by Robert Ellsberg, I have a detailed account of the meeting.

"The purpose of the present meeting is to reflect on whether this is really God's will," O'Connor said at the outset. "Is it in the best interest of the poor, of the Church? What should we do in this matter? . . . Cardinal Newman said, 'The tragedy is never to have begun.' So now we are beginning. If we decide to go forward it will be a lengthy and complicated process. I presume it will not be completed in whatever time I have left."

Responding to the issue of whether the time was right, Ellsberg pointed out that "Dorothy is a real saint of what Cardinal Bernardin called 'common ground.' She challenges the reformers and social activists to maintain their love for the Church and the Gospel. She challenges conservatives to be attentive to the radical social dimensions of the Gospel. She challenges both sides to resolve differences with mutual respect and love, for the benefit of the world."

Pat Jordan, another former managing editor of *The Catholic Worker*, said he felt it was important that the light shed by Dorothy's life "not be hidden under a basket." He stressed her purity, her modesty, her hope, her ability to go on even when things seemed hopeless, and doing so without institutional help. Her greatest sacrifice was "not being able to put the needs of her family first—she died totally to self to try to respond to Christ's love. She had to struggle, to forgive seventy times seven. She knew all the spiritual traps. She challenged us always to care for the weak, to love our enemy, yet she never claimed that everyone had to do it her way. In

"People talk so much about the meaning of life and the work is to grow in love, love of God our destination, and love of neighbor, our first step, our continuing step, our right road in that direction. Love means answering the mail that comes in—and there is a fearful amount of it. That person in the hospital, that person suffering a breakdown of nerves, the person lonely, far-off, watching for the mailman each day. It means loving attention to those around us, the youngest and the oldest (the drunk and the sober)."

—January 6, 1967

"Of course the church is corrupt! 'But this corruption must put on incorruption,' St. Paul says, so I rejoice as I have in my short lifetime seen renewals going on, or read of them, and see the excitement, the joy of this sense of renewal. Certainly I knew when I became a Catholic that the church was a human institution and at first I had a sense of my betrayal of the working class, of the poor and oppressed for whom I had a romantic love and desire to serve. But just as I in my youth sought them out, lived in their slums and felt at home, so the Lord was seeking me out and I could not resist Him. And I found Him in the Church, in the Sacraments, life-giving and strength-giving, in spite of the American flag in the sanctuary, the boring sermons, the incomprehensible and mumbled Latin, the Sunday Catholic, the wide gulf between clergy and laity, even the contempt for the laity which I often felt, and even heard expressed."—Diary entry, July 1969

this materialistic society, she showed us the simple beauty of sharing and of community."

O'Connor asked Jordan what Dorothy would think about being called a saint? "She would have none of it," he replied. "She knew that some people during her life wanted to call her a saint. She thought it was a way of letting themselves off the hook— Dorothy could do these things because 'she's a saint.' But she really took seriously the idea that we are all called to be saints. She wasn't embarrassed about saying that. She often quoted Leon Bloy, 'There is only one sadness: not to be a saint.'"

Was her objection to being called a saint due to humility, O'Connor asked. "Dorothy had a strong sense of her own sins, her weaknesses and failures," Jordan responded. "Her standards were so high that her failures stood out all the more sharply. But she had all the more sense of God's grace, of what it means to be forgiven. Her gravestone has the words '*Deo Gratias*,' as she had requested. She had such a sense of gratitude, a sense that what she had done was because of grace. This was one reason she didn't like to be called a saint, which implied that she deserved the credit for what she had done. She believed she was responsible for her failures. Everything else was due to God."

O'Connor noted that some people objected to the archdiocese seeking Dorothy's canonization because it would cost a great deal of money that could better be given to the poor. "I don't know where this idea comes from that a lot of money is involved," said O'Connor. "It's really a very small amount. The process of seeking the canonization of Pierre Toussaint [a Haitian-born New Yorker of slave descent], which has progressed now to the point of awaiting a miracle, has cost the archdiocese no more than three or four thousand dollars, including the cost of sending someone to Rome. [In 1996, Toussaint was beatified by Pope John Paul.] If the money were given instead to the poor, we wouldn't be giving them very much money."

Eileen Egan, Dorothy's friend of many years as well as a key figure in Catholic Relief Services, saw Dorothy as someone who "shows that ordinary people can live by the Sermon on the Mount. She tried to relate the Sermon on the Mount to everything she did. This makes her a tremendous inspiration for lay people. Most saints appear to be hedged in by vows or life style, but Dorothy wasn't hedged in by anything."

O'Connor wondered if canonization might trivialize Dorothy's memory—would it merely serve as a "superficial aggrandizement of the Catholic Worker movement? Would it let us off the hook? Would it be a way, as she said, of dismissing her too easily? Turning her into a holy card? Would it attract more people to know this life? The issue here is the holiness of her life. Holiness is expressed in a thousand ways."

Jordan said that Dorothy had taught him "how to see Christ in every person. This didn't come easily or naturally. It reflected tremendous effort. She was not always an easy person to get along with. There were times when I felt miffed by her decisions. But there was no question in my mind about her holiness. I've never met anyone like her. I doubt that I will ever meet anyone else like her."

Ellsberg commented that, "if Dorothy Day was not a saint, it is hard to know what meaning that word should have."

O'Connor said that the discussion had made it even clearer that "here was a holy woman" and that he would be failing in his duty if he were not to begin the canonization process. "I don't want to have on my conscience that I didn't do something that God wanted done." It seemed to him that the campaign the Claretians had begun in 1983 should now be taken up by the diocese Dorothy had belonged to all her Catholic life.

As he said goodbye, O'Connor remarked, "You are all so warm—you must have gathered around a wonderful fire."

The group met again in March, this time augmented by *Catholic Worker* artist Ade Bethune, Geoff Gneuhs (who, as a Dominican priest, had presided at Dorothy's funeral), Dorothy's friend and correspondent Nina Polcyn Moore, Phillip Runkel (curator of the Catholic Worker Archive at Marquette University), long-time Catholic Worker Dorothy Gauchat, George Horton of Catholic Charities, and Meinrad Scherer-Emunds, representing the Claretians. Tom and Monica Cornell were absent; they were at the Vatican for a meeting with Cardinal Joseph Stafford, then head of the

"Love is a matter of the will. . . . If you will to love someone (even the most repulsive and wicked), and try to serve him as an expression of that love—then you soon come to feel love. And God will hear your prayers. 'Enlarge Thou my heart that Thou mayest enter in!' You can pray the same way, that your heart may be enlarged to love again."

—August 6, 1937

Men entering St. Joseph House.
(Credit: Jon Erikson)

"Every morning I break my fast with the men in the breadline. Some of them speak to me. Many of them do not. But they know me and I know them. And there is a sense of comradeship there. We know each other in the breaking of bread."
—Diary entry, February 27, 1939

Pontifical Council for the Laity, who would have to approve Cardinal O'Connor's application to introduce Dorothy's cause in Rome.

The decision to begin the process having already been taken, the focus this time was on identifying next steps. In the coming months, O'Connor would send a letter to the prefect heading the Congregation for the Causes of Saints proposing Dorothy's canonization. Next would come the formal appointment of a postulator in Rome and a vice-postulator in New York who would interview people who knew Dorothy or were acquainted with her life. Next, a commission would write a historical report on Dorothy's life which would then be handed over to a theological commission. Finally a recommendation would be made to the pope that, as soon as there is a documented miracle linked to her, Dorothy Day be declared Blessed. A second miracle would open the way for her official recognition as Saint Dorothy.

In September 1998, O'Connor wrote to those involved in the meetings to let them know how things were coming along: "I have written to the Congregation for the Causes of Saints asking that the process for her canonization be initiated. Included in my submission are the letters submitted by those who attended our meetings in the spring. I have received an invitation to meet with the Prefect of the Congregation during my next trip to Rome. I may have more information for you following that visit."

Rome is well known for moving slowly. It wasn't until March 2000, eighteen months later, that Cardinal O'Connor announced the approval of the Holy See for the Archdiocese of New York to open the cause for the beatification and canonization. With this approval, Dorothy received the formal ecclesiastical title, "Servant of God Dorothy Day."

By then O'Connor knew he was living in sight of his grave. Two months later, on May 3, he died of cardiopulmonary arrest. He was eighty years old. A spokesman for the archdiocese said the cardinal's death was "the result of the tumor and the cancer that he was suffering from."

O'Connor's successor, Cardinal Edward Egan, formally established the Dorothy Day Guild in 2005 to advance the cause. (One way to join the guild is via its website: http://dorothydayguild.org.) His successor, Archbishop Timothy Dolan, enthusiastically supports the cause, which is headquartered in the New York Archdiocesan Offices.

Whatever comes of the canonization effort, the Catholic Worker movement is alive and continues to grow. Each house of hospitality that identifies itself with the Catholic Worker movement—currently there are more than a hundred and sixty—might be regarded as a monument to Dorothy Day, though Dorothy would stress they are first and foremost a response to the words of Christ: "What you did to the least, you did to me." There is also the more hidden testimony of the countless people who lead more hospitable and more peaceful lives, thanks in part to Dorothy Day. Who could count them all?

"I believe You are a personal God, and hear me when I speak, even my trivial petty speech. So I will tell You personally over and over I love You, I adore You, I worship You. Make me mean it in my life. Make me show it by my choices. Make me show it from my waking thought to my sleeping."
—Diary entry, August 21, 1952

(Credit: © Bob Fitch)

Dorothy Day:
A Personal Remembrance

Ifirst met Dorothy Day a few days before Christmas in 1960 while on leave from the U.S. Navy. After reading copies of *The Catholic Worker* that I had found in my parish library, and then reading Dorothy's autobiography, *The Long Loneliness*, I decided to visit the community she had founded. I was based not so far away, in Washington, DC.

Arriving in Manhattan for that first visit, I made my way to Saint Joseph's House—then in a loft on Spring Street, on the north edge of Little Italy in the Lower East Side of New York City. Discovering that it was moving day, I joined in helping carry boxes from an upstairs loft to a three-storey brick building at 175 Chrystie Street, a few blocks to the east. Jack Baker, one of the other people assisting with the move that day, invited me to stay in his apartment in the same neighborhood.

A few days later I visited the community's rural outpost on Staten Island, the Peter Maurin Farm. Crossing Upper New York Harbor by ferry, I made my way to an old farmhouse on a rural road just north of Pleasant Plains near the island's southern tip. In its large, faded dining room, I found half-a-dozen people, Dorothy among them, gathered around a pot of tea at one end of the dining room table.

At the time, Dorothy was only sixty-three, though to my young eyes she seemed old enough to have known Abraham and Sarah. But what a handsome woman! Her face was long, with high, prominent cheekbones underlining large, quick eyes, deep blue and almond shaped, that could be teasing one moment, laughing the next, then turn grave an instant later. Her gray hair, parted in the middle, was braided and circled the back of her head like a garland of silver flowers. She had a fresh, scrubbed look with no trace of cosmetics. The woolen suit she wore was plain but well-tailored and good quality. (I only recently learned from her goddaughter, Johannah Hughes Turner, that her suit was probably a gift from her sister, Della Spier. "Dorothy was tall and hard to fit," Johannah told me. "Rarely did she find anything in the Catholic Worker clothing room that she could use. Della enjoyed dressing Dorothy and could afford to provide her with solid, classic suits and dresses.")

I gave Dorothy a bag of letters addressed to her that had been received in Manhattan. Within minutes, she was reading the letters aloud to all of us.

The only letter I still recall from that day's reading was one from Thomas Merton, the famous monk whose autobiography, *The Seven Storey Mountain*, had held many people in its grip, including me. In 1941, Merton had withdrawn from "the world" to a Trappist monastery in Kentucky with a slam of the door that eventually was heard around the world. I had assumed that he wrote to no one outside his family. Yet here he was in correspondence with someone who was not only in the thick of the world, but one of its more engaged and controversial figures.

In his letter, Merton told Dorothy that he was deeply touched by her witness for peace, which in recent years had five times resulted in her arrest and imprisonment for refusing to take shelter during civil defense drills. "You are right going along the lines of *satyagraha* [Gandhi's term for nonviolent action]. I see no other way. . . . Nowadays it is no longer a question of who is right but who is at least not criminal. . . . It has never been more true than now that the world is lost in its own falsity and cannot see true values. . . . God bless you." Ten months later, Merton published an essay in *The Catholic Worker*—"The Root of War Is Fear"—and immediately got into trouble with his religious superiors and others both inside and outside the monastery.

Merton was one of countless people drawn to Dorothy and influenced by her. She had a great gift for making those who met her, even if only through letters or her published writings, look at themselves in a new light, questioning previously held ideas, allegiances and choices.

I was another of those whose life took an unexpected turn thanks to Dorothy Day. Five months after that first encounter, I was granted an early discharge from the Navy on grounds of conscientious objection. At Dorothy's invitation, I became part of the staff at Saint Joseph's House in New York.

One of my predecessors was Jack English, who had joined the New York Catholic Worker in its early years and remained close to Dorothy into her old age. Recalling his first impressions of Dorothy in a taped interview with Deane Mowrer in 1970, he said he was still impressed with Dorothy's ability to engage with so many individuals. "She occasionally talks in terms of the abstract, but she never talks or operates except person to person." Jack had learned from her that "each human being is unique, totally unique, and that each time I meet and have a real encounter with another human being, I am changed somehow, whether for good or bad."

The qualities that so impressed Jack were just as striking to me: her ability to focus on the person she was talking to, not to see just a young face but *your* face, not discerning just a vague, general promise, but *your* particular gifts. Through Dorothy, you glimpsed exciting possibilities in yourself that you hadn't seen before.

When I joined the Catholic Worker, there was just one house in Manhattan, Saint Joseph's. It was so cramped a building that only one person actually lived there as nighttime care-taker. The rest of us, Dorothy as well, lived in $25-a-month cold-water flats located nearby that were usually occupied by two people. By chance, Dorothy's room (shared at the time with a woman we knew as Saint Louis Marie) was next to

Folding papers at St. Joseph's House, 175 Chrystie St., 1962. (Credit: William Carter)

the one I shared with Stuart Sandberg, a recent college graduate who, later in life, was ordained a priest. We were on the sixth floor of a Spring Street tenement. There were four small apartments per floor, each with a bathtub next to the sink. The one toilet on each floor was in a closet-sized space in the hallway.

As I had discovered that first day at the farm on Staten Island, Dorothy was a tireless story-teller, often using incoming letters as a starting point. I recall her reading a letter aloud one day from the Gauchat family, founders of a Catholic Worker community in Ohio. Dorothy told us how the Gauchats had taken in a six-month-old child who was expected to die at any time. The child, they were told, was deaf and blind, with a fluid-filled lump on his head larger than a baseball. "Bill Gauchat made the sign of the cross over that child's face," Dorothy said, "and he saw those dull eyes follow the motion of his hand. The child could see! Within a year David—that was his name— was well enough to be taken home by his real parents. His life was saved by the love in the Gauchat home."

A letter from a Catholic Worker community that was trying to help a prostitute get free of her pimp reminded Dorothy of a prostitute named Mary Ann with whom she had been in jail in Chicago in the early 1920s. At the time, Dorothy had been living a bohemian life with no plans of ever becoming Catholic or joining any church. She hadn't intended to be arrested and was terrified of the guards. "You must hold your head high," Mary Ann advised her, "and give them no clue that you're afraid of them or

(Credit: © Vivian Cherry)

ready to beg for anything, any favors whatsoever. But you must see them for what they are—never forget that they're in jail, too."

Hearing stories like these, we were learning something about life that you don't get in newspapers, classrooms or even in many churches. At the core of each story there were always just a few people, perhaps just one, for whom following Christ was the most important thing in the world.

Stories gave Dorothy occasion to draw on her massive supply of sayings. How many times have I heard her repeat Saint Catherine of Siena's remark, "All the way to heaven is heaven, because Jesus said, 'I am the way.'" There was a passage from George Bernanos's novel, *Diary of a Country Priest*, that she often used: "Hell is not to love anymore." Just as often, she made use of a saying from Saint John of the Cross, "Love is the measure by which we will be judged." Another favorite was a sentence from

Dostoevsky: "The world will be saved by beauty." There was also Saint Augustine's declaration: "All beauty is a revelation of God."

Beauty! Dorothy had an astonishing gift for finding beauty in places where it was often overlooked—in determined flowers blooming in a slum neighborhood, in grass battling upward toward the sky between blocks of concrete, in the smell of an herb growing in a pot on a tenement window ledge, in the battered faces of people who survived on the economic fringes of society.

Music was important in Dorothy's life, especially opera. One had to have a very good reason for knocking on her door on a Saturday afternoon when she was absorbed in the weekly radio broadcast of the Metropolitan Opera, though she was willing to have company to listen with her so long as no attempt was made at conversation. (Dorothy said once to Willa Bickham, a member of the community at the time, "If I am reincarnated, I hope I come back an opera singer. Then I'll bring joy to everyone instead of always having to tell what's wrong with the world.")

More than anything else, Dorothy was a writer. There was always a notebook in her bag. She seemed endlessly to be taking notes and writing. Note-taking and journal-keeping were as much a part of Dorothy as breathing. Time and again every day she made note of something that had been said or jotted down a passage from the book she was then reading. During the weekly Friday night meetings at the Catholic Worker, Dorothy's note-taking was usually nonstop. When she traveled, she kept track of everyone she met and what had been said. Her notes in turn became raw material for her monthly column, "On Pilgrimage." (Dorothy's more substantial work, the several books she wrote, were mainly written at the several Staten Island beach cottages she had lived in over the years, places of retreat and solitude.)

Dorothy was an avid reader. She had loved books since childhood. She once told me that "the hardest part of living in community is the loss of so many books." In a 1952 diary entry, she reports with distress how she found her copy of the writings of Saint John of the Cross under an apple tree, soaked by rain. Her engagement in the world seemed only to fuel the reading side of her life—or was it that her reading fueled her engagement? She read certain Russian classics over and over again. She returned again and again to the novels of Charles Dickens. More than once she told young people like me that we could only understand the Catholic Worker by reading Dostoevsky.

Certain books had a huge impact on her life. One can wonder whether Dostoevsky shouldn't be regarded as a co-founder of the Catholic Worker, so much did his books help shape Dorothy's understanding of Christianity. In *The Brothers Karamazov*, the elderly monk, Father Zosima, made an exceptionally deep impression on her, especially his words, "Love in action is often a harsh and dreadful thing compared to love in dreams," a passage Dorothy recited so often that she made it her own.

I have never known anyone more disciplined in her spiritual life than Dorothy—daily

Mass, devotion to the rosary, frequent confession, times of private prayer and intercession each day. How often I have seen her on her knees at one of the nearby parish
churches or at the chapel at the Catholic Worker farm. (The Archdiocese of New York
permitted a chapel on the farm and reservation of the Blessed Sacrament within it.)
While praying, I noticed she often referred to pieces of paper. One afternoon, Dorothy
having been summoned from the farm chapel for an urgent phone call, I looked in the
prayer book she had left on the bench and discovered page after page of names, all written in her careful italic script, of people, living and dead, for whom she was praying.

It seemed to me Dorothy prayed as if lives depended on it, and no doubt some did.
The physician Robert Coles of the Harvard Medical School credited Dorothy's
prayers with the miraculous cure of his wife. She had been dying of cancer but—to the
astonishment of her physicians—recovered.

Dorothy had a special list with the names of people who had committed suicide. I
once asked Dorothy, "But isn't it too late?" "With God there is no time," she responded. She went on to say how a lot can happen in a person's thoughts between initiating
an action that will result in death and death itself—that even the tiny fraction of a second that passes between pulling a trigger and the bullet striking the brain might, in the
infinity of time that exists deep within us, be time enough for regretting what it was
now too late to stop, and to cry out for God's mercy.

I recall a story Dorothy once told me about persistence in prayer. For many years,
she said, she had been a heavy smoker. Her day began with lighting up. Her big sacrifice every Lent was giving up smoking, but having to get by without a cigarette made
her increasingly irritable as the days passed until the rest of the Catholic Worker
household was praying she would light up a cigarette. One year, as Lent approached,
the priest who heard her confessions at the time urged her not to give up cigarettes
that year but instead to pray daily, "Dear God, help me stop smoking." She used that
prayer for several years, she told me, without it having any impact on her addiction.
Then one morning she woke up, reached for a cigarette, and realized she didn't want
it. She never smoked another.

Without prayer and the sacraments, Dorothy felt, the Catholic Worker would be
blown away like dust in the wind. "We feed the hungry, yes," she told Bob Coles. "We
try to shelter the homeless and give them clothes, but there is strong faith at work; we
pray. If an outsider who comes to visit us doesn't pay attention to our praying and what
that means, then he'll miss the whole point."

Dorothy went to Mass every day until her body wasn't up to it and, even then,
received daily communion, carefully preparing before and giving plenty of time afterward for thanksgiving. She loved the rosary and prayed it often. "If we love enough,"
she once noted, "we are importunate: we repeat our love as we repeat Hail Marys on
the rosary."

She could be as fierce and determined as one of those resolute Russian women who repaired Moscow streets and kept going to church even in the years of Stalin. Her direct, at times electrifying way of getting to the heart of things was much in evidence one night when she was speaking to a Catholic student group at New York University in a packed and smoky room in a building near Washington Square Park. It was in the fall of 1961—the Cold War was at its most frozen. The

Jim Forest with Dorothy Day in the late 1960s.

explosion of nuclear weapons in the Nevada desert had become too ordinary an event to qualify as front-page news. A much repeated slogan of the time was, "Better dead than Red." Clearly some of those present considered Dorothy a Red, meaning a faithful servant of the Kremlin with its blood-red flag. One student demanded to know what Dorothy would do if the Russians invaded the United States. Would she not admit, in this extreme, at least, that killing was justified, even a sacred duty? "We are taught by Our Lord to love our enemies," Dorothy responded without batting an eye. "I hope I could open my heart to them with love, the same as anyone else. We are all children of the same Father." There was a brief but profound stillness in the room before Dorothy went on to speak about nonviolent resistance and efforts to convert opponents rather than kill them. Which of his enemies had Christ slain?

Dorothy had an intense devotion to the saints—Christ's mother Mary, first of all, but then to so many others. One of the least likely was Joan of Arc, famous for her military exploits (though, except in statues, she never wielded a sword) and finally for being burned at the stake for refusing to deny her visions. I once noticed a small statue of Joan, clad in armor, on the table next to Dorothy's bed. Responding to my surprise at her devotion to a military saint, Dorothy explained, "Joan of Arc is a saint of fidelity to conscience." This was, she said, her second such statue of Joan. The first had been stolen years earlier, but recently Bishop John Wright of Pittsburgh had given her another.

Dorothy in Milwaukee, 1968. (Credit: *Milwaukee Journal*)

Joseph, the foster father of Jesus and patron saint of all working people, was among the most important for Dorothy. The Catholic Worker house of hospitality I had become part of was dedicated to Saint Joseph. We had a finely carved wooden statue of him that the artist had donated. Under it, during periods when the community's financial well was dry or nearly so, Dorothy would place all the bills awaiting payment. "Keeping us going is your responsibility," she would remind Saint Joseph.

Dorothy had much in common with another of her favorite saints, Teresa of Avila. Both Dorothy and Teresa had animated the foundation of many communities, and both were tireless travelers. Both were reformers who went through periods of being regarded with suspicion by the hierarchy. Both were outspoken and fearless.

Another saint that greatly inspired Dorothy was Therese of Lisieux, a contemplative Carmelite nun of the nineteenth century who, after her death, came to be known as "the Little Flower." She lived an obscure life, never traveling and never founding anything, and had died only two months before Dorothy's birth. So significant was she to Dorothy that the only completed biography Dorothy ever wrote was about Therese and her "little way." What most impressed Dorothy was Therese's certainty that nothing, even the most hidden action, is ever wasted. As she put in her "On Pilgrimage" column for the December 1965 issue of *The Catholic Worker*: "Paper work, cleaning the house, dealing with the innumerable visitors who come all through the day, answering the phone, keeping patience and acting intelligently, which is to find some meaning in all that happens— these things, too, are the works of peace, and often seem like a very little way."

I don't know when or how often Dorothy made her famous remark, "Don't call me a saint—I don't want to be dismissed so easily." Very likely it was only once, but since her death even the briefest article about her is almost certain to include it. It is *the* quotation from Dorothy Day. But what was the context? Dorothy found great inspiration in the lives of those people—saints—who had been placed on the calendar of the Church, and she had done what saints do: attempt to follow Christ. At the same time she didn't want the word "saint" to be used in order to place people who attempted to live according to the Gospel in a special category of irrelevancy.

Dorothy believed we are all called to sanctity. In 1967, when Tom Cornell and I were editing the first edition of *A Penny a Copy*, an anthology of *Catholic Worker* writings, we read through thirty-four years of back issues. The front page that most impressed me had a banner headline—the kind of ultra-bold, all-caps headline that in a conventional newspaper would be used for the assassination of a president or the outbreak of war—that declared "WE ARE ALL CALLED TO BE SAINTS." The headline sums up what Dorothy regarded as absolutely basic. Why else would anyone attending the liturgy receive communion? Why receive Christ unless you hope to become more Christ-like? Why call yourself a Christian if you have no interest in trying to live the Gospel? If someday Dorothy is added to the Church calendar, one benefit is that we will have a saint whose sins and shortcomings will be impossible to air-brush out. She will be a saint who really bears witness to the possibility of flawed peo-ple, with pasts that embarrass them, never giving up in their efforts to rise from their falls and stumble along in the general direction of the kingdom of God.

Dorothy's embarrassment and sometimes annoyance in the face of admiration was only in part due to modesty. Rather she felt that many people would view her more critically if they knew her better—knew her faults, and knew more about her past. She felt she had helped create an idealized image of herself by leaving out of her autobio-graphical writings certain events preceding her entrance into the Catholic Church that she found particularly shameful, and also saying little about the faults she struggled with every day of her life.

Only years later did I come to realize that nothing in her past distressed Dorothy more than the decision to abort her first child, an event that took place in her early twenties, years before her conversion. I recall how distressed she was when I asked her if I might borrow her first book, *The Eleventh Virgin*. Somehow I had become aware that, as a young woman, she had written a novel with that title. She didn't have a copy, she told me, regretted that it had ever been published, appealed to me not to mention it again, and asked me not to look for it. It wasn't until late in her life that a friend who dealt in rare books presented me with a copy. Only when I read it did I understand why Dorothy had responded to my question with such anguish. The end point of this autobiographical novel was an abortion, carried out in the desperate hope that the man she was in love with at the time, her unborn child's unwilling father, would not leave her. He left her even so.

In a letter to a young woman written in February 1973, Dorothy refers to her abor-tion as well as to two suicide attempts she made as a young adult: "Twice I tried to take my own life, and the dear Lord pulled me through that darkness—I was rescued from that darkness. My sickness was physical too, since I had had an abortion with bad after-effects, and in a way my sickness of mind was a penance I had to endure." A few sentences later, Dorothy added, "I love you, because you remind me of my own youth, and of my one child and my grandchildren. I will keep on praying for your healing, writing your name down in my little book of prayers which I have by my bedside." (This is one of many letters by Dorothy included in *All the Way to Heaven*, edited by Robert Ellsberg.)

Dorothy once told Robert Coles about the effort she had made earlier in her life to find and destroy every copy of *The Eleventh Virgin*. Finally she brought her book-burning effort to the attention of the priest who was then hearing her confessions. He laughed. "My, my," he said. "I thought he was going to tell me to stop being so silly and mixed up in my priorities," Dorothy told Coles. "I will remember to my last day here on God's earth what the priest said: 'You can't have much faith in God if you're taking the life He has given you and using it that way.' I didn't say a word in reply. The priest added, 'God is the one who forgives us, if we ask Him; but it sounds like you don't even want forgiveness—just to get rid of the books.'"

Normally Dorothy went to confession every Saturday, not simply because it was, at that time, common Catholic practice, but because she always found that by the end of the week she had a lot to confess. A journal entry Dorothy made in 1951 makes a typ-ical summary note: "This after-noon [I had] glimpses of my own ugliness, vanity, pride, cruelty, con-tempt of others, levity, jeering, carping. Too sensitive to criticism . . . " Weeks later she added other sins: "flippancy, criti-calness, [a] gibing attitude, lack of respect and love for others." The following year she wrote: "I fail people daily, God help me, when they come to me for aid and sym-pathy. There are too many of them, whichever way I turn . . . I deny them the Christ in me when I do not show them tenderness, love. God forgive me."

Confession was part of the basic architecture of Dorothy's life. On the first page of her auto-biography, *The Long Loneliness*, she writes about what hard work

Dorothy in 1968 wearing a badge for the "Milwaukee 14." (Credit: Richard Avedon)

it was going to confession, "hard when you have sins to confess, hard when you haven't . . . you wrack your brain for even the beginnings of sins against charity, chastity, sins of distraction, sloth or gluttony. You do not want to make too much of your constant imperfections and venial sins, but you want to drag them out to the light of day as the first step in getting rid of them." Note that sins against love top the list.

Confession was, for Dorothy, a means of overcoming the sense that she was fight-ing a losing battle. She once gave Joe Zarrella a card on which she had written: "We should not be discouraged at our own lapses . . . but continue. If we are discouraged, it shows vanity and pride. Trusting too much to ourselves. It takes a lifetime of endurance, of patience, of learning through mistakes. We all are on the way." Rosalie Riegle tells me that Joe carried the card in his wallet until his death.

No one knew her shortcomings better than Dorothy herself, as has become clearer than ever following the recent publication of her diaries, *The Duty of Delight*. She was painfully aware that there were some who came to live in community with her who looked back on the experience with more pain than joy, nor could she blame them. She also felt that, due to the demands of leading the Catholic Worker movement, she had at times failed at being the ever-attentive, patient mother to her daughter Tamar that she so wanted to be. (On

Dorothy with her graddaughter Martha Hennessy. (Courtesy of Tamar Hennessy)

the other hand, given the circumstances and the fact that she was a single parent, it's remarkable how good a mother Dorothy was, and later how devoted a grandmother. In 1964, she spent four months taking care of her grandchildren in Vermont while Tamar took a course in practical nursing.)

One of Dorothy's most impressive gifts was that she was never reluctant to apologize when she felt she had been wrong or too harsh. She could do so with passion and without reservation or excuses. I am among those who received letters from Dorothy in which she begged forgiveness for something she had said or written or done which, on reflection, she deeply regretted. The last such letter I had from her along these lines was spattered with tears that had made the ink run. It had been written, she said, on her knees.

Confronted by a camera, Dorothy rarely smiled. If you study photos of her, you might form the idea that she had a dour personality. It's easy to see that she was at times a person of the utmost seriousness, but it's harder to imagine her warmth. In ordinary life, much of her time was spent sitting at a table, sipping tea or coffee, in comfortable conversation with whoever happened to join her—friend or stranger, sane or insane, young or old—often just listening, saying very little.

When Dorothy was present, she was completely present, but often she wasn't there at all. She was away visiting other Catholic Worker houses, speaking at churches and colleges, writing at her beach cottage on Staten Island, visiting Tamar and her many grandchildren, or enjoying the relative peace and quiet that reigned at Peter Maurin

Farm. In the New York house, her periods away left a hole that no one else could fill. Each member of staff had somehow acquired particular responsibilities: having charge of the kitchen, taking care of the address list, writing thank you notes, handling the household money, managing the paper—though, even in absentia, Dorothy was definitely the paper's editor and publisher. But no one was in a position to make a significant decision in her absence that everyone else would accept. In the New York house, in our somewhat splintered state, Dorothy alone could lay down the law.

I look back on being part of the Catholic Worker in New York City in those days as a major blessing, but it was not an easy blessing. In the early sixties, the New York house probably was one of the least happy communities in the Catholic Worker movement. In fact we were hardly a community at all. We had no community meetings and not all of us got along with each other. There was no formation program for the integration of new volunteers and few conditions of engagement. Nor was there any pay—though whoever handled community money could dispense small amounts as needed. It was exhilarating and exhausting, inspiring and discouraging.

I recall a decision made by our two-person kitchen crew that the occasional pound of butter or box of eggs contributed to the house would go to those on "the line" rather than to "the family." This was a change in custom, they recognized, but was, in their view, in line with the Gospel verse, "The last shall be first."

"The line" referred to those people who turned up for meals but whose names were unknown to most of us. "The family" was the much smaller group of people who had become regulars, were known by name, were living at the Catholic Worker and, in many cases, had chores to do within the household. "The family" ate after "the line." Traditionally anything special that turned up in small quantities was saved for them. As a result of this change in policy, members of the family, who had seen many volunteers come and go, were outraged, and the staff itself—six or eight people at the time—divided. Conflicting quotations from Dorothy's writings began to appear on the community bulletin board, each faction hurling verbal fragments of Dorothy at the other. On the one hand there might be a quotation from Dorothy declaring that we must be ready to roll up in old newspapers, giving our beds to those who needed them—and, on the other hand, a text in which Dorothy humbly reflected that voluntary poverty sometimes meant accepting one's limitations.

Dorothy was soon back again. Without bothering to sort out the paradoxes posed by the quotations from her writings, she said—with the finality of a monastery's abbess—that the butter and eggs were to go, as before, to the family. In the end, two people resigned, disappointed that Dorothy had failed to live up to some of her own quotations.

Such events, while petty and even comical when viewed from the outside, were grueling from the inside. There were many staff blow-ups during the forty-seven years

Dorothy in 1972. (Credit: Harriet Norris/WNET-TV)

that lay between the founding of the Catholic Worker and Dorothy's death in 1980, not to mention divisive controversies within the Catholic Worker movement as a whole, such as the debate about pacifism during World War II. It is an endless cause of wonder to me that, despite all these trials, she nonetheless retained her capacity for faith, hope and love down to the last day of her life. She occasionally spoke of "the duty of hope."

Perhaps her survival was not only thanks to remaining resolutely hopeful, but also to her taking time away, whether in the solitude of her Staten Island beach cottage or in Vermont visiting Tamar and her grandchildren.

It was in the aftermath of "the great butter crisis," late in 1961, that Dorothy appointed me as managing editor of the paper. She had to find someone—one of the two who had just left was my predecessor. Having just turned twenty, I was the youngest person ever to have held that post. Eventually, I too became a casualty of the early-sixties stress within the New York Catholic Worker community. When I was poised to get arrested for participating in an act of civil disobedience protesting U.S. resumption of nuclear weapons tests, Dorothy insisted that I instead go south to Tennessee and write about a civil rights project she admired. I said that, having been one of the organizers of the protest, I couldn't back out. I would have to go to Tennessee afterward. It wasn't a good moment to work out a compromise with Dorothy—earlier that same day she had been infuriated by the irresponsible actions of several other staff members. She gave me an ultimatum: "Either go to Tennessee or you are no longer part of this community." At the time, I felt I had no option but to do what I had helped plan and had promised to take part in. From Dorothy's point of view on that short-tempered day, I was simply being self-willed.

Only later in life, having gone through the white water of parenthood and having worked with many young volunteers in other contexts, did I realize that, had I gone back to Chrystie Street once I completed my month in jail, no one would have been happier to see me than Dorothy. But I was too young to realize the about-face adults can make after a good night's sleep. Moving timidly, it took me the better part of a year to renew my relationship with Dorothy.

Dorothy often described the Catholic Worker as a school. Certainly it was for me. One of the things I learned was that the poverty-stricken, the addicted and the insane—the people for whom our house of hospitality existed—were often easier to live with, and more patient and compassionate, than young volunteers who knew more about ideology than love. Yet for all our shortcomings and conflicts, we volunteers managed to get a great deal done: food begged or purchased, meals cooked and served, clothing received and given away, dishes washed, floors scrubbed, sheets laundered, the paper mailed out, those with medical needs assisted, hospital patients visited, and thank-you notes sent out to each and every donor, no matter how small the gift—all that and much more.

Not the smallest problem in the house was the noise. I recall one day trying to carry on a conversation with Dorothy about an article we were thinking about using in the next issue of the paper. We were at her desk in a tiny office next to the front door of the house on Chrystie Street, adjacent to the area in which meals were served, easily the noisiest part of the house. We could hardly hear each other. In the middle of a sentence, Dorothy got out of her chair, opened the door, and yelled, *"Holy silence!"* Silence briefly reigned at Saint Joseph's House such as a Trappist monk might admire.

One of Dorothy's striking qualities was her respect for Christians of other churches, especially those in the Orthodox Church. What was at the root of her affinity to Orthodoxy, I don't know. Perhaps it had to do with her Russian friendships and the special role Dostoevsky had played in the formation of her faith and vocation. The first time I visited an Orthodox church, it was with Dorothy, and the first time I attended the magnificent Orthodox Liturgy, it was with her as well. In the early sixties, she was a friend of a priest serving at the Russian Orthodox Cathedral on East 97th Street in Manhattan, Father Matthew Stadniuk from Moscow. (In 1988, having returned to Moscow some years before, he was the first priest in Russia who got his parishioners into publicly-visible voluntary service at a local hospital, thanks to the new climate of religious tolerance inaugurated by Gorbachev. For the first time since Lenin, religious believers were no longer excluded from openly performing the works of mercy.)

Dorothy's longing for the repair of the centuries-old schism dividing Eastern and Western Christianity drew her into the Third Hour group, founded by her Russian friend, Helene Iswolsky. This may have been the only association in America at the time in which people of various churches came together who had in common a deep respect, even love, for the Orthodox Church. I remember sitting next to Dorothy at a Third Hour meeting at an apartment in mid-town Manhattan, trying to make sense of the Russian words and phrases she and others used so comfortably. Among those present were the poet W.H. Auden, the Orthodox theologian, Alexander Schmemann, and Alexander Kerensky, who nearly half a century earlier had been prime minister of Russia in the brief period between the last tsar's abdication and the Bolshevik Revolution.

Dorothy's own commitment to the Catholic Church was never at issue—she wasn't window-shopping for another, "better" Church. In fact it disturbed many people, including many in the Catholic Worker movement, that Dorothy was so conservative a Catholic—so wholehearted in her acceptance of Catholic teaching and structure. She was critical not of what the Church taught, but rather of its failures in living out its own teaching. "I didn't become a Catholic in order to purify the Church," Dorothy once explained to Robert Coles. "I knew someone, years ago, who kept telling me that if we [Catholic Workers] could purify the Church, then she would convert. I thought she was teasing me when she first said that, but after a while I realized she meant what she was saying. Finally, I told her I wasn't trying to reform the Church or take sides on all the issues the Church was involved in; I was trying to be a loyal servant of the Church Jesus had founded. She thought I was being facetious. She reminded me that I had been critical of capitalism and America, so why not Catholicism and Rome? . . . My answer was that I had no reason to criticize Catholicism as a religion or Rome as the place where the Vatican is located. . . . As for Catholics all over the world, including members of the Church, they are no better than lots of their worst critics, and maybe some of us Catholics are worse than our worst critics."

Though there are millions of Catholics who seem to be more nationalist than Christian in their core identity, Dorothy found Catholicism the Christian body least contaminated by nationalism. Even the most nation-centered, flag-waving Catholic was at least vaguely aware of being part of a Church that was confined by no national or linguistic borders. Still more significant to Dorothy, it was a church crowded with the poor. Most important of all, it was a dispenser of sacraments without which life, for her, was barren. Part of the value of the Church for Dorothy was that it brought people together across many lines of division—political, ideological, economic, geographic, even the borders drawn by time. She agreed with G.K. Chesterton's remark that "tradition was democracy extended through time"—a democracy in which not only the living had a vote, but the dead as well.

Dorothy often stressed obedience (the root meaning of which is "listening"), insisting that if she were ordered by her bishop to stop publishing *The Catholic Worker*, she would do so, though not without trying first to change the bishop's mind. "Would that mean," I asked her one day, "if Cardinal Spellman says we have to give up our stand on

(Credit: © Vivian Cherry)

Funeral procession on 2nd Ave. led by Fr. Geoff Gneuhs, Bro. Bill Barrett, and Fr. Peter Raphael. Dorothy's grandchildren carry her coffin.

war, we give it up?" "Not at all," she said. "But then we might only use quotations from the Bible, the sayings of the saints, extracts from papal encyclicals, just nothing of our own." But she said that if there was no alternative but to stop publishing the paper, she would do so, hoping others might carry on in some way. Then she quoted the Gospel: "Unless the seed fall into the ground and die, it cannot bring forth new life."

Dorothy's devotion to the Church was rock solid but not without a critical edge. Borrowing from Romano Guardini, she sometimes spoke of the Church as being "the cross on which Christ was crucified." Though the metaphor sounds poetic, it was no compliment. Similarly Dorothy occasionally remarked that the net Peter had lowered into the human sea, once Jesus made him a fisher of men, "caught many a blowfish and quite a few sharks." There were priests and bishops who reminded her "more of Cain than of Abel."

Dorothy had very little sense of owning anything—she regarded what she possessed as being "on loan." What she had was often given away. A friend complained that none of the sweaters she had specially knit as gifts remained with Dorothy for long—sooner or later, usually sooner, each was given away. The same happened with many books. As far as I could see, Dorothy never indulged herself, though she often accused herself of being self-indulgent, as she did one afternoon when we had gone for a walk in the neighborhood. I don't recall any goal, only that it was a warm day. Passing a small kosher restaurant at a corner somewhere along Ridge Street, Dorothy suggested we stop for a glass of cold beet borscht with a spoonful of sour cream. Once it had been served, Dorothy was slightly scandalized at herself—"Borscht with sour cream! What luxury! This isn't voluntary poverty." But then she laughed. The voluptuous treat was only ten cents a glass.

Dorothy, who never seemed to be overly anxious about how little money there was in the community bank account, frequently set an example of passing on what was given as quickly as possible. In one memorable instance, a well-dressed woman visiting the Worker house one day gave Dorothy a diamond ring. Dorothy thanked the visitor, slipped the ring in her pocket, and later in the day gave it to an unpleasant old woman—Catherine Tarengal. Catherine, a bitter complainer second to none, was known in the community as "the weasel." She lived with her handicapped son and often ate meals at Saint Joseph's. We paid her rent each month. One of the staff suggested to Dorothy that the ring might better have been sold at the Diamond Exchange on West 47th Street and the money used for paying Catherine's rent. Dorothy replied that the woman had her dignity and could do as she liked with the ring. She could sell and buy whatever she wanted or take a trip to the Bahamas—or she could enjoy having a diamond ring on her hand just like the woman who had given it to the Worker. "Do you suppose," Dorothy asked, "that God created diamonds only for the rich?"

In the early days of the Catholic Worker, those who came to the door were often the unemployed rather than the unemployable. Dorothy's attitude toward hospitality, much admired during the Depression, often came under criticism in later years when those being helped struck many observers as considerably less worthy. We were no longer helping the "deserving poor," we were told, but no-account drunkards, addicts, loafers and thieves. Why did we have no employment or rehabilitation programs? Didn't we realize that the clothes the Worker gave away were often sold or bartered for drink or drugs? Dorothy responded by pointing out that those who ask such questions also use their money and possessions as they please, and often no more wisely than the down-and-out.

Another often repeated objection was, "Didn't Jesus himself say that the poor would be with us always? Why make such a fuss about them?" "Yes," Dorothy replied again and again, "but we are not content that there should be so many of them. The class structure is our making and by our consent, not God's, and we must do what we can to change it. We are urging revolutionary change."

There was a social worker who asked Dorothy how long "clients" of the Catholic Worker were permitted to stay. "We let them stay forever," Dorothy answered testily. "They live with us, they die with us, and we give them a Christian burial. We pray for them after they are dead. Once they are taken in, they become members of the family. Or rather they always were members of the family. They are our brothers and sisters in Christ."

While Dorothy was an enthusiastic and unapologetic borrower of other people's ideas, her way of seeing was very much her own. I think, for example, of what happened one day when my room-mate, Stuart Sandberg, and I were clearing out rubbish from a small apartment one flight up in a cold-water tenement on Ridge Street. Dorothy was having increasing trouble managing the five flights to the apartment on Spring Street. These two rooms could be reached without such a climb, but first many layers of linoleum and wallpaper had to be removed and white paint applied to the walls.

Stuart and I dragged box after box of debris down to the street, including a hideous—so it seemed to us—painting of the Holy Family. Mary, Joseph and Jesus had been painted in a few bright colors against a battleship gray background on a piece of plywood. We shook our heads, deposited it in the trash along the curb, and went back to continue cleaning. Not long afterward Dorothy arrived carrying the rejected painting. "Look what I found! The Holy Family! It's a providential sign, a blessing." She put it on the mantle of the apartment's extinct fireplace. I looked at it again and this time saw it was a work of love and faith, however crudely rendered. If it was no masterpiece of iconography, it had its own unlettered beauty, but I wouldn't have thought so if Dorothy hadn't seen it first.

Dorothy is no longer with us. We can't sit down and have a cup of coffee with her anymore, or send her a letter and await her response. But she remains a vital presence. Many regard her as a saint, and not as a way of keeping her at a safe distance or because of ignorance regarding the darker moments in her life. If by the word "saint" we mean a person who helps us see, by both precept and example, what it means to follow Christ, surely Dorothy is such a person.

Dorothy helped bring about a conversion of heart that greatly influenced many people in the Church, especially in America, but has reached far beyond it. It is not a reformation of theological doctrine, but one rooted in the sacredness of life. Dorothy has helped us better understand one of the primary biblical truths: that each person, no matter how damaged or battered by the events and circumstances of life, is a bearer of the image of God and deserves to be recognized and treated as such. She has reminded us of the real presence of Christ in the least person. "Those who fail to see Christ in the poor," Dorothy said, "are atheists indeed." Thanks to her, many have come to realize that the opposite of the works of mercy are the works of war. Dorothy gave an astonishing example of hospitality and mercy as a way of life. "We are here to celebrate Him," she said time and again, "through the works of mercy."

In my own life, every time I think about the challenges of life in the bright light of the Gospel rather than in the gray light of money or the dim light of politics, her example has had its influence. Every time I try to overcome meanness or selfishness rising up in myself, it is partly thanks to the example of Dorothy Day. Every time I defeat the impulse to buy something I can get along without, Dorothy Day's example of voluntary poverty has had renewed impact. Every time I give away something I can get along without—every time I manage to see Christ's presence in the face of a stranger—there again I owe a debt to Dorothy Day. Every time I take part in efforts to prevent wars or end them, or join in campaigns to make the world a less cruel place, in part I am in debt to

Dorothy Day
1897-1980

"We have all known the long loneliness and we have learned that the only solution is love and that love comes with community."

Card distributed at Dorothy Day's funeral.

Dorothy. What I know of Christ, the Church, sacramental life, the Bible, and truth-telling, I know in large measure thanks to her, while whatever I have done that was cowardly, opportunistic or cruel, is despite her. She has even shaped my reading life—one could do worse than to get to know the authors whose books helped shape and sustain Dorothy's faith and vocation. It isn't that Dorothy is the point of reference. Christ is. But I can't think of anyone I've known whose Christ-centered life has done so much to help make me a more Christ-centered person.

In 1997, seventeen years after Dorothy's death, one of her grandchildren, Kate Hennessy, wrote in *The Catholic Worker*: "To have known Dorothy means spending the rest of your life wondering what hit you. On the one hand, she has given so many of us a home, physically and spiritually; on the other, she has shaken our very foundations."

I am one of the many whose foundations were shaken. I am still wondering what hit me.

Sources and Resources

Collaborators

"It takes a village to write a book," Johannah Hughes Turner told me recently. Certainly it's true of this book. I am deeply indebted to a number of people who knew Dorothy and read all or part of this book while it was in typescript, providing corrections and timely advice.

First of all, there are Tom and Monica Cornell. Monica was born into a Catholic Worker family while Tom was drawn to the Catholic Worker as a college student after reading *The Long Loneliness*. Many of my favorite stories about Dorothy come from Tom and Monica. Their Catholic Worker vocations continue. After founding Guadalupe House in Waterbury, Connecticut, and remaining with it for many years, they are now living at the Peter Maurin Farm in Marlborough, New York.

Equally important is Robert Ellsberg. He and I were the two youngest managing editors *The Catholic Worker* ever had, though Robert was much longer at the job than I was. Robert was close to Dorothy in her last years and has an astonishing gift to recall conversations. This revised and expanded book would never have been written or published had it not been for Robert. The selections of quotations from Dorothy used in the margins of this book was also done by Robert. (The earliest edition of this book, with the title *Love is the Measure*, was published in 1986, thanks to the interest of Don Brophy, managing editor at Paulist Press. With minor revisions, that book was republished by Orbis Books in 1994 and went through eleven printings prior to this new edition.)

Phil Runkel, responsible for the Catholic Worker Archive at the Marquette University Library, again and again found papers I needed as well as many of the photos used in this book. He also read this book in typescript, spotting many errors which, thanks to him, have not made it into print. Never has an archivist been more committed not only to the papers in his care but to the spiritual values they represent.

Jim Allaire initiated the Catholic Worker website, which includes, among other resources, many hundreds of pages of Dorothy Day's columns and other writings <www.catholicworker.org/dorothyday>. It's a resource I have turned to countless times while working on this new edition.

Special gratitude is due to Johannah Hughes Turner (one of Dorothy's godchildren). I have seldom met anyone with such talent for research and fact-checking. My thanks also go to Father Gerald Twomey and Meghan Battle, both of whom helped make this a better book.

The late Fritz Eichenberg, whose wood engravings and drawings are well known to every reader of *The Catholic Worker*, shared with me his correspondence with Dorothy. His *Catholic Worker* art was published by Orbis in *Works of Mercy*. Not every *Catholic Worker* subscriber has the education to read the articles, but even the most unlettered person could understand what the paper stood for thanks to the art of Fritz, Ade Bethune and such other artists as Rita Corbin.

Last but far from least, words cannot express my debt to my wife, Nancy, who worked closely with me on each edition of this book and has cheered me along when cheering was needed.

Sources and Further Reading

My apologies to those readers who would have found endnotes helpful. I hope that the information that follows, in addition to references in the text itself, will help those interested find original sources.

Dorothy Day was a prolific writer. Her most enduring self-portrait, *The Long Loneliness*, was first published in 1952 and has been in print ever since. It follows Dorothy's life up to the time of Peter Maurin's death in 1949. It has become a classic of religious autobiography, yet one finds a cautionary note about the book among Dorothy Day's papers in the Catholic Worker Archive at Marquette University: "It is always called my autobiography but it is really a selection of periods of my life searching for God and not a story giving the whole truth. . . . I feel, to put it simply, that it is not the truth about me . . . only part of the truth." (It was only in her autobiographical novel, *The Eleventh Virgin*, published in 1924 by Albert & Charles Boni, that Dorothy described her abortion and her love affair with the unborn child's father.)

From Union Square to Rome (published in 1939, reissued in 2006 by Orbis Books) was still less candid about events Dorothy preferred not to recall, but introduces the reader to a younger Dorothy in the first years of the Catholic Worker movement.

Many of the blanks in Dorothy's autobiographical writings have been filled by her diaries, *The Duty of Delight*, edited by Robert Ellsberg and published in 2009 by the Marquette University Press. A second major source is *All the Way to Heaven: The Selected Letters of Dorothy Day*, also edited by Robert Ellsberg, published in 2010 by the same publisher.

Robert Ellsberg also edited a major anthology of Dorothy's writings, first published by Knopf as *By Little and By Little*, now available from Orbis as *Dorothy Day: Selected Writings*.

Dorothy's history of the Catholic Worker movement, *Loaves and Fishes*, was published by Harper & Row in 1963 and reissued by Orbis in 1997. Her biography of Saint Therese of Lisieux, *Therese* (Templegate), is not only is an excellent introduction to the life of Therese but provides a better understanding of Dorothy's commitment to "the little way."

From 1929 until 1975, Dorothy was an occasional contributor to *Commonweal* magazine. Patrick Jordan has collected her articles and letters in *Dorothy Day: Writings from Commonweal* (The Liturgical Press, 2002).

For almost half a century, Dorothy wrote a column for *The Catholic Worker*. Thanks to Jim Allaire, nearly all her columns and many of her other non-copyrighted texts are available on the Web via *The Dorothy Day Online Library*: www.catholicworker.org/dorothyday. Some of Dorothy's columns were also collected in books: *House of Hospitality* (Sheed & Ward, 1939), *On Pilgrimage* (Catholic Worker Books, 1948), and *On Pilgrimage: The Sixties* (Curtis Books, 1972).

An anthology, *A Penny a Copy: Readings from The Catholic Worker*, edited by Tom Cornell and Jim Forest, provides a sampling of important articles published in *The Catholic Worker* in its first thirty-five years; it was published by Macmillan in 1968. An updated edition, which cut some of the content of the earlier book to make room for newer material, was issued by Orbis in 1994 (editors: Tom Cornell, Jim Forest and Robert Ellsberg).

William Robert Miller was the leading Catholic Worker scholar—see *A Harsh and Dreadful Love: Dorothy Day and the Catholic Worker Movement* (Liveright, New York, 1973, reprinted by Marquette University Press) and *Dorothy Day: A Biography* (Harper & Row, New York, 1982). In *All is Grace: The Spirituality of Dorothy Day*, published by Doubleday in 1987, Miller gathered together extracts from Dorothy's journals, letters and retreat notes. (It had been an unfulfilled intention of Dorothy's to write a book called *All Is Grace* that would relate the story of the retreat movement that had been so important to her just before and during World War II and the priests and spiritual advisors who had played a role in her life.) It is large-ly thanks to Miller that an archive of Dorothy's papers and other Catholic Worker material is located at Marquette University. The archivist is Phillip Runkel.

Dorothy Day: Portraits by Those Who Knew Her by Rosalie Riegle (Orbis Books, 2003) provides interviews with nearly a hundred people who knew Dorothy. *Voices From the Catholic Worker* (Temple University Press, 1993), also compiled by Rosalie Riegle, is a massive outpouring of voices that bring to life the Catholic Worker movement, past and present, also giving voice to controversies still going on within and between Catholic Worker communities.

Dorothy Day: A Radical Devotion by Robert Coles (Addison-Wesley, Reading, MA, 1987) centers on Coles's wide-ranging conversations with Dorothy.

Easy Essays by Peter Maurin, one of the core Catholic Worker books, is back in print thanks to Wipf & Stock Publishers.

Peter Maurin: Apostle to the World by Dorothy Day with Francis J. Sicius (Orbis, 2004), a biography Dorothy Day worked on from time to time over many years, has now been completed by Francis J. Sicius. Also of note is *Peter Maurin: Prophet of the Twentieth Century* (Paulist Press, 1981) by Marc Ellis, both a biography and a work of reflection on Maurin's ideas.

A Spectacle Unto the World (Viking, 1973): Jon Erikson's wonderful photos of Dorothy and the New York Catholic Worker community as seen in the early seventies. The images are augmented with an essay by Robert Coles.

Dorothy Day and the Permanent Revolution by Eileen Egan (Benet Press, available from Pax Christi USA) is an attractively illustrated booklet by one of Dorothy's closest friends and collaborators. Among other things, Egan writes about her travels with Dorothy in Europe and Asia.

The Dorothy Day Book (Templegate), edited by Margaret Quigley and Michael Garvey, is a collection of some of Dorothy's favorite quotations plus a few chosen from her own writings. Illustrated with linocuts by Ade Bethune.

Dorothy Day: Meditations: A selection of shorter texts by Dorothy Day selected and arranged by Stanley Vishnewski (Paulist Press, 1970, reissued by Templegate in 1997).

The Catholic Worker Movement: Intellectual and Spiritual Origins by Mark and Louise Zwick (Paulist Press, 2005) looks at major influences on Peter Maurin and Dorothy Day, including the Benedictine monastic tradition, Saint Francis, Saint Catherine of Siena, Saint Teresa of Avila, Saint Therese of Lisieux, Dostoevsky, the liturgist Dom Virgil Michel, the Russian philosopher Nicholas Berdyaev, and Jacques and Raissa Maritain.

Dorothy Day and The Catholic Worker (State University of New York Press, 1984), by Nancy Roberts, focuses on the history of the newspaper.

The Life You Save May Be Your Own: An American Pilgrimage by Paul Elie (Farrar, Straus and Giroux, 2004) weaves together biographies of Dorothy Day, Thomas Merton, Flannery O'Connor and Walker Percy. Elie sees them unified as pilgrims moving along different paths that often interconnect.

Proud Donkey of Schaerbeek by Judith Stoughton (North Start Press, St. Cloud, MN, 1988) tells the life story of Ade Bethune, the first *Catholic Worker* artist. The book is profusely illustrated.

Fritz Eichenberg: Works of Mercy (Orbis, 1993) gathers Fritz's *Catholic Worker* art as well as text from Dorothy Day, Fritz Eichenberg, Robert Ellsberg and Jim Forest.

Dorothy Day and the Catholic Worker Movement: Centenary Essays, edited by William Thorn, Phillip Runkel and Susan Mountin (Marquette University Press, 2001), is a substantial collection of essays and papers presented in 1997 during a major conference at Marquette University in celebrating the hundredth anniversary of the birth of Dorothy Day.

A Revolution of the Heart, edited by Patrick Coy (Temple University Press, 1988), is a collection of essays on the Catholic Worker movement.

Breaking Bread: The Catholic Worker and the Origins of Catholic Radicalism in America by Mel Piehl (Temple University Press, 1982).

Catholic Worker Houses: Ordinary Miracles by Sheila Durkin Dierks and Patricia Powers Ladley (Sheed & Ward, Kansas City, MO, 1988) is a portrait, in word and picture, of seven Catholic Worker communities.

Dreadful Conversions: The Making of a Catholic Socialist by John Cort (Fordham University Press, 2003) is the engaging autobiography of an intellectual who went from Harvard to the Catholic Worker staff in its early years and went on to play an important role in the American labor movement.

The Catholic Worker After Dorothy Day by Dan McKanan (Liturgical Press, 2008) explores the Catholic Worker movement as it has developed in recent years.

Other Sources

I have drawn on many stories and memories that either were my own or have been shared with me by friends, especially Tom and Monica Cornell and Robert Ellsberg.

Deane Mowrer recorded numerous interviews with persons associated with the Catholic Worker movement. These have been transcribed and are among the Catholic Worker Papers at Marquette. They have served as helpful background reading in better understanding the earlier years of the Catholic Worker. The remembrance of Dorothy Day by Jack English is from one of the Mowrer interviews.

Quotations from speeches by Dorothy Day in the 1970s come from tape recordings in my possession.

For details of the FBI file on the Catholic Worker, see Robert Ellsberg's two-part article, "An Unusual History from the FBI" (*The Catholic Worker*, issues dated May and June 1979).

The Catholic Worker Today

The Catholic Worker movement is at least as vital today as it was when Dorothy Day was alive. A list of Catholic Worker communities, both urban and rural, can be found on the Web at www.catholicworker.org or obtained from the Catholic Worker in New York (Maryhouse, 36 East First St., New York, NY 10003). To subscribe to *The Catholic Worker*, write to the same address. A donation of any amount is all that it costs, but why not send as much as you paid for this book?

There are many other Catholic Worker journals published by various communities. One that I especially look forward to is *The Houston Catholic Worker*, published by the Casa Juan Diego House of Hospitality (Box 70113, Houston, Texas 77270; website: http://www.cjd.org).

The Catholic Worker, however, is found neither in books nor newspapers but mainly in houses of hospitality. Visit those that are within reach. Be aware, however, that each house is autonomous, no one authorizes or disqualifies a Catholic Worker community, and that not all houses are notably Catholic or even sympathetic to the Catholic Church. There are houses in which Dorothy Day's views on many topics would not be welcome—but there are also houses where she would be at home in every possible way.

Come and see for yourself.

Index